# THE LAST CHALKLINE

The Life & Times
of
Jack Chevigny

Jeff Walker

# Wasteland Press

www.wastelandpress.net
Shelbyville, KY USA

*The Last Chalkline:*
*The Life & Times of Jack Chevigny*
by Jeff Walker

Copyright © 2012 Jeff Walker
ALL RIGHTS RESERVED

Second Printing – June 2012
ISBN: 978-1-60047-712-6
Front cover photo – courtesy of Notre Dame Archives
Photo, page 3 – courtesy of Gege Chevigny Beck
Back cover photo – courtesy of Jack & Babs Chevigny

Printed in the U.S.A.

0  1  2  3  4  5  6  7  8  9  10  11  12  13  14  15  16

Blessed is the man who perseveres under trial,
because when he has stood the test,
he will receive the crown of life that
God has promised to those who love Him.
*James 1:12*

To my best friend and eternal love,
Paula Loree Nugent Walker
Because of my Puldeaux, I am.

To my son, Gabriel Dayson-Alexander Walker
Because of my Gabe, I am blessed.

To my daughter, Isabella Grace Ann Walker
Because of my Ella, I am joyful.

# Acknowledgments

First to be acknowledged is the original Jack Chevigny biographer, Maurice D. O'Hern. Maurice, the altar boy once lifted by his hometown hero's arms, dreamed of what has become.

This book took a village to create. Without any of the following persons assisting the author in research, information, funding, editing, or moral support, Jack's story could not have been told:

Jack Chevigny and Babs Chevigny, Munster, Indiana

George "Sonny" Franck and Helen Franck, Davenport, Iowa

Paula Walker, Katy, Texas

Tom Beck and Gege Chevigny Beck, Phoenix, Arizona

Eugenia Purdy Chevigny Brennan, Seattle, Washington

Terry Siddall and Sharon Siddall, Danville, Indiana

Joe Gaffney, Jr., Wheaton, Illinois

Marshall Law, Houston, Texas

Stephanie Ascherl, Fund for Teachers and Apache Oil, Houston, Texas

Armando Garcia of the Scarborough-Phillips Library at St. Edward's University, Houston, Texas

Elizabeth Hogan and the University of Notre Dame Library and Archives staff, South Bend, Indiana

John A. Lejeune Education Center Research Library, Camp Lejeune, North Carolina

Kathy Powers, the Dyer Indiana Historical Society

Dolph Briscoe Center for American History, Austin, Texas

Hammond Indiana Public Library

Bob Daily, Jamison, Pennsylvania

Al "Junie" Kleinhenz and family, Louisville, Kentucky

Hugh Wolfe, Stephenville, Texas

Paul Merriman, Houston, Texas

Jay Hickman, Houston, Texas

Cater Joseph, Austin, Texas

Ted Paulison, River Oaks, Texas

David Kornaus, Santa Barbara, California

Maureen O'Hern, Indianapolis, Indiana

John Maher, Austin, Texas

Joe Casey, MD, Fort Lauderdale, Florida

Chris Gunnell, The Woodlands, Texas

Pete Wright, Austin, Texas

Ray Damrel, Magnolia, Texas

Susan Giffin, Editor, Dearborn, Michigan

# Table of Contents

# Prologue

By the winter of 1944, the despotic triumvirate that was Germany, Italy, and Japan had fractured and was disintegrating. Though the core of the immoral alliance known as the Axis remained, its sphere of influence was shrinking.

In Germany, the Third Reich was being debrided on two fronts. Red retribution raced westward from the Soviet Union. From across the English Channel, the western allies battered Nazi resistance, liberating France and pushing eastward. Benito Mussolini, the Fascist father of Italy's black shirt movement and the man who would have restored Rome to its glory, had been arrested by his own government. Rome was liberated, and the third major Axis power, Japan, was being strangled by the combined forces of the United States Army, Navy, and Marines. The Land of the Rising Sun was losing the Pacific War; Emperor Hirohito's official patronage of militarist Prime Minister Hideki Tojo had ended. Tojo's final endowment for leading the war effort would be the sympathy of his god-emperor.

With the war's end edging over the horizon, the ultimate cost in blood escalated. In Europe, Axis resistance crossed over from a mission of defense to a manifesto that embraced a fanatical fight to the death. Hitler's inhumanity and Japan's national honor assumed a philosophical stance that guaranteed the extermination of their people and cultures.

Of the two totalitarian Axis powers, Japan would prove to be the more challenging enemy to force into total capitulation. Nine months prior to the Japanese attack on Pearl Harbor, President Roosevelt had approved Admiral Stark's 1940 plan designating Germany's defeat as the Allies' priority. In the Pacific, the United States would have to carry the war to conclusion with little assistance from its main allies, the British and Soviets.

Once the Pacific War progressed into its second year, the overpowering mobilization of America dulled the Japanese sword of aggression. Wave after wave of ships, weapons, and manpower forced the Japanese military into a containment and survival mode. In the first years of the war, the strategy of concentrating their forces to meet the invading forces near the beaches wasted men and material. Beginning with the defensive strategy at Peleliu, the Japanese began to embrace a more frugal defense, one of layered strongpoints and underground tunnels. No longer would Japanese Army commanders waste their soldiers' blood on banzai charges into a line of entrenched Marines supported by Browning machine guns. It had become the duty of every Japanese soldier to kill ten United States Marines in a fight to the death. The new objective was to bleed American boys to death on islands whose names their parents couldn't pronounce. As their enemy tightened the noose around the home islands, Japan's only hope was that America did not have the stomach to lose a generation in order to close out the war.

It was a sensible strategy. Domestic protests against the growing American losses in the Pacific gained momentum with each passing month. The Pacific War seemed be drawing to a foreboding conclusion. Military planners speculated that an American invasion of Japan would result in more than one million Americans wounded with over a hundred thousand American deaths. In contrast, the June 6, 1944, multi-national allied

2

invasion of German-occupied France had claimed approximately two thousand five hundred American lives. An invasion of Japan would cost the blood of a generation and with the casualty protests starting to unravel the fabric of the home front's morale, President Roosevelt could not be sure that the American people would accept an invasion financed by such a cost. Three years of total war on three fronts, two foreign and one home, had drained the country. Americans were tired of the rationing, tired of the gold stars, and tired of the tears.

Alerted to the new Japanese strategy of military entrenchment and the escalating human cost of the Pacific War, Roosevelt agreed with his Army Air Corps leaders. Before undertaking the cataclysmic task of invading the Japanese mainland, the United States must attempt to bomb Japan into submission. Prior to the beginning of land operations, millions of incendiary bombs would rain fire upon the paper houses of the Japanese people.

Assigned the mission of bombing Japan into submission was the B-29 Superfortress. With a ceiling of thirty-eight thousand feet, the heavily armed four-engine bomber could carry four tons of bombs three thousand five hundred miles. Based in the Marianas, the modern killing machine could embark on long-range missions to the Japanese home islands. It was the Air Corps' position that capturing a Bonin Island for use as a midpoint airstrip between Guam and Japan would make the B-29 raids more efficient in that crews would not have to detour these midpoint islands in order to safely execute their bombing missions. Additionally, a Bonin Island base could offer B-29s a refueling waypoint, which would allow for heavier payloads and deeper strikes into Japan. The Joint War Planners also concluded that capturing a Bonin way station would provide a base for P-51 Mustangs, long range fighters that could escort the bombers.

Of the Bonin Islands, only two were suitable for the construction of a runway large enough to handle the B-29 Superfortress. Early on, one of those islands was identified as most ideal to fill the needs of the Air Corps. The United States Marine Corps was assigned the mission of capturing it.

On the morning of February 19, 1945, three divisions were committed to the largest invasion in Marine Corps history. At 9:00 a.m., the first waves of fifty thousand United States Marines and supporting personnel, the best of America's greatest generation, would strike a narrow black beach on a small island in the middle of nowhere. With orders to repel the first enemy incursion into their homeland, twenty thousand entrenched Japanese prepared for a fight to the death.

For everyone touched by the events of that day, a lifetime of tomorrows would be forever changed. The island was Iwo Jima.

# CHAPTER ONE

# *The Last Circus*

During the second summer of the Great War just southwest of the Indiana Dunes in the exploding boisterous city of Hammond, anticipation enveloped a humid breezeless night. Hundreds of steelworkers' children dreamed of flying trapeze artists, snarling tigers, and roaring lions. Like those children whose fathers worked nearby in the Gary steel industry, thirteen-year-old Marie Chevigny and her eleven-year-old brother Johnny also would have looked forward to the arrival of the circus.

For both young and old residents of the Indiana state-line region, the circus offered a welcome distraction from the news of the European war and brewing labor unrest boiling in the hearth of heavy industry and American steel manufacturing. In the weeks prior to the troupe's planned arrival, teams of advance men invaded the nearby towns and communities distributing flyers and posting the one-sheet lithographs and posters that announced the coming of the circus.

*Saturday, June 22, 1918.* At three hours past midnight, it was a time too early even to be called a time of day. The younger residents of northwestern Indiana's Calumet region, the cauldron of America's steel manufacturing, would soon awaken to an excitement reserved for one of the two best days of the year—Christmas and the day the circus comes to town.

For now, the gleeful December morning of full stockings and presents was still a distant dream. Not so distant was the daybreak and the opening of the Hagenbeck-Wallace Circus.

Rumbling down the Michigan-Central line, the circus was coming to town in a series of twenty-six cars. With a full complement of equipment, animals, performers, and roustabouts, the extravaganza was due to arrive in Hammond aboard two separate trains. Both sections would stop near Calumet Avenue and 150th Street where the ensemble would disembark and work to set up before noon.

By 3:00 a.m., the animals in the first section were in place and waiting in Hammond for the second train of twenty-five cars and a caboose rolling west from Michigan City. On this train, performers and animal trainers slumbered aboard a series of outdated passenger sleeper cars. Approaching Ivanhoe, Indiana, the seasoned entertainers enjoyed the final dark hours before dawn. The soothing rhythmic roll of the rail was a siren of sleep in the rare tranquil hours. It was the troupe's last opportunity for rest prior to the frenzied, organized chaos of the morning's opening performance. With the fourteen flat cars, seven stock cars, and four sleepers approximately thirty minutes from Hammond, the artists in the four sleeper cars would awaken soon to begin their pre-dawn preparation for the afternoon show.

In his refurbished nineteenth-century Pullman sleeper cabin, circus manager Charles Dollmer fussed as he attempted to balance the teetering circus finances. A premier long-running circus, the Hagenbeck-Wallace Circus incorporated over twenty tents, and average expenses of their operation amounted to over $7,000 a day. Typical of any successful business, Hagenbeck-Wallace watched its bottom line closely. Mindful of what it took to balance the books, Dollmer knew his budget didn't include the frills of the modern steel Pullman sleeping cars.

In the sleepers, performers, animal trainers, and support personnel rested among a stacked arrangement of three berths lighted by kerosene lanterns, which hung over the center aisle. While not the most modern of facilities, these adequately maintained wooden sleeper cars met the needs of Dollmer's entertainers. They were seasoned, tough troupers.

Not all the performers traveled in the cramped sleepers. Rose Borland, the circus's feature equestrienne, slept elegantly in her very own private berth—one that allowed the personal space and privacy enjoyed by only a select few circus employees. As a highlight performer with the noted Hagenbeck-Wallace horses, Borland enjoyed numerous perks in addition to her seasonal salary of $25,000.

Hercules Navarro, known in the Midwest as *The Strongest Man since Sandow*, also enjoyed a private berth, as did the chief of clowns, Joe Coyle who was traveling with his wife and children. Occupying a separate sleeper were the lithe and limber members of the female dance company. Hagenbeck-Wallace's billing of *100 Dancing Girls, Count Them* would titillate and tempt more than a few hardnosed U. S. Steel employees into accompanying their families to the colorful circus carnival.

The Hagenbeck-Wallace Circus had something for everybody. If any amusement vehicle of the era could transport the common folk into a glorious world of galloping dreams, empowered invincibility, and felicitous imagination, it was the circus.

Dawn approached as the train railed westward. For the train's crew, the first glint of trouble in the night occurred near the pastoral village of Ivanhoe, five miles east of Hammond. An unmistakable burning smell drifted back to the caboose. It was determined that one of the flat cars had developed a hotbox, railroad slang for a mechanical malfunction typical of an overheated bearing of a car's axle.

In early twentieth-century railroading, axle bearings were friction devices. The axle rotated inside a journal box, an assembly at the axle's end that contained a brass brushing, packing material, and a supply of lubricant. If the level of lubrication fell below a safe level, the axle bearing would overheat. For an alert conductor or brakeman, a smoking box assembly was the first hint of trouble. Within minutes of a hotbox developing, the axle can snap like a dry twig. In the case of an especially inattentive caboose crew, the journal box could burst into flames and melt the end of the axle.

Servicing the box or diagnosing a potential lubrication deficiency was a relatively simple procedure. A hinged cover of the journal box assembly allowed for a quick inspection and lubrication check. Using a journal hook, a long metal device resembling a horse jockey's whip, the inspector opened the journal lid and checked the oil level.

Railroad statistics from the turn of the century show the hotbox as the most common cause of train derailment. Adherence to a set maintenance schedule prevented the mechanical malfunction, but the rail cars of 1918 often suffered from irregular preventative maintenance due to the capacity and urgency of wartime rail traffic.

Despite the clear starlit June sky, the darkness of the moonless morning shrouded any visible vapor trail. But for veteran conductor R. W. Johnson, the lack of any visual indicator was of little consequence. When the burning smell of the packing material drifted back to the caboose, conductor Johnson's experienced olfactory sense identified the developing problem. He notified the circus train's engineer to take emergency measures.

The engineer acknowledged the conductor's signal and slowed the train as he exited the main track to a siding where a complete inspection could be performed. The crippled circus train rolled to a stop near the Elgin, Joliet, and Eastern crossing, less than five miles from its final destination in Hammond.

Few passengers would be disturbed from their slumber. The hotbox had been detected before any serious damage was done to the axle hub, and repair measures began to get underway. At 4:00 a.m., the Hagenbeck-Wallace circus train sat immobile on the siding as the circus train's flagman, Mr. Trimm, ran eastward down the line to set up a secondary warning system of red flares.

For years, railroading had incorporated the concept of the siding, a section of track serving as a temporary safe zone. As the use of the telegraph and timetables became more standard, communication regarding separate trains traveling on the same line was made more efficient. With quick communication, train engineers could avoid potential collisions by making way for an oncoming or fast approaching train from the rear. The alternative loop of parallel track permitted the engineer of one train to pull over and allow a second train to pass. Slower freight trains could pull over for speeding passenger trains. With the effective use of time schedules, signals, and sidings, World War I-era troop trains and other high priority supply trains could move their cargo expeditiously from locale to locale as other lower priority trains surrendered the right of way.

As the circus train's crew worked to repair the hotbox, Alonzo Sargent engineered an empty troop train consisting of four steel Pullman sleeper cars westward toward Ivanhoe. He had cleared the Michigan City station twenty-seven minutes after the circus train's departure.

Minutes away, Engineer Sargent approached Ivanhoe and the disabled circus train. An automatic signal beamed caution.

Flagman Trimm was positioned eastward of his disabled train, his flares burning, while he stood ready to act as a failsafe warning system. Seeing Sargent's westbound trooper come into sight, Trimm realized that the oncoming engine was bearing down upon the circus train. The panicking flagman knew that his parked circus train was not completely clear of the main track. Waving his bright red lantern in wide sweeping arcs, Trimm hurled a burning red flare into the passing locomotive's cab in a last ditch attempt to stop the troop train. When Engine 8485 sped past the frantic flagman, Trimm was overcome with panic and nausea. No one was at the controls. Watching helplessly, Trimm saw the troop train cruise through the final warning light, a glowing red caution signal.

Engineer Sargent was dead at the throttle, asleep from a mixture of kidney pills and fatigue. Meanwhile, Sargent's fireman remained focused on his job and continued to shovel coal without noticing either the warning signals or the sleeping Sargent. At the moment of impact, the circus train's caboose and passenger cars imploded.

Headlines would record the wreckage as horrific. Many of the victims were crushed. Some burned alive as they cried for help. Among the victims and witnesses, confusion ruled the day.

The *100 Dancing Girls* were decimated. At the same moment, the entire Rooney family of bareback riders was killed as was another familial group of horsemen, the Cottrell family. The *Famous Meyers*, premier animal trainers, perished. Top-billed horsewoman Rose Borland was reported killed in the crash, but her brother-in-law learned later that both Rose and his brother Clinton had survived. Meanwhile, no such contradictory account would offer a reprieve for Hercules Navarro. Newspapers across the country printed ghoulish accounts of Hercules crushed into a bloody soup of bone and tissue from the waist down, begging rescuers to kill him on the spot.

Offering little value to clown Joe Coyle was the private berth in which he lost his children and his wife. Of the four passenger cars, nothing remained. Fueled by the kerosene lanterns of the wooden sleepers, fire converted the splinters into a derailed crematorium.

Women pleaded with God for their children's lives, while grown men weaker men than Hercules begged to be shot rather than left to perish in the fire. Those who weren't able to be pulled out of the wreckage were consumed in the wooden and steel pyre. In addition to the fifty-three performers later confirmed to be dead, almost two hundred other individuals were seriously injured. Chicago, Gary, Hammond, and nearby cities dispatched emergency personnel to the site to extricate and treat the wounded.

Some of the survivors thrown from the crash were rescued in their nightgowns as they stumbled throughout the wreckage. The condition of traumatic shock was unknown. Newspaper reporters noted the sleep-walking actions of those dazed survivors to be a bizarre consequence of experiencing such a tremendous collision in their sleep. Most of the survivors suffered severe burns to various parts of their bodies.

In 1918, America's involvement in The Great War had seriously depleted the availability of licensed medical doctors nationwide. During this time of the war, many of the area's best doctors and surgeons were stationed in military hospitals on the East Coast. One of those physicians absent from the scene was Julius A. Chevigny. He had been called to the service of his country in early June.

Originally from Quebec, the youthful physician migrated from Canada to Vermont in 1898. By 1914, Doctor Chevigny relocated to just a few miles south of Chicago where he had accepted the position of health officer of Dyer, Indiana. Although the $10 annual salary provided only a small supplement to his income, the position enhanced his civic stature in the rural rail stop on the Illinois state line.

After his brief wartime service on Long Island, New York, Doctor Chevigny returned to a region in turmoil with labor strikes and anti-unionist violence. America was experiencing a spasm of growing pangs as it took its place in the world as the defender of freedom and democracy. An increasing global awareness and the bitterness of losing jobs in the postwar economy combined to fuel the first American Red Scare. The principles of communism appealed to the millions of impoverished immigrants and native workers alike as American workers unionized to fight the perceived injustices of the postwar financial decline.

Soon, women would gain their long-denied rightful spot at the polls and experience their own liberation from society's tyranny. Workplace conditions would improve gradually while legalized child labor faded from practice as the final fruits of the Teddy Roosevelt's Progressive Era were picked. Before the close of the decade, the prohibition of alcohol combined awkwardly with a growing age of conspicuous consumption and the dismissing of traditional mores to create an unsteady beam upon which the decade of the 1920s would balance.

Hammond was one of the more promising cities in Indiana, just far enough from Chicago to be immune from the big city ailments but just close enough to be a spoke in the hub of the area's oncoming economic boom of the 1920s. After the circus train crash, Hammond left the front pages to return to the grind of the twenty-four-hour shifts in the steel mill, the sporadic labor strike, and the occasional thrill of local high school sports. The heart of the second industrial revolution and the birthplace of professional football in the Chicago area, Hammond and its sports fans had a love for games of bare knuckles and bloody noses.

For Johnny Chevigny, a boy with a fearless nature on and off the playing field, Hammond's blue collar world was the gateway to a celebrated life.

# CHAPTER TWO

# *Rally Sons of Notre Dame*

Before moving to 569 Sibley Street, Johnny attended a parochial elementary school in Dyer, eight miles south of Hammond. As sophomore at Hammond High School, Johnny Chevigny met his lifelong friend, Francis Meyer. The *Hammond Times* often sported weekly Chevigny banners heralding *The Flash*. Despite being a small athlete even for the 1920s, the dark-haired Johnny became recognized for his athletic prowess, as well as his charismatic personality. His athleticism notwithstanding on the courts, fields, and oval, Johnny exhibited a social presence that dominated the hallways and schoolyard.

In the 1920s, Hammond High School athletics enjoyed the talents of some of the best athletes in the Chicago area. Sports columnists and fans alike considered the Wildcats to be the Notre Dame of high schools. It was in this high-caliber setting that the All-American kid Johnny Chevigny demonstrated his athletic acuity and raw talent on the gridiron.

By the time of his enrollment as a sophomore, Johnny was both conversationally engaging and strikingly handsome, the centerpiece in any social gathering of his peers. As a student at Hammond High, Johnny maintained a diverse extracurricular schedule, participating on numerous committees, serving as the president of his class, and working on the yearbook. True to his personage, Johnny took center stage in two different school plays during his time at Hammond. And although he planned to become a doctor like his father and brother, creative writing appeared to be his significant academic strength.

Attending school in one of the more lively decades in American history brought a time of felicity in Johnny's life, and during his senior year, his creative pen illustrated the usual insouciant gaiety of a graduating class about to take on the world. As class president, Johnny was enlisted to pen the senior class prophecy. Lampooning the future of each class member was a traditional responsibility for the ranking class executive, and Johnny showcased his comedic ability, writing a Rip Van Winkle satire.

In the parody, Johnny falls asleep backstage at the prom and awakens in 1944. Of no small note to the roused Johnny is the destiny of Marguerite Cottrell, his longtime sweetheart. He finds that after his disappearance, a broken-hearted Marguerite enters a convent where she mourns the loss of her beloved.

What was Johnny's reaction to the news of his Evangeline's heartbreak? Go out and find his way in the surroundings of a modern Hammond "craving a much-needed breakfast."

Given the characteristic uncertainty of the future and the independent spirit of high school seniors, the 1924 Hammond High yearbook, *Dunes,* offered a smattering of obligatory senior dreams for a carefree future and Johnny's senior comment, "I'll have my lesson tomorrow!" exemplified his blithe attitude toward schoolwork.

Other than his aversion to academic accountability, if Johnny Chevigny had a flaw, it was the typical inner conflict that has afflicted most teenagers for centuries. It was a condition suffered by adolescents since before the Latin origin of the word, *ambition*. His parents wanted one thing; he felt called to another. While the senior class president of Hammond High School listed his ambition "to be a physician and a surgeon," his personal quote revealed a contradiction.

"On the football field he loved to be,
And few could play as well as he."
—*John E. Chevigny, 1924 Dunes*

Most of his senior classmates' quotes were nothing more than the wistful daydreams of a high school student. None of the senior quotes shared the subtle contradiction of aspiration revealed in the contrast between the Hammond class president's quote and stated ambition. Johnny Chevigny's dream was to be a physician and a surgeon, but his goal contrasted with the poetic insight of his true love—football.

Prior to the final procession of Hammond's 1924 graduating class, most of Hammond's high school faculty encouraged Johnny to attend Wabash College, a respected liberal arts college located just over a hundred miles south of Hammond. Founded in 1832, the non-sectarian school was led at one time by Caleb Mills, the father of Indiana public school education. Modeled after the Ivy League schools, Wabash College was a natural favorite of many faculties in the Indiana school districts. The Hammond faculty was no exception.

Instead of Wabash, Johnny and his father decided on nearby Notre Dame. The mission of the Congregation of the Holy Cross had an established national reputation and attracted Catholic boys from all parts of the country. Like many fathers of the Catholic faith, the Chevigny family patriarch believed his son would be best served at Notre Dame. No small factor in the Chevigny's choice of Notre Dame was the fact that Notre Dame was founded as a French Catholic university. To a French-Canadian Catholic living in the Midwest, no other university existed.

With Johnny's acceptance in the fall of 1924, Doctor Julius Chevigny realized a personal dream of having a son play football at Notre Dame. And the son would have undeniably shared his father's dream. After all, Wabash had defeated Notre Dame on the gridiron only once in the previous two decades.

In September of 1924, Johnny and Francis Meyer traveled east from Hammond to study at the university in South Bend. Johnny had committed to a course of study in premed, and best friend Frances followed suit. Classes opened on the ninth of September. The two hometown buddies were assigned as roommates in the freshman dorm, Bronson Hall.

Residing in what Meyer termed a "primitive sleeping quarter consisting of a bunk bed with heavy curtains supported on a pipe rack," the boys were now official Notre Dame men. Amenities such as lockers and washroom facilities were found in the basement.

South Bend, Indiana, was a life much farther from Hammond than the eighty miles shown on the map. While Hammond served as point for the nation's industrial caravan into the twentieth century, South Bend remained a rural outpost of Midwestern Americana.

After several years of a major postwar recession, prosperity had finally spread across the urban and suburban areas. By the midpoint of the decade, the Roaring Twenties had just begun to gain momentum.

Yet, while the stuttering growth of individual worth improved the standard of living near the large principalities, the economic growth for farmers and small town residents remained stagnant. Frustration and anger bred in these locales as the rural breadwinners of America looked for someone to blame. In northern Indiana, rural resentment found an easy target—Catholics. Most preeminent of the anti-Catholics was the Indiana Klan.

About seven hundred fifty thousand men, 30 percent of the nation's white male population, were members of the Ku Klux Klan (KKK) in 1924. The Indiana Klan was the strongest *klavern* in the nation. So malevolent were the nativist Klan's goals to expand their presence in the region and squash Notre Dame's influence, the sheeted harbingers of hatred entered into negotiations to purchase Valparaiso University, a small institution located fifty-three miles west of South Bend. In the eyes of the Klan leadership, the purchase would allow the Invisible Empire to challenge the growing presence of the hated papal university. In a reprieve for Valparaiso's legacy, the deal to sell the university to the Klan collapsed, and the Klan failed to capitalize on its momentum in the region.

In this tense environment, just prior to Johnny Chevigny's graduation from Hammond High, the KKK had announced its intention to hold a week-long convention in South Bend. From their assembly point near downtown, the planned march of more than two hundred thousand members was to end at the Notre Dame campus. As with many hate rallies sponsored by the Klan throughout history, the plan was unrealistically grandiose. The white-sheeted bark of the KKK proved to be worse than its bite, when the hundreds of thousands of expected Klansmen failed to materialize. Nevertheless, by Saturday, May 17, 1924, a smattering of expected Indiana Klansmen had arrived at the South Bend train station.

When it appeared that all who were going to participate in the demonstration had assembled, the group set out on its march. Intent on teaching the Imperial Knights a lesson of religious tolerance, groups of Notre Dame men planned to countermarch in protest.

The arriving Klansmen, many of them hardened farmers with families, were ready for the boys. Several students suffered severe beatings. With the local police assisting the Klansmen, the unarmed students were no match for the brutality and blunt instruments of the white-sheeted marchers. The worst altercation left injured students lying on the pool tables of Hullie & Mike's Pool Hall at 112 South Michigan, a popular spot for Notre Dame men. Blood stains darkened the green felt of proprietor Joe Claffey's pool tables.

Following the altercation at Hullie and Mike's, the students retreated. However, by Monday a wild rumor had swept the campus that a Klansmen had killed an undergraduate and that the police would seek no justice. Waves of anger roared from the dorm rooms as the students rallied to seek reprisal against the Klan and the South Bend police. Responding to the crisis, university president, Father Matthew Walsh, drove to the South Bend courthouse to calm the crowd and order the students to return to the campus.

In the following days, the Indiana Klan and its women's auxiliary of hate, the Queens of the Golden Mask, manufactured claims of reckless young Catholic thugs rioting throughout the South Bend streets and beating women and children. Thanks to the support of corrupted pro-Klan media throughout much of the Midwest, the Indiana Klan achieved a tactical victory in the encounter.

Later in Johnny Chevigny's freshman year, the Klan would threaten another attack. It was suspected that the threat was part of a political maneuver designed to assist the Republican candidate for governor, Ed Jackson. A crony of Grand Dragon D. C. Stephenson, Jackson received his political funding from the Klan's white robe pockets. Notre Dame's administration foresaw a fog of anti-Catholicism enveloping the state.

President Walsh was right to have concerns regarding the Klan's candidate. After Jackson's election by a large margin, he supported numerous anti-Catholic legislative proposals, including a bill that proposed the abolition of parochial schools within the state of Indiana.

In addition to Governor Jackson, United States Senator James Eli Watson was also an admitted Klan sympathizer. Saying that he sought the votes of not only the KKK but also every other order, church, and creed, as well, the Indiana senator defended his collaboration with the Knights of the Ku Klux Klan.

The native populous wasn't without voices that echoed sentiments of Watson being a charlatan and a disgrace to Indiana. Despite Senator Watson's support, some voters in Indiana despised the Klan and the politicians who hid under the pointed hoods.

Still, Senator Jim Watson's Klan-assisted reach knew no boundaries. After the Klan failed to establish a signature presence in the region with its purchase of Valparaiso, Watson flexed his political muscle with regard to the crown jewel of Notre Dame, the football program. In doing so, Watson reached out to former Notre Dame President Father John W. Cavanaugh in an effort to secure Knute Rockne's cooperation in scheduling the powerhouse Quantico Marines.

Cavanaugh responded by conditionally forwarding the senator's request to the eminent Rockne. Given the impunity of his power, Watson didn't realize the level of Father Cavanaugh's disdain for the senator's politics. Yet, the prudent former university president was careful to tread on the powerful

Watson's sensitivity. Cavanaugh agreed to be of service to the stalwart senator and pass on the scheduling request to Notre Dame's football coach.

The Quantico Marines were not associated with the Invisible Empire. However, if Watson were able to pressure Notre Dame to schedule a series with the Marine juggernaut, he would enrich his reputation both in the U. S. Senate and in his home state. Quantico's football program wanted the prestige of having Notre Dame on the Marines' schedule. With Rockne and his Ramblers on the schedule, the Marine base would legitimize its accomplishments on the field and set the stage to establish itself as a rival to West Point within the niche of college football.

Though Cavanaugh did ask Knute Rockne to consider a game with the Marines, in his dispatch to Rockne, a message lay between the lines. Obliquely stated that he wouldn't care so much as to shake hands with the senator, Father John W. Cavanaugh clearly stated his position on the matter to Rockne. Providing a covert clear hint as to what play he should run, Cavanaugh placed the ball in the coach's hands.

Rockne responded just as the priest expected. Rockne diffused the situation by blaming a veto of Watson's proposition on the university's Faculty Board of Control of Athletics, thereby denying the senator's request to schedule Quantico. The matter was settled; Notre Dame would not play the Marines.

Rockne had his own share of battles with the faculty board, so he was due a little cooperation. The Faculty Board of Control of Athletics was the last word on any athletic matter. Even though its members were reformist and its policies were usually a pain in Rockne's paw, he was known to be able to navigate the thorns in seeking his will.

With the Watson-Quantico dilemma dampened and a two-week eastern trip scheduled, Notre Dame football looked to earn a huge payday in 1924. On the road trip east, they would play Army at the Polo Grounds, then travel to Princeton. As good as the financial returns of the two gates would be the fourteen-day exposure of the team to the New York media. In terms of both the bottom line and media exposure, the most important game was October, 14, 1924, when Rockne's Ramblers met West Point at Yankee Stadium.

There, just before the end of the half, the Ramblers held a 6-0 lead at intermission. Other than witnessing the steady performance of the Notre Dame backfield, it had been a dull game with little action for the fans. With the game half over, famed sportswriter Grantland Rice needed an inspirational lead for the game's summation. The press box's long wooden counter was strewn with typewriters and notes as various journalists and press box spectators engaged in their usual boisterous conversations. At some point in the banter, a New York sportswriter, whose name is lost to history, expressed awe of Notre Dame's backfield.

Overhearing the accolade, Notre Dame press assistant George Strickler chimes in, "…just like the Four Horsemen…" Asked to elaborate, Strickler described a movie he'd seen, "The Four Horsemen of the Apocalypse." Based on the best-selling 1918 wartime translation of Spanish author Vicente Blasco Ibanez's *Los Cuatro Jinetes Del Apocalipsis*, the 1921 film starred Rudolph Valentino. With its powerful final scene, the movie and its intricate plot of wartime duty and personal redemption left a lasting impression on those who viewed it. Eventually named by many critics and many silent movie fans as the greatest silent movie of all time, the film had obviously hit a home run with Strickler.

It was George Strickler's remark, "…just like the Four Horsemen…" that Grantland Rice used, when he struck his lead for the game's outcome.

"Outlined against a blue, gray October sky, the Four Horsemen rode again. In dramatic lore, they are known as Famine, Pestilence, Destruction and Death. These are only aliases. Their real names are Stuhldreher, Miller, Crowley, and Layden. They formed the crest of the South Bend cyclone before which another fighting Army team was swept over the precipice at the Polo Grounds this afternoon as fifty-five thousand spectators peered down upon the bewildering panorama spread out upon the green plain below." — *Grantland Rice, New York Herald Tribune*

Not offended by Rice's plagiarized inspiration, George Strickler enjoyed the near fame of his part in the Sunday edition's front page story. To capitalize on the power of the passage, the young Notre Damer telegraphed South Bend and arranged for a photographer to capture a shot of the four Notre Dame backfield members on horseback once the team returned to campus.

The subsequent publicity photo becomes a sensational sports image unmatched in its power of recognition. The picture was an instant classic, and future Pulitzer Prize-winning sportswriter Red Smith, a Notre Dame student in 1924, noted that Strickler made a small fortune, selling hundreds of eight-by-eleven prints for $1 each.

A writer's keen ear, a slick phrase, and a picture worked together to provide four pretty good football players, self-professed as unremarkable in size, strength, and speed, a position of permanence and reverence in the eternal annals of college football. Although he was familiar with George Strickler and was a Notre Dame man through and through, Johnny Chevigny wouldn't have purchased the $1 print. Confident that he would soon make his own mark on the gridiron, he would become his own Notre Dame legend.

# CHAPTER THREE

# *The Odds Be Great*

Regardless of the national acclaim awarded the university because of the success of Knute Rockne's Ramblers, the good priests wanted Notre Dame to be known for more than its football program. When it came to a conflict between practice time and class responsibilities, Notre Dame faculty members were unconcerned that the afternoon classes and labs made it difficult for the players to attend football practice. At Notre Dame, the afternoon lab was a staple of the curriculum for all pre-med students. However, Rockne made no concessions; the afternoon was for football practice.

Such a scheduling conflict between the science professors and football coach may have contributed to Johnny failing both semesters of his freshman zoology lab. His chemistry marks were poor, as well, a seventy-three in the fall semester of 1925 and a seventy-eight in the spring semester of 1926. With his lowest grades recorded in the sciences, Johnny Chevigny began to have second thoughts about his high school goal of becoming a physician and surgeon.

Facing even stiffer academic requirements in the fall of 1925, Johnny Chevigny and Francis Meyer were in their second year at Notre Dame, and arriving in South Bend with the newest class was a big distraction, Hammond native Bill Kleighe. Standing over six feet and weighing more than two hundred pounds, the popular Kleighe was known around Hammond High as a tough kid.

In the vernacular of the day, Bill may have been described as a *Big Six*, a reference to the powerful six-cylinder engines then emerging on the highways. One afternoon, a playful Bill decided he would have some fun stuffing Johnny in a locker. He should have known better. Despite his small stature, five feet seven and weighing less than one hundred seventy pounds, Johnny Chevigny was no turkey and locker stuffing. When the scuffle ended quickly and a peace accord was negotiated, Johnny avoided the Kleighe locker treatment for good.

In a letter recalling the competitive nature of his high school buddy and college roommate, Meyer wrote, "Jack was not a bully and he was afraid of no one."

Jack owned his own rambunctious demeanor, a trait that set him apart from many of the other underclassmen.

Meyer recalled, "Jack and I shared a double bunk bed, and I had the top bunk. On one occasion, Jack asked me to look over the side of the bed. As I did so, he pushed the underside of my bed, and over I went. He caught me on the way down."

In his whimsical admiration, Meyer neglected to mention that Jack exhibited far more enthusiasm for dorm room horseplay than he did for his studies. By the conclusion of his freshman year, John Chevigny had bottomed out academically and was ruled ineligible to continue as an active member of the football program. He would not play football from the fall semester of 1925 through the spring semester of 1926.

Although Jack dropped the premed curriculum in the spring of his second year, he continued to falter. Failing four more classes in the spring, even his passing marks were less than impressive. Five of his eight credits averaged below a mediocre seventy-five. At that point, it looked as if the only Notre Dame legacy to which Jack Chevigny would be associated would be one of failure. After two years of a dismal academic performance, John E. Chevigny was suspended from Notre Dame. He had already missed one football season and now faced losing another. Only a stellar summer school could save him from expulsion.

Showing a marked improvement in the summer of 1926, Johnny earned consideration for reinstatement with high scores in two journalism courses, an education class, and a psychology course. He and his father were relieved, when, in September of 1926, he was reinstated to the University of Notre Dame and ruled eligible for football.

By the football season of 1926, John Chevigny understood that his laurels wouldn't be won in the afternoon lab classes. Both he and his father suspected that his notoriety wouldn't be found in a wooden desk or student lab coat. Rather than performing tests of alkalines and acids, Johnny gravitated toward the gridiron tests of mettle. At about the same time, the great pioneer of heart surgery, Michael Ellis DeBakey, began his freshman studies at Tulane University, a struggling Notre Dame sophomore turned his back on medicine and the pursuit of academic excellence. It would prove to be a decision that Johnny Chevigny and Notre Dame would never regret.

It was on the football field he loved to be.

And few could play as well as he.

# CHAPTER FOUR

## *Loyal to Notre Dame*

As Jack regained his balance, his famous coach managed to catalyze his own meltdown by way of the Columbia University affair, Knute Rockne's most infamous professional indiscretion. Sparking the Columbia affair was the despotic nature of the Notre Dame Faculty Board of Control of Athletics.

In December 1925, a rift between Rockne and the board resulted in his acceptance of Columbia's petition to bring his coaching talent to New York. Rockne's relations with the board had ruptured, when Rockne vehemently disagreed with their rejection of his proposal to continue the Nebraska series. Subsequent to that decision, Notre Dame's powerful football coach initiated a meeting with the interested parties from Columbia University.

A longtime stepsister of eastern football, Columbia was thin on talent but fat in the wallet. The Lions offered an endowed financial support system along with a Manhattan base of operations that provided a media-savvy coach with access to the pulse of the nation, the New York City media. Having grown tired of the prospect of continued mediocrity, Columbia offered Rockne a three-year deal with an annual salary of $75,000, the largest salary of any football coach. In reaching for the prestige enjoyed by the other eastern football elites, the Columbia principals felt they had made Rockne an offer that he could not refuse. Unaware of Rockne's underlying psychological motivation and his constant need for celebratory affirmation, the Columbia supporters left the deal's closing with the belief that they had hooked the country's greatest football coach. Then, in an overly exuberant expression of joy and relief over their catch, a Columbia football zealot leaked the terms to the press.

The news of the proposition leaked; Rockne was exposed. His Columbia option had relied on subterfuge and a closeted appeal to Notre Dame's administration to reconsider their priorities. When Rockne realized that the Columbia booster's leak put Notre Dame in a spotlighted corner from which they would emerge swinging, he rightly suspected the scenario would end badly.

Though the Columbia deal offered Rockne a raise of $15,000 and local access to the nation's media hub, he had no intentions of ever moving to Morningside Heights. Like other Rockne ploys for attention and gain, the gambit was just another double-slot reverse, pure deception.

It is a longstanding myth of machismo: gain attention from an attractive girl you've just met, and your longtime girl will work harder to please you. For Rockne, holding the myth to be true almost cost him his marriage to Notre Dame. When the story of his unauthorized contract discussions with Columbia erupted, Rockne worked frantically to spin the facts in order to mitigate his guilt. When he claimed that the unethical and technically illegal contract negotiations with Columbia were an exaggeration of the press, Rockne proclaimed that he was never serious about accepting the Lion backers' proposition.

In fact, the priests of Notre Dame muted the discourse by refusing any negotiation for Rockne's release. He would honor his contract, albeit with a slight tuck of the tail on his part. Sympathetic to Rockne, the New York media fabricated a fortunate conclusion to the incident, blaming overenthusiastic Columbia boosters for the encroachment across Notre Dame's property line. Meekly returning to his South Bend duties after a mild reprimand, Rockne was fortunate to have suffered only mild collateral damage from the ill-conceived venture.

After Rockne reneged, Columbia would likewise cut and run in an attempt to restore confidence in their new rookie head coach, Charles F. Crowley. After all, Crowley hadn't been so bad. Mildly successful in his first season, his only failing may have been the fact that he had the misfortune of following the abbreviated tenure of football's *Dean of the Ivy League*, Percy Haughton.

Haughton's hiring in 1923 was believed to be the master stroke that would put Columbia at the top of the Ivy League. Lion supporters were elated to see the Haughton investment show dividends as the 1924 squad, despite playing one of the toughest schedules in football, raced to a 4-1 record. The Haughton system was working its magic, but the curtain fell during a Monday's preparation for Cornell. Haughton experienced chest pains and collapsed on the turf. Just as the light of expectant glory had broken for Columbia, Haughton's death at St. Luke's Hospital cast a cloud of gloom over the program. Finishing the 1924 season, the Blue and White fought on in Haughton's memory and finished a modest 5-3-1 under an interim coach. Charles Crowley's 1925 squad followed with a respectable 6-3-1 over a decidedly weaker schedule.

The courting of Rockne gave Columbia a second opportunity to secure a proven winner, and with Rockne on the hook in December 1925, Columbia backers again huddled to call a signal that would acquire the product it needed for East Coast dominance. When Rockne withdrew abruptly from consideration, it was a turn nearly as cruel as Haughton's sudden passing. After Rockne's dalliance with their hearts, it would take Columbia years to land a field general who would take them to the top. Lou Little would eventually lead the Lions to a Rose Bowl victory over Stanford in 1933, but Little's teams couldn't sustain any length of dominance over the East. Despite an occasional run of good teams and the sporadic remarkable upset, Columbia football would drift toward mediocrity.

For Rockne, backing out of the Columbia deal was possibly the most important decision of his life. Most college football historians doubt that he could not have done anything to alter the future of Columbia football. Rockne's acceptance of tenure near Grant's tomb only would have defaced college football's sacred coaching idol.

Fighting his own battles, Johnny Chevigny wouldn't have cared much about the Columbia controversy. After a stellar freshman year in 1924 and a difficult year of ineligibility in 1925, Johnny was poised to challenge for a role in the varsity backfield as an understudy to Christie Flanagan.

Because the Columbia incident was over as soon as it had begun, most of Rockne's team never gave it a second thought. To the Notre Dame man, Rockne's resignation was a matter of impossibility. With his conversion to Catholicism on the eve of the Northwestern game in 1925, he had become a Notre Dame man. All Notre Dame men cherished the Notre Dame tradition.

If the Columbia affair caused Rockne's reputation as a square dealer to dip, the expected fortunes of a returning veteran squad in 1926 would restore the coach's vigor. The Columbia dalliance behind him, Rockne and the Ramblers opened 1926 with great promise, and another year of Notre Dame football usually meant another sports legend born.

# CHAPTER FIVE

# *Carnegie's Echo*

Awarded a probationary reinstatement in September of his third year, John Edward Chevigny continued his studies in the autumn of 1926. Dropping premed for prelaw may have disappointed the elder physician of the family, but dwelling in disappointment wasn't a Chevigny way. This father understood his son's goals and supported them with fervor. Doctor Chevigny's disappointment would have been supplanted by a larger enthusiasm for Johnny's true vision quest—football. Even with the loss of his premed scholarship money, he was on the right course. The future football star had charted his true North.

Anointed with a Rockne nickname, Chev would major in football and minor in the study of law. Thanks to his reinstatement, the name of John Chevigny, lost from its familiar place in the sports section during the last two years, was now found at a halfback spot on the reserve roster.

As for Rockne, the Columbia affair was far behind him. While pillaging his opponents by a total point spread of 197 to 7, Rockne had stitched his tattered prestige. After defeating Army 7-0 late in the 1926 season, Rockne's Ramblers were one game away from a showdown in Los Angeles with the Trojans of the University of Southern California (USC). They would be the final hurdle in the race for another national championship. But first was Carnegie Tech.

While the Carnegie Tech game of 1926 held its own place in sporting infamy, the events surrounding the game would rival the serpentine plot of the greatest crime novel. By the final gun, the only thing about that game that wasn't disputed was the final outcome: Carnegie Tech 19, Notre Dame 0. It was a loss that Johnny Chevigny would never forget.

Years after the Carnegie Tech loss, Irish alumni and fans continued to castigate the one person they believed to be responsible for the most embarrassing loss in Notre Dame history. Indelibly scapegoated for the shocking loss would be Heartley "Hunk" Anderson. For the rest of his life, Hunk would wear the albatross of Carnegie Tech about his professional neck. In reality, it was an albatross that belonged to Rockne alone.

Instead of traveling to Pittsburgh to direct his team against the lesser Tartans of Carnegie Tech, Rockne was in Chicago allegedly conducting scouting duties at the Army-Navy game. To Rockne, the Tech contest was an inconsequential contest against an out-manned squad. He confidently appointed his strategist and trusted assistant Hunk Anderson to lead the team in his absence.

Anderson was considered the preeminent line coach in the country, capable in directing every aspect of Rockne's strategies. A more devoted assistant than Hunk Anderson had not manned the Notre Dame sideline. Conversely, it was his loyalty that left him impotent in the face of a fluid crisis. Anderson was unyielding to any influence that suggested he should alter or adjust the master plan in mid-flight; his inflexibility was a key thread in the unraveling of Notre Dame that afternoon.

Anderson obeyed an absent Rockne's precise instructions to the letter. Later, in an attempt to explain the disastrous upset, Rockne would state that

Anderson's loyalty was partially responsible for the Rambler's undoing against the Tartans.

Though Rockne attempted to deflect the blame away from Hunk, the result for Anderson would be a lifelong scarlet letter. In the eyes of the media and fans, Anderson broke a trust. With the greatest team in America at his command, Anderson failed against a greatly inferior opponent. No one could believe the outcome. Hunk Anderson had choked.

In an attempt to mitigate Rockne's role in the debacle, publicist Christy Walsh instructed Rockne to say he had been away on a sacred scouting mission, a mission so important that he could entrust the task to no one. It was a plausible explanation. Carnegie Tech should have been no threat to upset the Ramblers. Leaving the team to scout a tougher upcoming opponent made sense. The hedgerow of lies was seeded.

Longtime Notre Dame trainer Eugene Scrapiron Young recounted that Rockne invited him to travel to Chicago as a tag-a-long for the trip. According to Young, he and Rockne traveled to Chicago to scout the Army-Navy game at Soldier Field, while their own Rambler Blue and Gold faced the Tartans in Pittsburgh. Recalling that he shivered in the cold bleachers as Rockne took notes of the Cadets' strengths and weaknesses, Scrapiron remembered Rockne insisting that they remain inconspicuous. They would avoid the warmth of the press box and prying eyes of the press, and simply blend into a mass of woolen overcoats and fedoras.

Scrap's oft-repeated tale makes for a great story, but the only truth of his blurred account is his memory regarding the score of the Army-Navy game. And that it was famed radio announcer Bill Stern who personally inspired Young to publish his memoir (with the Carnegie Tech yarn included) provides some clue as to how the fabrication was constructed.

Stern was a masterful storyteller, well known for his liberal boundaries regarding the ethics of sports journalism. An adherent of gee-whiz sports journalism, Stern wrote as if the truth was subject to his own creative anarchy. Consequently, in Bill Stern stories, neither fact nor fiction is easily identifiable.

Should the ghosts of Stern and Young ever be called to issue on their veracity, they would scoff at the suggestion of impropriety on their part. Gee-whiz journalism, the exaggeration of uplifting characteristics or the misrepresentation of fact, was a form of inspirational art. Such fabrication and misrepresentation in the 1920s sport print media was a critical cog in Notre Dame's football machine. Mythmaking was central to the establishment of the most colorful Notre Dame traditions, and Rockne was as a well-paid collaborator in the practice.

What was the truth of November 27, 1926? Was Rockne sitting incognito in the wooden bleachers of frigid Soldier Field, hoping only to maintain anonymity as he charted the mighty Army squad's tendencies?

One flaw in Scrapiron Young's account is that he said Rockne was in Chicago to scout Army on that day, two weeks after the Irish had already defeated the Cadets. When Young explained the unrealistic timing of the scouting trip, he insisted that Rock, as he was known to his friends, was in Chicago to scout the Cadets for the following season, an implausible if not ridiculous justification.

Too embarrassing to circulate, the truth is that Rockne was in the press box at Soldier Field, but he wasn't scouting anyone. He was making a publicity appearance in full view of numerous sportswriters. Rockne's real purpose for the trip to Chicago was to publicize the upcoming All-American Team selections, feed the Christy Walsh-Rockne publicity machine, and fill his pockets.

In staging a photo opportunity with the two other top college coaches of the year, Tad Jones of Princeton and Pop Warner of Stanford, the buoyant Walsh explained to Rockne that the trio would score a public relations coup with a group photo. Although Walsh voiced his apprehension about Rock's planned absence from the Carnegie Tech game, the coach calmed Walsh's fear of a public relations backfire. Reassuring his longtime agent, Rockne dismissed the Carnegie contest as unimportant. The Tartans weren't good enough to stand against a rolling blue wave of undefeated (8-0) Notre Dame men.

As it turned out, the Skibos, as they were often called in honor of Andrew Carnegie's Scottish castle, were enough. The Tartans' part-time coach, Walter Steffen, was no dunce. Balancing his full-time job as a judge in Chicago and his position as the head football coach at Carnegie Tech, Steffen was an inconsiderate irritation to Rockne. For example, Steffen rarely yielded to Rockne's demands in the selection of game officials, an act that, in Rockne's eyes, was a particularly irksome show of disrespect. Hunk Anderson remembered that Steffen pounced on Rockne's absence as a motivational tool for his Skibos. That afternoon in Pittsburgh, Steffen had his squad motivated and prepared.

On the opposite sideline without their head coach, the unbeaten Rambler squad was flat and uninspired. Most accounts of that weekend support Hunk's claim that his orders included Rockne's edict that the pregame strategy was to be strictly followed. No variations or liberties were to be taken. Rockne's philosophy was simple if not simple-minded. Stick to the plan, and the superior team would win. As the game progressed, the first assistant in rank had no flexibility in adjusting the plan to compensate for the deteriorating play of the Irish.

Some coaches like to pontificate that losing is an indication of a lack of character. On this day, the coach would fail because of his wealth of character, not his lack of character.

Anderson often recounted the principal feature of Rockne's plan. Start the shock troops (Johnny Chevigny was in that group) and play them for a quarter, then bring in the regulars to seal the win. It should have played out as just another Notre Dame victory march, but Carnegie struck the first blow, punching in a first-quarter touchdown. Anderson remembered that the first string did little to alter the tide, and the starters' quality of play degraded further as the contest continued. Rockne had coached the defenders to stay wide, but instead of performing as they had been coached, the sleepwalking Irish pass defenders showed no reaction as the Tartan quarterback connected at will. Nothing Hunk said could wake the Notre Dame secondary out of their trance.

Fairly or unfairly for Hunk, this loss would blot his coaching legacy. The price of loyalty was something his legacy would be charged for all time.

How big was the Carnegie Tech upset? The answer can be found in the fact that current Carnegie Mellon players continue to draw strength from that day in 1926. Today's Carnegie Mellon Tartans play in the lowest division of National Collegiate Athletic Association (NCAA) football, but on the day of every home game, the Tartans walk through the Howard Harpster Hall of Fame to view the hallowed Notre Dame game ball. As they pass slowly by the trophy case in reverence of that day in 1926, the modern Tartans see indisputable proof that on any given Saturday, the least of the underdogs may defeat the greatest of the giants. Like a chalice of glory, the ball remains for those to drink of its message.

The blame for the loss should have been nailed to Rockne's wall, but it never was. Rockne neglected to remember the axiom of the underdog:

motivation is a decisive force for victory. His poor judgment in late November 1926 will be listed as one of the greatest coaching blunders in the history of all sports. Rockne's negligence gave Carnegie Tech the winning edge, and despite the efforts of Scrapiron Young, Bill Stern, and numerous other Irish purists over the decades—it didn't matter what version of the fable was told—the ending was the same; a national championship was lost.

In Los Angeles the week following the Carnegie Tech upset, Notre Dame and Rockne applied a mildly redemptive salve to their wound with a victory over USC to close out the season. Possibly more redeeming was the game's payout of slightly over $75,000, which brought the 1926 season's profits to over $250 million. In a time when the president of the United States maintained that "the chief business of the American people is business," the chief business of college football was Notre Dame.

On New Year's Day, an unbeaten Alabama played an unbeaten Stanford in the 1927 Rose Bowl for the unofficial 1926 national championship. The game ended in a 7-7 tie.

After a noteworthy year as a shock trooper and effective backfield reserve, Jack Chevigny readied himself for his breakout junior season of eligibility. He was one year away from being christened the toughest player Rockne would ever coach.

# CHAPTER SIX

# *Flanagan's Fighting Irish*

It was the 1920s, the Golden Age of Sports. Exhibiting a national sports mania emblematic of the decade's economic giddiness and mass enthusiasm, America basked in its celebration of the athlete-hero. Basketball's Harlem Globetrotters played their first game in Hinckley, Illinois. In major league baseball, Babe Ruth boomed homeruns, while pitcher Walter Johnson recorded his one-hundred-and-tenth shutout victory. In swimming, Johnny Weissmuller's one-hundred-yard freestyle time of fifty-one seconds set a mark that would stand for seventeen years; like Johnson's shutout record, Weissmuller's record of fifty-two national championships may never be broken. On the links, Bobby Jones earned a rain-soaked trophy in the U. S. Amateur Championship at Minikahda Club in Minneapolis, while Walter Hagen, one of golf's greatest celebrity and match players, continued to lift professional golf toward its eventual penthouse of Sports Americana. And in 1927, the greatest era in heavyweight boxing reached its zenith, when over one hundred thousand Soldier Field fight fans witnessed the infamous long count heavyweight victory of Gene Tunney over Jack Dempsey.

The November 7, 1927 cover of *Time Magazine* depicts Knute Rockne, standing patronizingly confident with his arms crossed. With the exception of the 1925 squad, no Rockne team has lost more than a single game. As the 1927 season opens, the Rock is a sports celebrity second only to Babe Ruth and Jack Dempsey; his Notre Dame football team plays second chair only to the great New York Yankee dynasty. In an obligatory reverence to Rockne's status, the stationery of his agent Christy Walsh sports a graphic header of numerous five-pointed stars. Rockne's star is near the center of the page next to Ruth's. By the year considered to the pinnacle of the decade's Golden Age of Sports, Knute Rockne's record is a phenomenal seventy-four wins offset by just eight losses. It's a great time to play football at Notre Dame.

In the third decade of twentieth-century football, Notre Dame is the emotional flag bearer for American Catholics. Rockne and his boys are on top of the world, and the Rockne style of play employed by Notre Dame is the benchmark of football strategy.

The celebrity came with a price. Conjunctive to Notre Dame's privileged athletic status was an intensified scrutiny regarding the academic accountability of Rockne's program.

As he continued his bumbling academic ballet, but projected to be a starter at halfback, Chevigny was in his fourth year on campus. Unfortunately for Jack, 1927 was a bad year to be an academic slacker. Notre Dame sought to improve its academic reputation through a slow but steady separation from the loose cattle-call recruiting methods prevalent during that decade of college football. President Matthew Walsh was growing tired of fielding inquiries from influential alumni asking for his confirmation that Notre Dame was not, as its detractors alleged, just a renegade football factory. In response, Walsh intended to prove that Notre

Dame football was worthy of any academic accountability test put forth by the Big Ten or any other conference.

Coincidental to President Walsh's concern was a statement of the Big Ten's athletic manifesto of January 28, 1927. The manifesto originated from a committee consisting of trustees, presidents, athletic directors, football coaches, and alumni from the member institutions, calling for the Big Ten Conference to eliminate any financial aid or loans based on athletic skill. Though the loss of financial incentives for the prospective athlete was a disturbing turn for many coaches, the committee didn't stop at limiting funds. It went on to further ban all mechanisms designed to distribute correspondence aimed at the recruitment of student-athletes. In effect, both the means and the end were cut from the coaches' ability to improve their reserve of athletes on campus.

In an era in which fifty-five different concrete Romanesque stadiums were constructed for college football spectators who added approximately a half million dollars a year to various university budgets, the Big Ten move was one of characteristic hypocrisy. Rockne reacted to the Big Ten's proposed direction with contempt.

To selectively argue his counterpoints to the hypocritical reforms, Rock enlisted his second voice, sportswriter Francis Wallace. Writing for *Scribner's Magazine*, Wallace, a Notre Dame alumnus and unofficial co-author of the "Fighting Irish" nickname, stormed the Bastille of reform. Wallace's scathing article, THE HYPOCRISY OF COLLEGE FOOTBALL REFORM, breeched the parapet of hypocrisy and left no doubt as to the lack of transparency and backbone in the Big Ten's reformation. Rockne couldn't have been more pleased with his covert countermeasure to the reformist's agenda.

Although Wallace's expository cut to the heart of Big Ten reform, the general athletic reformation movement continued to garner sympathy and support throughout the nation's ivied halls. In the months following the Wallace article, the spider had welcomed the fly, when Rockne was invited to be a guest speaker at a forum held at Georgetown. The main topic of the conference was academic reform.

Of course, the masterfully obtuse Rockne gave his full support to the Carnegie Foundation's objective of cleaning up college football. Though he was an opponent of any substantial legislation regarding institutional oversight, Rockne appreciated the Carnegie Foundation's significant clout as a financial force behind his university. As adept at public relations as he was between Saturday's chalked lines, Rockne possessed acuity for recognizing the value of the dollar in the equilibrium of power. In appreciation of the size of the Carnegie watchdog pulling at its chain, Rockne gave the dog a wide berth.

For the present, Notre Dame football recruiting would take on the look of a more localized operation. Meanwhile, the self-propelled recruiting machine continued to harvest crops nationwide as Rockne received more inquiries from prospects than his program could ever hope to utilize.

Thanks to the effort of Christy Walsh and Francis Wallace, the media continued its fabrication of a missionary's creed regarding Rockne and his methods. Portrayed as the immigrant coach who acted as an angel for the tough impoverished boys of the back alleys, Rock was seen as giving boys a chance they would never have outside of his program at Notre Dame. What wasn't so publicized was the coach's true intent in recruiting and sequestering all of the available football talent in his own private South Bend football monastery. Whether the talent was heir to a New York City tenement or a Milwaukee beer fortune was of equal unimportance to the coach. Rockne's true recruiting policy and practice was that if he came across a prospect, even one who was talented but not talented enough to excel at Notre Dame, he would make sure no one else obtained that athlete. This policy prevented Pitt, Minnesota, and other rivals from gaining the use of that athlete against his own program. During most of his tenure at Notre Dame, Rockne would carry over a hundred players on the squad, knowing many would never see the field in a varsity game. He was heard to say that if they weren't playing for another coach, they couldn't beat Notre Dame's coach.

Not all Notre Dame men looked upon Rockne's talent hoarding with admiration. Former student-athlete Frank Leahy, who rose to rival Rockne's iconic status in the annals of Irish football, recalled his mentor's philosophy in the numbers game. Leahy called it a deplorable waste of fine young athletes. During the highpoint of the Rockne era, spring football would begin with nearly four hundred squad members. Consequently, Notre Dame's stockpiling plan resulted in the development of a two-deep roster that was usually more talented than most starting rosters in the country.

Rockne was a visionary. Modern football would build dynasties according to the Rockne model until 1977. Only then did the NCAA begin restricting the allotted number of scholarships and put an end to the meat-on-the-hoof mentality of major college football.

Notre Dame carried thirty-five players on its varsity traveling squad. The reserve squad, Jack Chevigny's main team in 1926, carried thirty-five additional players. A practice squad consisted of another ninety players or so. Additionally, in the 1920s, Notre Dame's freshman football roster numbered about eighty players. Remarkably, these large numbers served Rockne's program in a time when football was a one-platoon game, meaning the same eleven players played both offense and defense.

Rockne's indirect recruiting reached into every crevice and high school cupboard of the Midwest. Former players and coaches, who knew his system and its demands, spotlighted their area's top talent and helped to channel those players' interests toward Notre Dame.

Despite Rockne's unrestricted network and prospect hoarding, the 1927 Carnegie Foundation probe into college football cleared Notre Dame of any violations regarding recruiting. Rockne's insiders, a tight-lipped group of former players and knowledgeable friends of the program, numbered just around a dozen. It was a tightly knit family with a level of secrecy and trust rivaling that of the Chicago gangsters. Though the Carnegie examiners would bite numerous other programs, Notre Dame stayed out of the reformist doghouse.

A clean bill of health from the Carnegie review didn't mean Rockne had no indiscretions. As with most university athletic programs of the day, Notre Dame provided paying positions at the university, and the better players earned top dollar, working at off-campus jobs. In addition to locating off-campus paid positions for his boys, Rockne guaranteed the best players remunerative fluff jobs, sweeping the gym and parking cars on campus. As a key player in 1927, Jack Chevigny was no exception to that rule.

Another concern for the reformists was in the area of academic fraud. From the likes of the Big Ten and other major forces of college football, charges of permissiveness and creative academic practices were often slung at Rockne and Notre Dame. Though perpetually alleged, these charges were unfounded. In fact, Rockne felt handcuffed by the strict scrutiny under which he was forced to operate.

Despite his guile, Rockne had a soft spot for the kid who couldn't quite reach the rung of opportunity, and, in one of these lost opportunities,

Rockne's true character and personal depth matched the fiction of the his hyperbolic legends. During the 1926 season, Paul Danculovic had been projected as the second team right halfback behind team captain Thomas Hearden. John Chevigny and Bucky Dahman were listed as third and fourth teamers. Rock dreamed of the gifted Slovakian, Danculovic, in the same backfield as the transplanted Irish-Texan Christie Flanagan. Not to anyone's surprise, the academically challenged Danculovic fell short in his second chance at reinstatement to the university. Though never would Danculovic see his name recorded on the all-time roster, Rockne didn't abandon him. Rock forwarded the talented Minnesota prep star to his former right-hand man, Hunk Anderson, at St. Louis University.

Few anecdotes illustrate the complexity of Rockne's character more than his diligence in helping the failed Danculovic. In placing the academically deficient superstar with another university, the coach's efforts showed a side of him contrary to Frank Leahy's assessment of Rockne as an unsympathetic miser of football talent. Given his faults, the harsh taskmaster Rockne was intensely loyal when it came to his boys. He would do almost anything for any one of them. And while the coach's win-first coaching priority may have conflicted with a fatherly devotion to all of his boys, the Danculovic story offers a window into appreciating Rockne's complex personality and drive. The complexities and contradictions defined the man whose essence was revealed to few, yet loved by many—especially, Jack Chevigny.

His charismatic leadership aside, Rockne's tactical impact on the game had few peers. Before the tactics and phraseology of the West Coast Offense, the Spread Offense, the Flexbone Offense, and the 46 Defense, the dominant style of football was Rockne-ball. Every school administrator and alumni association wanted to hire a coach who understood it. To anyone associated with any level of football, Rockne-ball was the holy lance of football coaching. It would empower the weak and make the strong unbeatable.

In 1927, the St. Louis Billikens wanted football's holy lance. Consequently, they hired Rockne's right-hand man, Hunk Anderson, the same Hunk Anderson blamed for the Carnegie Tech disaster. Soon after Anderson arrived on campus, he found the Jesuit administration's goals and policies to be contradictory and counterproductive to his aims for the university's program. In just a single season, the aimless Jesuit leadership quickly broke Anderson's morale and sent him back to Rockne with his hat in his hand.

At St. Louis, Hunk had realized that he couldn't be appreciated unless he was in an environment that supported his goals, both professionally and financially. A practical man, he also appreciated the value of a dollar. In 1928, Rockne offered him $8,500 to return. It was the same salary he had received as head coach at St. Louis, a job that had driven him mad. After his one-year foray as head coach of the underfunded Billikens football program, Rockne's former player and trusted assistant knew where he belonged. He needed to be back with the Rock.

Johnny Chevigny also knew where he belonged. Since his note-taking days in Rockne's freshman football class, the Hammond speedster's life and actions had grown symbiotic to those of his coach. With this symbiosis nearly complete by Jack's junior year, the Chevigny star was ready to shine just as brightly as those stars arcing across the top of a Christy Walsh correspondence. In 1927, Jack was poised to make his mark as an international star of the Fighting Irish. Team captain of the 1926 squad Thomas Hearden had graduated, and Chev hoped to earn Hearden's right halfback spot. His only challenge would be his good friend, Bucky Dahman.

An all-star basketball player for the Blue and Gold, Bucky Dahman hailed from Youngstown, Ohio. With achievements in the previous season that included coming off the bench and breaking a seventy-yard touchdown run against Minnesota, Dahman posed a significant obstacle to Jack achieving his goal, but at least the goal was achievable now that Paul Danculovic had transferred to play for the Billikens. When on the field, Danculovic was said to have been the legendary George Gipp reincarnated.

For Rockne, the usual irons were heating in the fire. Of these topics, scheduling was typically one of the hottest. Although both Rockne and the Notre Dame administration had grown comfortable with the Irish remaining an independent without conference affiliation, Notre Dame had been petitioned to join the newly formed Missouri Valley Conference. Rockne graciously refused. From this point, no conference would be big enough. Notre Dame would remain a national team.

As if to emphasize the point that Notre Dame was in a league of its own, the Irish defeated the Kohawks of Coe College 28-7 in front of less than ten thousand fans at Cartier Stadium in the 1927 home opener. Rockne knew that if Notre Dame were to play those types of teams week to week, it would have downgraded its football program. If Notre Dame had joined the Missouri Valley Conference in 1927, the long-term consequence would have rewritten the history of college football.

A visit to the Jesuit-founded University of Detroit and their new stadium followed the Coe College meeting. In the week prior, mighty Army had narrowly escaped a loss at home to Detroit. The Notre Dame game was something of a favor to Gus Dorais, college teammate and best man at Rockne's wedding in 1914. Rockne was known to throw a bone to an old friend, but in this case the dog could not only bark; it could bite. Detroit had a good team and ran the Notre Dame box offense. Rockne and his boys staved off the planned ambush with a solid 20-0 shutout of Dorais's red and white Titans.

Both the Coe College and University of Detroit games generated no more than a ripple in the current of nationwide interest. Decades later, evidence testifying to the insignificance of the contests with the Kohawks and Titans could be found in the absence of news clippings in Jack Chevigny's scrapbook.

Numerous pages of the scrapbook contain multiple news accounts of the Navy games, Army games, and USC games. Jack's scrapbook confirmed Rockne's belief that these games generated the enthusiasm of the players and the subway alumni. These were the games of which memories were made.

After the 2-0 start on the 1927 slate, Jack and his teammates met Navy at a neutral site, Baltimore. Navy, one of the most prestigious football programs of the era, added a significant kick to Rockne's schedule, and the meeting would be the first in a long historical series. Partially because of the densely populated Catholic neighborhoods of Baltimore, the Fighting Irish were favored against the hometown Midshipmen. Playing the Midshipmen was always a newsworthy experience, but this time it was the way the Fighting Irish dressed that made this Navy-Notre Dame game an instant classic. While Notre Dame's freshmen typically wore green, the upperclassmen normally took the field in blue. It was a tradition, which continued against Navy, when Rock started his usual shock troops clad in the traditional Notre Dame blue. An unorthodox decision to incorporate green into the game plan headlined the newspapers, when a switch from the blue to green jerseys was made during the game.

George Trevor of the *New York Sun* reported that after the Middies jumped out to a quick touchdown lead on the blue-clad shock troops, Rockne ordered in the regulars. As reported by the *Syracuse Herald,* the "racket was terrific" until the Rockne substitution of the regulars.

Sending in the regulars after the shock troops was the traditional Rockne-ball strategy, yet George Trevor also noted the psychological aspect of the jersey switch.

Trevor wrote, "Instantaneously, the Notre Dame regulars yanked off the blue outer sweaters and like a horde of green Gila monsters darted onto the field. From that moment on Notre Dame held the initiative, and imposed its collective will upon the Navy."

Following the deployment of the green jerseys, Christie Flanagan and John Neimeic exploited the Navy ends with wide sweeps for large chunks of yardage. Notre Dame was unstoppable in its brilliant green sweaters and shining golden silk trousers.

After Notre Dame moved the ball with Ray "Bucky" Dahman and Neimiec at the halfback positions, Johnny Chevigny entered the game for Dahman and Flanagan replaced Neimiec. From that point, Flanagan's end sweeps led by Chevigny's blocking rolled the Midshipmen down the nine yard line for a first-and-goal situation. A six-yard gain by Flanagan put the Fighting Irish at the Middies' one yard line. From the Midshipman one yard line, Indianapolis native Charlie Riley took it over for the go-ahead score. With Bucky Dahman's second missed point-after-touchdown kick, Navy still had life, but time was running out.

Notre Dame controlled the momentum, and the Irish, more commonly known to the eastern media of that day as the Westerners, planned to wear down the Navy interior. For Rockne, it was a practical strategy that called for Chevigny and Dahman to substitute for each other, while Niemiec and

Flanagan similarly replaced one another. As in most years, Rockne's 1927 team enjoyed a thoroughbred stable of exceptional halfbacks. Flanagan, often called the best back in the country, eventually left the field for good in a final substitution. Navy fans roared in appreciation.

One sportswriter in the press box remarked that it should be John Niemiec's exit that the Navy fans cheered. As far as the more learned observer was concerned, Niemiec was "just another Flanagan."

With Navy sunk by a 19-6 final score, the Fighting Irish headed homeward to greet their fans and prepare to meet their fellow Hoosiers of Bloomington. Three thousand fans waited at the South Bend train station for the late arriving Irish. Mixed with loud chants of "We want Flanagan!" a rousing ovation rolled out the welcome mat for Rockne as he exited the train.

Excused from Monday's practice were Flanagan and his fellow starters, along with other key players such as Jack Chevigny. Chev had suffered one of his many career concussions. On Tuesday afternoon, the battered and bruised Irish ran through a light workout, while the remaining team members underwent a gauntlet of contact drills. Wednesday, Rockne felt the squad was again synchronized and on track to face the surprising Crimson of Indiana on Saturday.

Notre Dame would face Indiana at Bloomington. At 1-1-1, the Hoosiers had tied a tough Minnesota team the previous week. Normally outmanned against the Irish, the Hoosiers were a perpetual, yet dangerous, in-state underdog to Rockne's boys. Indiana had not defeated Notre Dame since 1906, but their tie with Minnesota raised eyebrows in South Bend. In fact, Minnesota's Golden Gophers had run roughshod over their two earlier opponents by a combined score of 97-10. Holding Minnesota to a 14-14 draw sent a message that the scrappy Hoosiers were a team to be taken seriously.

In Bloomington, Flanagan and Niemiec again engineered the substitution train. As recorded in the sports pages of the day, Niemiec stole the show from Flanagan as Dahman's inconsistency in the kicking department continued. Having missed two point-after touchdowns against Navy, the tough Ohio native continued to struggle.

Nothing came easy for the Irish. On the third play from the opening whistle, Indiana jumped out to a 6-0 lead against the Irish shock troops. Then Notre Dame responded with a scoring drive that culminated with a Niemiec touchdown run on the first play of the second quarter. The point-after touchdown was good, and the Irish held a 7-6 lead.

In the third quarter, Christie Flanagan scored the Irish's second touchdown with a short run. After Bucky Dahman missed the extra point, the score read Notre Dame 13, Indiana 6.

In the final quarter of the game, Notre Dame flexed its muscle, when Flanagan plunged over the goal line for another score and increased the lead to 19-6. Time expired as Indiana stalled out deep in Irish territory.

The Crimson's Chuck Bennett, who in the following year would become Indiana's first Most Valuable Player of the Big Ten Conference, couldn't carry the Hoosiers to a comeback. With Irish dominance of the series secured, Notre Dame left Bloomington with a perfect 4-0 record.

Up next for Flanagan, Niemiec, and company was the Golden Tornado of Georgia Tech. Rockne had good reason to expect an easy victory. The Fighting Irish enjoyed a six-game win streak in the series, and the southerners would be traveling north to Cartier Field. Rockne had never lost to the squad from Atlanta. Sunday morning papers on October 30, 1927, headlined the possibility of a "one-sided battle taken by Irish."

After Notre Dame spanked the southern invaders, the Associated Press wired NOTRE DAME NOW LOOKS GOOD TO WIN NATIONAL TITLE IN FOOTBALL.

The account cabled from South Bend heralded the "technique of super football as taught to the Irish of Notre Dame by that old Danish master of the pigskin art...all of the wind was taken out of the vaunted Golden Tornado." In the manner of the sports reporting of the day, the Midwest accounts of the game were far more colorful than the game itself.

As expected, southern newspapers were less prismatic in their prose, the *Charleston Daily Mail* informing its Sabbath Day readers that, for Notre Dame, the game was "one of those hollow victories, a dull...game."

Indeed, the contest had started out slow. Both squads remained scoreless after the first quarter. As usual, Rockne replaced his reserves with starters at the start of the second quarter. In addition to Jack's stellar defensive play and blocking from his right halfback position, the usual names dominated the flow of the game; Tim Moynihan at center, John Law at right guard, and John Niemic at quarterback. In the days of one-platoon ball with players playing both offense and defense, these four accounted for what in the modern game would be eight players. Meanwhile, Fred Collins, returning from a broken jaw suffered during the prior season, stole the day with two touchdowns.

Despite the exalted tradition of Georgia Tech football and the legacy of John Heisman leading college football's first southern team to a national championship in 1917, the Associated Press could not help but point out "Rockne's men knew entirely too much football for the southerners."

Even though the record showed the Georgia Tech game to be something of a nondescript event, the Irish win was a giant step toward the national championship. Georgia Tech had already defeated Alabama, a clear contender for the national title. On this day, Notre Dame's convincing win combined with Georgia Tech's earlier upset over the highly regarded Alabama squad to put the Irish in control of their own destiny.

With Georgia Tech handled, Notre Dame stood tall at a familiar 5-0. As a date with Minnesota and future gridiron immortal Bronco Nagurski approached, Rockne was casual in his confident outlook. Notre Dame had won the last two previous meetings with Minnesota by at least twelve points.

When game time arrived and the two teams took the field, the weather in South Bend was miserable. Warren Brown, *Universal Press* staff correspondent, reported that the Irish met the Gophers in what he described as a blizzard that "made the crowd of thirty thousand sigh for California, Texas, Florida or some of those other places where the sun shines even in football season."

In his own version of Rockne-ball, Minnesota head coach Doctor C. W. Spears started the game with his second string. The Irish countered with its regular starting line and second team backs. With both teams stalemated, Notre Dame seized momentum after ten minutes of play, when a fumbled punt return bounced off Gopher Fred Hovde and the Irish recovered at the Minnesota twelve yard line. From that point, John Niemiec scored on the first play from scrimmage and added the point-after to give the Irish a quick 7-0 lead.

Associated Press sportswriter Morris Edwards reported that the "penetrating cold" caused numerous fumbles, and neither team could advance the ball. In his attempt to play to the weather conditions, Minnesota's coach Doc Spears grew more conservative in the second half. What remained of the crowd saw a stale offensive strategy utilizing punts on first down. Because of the poor footing, the Irish speed of Flanagan, Dahman, Collins, and Niemiec couldn't exploit the Minnesota strategy.

As the weather strengthened, so did the Gophers. With each Minnesota drive that pushed deep into Notre Dame territory, Irish hopes of a perfect season dampened. But because the Gophers were set back on each opportunity, Rockne remained encouraged. Of the threatening Minnesota drives, the Gophers' most serious threat came early in the final quarter, when Minnesota's two-sport star Mally Nydahl swept the right side from the three yard line, but was stopped short of the goal line on fourth down. Some accounts credit Jack Chevigny, who had substituted for Dahman, with the stop; others credit George Leppig.

With Notre Dame All-American Christie Flanagan held silent for most of the afternoon, the game became a slugfest. After Chevigny, or Leppig, thwarted Minnesota's last gasp at the goal line, the Irish still could not move the ball, and Niemiec was forced to punt from near his own end zone. At that point in the game, Bronko Nagurski would make what he recalled as the play of his life to resuscitate the dying Gophers.

With the Irish aligned in a tight kicking formation, Notre Dame's deep-snapper passed the ball back toward the punter. Accounts are sketchy as to whether the future Hall of Famer Nagurski blocked the punt or forced a bad pass from center, but most newspaper accounts indicate that Nagurski disrupted the snap from center. Whatever the details of Bronco Nagurski's action, the fumble recovery gave the exhausted Gophers new energy deep inside Irish territory with the clock winding down.

For the rest of his life, Nagurski was exceedingly proud of the moment. "Nothing I did afterwards in college could compare with causing and recovering that fumble."

Despite Nagurski's heroics, the Gophers' initiative again stalled, when Notre Dame stuffed the Minnesota offense on three consecutive goal-line rushes. And with the freezing weather and Jack Chevigny back in the game, what had become difficult for the Gophers (rushing around the ends) was now impossible. Minnesota had to go to the air if they were to tie the game. On fourth down with the game on the line, All-American Herb Joesting lofted a pass to six-footer Ken Haycraft. The touchdown catch and the point-after touchdown by the left-footed Arthur Pharmer tied the score at 7-7.

Notre Dame's final moments were spent desperately attempting to pass the ball down the field in a blinding snow. The game ended in a tie, when John Niemic was thrown for a loss on the final pass attempt. For Notre Dame, it was a crushing tie that was good as a loss. Irish hopes for a national championship boarded the next train north to Minnesota.

On the following Monday, a stunned Rockne stumbled about his office incoherently mumbling. The pain of the Minnesota contest was unbearable. Days later, when Rockne was asked by Grantland Rice to provide his customary input as to the sportswriter's All-American team, the coach cited a long list of Minnesota players.

Rockne and the Irish had little time to cry. West Point, exhibiting one of its toughest squads in recent years, was next on the schedule. For the Notre Dame athletic program, this was more than just a game; it was the money game.

Demand for tickets to the 1927 Army-Notre Dame game was so great that Yankee Stadium did not put any up for public sale. The entire allotment was reserved for the connected and socially active favorites of the sporting world. It was estimated by the *New York Sun* that Yankee Stadium managers refused over one hundred thousand ticket requests made by the general public. It wasn't just a game; it was a national event.

Still, Rockne's morose mood couldn't be sparked. Following the stalemated outcome of the Minnesota game, Rockne's confidence waned. His depression had validity. Army, with its unique eligibility waiver, started nine players with previous college experience. Red Cagle, their main offensive weapon, was playing in his sixth season of college football. At the end of the 1927 season, Cagle would earn All-American honors. Eventually, he would land in the College Football Hall of Fame.

In order to provide more contrast from the dark blue Army jerseys, Notre Dame again brandished the green uniforms. In addition to the green jerseys, Rock would bring with him the usual bag of tricks. He hoped to confuse the Army keys and coaches by secretly switching the players' numbers from those he had posted in the game program.

Once the game was underway, Rockne realized that changing both the jersey color and numbers wouldn't help against Cagle and his Army teammates. There would be no repeat of Christie Flanagan's 1926 heroics in this meeting as Army controlled the tempo and ruled the day with an 18-0 shutout. Cagle was a player for the ages.

After the Minnesota disappointment and the beating administered by Army in Yankee Stadium, Rock's boys hoped for something of a respite. Against an outmanned Drake in Des Moines, they found it; Notre Dame crushed Drake 32-0 before a small crowd of eight thousand four hundred fans. After playing two of the toughest college football teams in the country, most of the Irish nation considered the Drake contest to be nothing more than a scrimmage for the Irish, a practice for upcoming University of Southern California.

Like Army, USC was a high caliber team. In the first notable visit by a West Coast team to Chicago's Soldier Field, the Trojans and their 7-0-1 record brought considerable clout to the pre-game ticket sales.

The 113,000 fans in attendance saw both teams strike early in the game with touchdowns, but only Notre Dame executed its point-after-touchdown kick. Included in the game's drama was a controversy that emerged when a Notre Dame defender intercepted a Trojan pass near the goal line and subsequently fumbled the ball backward through the end zone. Although USC argued that a two-point safety should have been called, the officials—all of them chosen by Southern California coach Howard Jones—ruled the play to be a touchback, and a 7-6 Irish victory was sealed.

Notre Dame finished 7-1-1. For Rockne and his Irish, another successful season was in the books. As important as the winning finish was the winning bottom line. Thanks to the two big games versus Army and Southern Cal, Notre Dame earned over $300,000 in profits for the season.

Due to Jack's solid weekly performances as a defender and backup halfback, the Chevigny name combined with his Canadian roots to give him a Ruthian status of *célèbre* in the Montreal newspaper. Recognized internationally for his vicious hits and airborne blocking, the second-generation French-Canadian looked to bloom in 1928.

By the end of the 1927 season, Rockne had grown tired of the university's inaction on the matter of building a new stadium to showcase Notre Dame's prestige. His dream stadium seemed grounded in the murky waters of inefficiency. The Rock felt that the constant shuffling of committees and circuitous meetings resulted in needless obstacles to the immediate action he needed on the stadium's construction. His frustration reached a boiling point after the USC game, when he realized the profits lost by having to use the Soldier Field venue instead of a similar stadium located on campus and managed by the university. Two days after the University of Southern California game, Rockne tendered his resignation as head football coach at Notre Dame.

# CHAPTER SEVEN

# *One for the Gipper*

Rockne's resignation would have resulted in Jack facing his senior year without his foster father and mentor. If Chev knew that Rockne was leaving for another school, the stalwart Notre Dame man and devout Catholic junior halfback would have prayed for intervention. Losing Rockne wasn't something the star defensive halfback could tackle alone.

Few of the Irish would have known of Rockne's resignation letter. Other than to make a single recommendation to the various ad hoc committees responsible for putting together the stadium plans and financing, President Walsh took no responsive action. And as a precautionary measure against just such a move on Rockne's part, Walsh had made it clear to the stadium committees that the university would not be bound to the stadium plans, should an unforeseen circumstance, such as Rockne leaving, occur. Luckily for Jack and Irish football fans everywhere, Rockne's resignation was just another tired ploy to force the hand of the various development committees.

The coach felt that his threat would meld the desires of the pro-stadium group with the concerns of the anti-stadium group. Announcing his resignation, Rockne planned to force his detractors out in the opening.

Betting his future that he was right, he was sure that his threat would act as a coercive hammer in making the stadium argument more malleable. Once some shared ground could be gained, the arguments would dissolve in a solution, which was acceptable to all.

Rockne's gambit achieved its goal, when the university responded with a firm commitment to the new stadium. Even President Walsh felt the stadium was necessary, if not for exactly the same sentiment that Rockne and the interested alumni held.

By the mid-1920s, Notre Dame football, in order to continue to generate the income that was needed and expected of the program, had to play its more prestigious opponents at a neutral site such as Soldier Field or Yankee Stadium. And even when the Irish played all of their big games at a neutral site, the revenue grew each year. Home games at the outdated Cartier Stadium inhibited the flow of that revenue. In order to continue its yearly financial growth, Rock scheduled games at neutral sites when he could have scheduled home games. Both he and the Notre Dame administration couldn't accept losing thousands of dollars of revenue just to have more home games on the Cartier bluegrass.

In that the home team was entitled to a much larger cut of the game's ticket sales, the new stadium was sound planning on the part of President Matthew Walsh and the university. Walsh knew that if Notre Dame built a home stadium rivaling those of the larger Big Ten schools and USC, the yearly net would be in the millions.

It was no secret that nicknames such as Ramblers, Wanderers, and Ghosts of the West made the administration cringe. Sarcastically expressing their doubts as to whether actual university campus existed in South Bend, hostile members of the press had long derided Notre Dame's traveling football show. It appeared that the football team from South Bend lived on the rails during most of their season. As one sportswriter put it, Notre Dame should have purchased stock in the Pullman Company. A new home stadium and the discontinuance of the traveling Irish football road show would deflect the sharp-tongued jabs directed at Notre Dame's success on the gridiron.

Ironically, Rockne's threat to leave delayed the progress of the debate. Because the school's administration felt the self-promoting coach's presence to be a vital thread in the fabric of Notre Dame's national following and football star power, Rockne's gambit dampened the resolve of the pro-stadium clique. The possibility of Rockne's leaving for another school disturbed President Walsh. Should Rockne follow up on one of his yearly threats in the near future, Walsh knew the university would be stuck engaging in a construction that would become just another white-washed concrete elephant on a small campus.

In short time, Albert Erskine, president of Studebaker, stepped in to soothe Rockne's frustration and ease the university's concerns. When the South Bend automaker introduced a plan for the university to self-finance the project, his promise to chair the funding committee sparked the fizzling construction plans. Under-funded stadium projects had become the newest plague of college budget concerns, and Studebaker's pledge to coordinate a debt-free building plan removed the last stumbling block.

Though the stadium construction migraine plagued Rockne, the coach had an even bigger problem. In the fall, the most vulnerable squad of Rockne's career was taking the field. Facing a firing squad of ranked opponents in Wisconsin, Navy, Georgia Tech, Army, and USC, the coach felt the season's prognosis to be truly grim. Of the two-way starters from 1927, nine had graduated. A paltry seven seniors remained. Two seniors who Rockne expected to make a difference were Jack and his close friend, Fred Miller.

No knowledgeable fan could expect his football team to have a winning season with only two starters returning on each side of the ball, but such was Notre Dame's lineup in 1928. On September 29, the Irish opened their season at home against Loyola of New Orleans.

Rockne scheduled Loyola for the traditional tune-up game as a favor for the Wolfpack's head coach Clark Shaughnessy. One of the game's master strategists of the era, Shaughnessy would use his expertise to present a serious challenge for Rockne's preparation and a valid test for the rebuilt Irish.

After the Wolfpack from New Orleans arrived in Elkhart, Indiana, on Friday afternoon, they practiced at a nearby athletic facility. At noon the following day, Loyola arrived in South Bend just minutes before their three hundred loyal fans that had made the trip from up the Big Easy. As they exited the passenger cars with an air of confidence, Shaughnessy and his team expected to win at Cartier Stadium.

As *News Times* sportswriter Franklyn E. Doan wrote,

> "In past years, the first opponents have come here with a kind of inferiority complex shadowing them…Loyola comes to battle Notre Dame with a different psychology. Defeated but twice in the past two years, once by the Quantico Marines and once by the Haskell Indians [two teams who neither resembled much of a traditional university when it came to eligible players]; the loyal warriors feel that they are the equal or superior of the Irish. They will enter Saturday's game knowing that a victory carries with it more prestige than an entire season of winnings over less renowned opponents."

Loyola had other reasons to be confident. The squad consisted of fourteen three-year veterans. Shaughnessy's stable of Southern-fried players popular with their New Orleans fan base included: speedster Bucky Moore, defensive specialist Peter Miller, the big back Don Maitland (better known as the battering ram), and two-hundred-pound tackle, Ray Drouhilet.

In the Notre Dame program flyer made available to the thirty thousand fans seated in Cartier Field, one paragraph read,

> "The Notre Dame team which plays today is mindful of the tradition to which it is heir; it is the earnest hope of the 1928 squad that the unsullied heritage of years past will be made more worthy by the game this afternoon."

Printed on the program in his remarks to the fans, Captain Frederick C. Miller had written,

> "The team pledges anew its loyalty to Coach Rockne and Notre Dame, its willingness to expend a supreme effort in seeking an honorable victory, and its desire to be worthy representatives of a noble University. To our opponents we pledge a sportsmanship that knows no flinching."

Centered atop the program published for each home game played at Cartier Field were the names of the Football Program Concessions Committee: Frederick C. Miller, Frederick Collins, George P. Leppig, John W. Doarn, and John T. Connor. In the left corner was a popularly posed shot of the day—a grimacing lineman. On the day of the Loyola game, the picture showed Fred Miller down in a three-point stance, knuckles in the grass, and ready for action.

On the Thursday night before Loyola's arrival, at the kickoff pep rally, university officials and student leaders reminded the student body of their duty to manifest the nationally known spirit of Notre Dame throughout the contest. It was a usual start for an unusual Notre Dame team.

Officiating the game were Walter Eckersall, John Schommer, and Nick Kearns. The three were one of the top officiating crews in the nation. By kickoff Saturday, all home team stations were alert and ready.

As Rockne normally decreed when the Irish faced a team clad in navy blue, the Irish dressed in green. Two Millers from opposite worlds faced each other at the coin toss, Pete Miller of Loyola and Fred Miller of Notre Dame. Pete Miller won the toss, and Loyola elected to receive.

At the kickoff, what should have been a walk in the park, even for this lightly respected Irish squad, morphed into a hard-fought battle at Cartier Field after Loyola returned the opening kick to their thirty yard line. Both teams struggled early, each failing to put together a productive drive. The first quarter ended in a scoreless tie.

At the start of the second quarter, the Wolfpack gained possession of the ball near midfield as Loyola looked to break the deadlock. Executing with precision, the New Orleans offense penetrated Notre Dame territory. Rockne's Irish were reeling from the Wolfpack assault. Taking advantage of Notre Dame's stunned frontline, Loyola fullback Aubrey Budge bulled into the end zone, giving the talented New Orleans squad a 6-0 lead.

After Loyola's point-after attempt was blocked, the Irish returned the kickoff to their own twenty-eight. Following a series of short scrimmages between the two squads, the first half ended with Loyola still clinging to its one-touchdown lead.

Jack Chevigny returned from halftime as a backfield starter at the right halfback spot. Morrissey stepped in at quarterback; Shay aligned at fullback; and Elder moved to the left halfback spot. Living up to his reputation for physical blocking and tackling, Jack threw one of his trademark flying body blocks to spring Elder on a forty-eight yard touchdown run. But when

Elder missed the point-after, the Irish were locked in a 6-6 tie with only a quarter to play.

With the clocking ticking down, neither team could consistently gain field advantage. Finally, it would be Jack from his right halfback spot who took control in the fourth quarter with hard surgical slashes through the Loyola line. Thanks to the *Hammond Flash*, the Irish were able to mount one final Rockne-like drive toward the Wolfpack goal line. Yet again, the Irish were unable to punch the ball over for the go-ahead score. With the Irish stopped short of the end zone, the ball changed hands.

In an attempt to preserve the tie, underdog Loyola downshifted into ball-control mode late in the game with the ball still deep in Wolfpack territory. Time was running out. The Irish had to find a way to force a turnover or the game would end in a tie.

The luck of the Irish prevailed when future Loyola Hall of Famer Don Maitland fumbled and Notre Dame's Fred Miller recovered. With less than three minutes to play and the ball inside the Loyola twenty yard line, Niemiec passed on three straight downs. The first pass was incomplete to Frank Carideo; the second was complete to Johnny O'Brien to the eight yard line; and the third was complete to Billy Dew at the two yard line. From there, with just seconds remaining, Niemiec smashed over for the winning touchdown, and the game was over.

In a chilling omen for Irish fans and the media, Notre Dame had managed a last-second 12-6 victory over a supposed warm-up team. If there was any doubt left in South Bend that this season would be the toughest autumn Rockne had ever experienced, Loyola carried it with them on the way back to New Orleans.

The upcoming week, Rockne had no illusions about taming the Badgers of Wisconsin. Prior to game time on October 6, the gamblers named Wisconsin a big favorite. Across the Midwest, newspapers trumpeted the upcoming clash with a half-page montage of Rockne and the six key athletes of his rotating backfield. Inset just below an image of Jack Chevigny was an oval-shaped head-and-shoulder shot of Notre Damer Fred Miller and Wisconsin's Rube Wagner.

In an improbable coincidence, left tackle Fred Miller met left tackle Rube Wagner at midfield for the coin toss. Rarely does a lineman generate the awe of leadership and charisma that earns them the position of captain, but in this peculiar midfield meeting, both of the elected captains of the team were left tackles. Considered one of the best captains in Wisconsin history, Rube Wagner was known to be a tough character on the field but the truest gentleman off the field.

When Rube regarded his opponent on Saturday, he had remarked earlier, "I don't know who will win as both teams are strong, but I will say that Notre Dame will know they have been in a football game when the final whistle blows. I hope for a victory, naturally, and with the 'breaks' we may upset the dope. But win or lose we'll fight hard."

As he did against Loyola a week earlier, Miller came out on the short side of the coin toss. And in a strategy not that unusual for the era, Wisconsin optioned to take the advantage of the wind at their back instead of choosing the first possession of the ball.

The game opened with Jack Elder fielding the Wisconsin kick. On the first play from scrimmage, Elder flanked the Wisconsin defensive line for a nice gain of fifteen yards. Then Jack Chevigny attempted two consecutive hard dives but was hit by Wisconsin's team captain Wagner. An attempted pass to Chevigny fell short, and the Irish were hit with a penalty. Facing a conversion down to keep the drive alive, Notre Dame's Elder launched a long pass to a wide-open Ed Collins. Running alone with a clear path to the end zone, Collins let the ball slip through his fingertips, and the Irish were forced to punt.

The two teams continued to play tug-o-war for most of the first quarter, with Notre Dame gradually losing field position. As Chev faced third down and eight yards for a first, he gained one yard up the middle, but the Irish were called for holding and penalized fifteen yards.

With the ball on the Irish fifteen yard line, Frank Carideo stepped back to punt to the Badgers. When he drove his foot forward into the ball, a Wisconsin roar erupted. Four Badgers had rushed in to block the punt.

After the blocked punt earned a safety for the Badgers, Wisconsin led 2-0. That score would stand for the remainder of the quarter as the two teams slugged it out in a static battle of smashing line charges.

In the second quarter, the wind shifted to the northeast as both coaches called for multiple substitutions for many of the two-way players. Most notably for Notre Dame was the substitution of Ted Twomey at right tackle. Soon after the substitutions were complete, Irish hearts sank, when Frank Carideo was injured and removed from the contest. Replacing Carideo was Joe Morrissey.

Notre Dame regrouped from the loss of Carideo when a Badger drive was stopped on downs at the Irish fifteen yard line. The Badgers were disappointed, but in pushing deep inside Irish territory, Wisconsin had demonstrated the ability to flex its offensive muscle.

When Jack Chevigny opened the next series, he dove behind Fred Miller for four yards, and Shay followed with an end-run around the Badgers' left side for a gain of twenty yards. With the Irish moving the ball out to near midfield, fans and sportswriters noticed an increased intensity in the collisions on the field. Several players were removed for injuries as the contest began to resemble a trench-like warfare of fullback bucks and halfback sweeps.

As the second quarter ebbed, Rockne's troops took to the air. Following an exchange of possessions, the Irish had moved out to midfield. With the Badgers rattled by the passing success of the Irish, Notre Dame exploited their confusion with another Chevigny dash off the right side for seven yards. The Irish utilized a series of punching strikes to the Badger defensive midsection, grinding their way down to the Wisconsin five yard line. When a penalty moved the ball to the Wisconsin ten yard line, Chevigny swept right for eight yards. Then from the Badger two yard line, Niemiec pushed the pile forward for the score.

The first half ended with the Irish on top of the Badgers by a score of 6-2. Notre Dame had gained the momentum.

Notre Dame fans were just back in their seats for the opening of the second half when Rockne's boys bungled their opening drive and were forced into punt formation at its own ten yard line. In a repeat of the first half miscue, the Irish punt was blocked and recovered by Wisconsin.

Rockne was dismayed to see that it would take the Badgers only one play to punch over the go-ahead touchdown. When the Badger point-after was blocked, Wisconsin now held a two-point lead, 8-6.

Irish fans roared when Jack Chevigny returned the following Badger kickoff to the Irish twenty-three yard line where Rockne expected his box formation to finally get to work at dismantling the Badger line. However, on the first play from scrimmage, fullback George Shay was tackled for a loss. Then on the second play, Jack fumbled and the Badgers recovered.

Eight plays later, the Badgers crossed the goal line. Following the successful point-after kick, Wisconsin led 15-6.

The game continued in a series of smashing power plays, misdirection plays, and fullback bucks. Notre Dame made some progress with Chev exploiting the flanks, but Jack was able to pick up yardage only in small partitions. With the Irish running game stifled, Wisconsin reloaded and blasted the Irish with a third touchdown to pad the score to 22-6. From that point, it seemed Rockne's boys could do little but put the ball in the air and hope for the best.

No luck of the Irish would be seen against the Badgers. Captain Fred Miller's pre-game scowl had no effect on the home team Badgers as Rube Wagner and his Wisconsin Badgers humiliated the Irish. Notre Dame would need to regroup if they were to defeat a struggling Navy in the following week.

Sputtering offensively, the Midshipmen carried a 0-2 record to Chicago on October 13. A solid defensive squad, Navy's losses included a two-point shutout and six-point shutout.

In his usual manner, Rockne distributed the allotment of free tickets to the various mouthpieces of the press corps. Before an unofficial attendance of one hundred twenty thousand spectators, the largest crowd ever to see a football game, Knute Kenneth Rockne's faltering Irish faced Navy in the "vast somber, dignified war memorial" that was Soldier Field.

Perhaps distressed from the sloppy offensive performance against Wisconsin, Rockne chose an unusual strategy to start the Navy game. He would not use his shock troops. As John Stahr of the *South Bend Tribune* reported, Rockne used replacements at only three positions during the entire game, while Navy's coach Bill Ingram substituted freely.

Referee Walt Eckersall saw Notre Dame's John Niemiec and Jack Chevigny rip the Navy line at will, but the Irish fumbling plague continued. Navy gambled by going to the air during a sustained ground attack, and

Jack intercepted at the Notre Dame eighteen. Then, as if he received a telepathic cue from his head coach to make his interception count, Jack burst off-tackle for a sixteen-yard gain. And when his number was called again, Jack struck the Middies with another searing run, this time a fifteen-yard gain. After suffering a fifteen-yard penalty, the boys in the green jerseys faced a long back stick of the down marker when Jack's number was called a third time. Niemiec to Chevigny, the pass was complete for twenty-one yards. After crossing midfield into Navy territory, the Irish machine appeared to be unstoppable. Yet again, the drive stalled, and the Irish were forced to punt. Niemiec pinned the Midshipmen deep on their own three yard line.

Inside the trenches, All-American Tim Moynihan was having the game of his life both at center and at defensive tackle. It seemed as if the seesaw wouldn't end when Notre Dame fielded a Middies' punt at midfield but failed to take advantage of the field position.

The second quarter opened with a Navy punt downed on the Irish thirty-nine yard line. After Bellaire, Ohio, native John Niemiec sliced off-tackle for three yards, Chev retook control, shattering the Navy defense on three consecutive plays. First, Jack pounded out twelve yards and a first down. Next, he caught yet another pass from Niemiec for ten yards. On the third consecutive snap, Jack rounded left end for twelve yards and another first down. It was Niemiec and Chevigny, then Chevigny and Niemiec; the Fighting Irish marched downfield. Owning a first down at the Middies' ten yard line, Notre Dame had pushed within striking distance. After advancing to the five yard line, the Irish faced a fourth-and-goal. On the final play of the drive, Niemiec lofted a pass to Johnny Colrick.

Irish fans moaned when the fourth-down attempt was knocked away by Navy's Art Spring. The Irish had failed to score.

For the rest of the period, Jack continued his personal assault on Navy. The third period ended with Notre Dame penetrating to the Midshipmen's twelve yard line.

In the fourth quarter, Chevigny and Niemiec rushed in tandem until the Irish moved near the eight yard line. Navy, lured into a trance by the punishing duo of Chevigny and Niemiec, was caught flat-footed when Niemiec rose and hit Colrick on a slant from the left side.

Eckersall signaled touchdown! Frank Carideo added the important extra point, and Rockne's Ramblers led 7-0.

The Middies, who were possessed by the spirit of John Paul Jones, fought back when, in the fourth quarter, Navy's Fred Beans downed the dropkick of teammate Harold Bauer inside Notre Dame's one yard line. Rockne, pinned in a precarious position, played conservative and communicated illegally to Carideo, telling him to immediately punt the ball out of the hole.

When Navy took possession of the ball just inside the Notre Dame forty-two yard line, they would have one final opportunity to tie the game. Bauer completed a first-down pass to Whitey Lloyd on one of Navy's many passes that afternoon, and the Midshipmen were on the move as John Castree and Harold Bauer battered the staggering Irish line.

Forty-five feet from the goal line and down 7-0, Navy faced a fourth-and-one at the Irish seven yard line. The Middies' John Castree got the call. When Notre Dame's George Leppig stuffed Castree short of the first-down marker, a cacophony of conflicting groans and cheers rolled over Soldier Field.

On the Notre Dame sideline, the hit revived memories of Leppig's goal-line heroics in the 1927 Minnesota game. Just as he was during the 1927 Minnesota game, Jack Chevigny was in on the hit with Leppig. This time, Jack is injured and carried from the field as his teammates take possession of the ball on their own seven.

In keeping with the strategy of college football of that era, with field position being the priority in game planning and execution, Rockne ordered Frank Carideo to punt immediately, even with time expiring. He got the punt off cleanly, but it netted only thirty-five yards, giving the Midshipmen an unexpected second chance near midfield.

The Middies opened their offensive series. On the opening play, Harold Bauer was sacked for a five-yard loss by Notre Dame guard Jack Cannon. Navy regrouped by quickly moving downfield via short passes. The Midshipmen were still afloat.

Then after a series of Navy completions, Notre Dame's Jack Montroy, Jack Chevigny's substitute, turned back the Midshipmen when he intercepted the final Bauer pass at the Notre Dame seventeen yard line. With little more than seconds remaining, the Irish ran out the clock. In one of the most thrilling games of the century, Notre Dame captured a shutout over the Midshipmen.

After the game, Knute Rockne wrote that John Paul Jones's spirit was evident in Navy's fight. He spoke of "irrepressible sailors" and "plucky Middies." For Jack Chevigny, it was the game of his life. Letters and telegrams from across the nation flooded his Notre Dame residence hall.

October 16, 1928

Dear Jack,

....I could not attend the game nor see you in action, but my ear was glued to the radio and the joy you gave me was far greater than the lines in this letter can indicate. I don't know how you ever succeeded in doing so well the frightful job assigned to you, and I just want you to know that I'm very proud of you and wish to offer my sincere congratulations. I know you must be frightfully battered and crushed almost beyond description, but our prayers will be with you to give you new strength and to restore you speedily your former fighting vigor. One of the Minneapolis papers mentioned before the game that the Notre Dame team was to the football world was what Dempsey was to the ring, that win or lose both were held in the hearts of the American people. Whatever was true before the game is doubly true now. Wishing you every success and every help human and divine in the hard battles awaiting you, I am,

Cordially yours,

Signed Joseph Boyle CSC

Another letter to Doctor Chevigny in Hammond spelled out the pride that Jack's friends felt in his performance. Dated October 15, from Joliet, Illinois, the correspondence read:

Dear Doctor,

Just a note to say that the entire Foot-ball World joins with you in being proud of your fine son and I am proud as well as the Mrs. and Junior to call John Chevigny a friend.

Wasn't he marvelous? You sure can justly be proud of such a fine son, and may God spare him and all your children to a grand old age. A boy like Jack is sure an incentive to the youth of our land.

With kindest personal regards in which Mrs. Dunn and my son joins me, I am

Very truly yours,

Signed Frances J. Dunn

The *South Bend Tribune* account of the game included verses of a chant for the partisan Notre Dame reader.

"He's a man!

"Who's a man?

"Chevigny!

"Say it again!

"Chevigny!"

Two-inch bold headlines, **NOTRE DAME SCUTTLES NAVY** proclaimed victory in *the South Bend Tribune*. Smaller headlines proclaimed ROCKMEN REPEL MIDDIE ATTACK AND WIN, 7-0. Another article heralded the reign of the great coach, KING KNUTE PROVES HIS MASTERY. In the center on most papers was a fourteen-inch by five-inch panoramic photo of Jack rounding left end, his left quadriceps tightly bandaged as he digs into a hard cut upfield. With Jack looking over his right shoulder to take account of the Midshipmen's pursuit angles, determination is etched on his face. Above the photo is a caption in unique script, Monsieur Chevigny sets out to go places.

Jack Chevigny would not be the only immortal of that afternoon. A footnote to the character and spirit of the athletes battling on Soldier Field was the story of Navy's Harold Bauer. On November 14, 1942, Lieutenant Colonel Joe Bauer, a Marine ace with ten kills, was shot down near Guadalcanal. He was last seen swimming from an oil slick approximately twelve miles north of Russell Island.

In his technical evaluation of the 1928 Navy game, Rockne stated in his column,

> "It was a splendidly played game of football for early season and it was my impression that both teams played over their heads. The blocking and tackling was decisive, clean cut,

and deadly. Both teams played smart football, and the flaws in technique were few."

Rock closed his post-game assessment with the following words,

> "It is my belief that this game will make the Notre Dame team—a victory of this kind was necessary to build up confidence, team play, cohesion, and that intangible thing known as team spirit."

Meanwhile, it was the Irish fans' apparent lack of spirit that had been eating at Rockne since the Wisconsin game. Remarkably thin-skinned, Rockne had little or no patience with anyone questioning his insight and expertise. Following the Navy game in which Rockne lauded the efforts of both teams, he was less generous with the Irish fans. Attending the packed alumni dinner, he was deafeningly applauded. In response, he chided those in attendance for their fair weather support of his boys and by default, their coach.

In looking deeper at his character makeup and the facts of his career, Rockne did have a harbinger or spark of resentment for those who dared to fail him, whether intended or unintended. As a brilliant man, he had little tolerance for those who could not understand how things were supposed to be done. And as a hard-working man, he had little tolerance for those who did not appreciate the effort as much as the outcome. Strangely insecure, Rock held little regard for those who failed to appreciate his charismatic potential. The great Rockne would tolerate nothing less than full devotion from the fans, the press, and the world, especially during the tough times when his boys needed them most.

Following the Irish's narrow escape over Navy was a tough intersectional game, the Georgia Tech-Notre Dame meeting. It was to be broadcast on NBC network radio stations throughout the South on KPRC in Houston and on WHAS in Louisville. Midwesterners would hear the game on WLW in Cincinnati.

Despite an unblemished record in the series, the Irish would face one of the more talented Georgia Tech teams on record. To the 1920s Georgian, Notre Dame was the school synonymous with papalism.

The presidential campaign of Irish-Catholic Democratic Party candidate Governor Al Smith of New York heightened anti-Catholic sentiment in the South. Consequently, a particularly hostile environment welcomed the Fighting Irish to Atlanta on October 20, 1928.

Heightening Rockne's anxiety was the fact that his team had just come off an emotionally draining win in front of the largest crowd to ever see a football game. In Atlanta, Notre Dame would take the field in front of just thirty-five thousand, but they were thirty-five thousand unfriendly Georgians. For most of Rock's boys, the South was a foreign land.

A perplexed Rockne was frustrated that his boys appeared to not appreciate the asperity of the environment. Partially because of his squad's lack of appreciation of the Golden Tornado's depth and talent, Rockne chose to forgo the inspirational pre-game talk. Rock felt that their ears, clogged with the accolades and acclaim of the previous week's victory over Navy, would not hear what he would say. As the locker rooms emptied for the kickoff, an amazingly overconfident Irish took the field.

Two contrasting styles of offensive football met in Atlanta that day. Rockne's patented, simultaneously shifting backfield confronted a Georgia Tech squad that utilized a style very similar to a later style of football, the Delaware Wing-T. Although Georgia Tech positioned its quarterback under center in a manner similar to the futuristic wing-T, the Georgia Tech quarterback faced the backfield instead of the opposing defense. Taking the snap from between his legs, the quarterback was already in position to fake to the crisscrossing backs.

The Fighting Irish had operated from the Notre Dame shift for many years; its development predated Rockne's tenure of leadership. However, if Rockne's predecessor and mentor, Jess Harper, originated the shift, Rockne perfected the concept. To the observer, the shift resembled dance steps. Previous to the snap, the four backfield members stepped in the appropriate direction. Stepping in a cross-over pattern, their last step planted in the sod just as the ball was snapped. The quick shift gave the offense a flanking advantage against a defense. Each halfback spot was a position with significantly different duties. Depending on the direction, the shift invariably ended in what was termed the Notre Dame box formation. Similar to the famous single-wing set, the formation was termed a box because the final alignment of the collective backfield formed a figure that could be more accurately described as a skewed box, a parallelogram.

If the backs moved to the right in a three-step shift, the right halfback Chevigny moved from an alignment four yards behind the center to an alignment at the wing, one yard outside the end and one yard deep in the backfield. From the wingback position, Jack would perform one of five actions: he would shoulder block from his alignment on the right side; he would slip out into the secondary for a pass; he would swing around in a quick pre-snap motion to carry the ball on a wide sweep to the left; he would slice left across the formation on a cross-buck play off-tackle; or he would dash laterally across the formation in order to block for the quarterback on a drop-back pass.

If the backs moved to the left in a three-step shift, Jack moved from the wing to the alignment behind the center. From that position, he could receive the snap for a pass, run a direct-snap sweep or dive, or half-spin and hand the ball to another back on a misdirection play.

The 1928 season would prove that the merit of the Notre Dame shift was not in the actual direction and timing of the backfield movement; the merit was in *who* were doing the actual shifting. Christie Flanagan's backfield of 1927 shifted more efficiently than the 1928 backfield. If the first three games of 1928 had indicated anything, they showed that Notre Dame would need more than the will and spirit of a single Jack Chevigny. If they were to end the season as winners, Rockne's boys needed to play in a highly motivated team each time they stepped onto the field.

With the boys disjointed and flat against Georgia Tech, Rockne undertook all measures to get his team back in the game—tricks, long passes, and reverses. Still, the Irish could maintain no consistency on offense. Under pressure for most of the day, Niemiec suffered four interceptions. All day, a jeering Atlanta crowd taunted the Irish with regard to their faith, their ineptitude on the field, and even the satin material from which their uniform's pants were made. The Yellow Jackets (the increasingly popular moniker for the yellow-clad Georgia Tech fans) cheered the final gun as Georgia Tech notched its first victory in the seven meetings between the two schools.

It couldn't be overlooked that Rockne's boys had played another sloppy contest. His reserves, the vital shock troops, had failed in their collective role. The 13-0 outcome could have been different, but the Irish misfired on two opportunities near the goal line.

Even though the Georgia Tech squad was one of the nation's finest college football teams, Rockne was stung by the Atlanta sportswriters' criticism of his preparation and coaching. Upon returning to South Bend, he would fire off a southbound letter of protest.

Provided little satisfaction over his voiced displeasure with the Atlanta press, the nonplussed coach had little time for self-pity. An undefeated Drake team was not one to be overlooked in the upcoming home stand. A loss to lowly Drake would sting far worse than the insults of the yellow-jacketed fans of Georgia Tech.

Drake followers were spirited as to their chances.

In speaking of the Ramblers, the *Waterloo Evening Courier* wrote, "So far they have lost two games out of four, which for a Notre Dame football team is somewhat of a disaster." Rumors flew that a combination of six injured Irish starters and reserves would be inactive against the Bulldogs in South Bend.

Despite the gloomy prognostications, Rockne would find his missing fullback. Since the Navy game, critics had continued to cry that the Irish lacked a true fullback, and Rockne was failing in his perseverance to find one. Against Drake, he found one in Larry "Moon" Mullins.

As if the pundits themselves were the proud papas of the newly discovered skills of Mullins, Chicago's United Press Staff Correspondent Dixon Stewart declared Mullins to be "the man Rockne needed to give the backfield the necessary spark."

As it turned out, Drake wasn't much of a problem for the Irish. Rockne repeated his Navy strategy of using the starters from the opening kickoff, and Notre Dame ran roughshod over the Drake Bulldogs, 32-6. The November 2, 1928, morning issue of the *Burlington Hawk-eye* headlined a photo of Jack's number-twelve jersey being tackled by a host of Drake players. Rarely was Jack tackled by a single defender, especially a Drake defender. Although impeccably uniformed with their front vertical stripes and ringed collars and arm sleeves, the Drake eleven were hopelessly overmatched against even this mediocre Irish edition.

The hoopla of the upcoming showdown with the Cadets at Yankee Stadium notwithstanding, Penn State was lying in wait in Philadelphia at historic Franklin Field. With a seating capacity of eighty thousand, Franklin Field was an exclamation point to Rockne's argument that Notre Dame's Cartier Field was an illegitimate venue for big-time college football.

In spite of the performance of Larry Mullins in the previous week, the story of the day was the tube of plaster over the right forearm of Fred Collins. Against Drake, Collins had re-injured an earlier fracture. Spectators strained to see what appeared to be a concrete drain pipe taped around his arm.

The evening before the game, a wild nor'easter carried in rains heavy enough for the grounds crew to position a rain blanket over the turf. Through the blanket's seams, water leaked through to form patches of puddles on the field that combined with the turf to create a field texture that *Chicago Tribune* columnist Westbrook Pegler described as "gummy." Watching the teams pre-game drills, Pegler noted that Jack Chevigny was having trouble with his footing.

During the game, Pegler saw Penn State utilize several trick plays. The first was the "whisper play." In it, the official marks the ball ready to snap, but the offensive team acts confused. They look to each other with their hands held out, whispering about what to do. When the opposing team also becomes distracted, the ball is snapped to speedy back. In the manner of a surprise attack, the jackrabbit player has the advantage before the defense recognizes the ruse.

Penn State's Cooper French was the rabbit. Pegler reported that the Rockne's boys were ready, but French was slippery and managed to advance the ball down to the Irish ten yard line.

Later in the series and facing a fourth and goal, Penn State aligned for a field goal. Right halfback Allie Wolf held for the kicker. Expecting trickery, Notre Dame wisely deployed for the fake. As the Irish expected, Wolf faked the hold as the kicker went through the kicking motion. Wolf then leapt and fired a pass to a spot in the end zone, a spot where some Penn State player was supposed to be, but wasn't. Wolf's incompletion was the end of the magic show for the day.

With the exception of the Penn State high-jinks, the game was primarily a mud fest played in dreary weather. The Irish exerted its physical superiority over the Nittany Lions, something the Irish had shown in their victory over Drake. By the time the gun fired, Jack and his teammates had punched the Penn State defense into a stupor. Notre Dame 9, Penn State 0.

Finally, it was time. The big dance was here—Army. To the Irish, the sportswriters, the alumni, and the fans, nothing counted until now. Even though the Irish had earned a record of 4-2, Rockne was acutely aware that his boys still faced the prospect of a losing season. Three games against the toughest competition of the season remained to be played. Rockne and his four assistant coaches, John Polisky, Tom Mills, John "Clipper" Smith, and Ike Voedisch, buckled down in preparation for the undefeated Cadets.

Back at West Point, Army prepared for what would be a tough fight in spite of the prognosticator's odds. Taking charge of one of the Army practice drills, Lieutenant Ralph Sassi instructed the Cadets as to the technique required to defeat the expertly executed cut-blocks of the Notre Dame players.

Sassi educated his troops saying, "Some of the Notre Dame men may drop in a heap, trusting that you will trip over them. I would suggest that you do not trip. I would suggest that you dive over them. But when you are diving, the interfering backs may throw themselves at you from the sides.

Still your purpose will be to ignore these distractions, grasp the man with the ball by his knees and hug."

To J. Arthur Haley, business manager of athletics at Notre Dame, there was but one game. His main complaint was that the fifty yard line did not extend from end zone to end zone. Telling an acquaintance that the university had to refund $1,000 a day because tickets were unavailable, the Army game was at once a windfall and a nightmare for Haley. So overwhelming was the demand of tickets, Notre Dame reached out an altruistic hand to its fans and alumni, allowing the two radio networks, CBS and NBC, to air the game for free.

Telegrams poured in not only to Haley and Rockne but also to others as well. Most consisted of some type of personal plea.

"We are friends of John Chevigny and would like a seat where we could see Johnnie without having necks like a giraffe. Thank you." —Donahue

Twelve-hundred Cadets marched into Yankee Stadium on the afternoon of November 10, 1928. Greeted by eighty-five thousand fans, the long gray line gave a brief demonstration in the dry Bronx air.

Once the Cadets cleared the field, Irish team captain Fred Miller met Army team captain Bud Sprague at midfield for the coin toss. Like the Miller and Rube Wagner meeting at Wisconsin, both of the team captains played the tackle position.

Heir to the Miller Beer fortune, Fred Miller saw his family invest wisely and survive Prohibition, thanks to their savings, soft drinks, and non-alcoholic beer. Although he was one of the wealthiest students in America, Fred Miller had none of the characteristics of the pandered rich kid. Twenty-two years of age, six feet, and nearly two hundred pounds, Miller was a premier All-American.

Native Texan, Mortimer "Bud" Sprague was the first of four Sprague brothers to captain his college football team. As most Army football stars, Sprague was a product of the West Point system of engaging college stars who transferred, sometimes without any years of eligibility left, from other college programs. Sprague had played football at the University of Texas from 1922-24 where he lettered two years. Then he transferred to West Point where he lettered four more years. Like his Notre Dame rival Fred Miller, Bud Sprague one day would be enshrined in the College Football Hall of Fame.

Just prior to 2:00 p.m., Army, dressed in their black jerseys with five horizontal black, gold, and white stripes across the chest, took the field for some group calisthenics and stretching routines. Notre Dame, dressed in their blue jerseys and dark satin pants, entered single-file into the stadium.

Sprague won the toss and chose to receive. Miller chose to defend the west goal. Irish quarterback James "Jim" Brady returned the Army kick to the Notre Dame thirty-six yard line. On the first play, John Niemiec tried to sweep right end but was hit by Army's Carl Carlmark. On the following play, a cross buck, Sprague dropped Fred Collins for a loss. Then Jack Chevigny attempted to flank the Cadet's right defensive side but was stopped near the line of scrimmage. Facing a fourth-and-twelve, Niemiec punted. After Miller downed the punt at Cadet forty-one yard line, the heavy favorites were already near midfield on their first possession.

College Football Hall of Fame member Christian "Red" Cagle couldn't help the Cadets cross midfield, and Army was forced to punt.

In December, Cagle—the force behind the Cadets 18-0 spanking of Notre Dame the year before—would be named All-American for the third consecutive season. Like Sprague, Cagle had played for another college from

1922-1925. At Lafayette's Southwestern Louisiana, Cagle would hold the career scoring record for six decades.

Niemiec opened Notre Dame's second offensive series with a one-yard gain off-tackle, but on second down, Chevigny dropped a Niemiec pass, and the Irish faced third-and-long. On third down, Niemiec again went to the air, but the pass was deflected by Army's John Murrell. Facing a fourth-and-long, Niemiec boomed an eighty-yard punt. As a result of the touchback, the Cadets gained possession of the ball at their own twenty yard line.

Eventually, the Irish found their rhythm with a Brady-to-Jack Chevigny pass. Gaining yards after the catch, the hero of Montreal carries the ball down to the Army forty-three yard line where he was stopped by Cadet William Hall. Fans sat tensely quiet as a sequence of Irish gains and losses again forced Rockne's boys to punt.

The consistent Niemiec drove a booming kick down to the Army fifteen yard line. Playing field position, Army immediately punted back to Notre Dame. Team captain Sprague downed the punt at the Army forty-six yard line, and the game remained scoreless.

Time after time, Notre Dame opened their offensive series with a John Niemiec carry. The next drive was no exception, and Army expected it. Niemiec gained only a yard behind center on first down. After Army's Carl Carlmark broke up his second pass of the day, the Irish were forced to punt. In his third such opportunity of the first quarter, Niemiec pinned the Cadets deep in their own territory.

Starting at their own fifteen yard line, the Cadets had little time left to win the first quarter. "Onward Christian" Cagle, as Red was sometimes called, tried running behind his right tackle, but gained only a few yards before being knocked backward by Jack Chevigny and Tim Moynihan.

Cagle then probed the right side, but George Leppig was there and Cagle went nowhere. John Murrell's punt to Notre Dame's Brady at the Army forty-eight yard line placed the Irish near midfield.

After a few hard drives from the shifting Notre Dame box formation, the first quarter ended with the score: Army 0, Notre Dame 0. The media and crowd had hoped for an exhibition of lightning strikes, but the first-quarter action was less entertaining than a schoolyard shoving match.

Facing fourth-and-five at the start of the second quarter, Notre Dame punted. Because Niemiec had managed to angle his kick out-of-bounds at the Army two yard line, Army quickly punted the ball out their end zone in order to improve their field position. The downside of that strategy was that it placed the Cadets back on defense on their side of the midfield stripe.

Starting at the Army thirty-eight, the Irish had captured their best field position of the day and soon set out to exploit their advantage. Fred Collins ripped the Army line off left tackle for eighteen yards. Tackled by Cagle on the first long run, Collins got the signal again and garnered another five yards. After a run by Chevigny, the down-marker read third-and-goal inside the five yard line. The Irish were rolling, and Rockne's typically enthusiastic grin had hardly creased his lips when disaster struck. On third down, Collin fumbled as he attempted to cross the goal line. Army's John Murrell recovered in the end zone for a touchback. Rock's boys were turned away.

Though the Cadets started a new set of downs at their own twenty yard line, Army was forced to punt. This time the ball was downed on the Notre Dame thirty-five yard line, and the field position had effectively flipped. The Army strategy of playing for field position worked.

Still, both coaches realized that despite the most recent positive outcome for Army, the leg of Notre Dame's John Niemiec continued to be an effective counter-measure to the Cadets' cat-and-mouse strategy of playing for field position. When the Notre Dame series failed to bear fruit, Niemiec again got off a beautiful punt that was downed back at the Army twenty-four yard line.

In the streets of New York standing near the wires and radios, the subway alumni cheered. On the Irish sideline, Rockne worried that Army's Red Cagle appeared ready for a breakout. His worry was warranted when Cagle rounded left end where Jack Chevigny stopped him after a gain of eight yards. On the next play, Army tried a hidden ball trick, but Moynihan snuffed it out and Murrell was stopped for no gain.

The crowd sat quietly. They grew restless when Army punted. Notre Dame's Jim Brady added a little electricity to the atmosphere by returning the punt to within thirteen yards of midfield, but after Brady's run, a timeout was called.

During the timeout, a sportswriter commented that the Army team was being served by some type of new water conveyance cart, a "cumbersome contrivance with everything necessary for first aid when their team calls a timeout."

Notre Dame appeared to be regaining momentum, but as the closing minutes of the second quarter ticked away, both teams continued to play conservatively. The half ended in a deadlocked scoreless tie. Feeling the game within his grasp, Rockne left the field, feeling the increasingly restless crowd had yet to see the best of boys. Entering the locker room, he had a plan to bring it out of them.

Behind a closed door, the stage was set for one of the most memorable phrases in cultural history, "Win one for the Gipper." Although academicians and sports historians boundlessly challenge the authenticity of Rockne's halftime speech, the message and its time of delivery lend it immortality as one of the most inspirational and recognizable moments in sports history.

The "Win one for the Gipper" legend began with a ballgame. It's the 1920 season. In front of a crowd of over twenty thousand, Gipp led Notre Dame to a win over Northwestern by the final score of 33-7. Gipp, the club's star, played the entire game, enduring a fever and battling an infection. The following week, Gipp became seriously ill and didn't suit up for the final game against Michigan State Agricultural. As the days progressed, Gipp's fever didn't subside, and he became gravely ill. On December 14, 1920—nine days after the season ended—George Gipp died.

Eight years later on November 10, 1928, it was halftime. George Gipp the legend was about to be cemented into the lore of Notre Dame football.

Crowded together in the locker room, anxious but proud faces looked to a confident Rockne and his staff. It was moments before time to retake the field for the second half. Most of the team stood or sat on benches, facing the coach. Several guys, Jack Chevigny included, sat to the coach's right with their heads turned toward him. They intently focused on his face. The adjustments had been made. The questions had been answered. Now, it was time for the old man to say a few words. In refreshing the memory of Gipp and setting the stage for the characterization of the ideal Notre Dame man, Rockne spoke softly of Gipp's talent and his sudden illness, describing in detail his visit to Gipp's hospital room. He was setting the stage for the best known sports soliloquy of all time.

> "On his deathbed George Gipp told me that some day, when the time came, he wanted me to ask a Notre Dame team to beat the Army for him. He turned to me. 'I've got to go, Rock.' he said. 'It's all right. I'm not afraid. His eyes brightened....'" 'Some time, Rock' he said, when the team's up against it; when things are wrong and the breaks are beating

the boys – tell them to go in there with all they've got and win just one for the Gipper. I don't know where I'll be then, Rock. But I'll know about it, and I'll be happy." — *Words purported to Knute Rockne, November 10, 1928*

In the locker room, not a dry eye was seen.

The fiery, senior halfback Jack Chevigny was said to have yelled, "Let's go!" Following Chev, the rest of the boys leapt to their feet and charged outside.

Notre Dame kicked to start the second half. Cadet O'Keefe had returned to action and was marked down at the Army twenty-seven yard line. When Bud Sprague was seen lying immobile on the field, Army fans noticeably gasped.

Army called a time-out to evaluate Sprague, the team captain and cornerstone of the defensive line. To the joy of the Army fans, their team captain was allowed to stay in the game.

When play resumed, Red Cagle tested the left side of the Notre Dame line but wasn't successful. Not to be deterred, Cagle's signal was flipped and repeated. This time the strategy worked. Cagle gained twenty yards and a first down at the Army forty-seven yard line.

Following the All-American's assault on the Notre Dame defense, a long looping pass from Cagle to Messinger was complete, but Notre Dame's fleet Niemiec prevented the touchdown. With the Cadets marching for the go-ahead score on their very first possession of the half, it now seemed that the air had been taken out of Rockne's halftime pep talk. Possibly during the break, Army coach Biff Jones delivered an equally compelling charge to his men. Clearly, Cagle and company were motivated and prepared to strike first.

After another Army timeout, Notre Dame, with their backs to the wall, sent Jack Cannon into the game for George Leppig. Rockne must have seen an Army strategy developing and countered with the Cannon substitution. After Cannon dropped Richard O'Keefe for a nice loss, Hunk Anderson slapped Rockne on the back in approbation of his mentor's timely substitution.

With the game on the line, Army saddled their racehorse, Cagle. But Cagle was surprisingly stopped for no gain.

Finally, with fourth down at the Notre Dame four yard line, it was do-or-die time for the Cadets. It had to be Cagle, and it was.

As Walt Eckersall and his crew measured, Notre Dame celebrated. To the boys in blue, Cagle was obviously short. Both teams felt they had won the down, but only Army was right. With a fresh set of downs at the Notre Dame three yard line, Army was postured to cash in on the fourth-down gamble. Cagle, O'Keefe, and Murrell had combined to manufacture a seventy-yard drive.

While attempting to cap the drive with a score, Cagle rushed to inside the one yard line, but was injured on the play. To the delight of the subway alumni, the Army tea wagon carried Cagle off the field.

Their jubilation was brief.

On the next play, Murrell thrust over the goal line. Although Sprague missed the point-after, Army had broken the tie and now led 6-0.

Irritated over his missed point-after, Sprague removed his lineman's nose protector. He had decided that it interfered with his sight and thus his ability to kick; he must have been right because on the following kickoff, Sprague got off a nice one. It was fielded by Notre Dame's Colrick on the ten yard line. But it was the era of one-platoon football, and Sprague had out-kicked his coverage. Colrick returned the kick twenty yards.

Though Jack Chevigny may have been wondering if the spirit of George Gipp had stayed in the locker room and forgotten about the game, he responded to the Army score with a dash off-tackle for eleven yards and a first down. Not to be outdone by Chev, Niemiec tried the left side for two. On second down, Fred Collins, still playing with his arm in a cast, split Army defenders Louis Hammack and William Hall for a first down at the Notre Dame forty-five yard line. With Notre Dame marching for a first down, Collins again heard his number and rumbled behind right guard for three.

He was met in the hole by Army's Bill Hall. Cadet Hall was able to return to his feet but appeared wobbly. Hall then made his third tackle in a row when he took down Jack Chevigny on a short reverse. Again, Collins moved the chains, this time forward to the forty-five. The Irish were on Army's side of midfield.

After the whistle ended the next play, Army's Charles Humber staggered from the field. He had been the first to make contact during two consecutive violent collisions. The crowd roared its approval of the up tick in intensity as Notre Dame continued to run right at Army.

Rockne knew his boys were mistaken if they thought Army would lie down for them. In punishing the Irish ball carrier on cue, Cadet Sprague and Cadet Messinger halted Notre Dame's march, and Niemiec was forced to punt.

While nursing a six-point lead, Army chose to shift into a more conservative gear. After a short run by Cagle, Murrell punted to Notre Dame's Jim Brady.

Across the country, Irish fists pounded the radio when the play-by-play man yelled out that Brady had muffed the catch. A nation of Blue and Gold was relieved when Jack alertly jumped on Brady's fumble.

With the Irish starting their drive at the Army thirty-seven yard line, Jack contemplated Rockne's halftime words. Maybe the Gipper's spirit had taken the field with the Irish, after all.

When quarterback Jim Brady started the drive with a run, he called upon Fred Collins who responded with a three-yard rush off-tackle. After Collins received the call a second time on an end run around Army's left side, his blockers opened an alley just outside his right end. Collins gained twenty-one yards. Brady realized he had something and stayed with Collins. Notre Dame picked up another yard.

On the following play, Jack Chevigny slipped through the Army line for another eleven yards. The Irish, down by six in the third quarter, had earned their second scoring opportunity of the day.

Fred Collins hoped to regain the spotlight on another sweep, but the Cadet line stiffened. On the following down, John Niemiec bucked for no gain.

Next, the Irish call was for number twelve to carry the ball. Jack plunged over center, tackled at the three yard line. At the three, the powerful Fred Collins was given the assignment to take the ball over for the score. Because Collins was unable to use his immobilized arm to stiff arm the defender, he was unexpectedly knocked backward for a two-yard loss.

Brady decided to push forward again with Collins, and Fred got the signal a second time. On the carry, he moved the ball near the one yard line. At the one, the ball lay. It was fourth down.

All in attendance were on their feet. New York street corners were silent. At the wire station, the gourd used to specify the ball's position dangled near the end of the makeshift line. In living rooms across the country, the only extraneous sound was the dull hum of the radio's vacuum tubes. Army led, 6-0. If the Irish were to win, they would have to make their statement now.

In the Notre Dame huddle, it was decided that number twelve should get the call. For Jack Chevigny, Yankee Field's chalked goal line would determine his mortality or immortality. Newspaper reports said a "pile" of Army defenders rose to stop Chevigny from crossing. But Jack wouldn't be denied.

Someone said that after he crossed the goal line, Jack yelled, "That's one for the Gipper!"

Most people say that the game might as well have ended at that point. Yet, the two teams still had much football—an entire quarter, in fact—left to play.

With the extra-point blocked, the score remained tied, 6-6. Though All-American Chris "Red" Cagle had yet to erupt, Army's offense had dominated the Irish on its last scoring drive. Army fans had no reason to believe the Cadets couldn't score at least twice more. While the game was now tied, Army remained undefeated and a three-to-one favorite over the Irish. Army wasn't familiar with failure; Notre Dame's third-quarter score would not have affected the morale of the "dope favorite" Cadets.

After the tying touchdown, John Niemiec kicked to Red Cagle. He brought the ball out to the Army twenty-five yard line where he was dropped by a Notre Dame tackler who was fueled with an adrenaline rush; it was Jack Chevigny.

With Army now in possession, Cagle opened the series with a sweep around left end where he was hit viciously by Brady's replacement, Frank Carideo. Though Cagle lost a yard, most fans were shocked that he held onto the ball. The Cadets were reeling. Knowledgeable fans felt it was time for a little trickery, and L. M. "Biff" Jones, who possessed the rank of Army captain as well as head coach, agreed. From the sideline, Jones watched his troops try a hidden ball trick that was sniffed out by Tim Moynihan. Stifled by Notre Dame's pesky defensive stand, Army called another timeout and decided to punt.

After regaining possession, the Irish decided to strike hard at the Cadets' edges, and in an alternating sequence, Fred Collins, Frank Carideo, and Jack Chevigny carried the ball across midfield where the drive stalled. From there, Carideo attempted a field goal, which fell far short. Army took possession on its own twenty yard line.

A coach's duty is to stick with the game plan, particularly in a tight game. Coach Jones was a great coach, and his soldier-players were well-trained. They stuck to the game plan; field position is the key to winning. By punting the ball back to the Fighting Irish in an attempt to flip the field position again, the Cadets hoped to regain the advantage. This strategy had worked for Captain Jones and his men all year, but after a few sequences of punt-back, Notre Dame had gained field position.

Jack Chevigny opened a new series for the Irish with a sixteen-yard gain as the Irish marched down to the Army fifteen yard line. Then a catastrophic miscue occurred between Moynihan and Niemiec.

Moynihan's snap skirted free and rolled sixteen yards backward. After a scramble for the ball, Notre Dame maintained possession, but not without cost. In recovering the fumbled snap, Jack Chevigny suffered a concussion, staggering from the field apparently unaware of his own name and surroundings. As Notre Dame's star halfback was helped from the field, his physician father listening on the radio back in Hammond may have taken note that it was Jack's second major concussion of the season.

Facing a long-distance conversion in order to keep the drive alive, the Irish confronted an unquestionable passing situation. After having scouted

Notre Dame thoroughly and owning the knowledge that Johnny Niemiec was one of college football's passing leaders of 1928, Army should have been aware of the pass threat. Perfectly executing the impossible play, Niemiec deftly dropped in a touchdown pass just across the goal line to a substitute described by the press as a real Notre Dame man with a Notre Dame name, Johnny O'Brien. The newspapers recorded that a silence fell over the Corps of Cadets and their supporters as the partisan Notre Dame fans went wild. After another missed extra point, Notre Dame led late in the fourth quarter, 12-6.

Sportswriter W. O. McGeehan reported that despite the situation, fight remained in the Cadets. Cagle broke loose on the following kickoff return. For a moment, it appeared that he would go the distance and crush the Irish's hopes for an upset. After he scrambled through the broken field for a fifty-five-yard gain, Chris Cagle was finally tackled deep in Notre Dame territory. With about a minute to play in the game, the winded Cagle again got the call, and the Irish hit him hard. Onward Christian Cagle was forced to leave the game.

In spite of Cagle's absence, the fighting spirit of the Long Gray Line refused to fade away. Previously not heard from for most of the day, Cadet Richard Hutchinson completed a pass to Cadet Charles Allan. Cadet Allan's reception moved the ball inside of Notre Dame's one yard line.

With the ball placed less than twelve inches from the goal line, the Cadets set their formation. As if on cue, thousands of program-waving Notre Dame fans, subway alumni, and tens of thousands of Catholic homes fell silent as the Corps of Cadets "chanted prayerfully." It was nearing dusk, and the temperature was dropping. Inside the one and inches to go in order to tie the score, the Army center placed his hands on the ball for the inevitable direct snap to Cagle.

W. O. McGeehan wrote that "he held it there for just a few palpitating heartbeats, just the few movements of an eyelash."

The snap was intended for Cagle, but Cagle wasn't in the game. Perhaps, that's the reason for the center's slightest delay in snapping the ball. Army's go-to-guy was out; the center hesitated.

As the mass of an estimated eighty thousand tiptoed to see the dramatic moment, a shrill whistle sounded just before the delayed snap. The ball game was over. The men in the striped black jerseys and "gleaming yellow satin breeches" lost, 12-6.

An Army tie or win would have muted any record of Rockne's Gipper speech. Jack Chevigny's "That's one for the Gipper" exclamation would have been overlooked. No hint of an unfulfilled halftime evocation on behalf of a long-dead football hero would have come forth, and the memory of a Johnny-on-the-spot performance of a reserve end with the perfect Irish surname would have eroded over time. If Army had ruled the day, George Gipp, Jack Chevigny, Johnny O'Brien, and the memorialization of Knute Rockne would have been marginalized. In a butterfly effect, the frayed thread of an Army victory would likely have unraveled a fabric of sports history and diminished a large part of the Notre Dame football mythos.

Yet, the ball wasn't snapped, the whistle did blow, and the time did run out. Whether for Gipp or not, the Fighting Irish held on for the win.

Whispered accusations that the Cadets were victims of a fix seeped through the sports underworld. Many observers called foul, stating that there was more time left, but the game had been cut short. The alleged proof of the timing error was that the Army players were in no hurry. If the Cadets had suspected that the final seconds were about to lapse, they would have gotten a last play off easily.

Despite the grumbling, neither Walt Eckersall nor any of the other white-clad officials was formally challenged. Eckersall, a single man best known for two things—a deep emotional dependence on his mother and a hard-drinking lifestyle—would die just two years later at the age of forty-three. If the fix was in, Eckersall took it to his grave.

With the climactic Notre Dame victory, the Gipper game moved from the vague recollection of a motivational talk that may or may not have occurred to an evincible certainty, a peerless legend of triumphal inspiration. In the movie "Knute Rockne All American," Pat O'Brien as Rockne delivers the greatest speech in football history, just as Rockne would have. A thirty-three-year-old actor wearing a number twelve jersey sits near O'Brien's right hand, just as Jack Chevigny would have. Following the conclusion of O'Brien's speech in the venerated locker room scene, the boys leap from their seats and push through the locker room, while the actor leads the way.

Actor Steve Pendleton was just two years younger than Jack Chevigny. Although he received no credit in the film, Pendleton would enjoy a distinguished career in Hollywood, performing for five decades.

Whether Jack really consecrated his touchdown run with homage to the George Gipp remains an issue of debate. However, no historian can question that the exclamation and its timing fit Jack Chevigny's known passion for the game and the intense fealty he felt for his teammates and their cause.

An account of the halftime oration wasn't revealed in the press for days, and it wasn't recorded in a magazine or book for years. The printed 1930 version was likely a concoction of a known Rockne ghostwriter, but it would seem reasonable to believe that some version of the speech was heard that day in the locker room. At least one witness, Joe Byrne Jr., claims to have heard Rockne's talk. The proliferation of two distinct legends, Rockne's Gipper speech and Jack's touchdown exclamation, from a single fabrication is somewhat illogical. And for those who want to believe, the logic lies in the corroboration offered by the alleged Chevigny exclamation.

Many modern sportswriters and media commentators still rank the 1928 Army-Notre Dame game and the Gipper speech as the top moment in college football. In any case, the undisputed outcome was that Army's chance for a national championship in 1928 was over.

Upon the Irish's arrival in South Bend, the team was enthusiastically mobbed, the chaotic scene leading to tragedy when a student fell from the train platform and died.

For Rockne, the celebration was over. Given the combined effect of a student's death and the impending letdown of having just participated in the most memorable game in college football history, the coach would have to resurrect his team's spirit and enthusiasm to face the best team Carnegie Tech had ever fielded, a team that many experts considered to be in the top five in the nation.

It wasn't long until sportswriter Franklyn Doan, in one bold sentence, repudiated the significance of one of the century's greatest games and the Notre Dame win over Army when he announced, "Carnegie Tech is better than the Army!" To many observers, no statement made could have been more blasphemous of the event at Yankee Stadium on November 10, 1928. Up until the Notre Dame victory, the Cadets had run off six consecutive victories in a row by a 164 to 31 margin.

A closer look at the statistics of the season indicated that Carnegie Tech was a team that demanded enormous respect. Prior to the Notre Dame showdown, Army had dominated their competition, but Tech exhibited its own dominion over their opponents by a margin of 174 to 20. Franklyn Doan was right. Carnegie Tech was better than Army.

Whether Notre Dame felt Carnegie Tech was better than Army would be a question for further consideration. Thomas Mills, assistant coach and chief scout for the Fighting Irish, felt the Skibos, or Tartans, to be dangerous.

In presenting his report to the squad at noon on the Tuesday before the Tech meeting, Mills warned,

> "We thought they were tough and now we know it....The Carnegie line will average 190 pounds and it charges faster than a torpedo. The Skibo backfield can run, buck, and pass. Captain Harpster is one of the best punters in the game today and Karcis, the sophomore fullback, or Letzelter, a heavy halfback, can hit the line or skirt the ends. If you fellows thought that the Army would be a hard nut to crack, just double your expectations."

Before Mills could finish, Rockne took the platform and greeted his squad, saying, "Carnegie might be as efficient as Tommy says, but we'll be ready for them."

From that point in Tuesday's skull session, Rockne outlined a game plan remarkably similar in all facets to the plan that brought home the victory from Yankee Stadium the week before. The coach explained that although the Carnegie team was stronger than the Army Cadets, he was confident in the plan and expected a favorable outcome on Saturday.

Tuesday's practice was light and loose. Reserves refined their assignments in running the Skibo plays. The first string players, who hadn't played in the Army game, were assigned to scrimmage the reserves.

Highlighting the acting bill was Joe Savoldi who acted as the 221-pound fullback Johnny Karcis of Carnegie Tech. Joe Morrissey played the role of Skibo team captain and star Howard Harpster. Disoriented and fatigued from the head injury that he suffered late in the Army game, Jack Chevigny remained out of all drills. Chev's return to practice duty wouldn't be expected until Thursday.

By game time, Cartier Field was bursting at the seams with thirty-five thousand fans in attendance to see Notre Dame's final home game of the season. In South Bend, all of the hotels had been sold out for months. In the last weeks prior to the game, over five hundred requests for reservations had to be declined for lack of space.

After a week of some recovery and reconstitution, the Irish hoped to hit the field in fine form. They were restless to prove that the previous week was no fluke.

Despite near perfect weather all week, by game time the field was slushy and the temperature dropping. Unfortunately for the Irish, the foul weather didn't stop the Skibos from striking quickly through the air. On the second play from scrimmage, John "Bull" Karcis tossed a short pass to Ted Rosenzweig who scooted thirty-five yards to the Irish eleven yard line. On the very next play, Letzelter burst through the stunned Irish defense and scored. Carnegie Tech All-American Howard Harpster failed on the point-after, but after only three plays from scrimmage, Carnegie Tech led, 6-0.

The Irish attempted to strike back via the arm of John Niemiec, but they were turned back when the Ohio native's pass was intercepted near midfield. A quick pass from Bull Karcis to Howard "Dutch" Eyth and the Skibos were again in business at the Irish thirty-eight yard line. After a series of Skibo bucks, Carnegie Tech had the ball on the Notre Dame twenty yard line. Sky high and ready to put the Irish away, the Skibos rushed four times toward the goal line with Harpster capping the drive from the one yard line.

This time, Harpster's point-after was successful and Carnegie Tech led 13-0, with time left in the first quarter.

It was turning into a rout before Notre Dame Captain Fred Miller and his mates quelled the Skibo onslaught. A punting feud between the two teams soon dulled the senses of the sellout crowd as neither team could advance against the stiffening defenses. Still, Carnegie appeared ready to blow the game open. When the first quarter ended, the score was Carnegie Tech 13, Notre Dame 0.

The quarter break offered no respite for the reeling Irish when Ted Rosenzweig immediately struck again for the Skibos third touchdown of the first half. Harpster's point-after was good, and Carnegie Tech led the stunned Irish 20-0. Penalties, punts, and failed offensive penetrations ruled the remaining minutes of the second quarter as both teams struggled to move the ball. At the halftime gun, a perplexed Cartier crowd watched their shell-shocked Fighting Irish leave the field with their heads hanging.

Eventually, Carnegie Tech's running game pounded the smaller Rockne men. Although some valiant efforts were attempted by several Irish, Carnegie Tech effectively crushed Notre Dame, 27-7. It was Notre Dame's first home defeat in twenty-three years.

In order to better the 1905 team's record of 5-4, the Irish would have to defeat the unblemished Trojans of Southern California in Los Angeles. It wasn't going to be easy.

In addition to an unbeaten record of 8-0-1, Southern Cal carried with them the bitter taste of the controversial loss to Notre Dame at Soldier Field during the previous season. An additional obstacle to the Irish objective was the fact that the USC contest would be in Los Angeles, the ultimate road game for 1928.

The Irish traveled from Chicago, stopping in Tucson, Arizona, for several days to practice at the University of Arizona. Other than the placement of an inappropriate orange-colored "Welcome Irish" sign ordered by local merchant James Patrick Greaher, Tucson saw the arrival of the Notre Dame squad as a celebratory event. Probably not lost in the city's motivation was the fact that USC had maliciously trampled Arizona 78-7 earlier that year. The Associated Press reported that "two stiff workouts" convinced Rockne his team was in shape for USC. Also of note was the fact that only six of the Notre Dame players had been with the team on the first trip out west in 1926. They were Miller, Leppig, Niemiec, Colrick, Moynihan, and Chevigny.

A headshot of Jack was inserted in a November 29, 1928, news article proclaiming him as the team's spiritual leader. Jack's prowess as a defender was noticed by all in attendance at the practice.

The report read, "While Rockne was piloting the Irish subs in Trojan formations Chevigny broke up the plays with startling regularity."

Using the Southern Cal trip as a dual fundraiser and goodwill tour, the Irish were toasted at a banquet in Tucson. The USC trip was an important public relations tour as well as a big game. Rockne's openness backfired when, upon the team's arrival in California, he saw diagrams of his plays in the area newspapers. Following the nationwide publicity of Jack's heroics against Army two weeks prior, the Southern California press headlined the need for the Trojans to contain Chevigny if they were to prevail.

Back in Hammond, Jack's beloved sister Marie tended to his scrapbook, gluing in the pages heralding Jack's tenacity and toughness.

In applauding Jack's play, Maxwell Stiles of the *Los Angeles Examiner* wrote,

"John Chevigny—remember the name. He is slick as a whistle, as swift as a hare, takes passes on the dead run, sears a blazing trail off tackle, and is just about the whole Notre Dame secondary defense wrapped up in the sinewy frame of one man. It will take a man of the capabilities, and, unerring reliability of Lloyd Thomas to rise to the crisis that will strike like lightning at the Coliseum next Saturday afternoon when this John Chevigny person breaks out into the wide open spaces beyond the line of scrimmage and prepares to take one of John Niemiec's spirals out of the California climate. And it will take a bank-up tackler of the aggressiveness of Nate Barragar or Harry Edelson, or of Captain Jess Hibbs, when he's in the mood, to take this John Chevigny person in hand when that scintillating star of the Irish backfield streaks off tackle."

The Trojans expectedly pummeled the Fighting Irish, 27-14. Nursing an injury suffered in the Carnegie Tech game, John Niemiec carried the ball only twice. Most Irish rooters in attendance attributed the Trojans' dominance to Niemiec's limited ability to perform, but to the professional writers in the press box, it was Southern California's superior athleticism, not Niemiec's injury, that rendered Notre Dame's normally effective passing game stale and impotent.

The Trojans' opening drive of 54 yards set the tone as USC rolled to 310 total yards of offense, 194 rushing and 116 passing. Given those numbers, the average fan might not have realized that it was the Trojan defensive effort that effectively had ruled the day. Team captain Jesse Hibbs authenticated his All-American status with countless bone-jarring tackles. For the Irish, the one bright spot came not from the Southern California sun but from Jack Chevigny. Notre Dame's lone score came in the third quarter on a fake reverse in which Jack slashed off left tackle for a fifty-one-yard score.

It was the first victory for the Trojans in the young series, and the Los Angeles press gloated. During an era that held sportsmanship as a goal of intercollegiate competition, quotes of opposing players normally were subdued and complementary.

Trojan captain Jess Hibbs did speak well of the Irish, but the *Los Angeles Times* made sure that he appended his favorable comments with a cutting jab. Hibbs expounded on the outcome, "Yes, they're a good team, all right. Not as good as last year, but still they're good. We've had harder games, though."

The controversial loss to Notre Dame at Soldier Field during the previous year remained a bitter pill that the Trojans tasted even in victory. From that point forward, the series would mean more than just a win or loss in the column. For decades, both football programs would use the Notre Dame–USC game as a benchmark for success.

After the game, Rockne rushed to Central Station. His son Jack, having inhaled a peanut, was hospitalized back in Indiana. Rockne's assistants would accompany the team back to South Bend.

At 5-4, the Irish finished the 1928 season as the worst Notre Dame team in twenty-three years. The four games lost equaled one-third of the games Rockne lost in his entire career. Yet, the team that Rockne called "terrible" would provide Notre Dame and college football with its most dramatic moment, the Gipper game.

With Jack Chevigny's senior season behind him and with his academic performance still faltering, his vision of the future became transparent.

At the same time, Knute Rockne realized that Jack was unique. The coach had long recognized that Jack was more than just a good player. Rock always had good players, but Jack Chevigny was his premier football graduate. Here was the boy destined to be Rockne's prophet.

# CHAPTER EIGHT

# *Just Before the Crash*

Since that springtime day as a Notre Dame freshman in 1925 when he first took notes in Rockne's football class, "Tactics and Strategy," Jack had grown in the game. From his notes on foods to avoid—chocolate and fried foods—to the ten deadly sins of a football team, the Notre Dame halfback had embraced the Rockne platform. It was confirmation of the natural order. Chev was the chosen one.

Forced to attend classes in the summer of 1928 in order to remain eligible for his senior year at Notre Dame, Jack nonetheless exhibited a relentless nature and a dedicated commitment to excel on the field. Pulling things together in the fall of 1928, Jack managed to pass four of five classes. With his senior season and playing career behind him, he was rewarded with an appointment to the coaching staff in the spring of 1929. While his playing days were over, Jack continued working toward his bachelor of law degree in the midst of spring football practice. By the end of the spring semester of 1929, Jack had amazingly passed every class, albeit with extraordinarily mediocre grades.

In March 1929, Jack accompanied Rockne on many of his coaching school circuit stops. Coaching schools had been a standard of Rockne's operation since the early days, and his Midas touch as a coach ensured that the coaching schools brought in large sums of extra income. It was a lucrative field for the forty-one-year-old Socrates of football. With many disciples and every football coach in America anxious to learn Rockne-ball, Rockne reciprocated their loyalty and interest with appearances at numerous coaching schools, which took place throughout the country.

For him, the art of making money was on equal footing with the art of coaching, and the concept of striking while the iron was hot was not lost on the Norwegian-born All-American. As hard as Rockne worked at football, he worked even harder at developing a sound financial portfolio. Rockne historians point out that the coach was a product of his time, the stereotypical hard-working immigrant who worked to guarantee that he would never relive the sparse days of his childhood. Like a lot of successful entrepreneurs, the days of good and plenty would never lull Rockne into thinking he had it made. Coaching was the vehicle of personal fulfillment, but financial security was the driver that guided his decisions. Along with maintaining his success in coaching, he wanted to insure his family's future against the unforeseen circumstances of an economic decline.

No doubt, Knute Rockne was more than just a legendary football coach in his time. He was a pioneer of his profession in the arena of media manipulation and marketing. With a profitable contract as the motivational speaker for South Bend automaker Studebaker, Rockne used his success on the field as a means to gain personal wealth. In Rockne's world, the marketing of his endorsements was the natural progression of his on-the-field accomplishments.

As one of several big-name coaches who capitalized on the concept of coaching schools in developing a substantial source of revenue, Rockne used the coaching school model to spread the gospel of the Rockne-ball and the

Notre Dame way. Novice coaches, who attended his summer coaching schools, would use his techniques and emulate the Rockne theories of coaching, seeding the concepts of Rockne-ball in every field of organized ball. Having refined his coaching school model at Culver Academy, located just a few miles south of South Bend, Rockne traveled the lecture circuit of coaching schools and built on his early 1920s gridiron achievements. In the latter part of the decade, Rockne's coaching schools were the most popular instructional sports clinics in the country, grossing the coach at least $35,000 annually. Not bad for a summer job in the Roaring Twenties.

Nationwide, over ninety thousand high school and college coaches attended Rockne's yearly spring and summer coaching schools, while Jack, as Rockne's understudy, learned the master's strategy and marketing of the game. So adept did Jack become at managing the schools, the twenty-three-year-old understudy played the central role in the daily administration of many various summer coaching schools by the summer of 1929.

Attending one such clinic in Chicago with his young partner Chev, Rockne took time out for a photo op in Jack's hometown. On Friday, March 22, 1929, the *Lake County Times* pictured Rockne and Jack side-by-side in a full-page spread. Knute dressed in a dark two-piece suit and tie; the slightly taller Jack dressed in a white woolen three-piece suit accessorized with a dark necktie.

In speaking of Jack to the Hammond Chamber of Commerce, Coach Rockne declared him to be "…one of the greatest team men I ever had." Rockne elaborated,

> "I took Chevigny out of a game three times last fall because he played himself out entirely. He absolutely gave every ounce of strength he had to the game. Johnny is a fighter, and I am certain that, no matter what business he goes

into in Hammond, whether it be law or anything else, he'll make good."

Rockne added,

> "I believe the imperative need in trying to stress character in students has never been so great as it is in this day and age. If students were going to successfully combat the hip bottle evil and the automobile craze they must do it by a strong will."

The *Lake County Times* remarked that Coach Rockne's address continued with "many epigrams, bright gems of philosophy, and pithy sayings."

From Hammond, Rockne and Jack would have made the short drive into Chicago to meet the director of the Chicago area coaching school, Sam Hill. Also present at the meeting with Hill would have been track coach Cliff Gallagher and Dutch Lonborg, a university basketball mentor. Rockne would have delivered the last-minute *dope* as to how the camp would be facilitated and coordinated.

Coaching schools provided an opportunity for all coaches to learn the Notre Dame system; it was Johnny Chevigny's 1925 freshman "Tactics and Strategy" class taken nationwide. After paying a small tuition to learn the tricks of the trade and study the Notre Dame system, all coaches were welcome to attend a Rockne coaching school.

All *white* coaches were welcome to attend.

When his secretary answered a query as to whether staff members from an established black institution, Texas College, could attend a Rockne coaching school at Southern Methodist University in Dallas, she affirmed that "Mr. Rockne will be very pleased to see you."

A few days following the Texas College inquiry, both Rockne and his secretary were taken aback when a communication arrived from Southern

Methodist University (SMU), alerting Rockne to the fact that Texas College is a "Negro institution." In their telegram, the SMU officials stated that Rockne apparently was unaware of the "nationality" of Texas College.

Although an SMU coach named Hayden Fry would turn racism upside down when he recruited Jerry Levias in 1965, SMU officials in 1927 made it clear to Rockne and his coaching school cartel that the "negro would not be popular attending coaching school here."

Considering Rockne within the scope of his essential character, it would seem that such a forward-thinking man, an immigrant and newly professed Catholic who knew something of discrimination, would have taken the opportunity to use his influence to act on the opportunity to invalidate racial prejudice in sports. However, in that Rockne's goal was to enhance his financial portfolio, he would have no part of a 1920s civil rights struggle in a country with over one million registered Klan members. Given the downside of challenging the racist stance of Southern Methodist University toward a fellow group of Texas coaches, Rockne felt it decidedly inappropriate to attempt to set straight southern attitudes or SMU's policies. Despite Rockne's contempt for the hatemongering Ku Klux Klan presence in 1920s Indiana and his resentment for the anti-Catholic riptide and rampant racism of the early twentieth century, Rockne was still a contemporary businessman.

Decades earlier, the U. S. Supreme Court in *Plessy v. Ferguson (1896)* had itself affirmed segregation, making it the law of the land. In Texas and in the Deep South the 1920s and 1930s, the lynching of African Americans was a prevalent threat, if not a frequent occurrence. Often supported and even perpetrated by local law enforcement, the lynching of black citizens occurred for such documented offenses as arguing with a white man, inciting trouble, quarreling, demanding respect, using obscene language, trying to vote, acting suspiciously, throwing stones, and unpopularity. Jim Crow racism ruled in the South.

Considering the social climate, Knute Rockne chose to ignore Texas College's request to attend the coaching school. Rockne's secretary closed the matter by providing an unsettling curt response to their registration. The Negro college coaches were told that their invitation was regretfully rescinded, and that they should not attend. Unequivocally, Rockne's favorite color concern was green, not black or white.

Both Rockne and Jack lived in an era when whites and nonwhites lived separately in all aspects of life, and as Rock's apprentice and a man of his time, Jack had no problem following Rockne's policy of turning a blind eye to the racial division in coaching and in society in general. Regrettably, Jack's faithfulness to his mentor's values would lend no help to Jack in his own critical face-off with racial discrimination just a few short years down the road.

While social reform in the South stood still, things in Indiana were changing drastically for Rockne and Notre Dame football in 1929. The long-demanded stadium was now slated for the critical construction phase. As a consequence, Notre Dame would be forced to schedule all of their 1929 games on the road. On the heels of the most disappointing season in Rockne's career, his squad faced nine straight games on the road—an imposing obstacle for practically any football team.

For Rock, some consolation would come in the ripening of the fruits of the previous season. While Jack and his fellow seniors struggled through 1928 without experienced reserves, Rockne used the season to enroll the underclass talent on a fast learning curve. The product of that curve was a backfield consisting of Frank Carideo, Jack Elder, Larry Mullins, and Joe Savoldi. Anchoring the line were John Law, Ted Twomey, and Jack

Cannon. Transfer Marty Brill added another warhorse to the stable. Tom Lieb, returning to Notre Dame as the first assistant, found the Fighting Irish to be loaded, coaching parlance for stocked with top players.

For the university's football fortunes, Lieb's return to Notre Dame proved to be providence blessed. Early in the fall, Rockne was diagnosed with a severe illness. Phlebitis, an inflammation of the veins of the leg, would cripple the coach for most of the 1929 season.

The historical description of Rockne's symptoms indicates a likely diagnosis of the most serious form of phlebitis, deep venous thrombosis. Deep venous thrombosis is a potentially fatal condition in which a blood clot forms in one of the major deep veins of the leg causing inflammation and irritation. This blockage causes a feverish feeling to the leg, swelling, and extreme pain. Should the clot break free, the patient can die from a lung embolism.

Rockne's condition has been linked to a 1926 game with Indiana. During that game the coach received a hard blow to the legs when he was struck by a Hoosier ball carrier tackled out of bounds. Violent sideline collisions have always been a part of the game, but in 1926 this type of occurrence was more rule than exception. In certain circumstances, the pre-modern game played in Rockne's era called for the ball to be spotted near the sideline. Before the hash mark was implemented as a field marking, pre-modern offenses would often find themselves snapping the ball just a few feet from the sideline. Only when the ball carrier went out of bounds could the ball again be repositioned in the center of the field. Thus, it wasn't uncommon for teams to waste a down by purposely running the ball out of bound, so that the playing field would again be balanced. Rockne's collision could have been the result of this strategy.

Another more plausible theory related to his practice habits. Rockne's phlebitis could have been a result of his daily practice of participating in contact drills. At almost every practice, he could be seen holding a dummy or bag, placing himself in harm's way against some of the best football players in the country. Numerous photos give witness to Rockne's active participation in the drills. And even though most of the photos were staged, Rockne's trademark was the active demonstration of a technique in live contact situations. Just such an active coaching style was typical of most coaches in Rockne's era. In later years, Jack would mimic his coach's theory and practice style, taking an active part in his squad's preparations.

Due to Rockne's delicate health, Lieb quickly stepped in as Rockne's proxy, and with Rockne listening to the radio in South Bend, the former Wisconsin assistant led the Irish to victory over Navy. Demonstrating why he would be named to the Hall of Fame, New Yorker Frank Carideo rallied Notre Dame from a six-point deficit.

The following week, Notre Dame met Wisconsin at Soldier Field; Rockne remained home. As would be expected, Lieb's inside knowledge as a former Badger assistant gave the Irish a psychological edge in preparation for the Badgers. Joe Savoldi and Jack Elder led the Irish to a 19-0 shutout.

Remaining flat on his back as much as possible, Rockne arranged to have a local hearse transport him to practice each day. With the infamously tough Skibos from Carnegie Tech next on the slate, Rockne was acutely apprehensive of missing the game. Mindful that his absence from the 1926 contest was generally acknowledged as the reason the Irish lost not only the game but also a national title, Rock was reluctant to turn over the reigns to even his most-trusted assistant, Lieb. Traveling to Pittsburgh, Rockne would manage the substitutions from a sideline wheelchair.

In coaching a game in 1930, a head football coach had considerably less game input than the coach of today. Coaches in Rockne's era weren't allowed play-to-play communication to their players. The quarterback was responsible for directing the team according to the coach's plan. In that he rarely left the field in the days of one-platoon football, the quarterback memorized the game plan in order to adjust the strategy independent of the coach's input. Measured by his ability to direct the offense, the quarterback was characteristically the field general of the football team.

Considered one of the best quarterbacks in the history of the game, Frank Carideo was an expert field general. The always tough Tartans made a game of it, but Carideo and the Irish edged the Pittsburgh squad, 7-0.

Following the Pitt victory, Notre Dame boarded the train for their annual ride deep into Jim Crow country. Awaiting the perfect 4-0 Irish in Atlanta was a significantly weaker 1929 version of the defending national champion Georgia Tech squad.

For the Irish, sweet revenge ruled the day. There would be no jokes about the satin pants after Rockne's 1929 model crushed the Yellowjackets' hopes for a repeat victory, 26-6. Because of Rockne's bitter memory of the taunting Atlanta press, this win was particularly enjoyable, even though it was witnessed through his mind's eye as he listened via radio from his home in South Bend. Though his health continued to improve, Rockne's doctors ordered him to remain home the following Saturday when his team traveled to Soldier Field. It was the first full week following Black Tuesday, the stock market crash of 1929. Nevertheless, fifty thousand fans showed up to see Notre Dame defeat Drake, 19-6.

By October 1929, Jack Dempsey was no longer the Manassas Mauler, and a knee injury had stolen Red Grange's legendary gallop. Babe Ruth's Yankees had failed to make the World Series, and the Golden Age of Sports had tarnished with age. Outside of sports, Black Tuesday signaled a reversal of the unprecedented prosperity America had enjoyed during the 1920s.

Throughout the decade, an extended stock market boom had pushed stock prices to all-time highs. As a result, stocks bought and sold on stock exchanges such as the New York Stock Exchange (NYSE) quadrupled in value. On Black Thursday, October 24, investors saw the stock market teeter toward disaster when 12.9 million shares (over three times the normal volume of shares) were traded. Exchanges across the country were overwhelmed as hysterical false reports of nearly a dozen suicides ran over the wires like wildfire.

Calm returned when the extraordinary action of Richard Whitney, vice-president of the NYSE, shocked the floor with an announcement that he was purchasing ten thousand shares of U.S. Steel, the Gary, Indiana, employer of Hammond's Dr. Julius Chevigny. With order temporarily restored, thanks to Whitney, the NYSE stock prices rose. Before the close of market on October 24, the market impressively rebounded. Suffering only a slight hint of a cough, stock prices awakened Friday morning in much better health.

Monday, investors heard an unexpected knock at the front door. The downturn had returned with the economic undertaker. When the trading volume reached over nine million shares, the market failed to rebound as it had on Black Thursday. Investors realized that they would see no firm recovery, no resurrection of the Jazz Age boom. By the close of trading, it was the worst day in NYSE history. That Monday, with Thomas Edison's patented ticker lagging significantly behind real time information, panicked investors sold their holdings blindly with no idea of the price.

On Tuesday, the coffin was nailed shut. The ticker, lagging more than two hours behind, recorded over sixteen million shares traded. On October

29, 1929, stock prices nose-dived. No help from the nation's largest banks was in sight. By November, over $100 billion in assets had been lost by investors. The stock market lost approximately 40 percent of its value. The Reaper stood ominously over Capitol Hill as a recently inaugurated President Hoover took center stage to reassure investors that the downturn was cyclical.

Rockne, having recently acquired a high-paying position with Studebaker, would have gasped when he read his morning paper on Wednesday, October 30, 1929. Though Rockne's business in early November was football, the added stress of the stock market crash would have exacerbated his poor health and threatened his future as a coach. By lunchtime on Wednesday, Rockne would have had a plate full of worries.

One of those worries was Notre Dame's next opponent, USC. The rivalry between the two schools had increased in intensity each year since the opening of the series in 1926. Fueling the passion of the grudge match were the pens of the West Coast journalists who resented the Eastern college football bias of the *New York Times* and *Chicago Tribune*.

After the Los Angeles press rubbed the Irish's nose into the memory of the 1928 beat-down, freshman coach Jack Chevigny and the returning members of the 1928 squad longed for some payback. This year, the Irish wouldn't have to worry about falling victim to the letdown, which normally followed the Army game; the Southern Cal meeting was two weeks before the Army game.

Having lost only to California by a score of 15-7, the Trojans were a fearsome force. In September, Howard Jones's squad annihilated UCLA, 76-0. In October, they crushed Washington, 48-0. In November, the week prior to the Notre Dame showdown at Soldier Field, USC destroyed a hapless Nevada, 66-0.

Nothing short of death would stop Rockne from being on the Irish sideline in Chicago. As expected, the game would be witnessed by a capacity crowd similar in size to the 1928 Navy game at Soldier Field.

With each team struggling to gain momentum, the Irish and the Trojans battled to a tied halftime score of 6-6. By 1929, Rockne's trademark halftime speech was so thematically consistent in both substance and style, it seemed as if he rehearsed regularly. Given the similarities of his Saturday afternoon exhortations, his players had come to appreciate Rockne's consistent message. In fact, they expected it. And while each new class of Notre Damers revered Rockne's halftime exhortations, another group of individuals had become tired and unappreciative of Rockne's repetitive locker-room elocution.

Some members of the sports writing press no longer bought into the gee-whiz promotion of Rockne. A newer element of the press had grown cynical of Rockne's consistently tearful pleadings and perceived grandstanding. With his ongoing battle with phlebitis serving to target Rockne for even more cynicism, he was accused of using the illness and wheelchair to inspire the boys to go out and win for old Notre Dame.

Rockne's temperament held no room for aspersion originating from the press box. Snapping back, Rockne decried the negative reporting as "Klanism."

As on many Saturdays in college football, the outcome of the Southern California contest would come down to the kicking game. But as long as Frank Carideo wore the blue and gold, Notre Dame held a slight edge in that department. Converting on the point-after-touchdown attempt following Joe Savoldi's go-ahead touchdown six minutes into the third quarter, Frank gave the Irish a 13-6 lead.

After the Trojans quickly struck on a ninety-five-yard touchdown run, Southern Cal missed the extra point that would have tied the game. Notre Dame won, 13-12.

On the following Saturday, the Irish would be back in Chicago but without Rockne. Worn from the USC week, he entrusted the Northwestern game to his assistants. Interim head coach Tom Lieb led the Fighting Irish to a 26-6 victory.

Though not having played a single home game, Notre Dame remained undefeated. The date with Army was now at the undefeated Irish's door.

In just one year, the table of fortunes for Army and Notre Dame had flipped. By the date of the Notre Dame match-up, the 1929 edition of the Cadets had already suffered three losses. With the Fighting Irish perfect for the season, New York bookies laid the odds heavily in favor of Notre Dame.

It was late November 1929, and the financial clouds had begun to shower despair throughout the city of New York. Already suffering from the market's collapse, the city welcomed any respite. Notre Dame-Army was the city's ticket out of despair.

In accordance with the hopes of the quintessential subway alumnus Mayor Jimmy Walker and the collective athletic departments of West Point and Notre Dame, fans of both teams were undeterred by the inequity of the two teams and the growing deflation of the dollar. Scarce tickets skyrocketed in value as scalpers got $50 apiece.

At his home in South Bend, Notre Dame's head football coach was forced to join a nationwide radio audience listening to the play-by-play from their living rooms. Meanwhile, frozen in the Bronx, fans of both teams found the highlights of the game to be as sparse and few-between as the smiles on Wall Street. In closing out his long multi-college career with a disappointing moment, Army's Chris "Red" Cagle was intercepted.

In a game played in ice and subzero temperature, Jack Elder's interception return broke the scoreless tie and provided the Irish victory. At Yankee Stadium, Elder's school record interception of one hundred yards won the day. Notre Dame prevailed, 7-0.

Blemishing the win and subsequent perfect season was a subsequent wave of disapproval that washed across the sports pages when the media criticized Notre Dame's strategy of taking the air out of the ball and playing close to the vest. An alarming amount of money had been lost in both large and small wagers when Notre Dame failed to cover the sizable point spread. So strident were the voices of criticism, those sportswriters favorable to Rockne felt it incumbent to respond by writing columns in support of the Notre Dame offensive strategy. Eventually, the cries of the insatiable malcontents faded.

Though no Irish home games were played on the South Bend campus, another national championship was claimed by the boys from Notre Dame. With the construction of the new stadium on campus, 1929 would be remembered as the final edition of Rockne's Ramblers. Notre Dame would no longer be forced to play their big-draw games on the road for money. The ignominious team nicknames would fade into obscurity. By the fall of 1930, the Fighting Irish, the most recognizable trademark name in college football, would have their own modern, large-capacity stadium.

After the season, Rockne's phlebitis continued to worsen. Encouraged to seek treatment at the Mayo Center in Minnesota where he would receive the best medical care available, Rock traveled north.

The lead physician for his case was Doctor Clifford J. Barborka, a well-known expert in nutrition and personal acquaintance of Rockne. Doctor Barborka's 1934 textbook, *Treatment by Diet,* would become the authoritative text on the treatment of ailments with nutrition.

Personal letters prove that Rockne and Barborka enjoyed a close personal bond. In those letters, Doctor Barborka referred to the coach as "Rock," the preferred name of address used by Rockne's friends.

While history records each of Rockne's assistants as having a peripheral interest in his treatment and progress, it was the former player and mediocre law student, not the trusted Tom Lieb or indispensable Hunk Anderson, who wrote a note of thanks to Doctor Barborka. Not bothering to register for any classes during the spring of 1930, Jack spent most of his waking hours by Rockne's side in Minnesota.

Bonnie Rockne would remain in South Bend with the children. From this intersection of Jack's devotion and Knute Rockne's health crisis, the Rocknes, especially Bonnie, would come to rely on Jack during a time of crisis. An unofficial coach with no specific spring duty, Jack had become indispensable to the Rockne family. From this point on, he was as much a Rockne as a Chevigny.

Giving evidence to Chevigny's close personal relationship with his former coach and boss was a news photograph of Jack at the Mayo Clinic bedside of Rockne. The purpose of the photo was to reassure a nation that the coach was indeed receiving the finest medical attention available at the time.

In South Bend during the midst of spring drills, Jack received the following letter from Rock's attending physician at the Mayo Clinic.

Mayo Clinic
Rochester, Minnesota

My dear Jack:
I appreciate your note of May 2.
I hope to be able to send Rock away from here Friday evening. I know he is looking forward very much to seeing the

finish of the spring practice. Be sure to notify me should your sister decide to come here.

God be with you in all your projects. Mrs. Barborka and Von join me in sending regards.

As ever,
(signed) C. J. Barborka
*CJB:AL*

As the May 6, 1930 letter to Jack indicates, Doctor Barborka was a close friend of both Rock and the Notre Dame family. While the Mayo physician and the Hammond doctor's son probably didn't develop a close friendship, their acquaintance developed into one from which personal letters emanated. The letter, lending credence to the fact that Barborka knew Jack well, is a testament to Jack's charm, a personality who could engage anyone on any subject.

Living the life of the big-man on campus, Chev was also the quintessential Jazz Age gentleman and party-goer. Selected as Grand Knight of the campus Knights of Columbus Council, the preeminent Catholic men's social and service organization, Jack Chevigny was a fraternal man in a time when social networking occurred face-to-face through group settings. In an era when the entire social fabric of society was sewn with personal interaction, panache was an essential part of the successful individual's skill set.

Doctor Barborka and the Mayo Clinic staff weren't lone explorers in the field of circulation problems. Tulane Medical School legends Doctor Alton Ochsner and Doctor Michael DeBakey ascertained the distinction between two types of venous thrombosis—thrombophlebitis and phlebothrombosis. As Oschner and DeBakey would later confirm, the most common cause of thrombophlebitis was tissue injury. In the prevention of pulmonary embolisms emanating from both conditions, Ochsner and

DeBakey emphasized prophylactic measures such as wrapping the lower extremities, early ambulation, electrical stimulation of calf muscles, resting in a head-down position, and the use of anticoagulation. In further testament to their vision and advanced medical postulation, Ochsner and DeBakey in 1939 identified a link between smoking and lung cancer.

Prescribed a rubber legging, Rockne managed his phlebitis of the calf area with compression and rest. Other treatment options for phlebitis were leeches and citrates. Leeches secrete a nontoxic substance known as hirudin, which has anticoagulant properties. Citrate had been used since 1914 as an anticoagulant, but the patient could tolerate only small quantities. Oral anticoagulants for the treatment of phlebitis, such as dicumerol, would not appear until the 1940s. Thus, the disease would have incontrovertibly plagued Rockne for another decade. As confirmed by Rock's own quips about "his spare tire," the rubber bandage was the primary long-term prescriptive measure for his ailment.

Rockne's constant traveling over long distances throughout the off-season would have aggravated his condition and further endangered his life. At the Mayo Clinic, physicians discouraged Rockne from taking extended train excursions. Likewise, the cramped cabins of the airplanes that serviced interregional and bicoastal air travel would have negatively affected Rockne's health.

With his numerous endorsement commitments, the million-dollar coach was a constant traveler during the off-season. Preferring to commute long distances in the cramped conditions of the small passenger planes of the day, Rockne took trips that were not only bad for his condition, but bad for his relations with his superiors at Notre Dame. The trips and Rockne's long and frequent absences from campus created friction between the coach and the administration.

Despite the severity of his condition upon his arrival at Mayo Clinic, Rockne improved. After receiving treatment, it was possible for him to see the conclusion of the spring practice. By this time, Jack had been promised a varsity backfield coaching stipend with a fulltime staff position at the university, an offer that convinced Jack to disdain the entreaties of rival USC for his services as an assistant coach. Chev would help lecture in the university's physical education department. Although he had not yet completed his law degree, Jack planned to return to school in the fall to finish what he had started.

Ironically, other than Jack Chevigny's scrapbook of letters and telegrams, no written documentation proves Rockne to be intrinsically closer to Jack than he was to any of the other former Notre Dame players. Innumerable first-person narratives from Rockne insiders make a point of magnifying the bond between the coach and his former players, but none of the testimonials distinguish any one player as the most intimate of Rockne's boys. Notre Dame's Francis Wallace explained what he felt was the reason for the lack of a coronation of one single player. Wallace stated that Rockne was a consummate politician who traditionally pledged allegiance to everyone who ever played for him. Wallace remarked, "He had a habit of saying to the hometown friends of one of his coaches: 'If I should ever leave Notre Dame, I'd like Joe here, to succeed me.' This led to confused nominations for his job after he died."

In attendance at many of those rubber-chicken outings with Rockne, Jack would have felt that the "Joe" of which Rockne spoke was Jack Chevigny. Only a few of Rockne's closest assistants would have earned a spot on the short list: veteran Tom Lieb who left for Loyola in 1930; Hunk Anderson, often considered Rockne's closest confidante and strategist; and

Jack Chevigny, Rockne's youthful apprentice who knew no other home but Notre Dame.

Rockne had no macabre Abraham Lincoln visions of death. When he spoke of who would succeed him, he was speaking of a time far distant from that moment. His plan was to continue to coach for several more years, perhaps another decade if the phlebitis could be controlled. In 1930, Rockne had four children at home and reigned over a marketing empire rivaling any future sport superstar. The imminent financial onslaught of the Great Depression would have sparked not a surrender but a renaissance of Rockne's determination to provide for his family. With the exception of the burden of the health issues, it is difficult to believe that Rockne would have considered leaving football in the near future. Even as the Great Depression deepened, Rockne foresaw his portfolio growing as his star continued to rise.

In 1930, the forty-two-year-old coach was still a young man. For certain, Rockne believed that Jack would remain at Notre Dame by his side for another decade. Hinting of how the future cards were to play, Rockne reassured Jack of his future at Notre Dame on at least two occasions, making sure his understudy didn't leave for USC and one other university. For Rockne, everything was centered on preparation. Everyone close to Rockne knew of Jack's preordainment. Promoting Jack Chevigny was an evident part of the master's plan of eventual succession.

Given the precarious health of the university icon, in 1930, the Notre Dame administration yielded to Rockne's persistent demands for a larger football infrastructure, adding to the number of professional support personnel and increasing the size of the coaching staff. With Hunk Anderson back from a frustrating stint as the head coach at Saint Louis University, Jack was added as a fulltime backfield coach. Ike Voedisch was made the end coach, and Tim Moynihan was appointed assistant line coach. Manny Vezie and Bill Jones rounded out the staff as freshman coaches. And with Hunk promised twice as much as the highest paid professor on campus, President O'Donnell also upgraded the coaches' salaries.

September of 1930 began a new era in Rockne's new stadium as the Fighting Irish defeated Southern Methodist University on the transplanted Cartier grass. Given the excitement surrounding the stadium's opening and the return of an improved version of the national champions from the year before, a sellout crowd was expected; however, despite the return of autumn football madness, the despair of the decade had already begun to insidiously erode the pageant and fanfare of spectator sports. The gate receipts proved that even Notre Dame football wasn't immune to the Great Depression when only 14,751 supporters attended the new stadium's opening day, far less than the 54,000 capacity.

Disappointed that the first week's gate wouldn't have filled half of old Cartier Field, the university amplified its effort to attract fans for the new stadium's formal dedication against Navy the following weekend. The promotion paid off when the athletic department was rewarded with improved receipts and an official attendance of 40,593. Though significantly smaller than the anticipated sell-out, the crowd enjoyed a grand dedication ceremony in which George Gipp was eulogized as a gridiron saint. At the report of the referee's final gun, the Irish had sunk the Midshipmen and notched its second win of the season, 26-2.

After the game, Navy coach Bill Ingram offered the following: "Not only was a fine stadium dedicated but there was ushered in the greatest Notre Dame team in the history of football."

Following Navy was Carnegie Tech, the only team of the last twenty-five years that had beaten Notre Dame at home. With Tech for a repeat of the miracle upset of 1926, it was not to be. The Irish easily handled the Skibos, 21-6.

Then on October 25, 1930, Rock and his boys opened another new stadium, this time in Pittsburgh against Pitt. Dampening the celebratory atmosphere for the Pitt fans were Notre Dame's five touchdowns in twenty-five minutes as the Irish caged the Panthers, 35-19.

After Rockne's boys left Pitt face down in the turf, in an all-Hoosier event the following Saturday, Indiana traveled to South Bend. With the Great Depression sinking the American dream and the value of the dollar, few sportswriters could discern what was more anemic, the Indiana football squad or the attendance numbers in the house that Rock built. Though tied at halftime, Notre Dame eventually demolished Indiana before a paltry 11,113 spectators. The small home crowd for the nation's premier program was an emerging sign of the time. Across the country, university presidents discussed discontinuing interscholastic competition due to low attendance and the need for fiscal restraint.

Showing no restraint in whipping its opponents, Notre Dame and its prowess ventured to Philadelphia's Franklin Field to meet a tough Ivy League member, Penn. Adding to the game hype, Eastern football fans anxiously anticipated the appearance of Joe Savoldi and his backfield teammates: Marchmont "Marchy" Schwartz, Marty Brill, and Frank Carideo. The day was distinctly special for Brill, a Jewish hometown football hero whose talents had been snubbed by Penn. Also significant to the press was the fact that the nation's premier Catholic university was winning football games with two members with the cultural heritage and religious identification of Schwartz and Brill.

Rockne commented that Schwartz was "smart from the Jewish blood in him."

In an unusual Rockne-coached rout, the Irish embarrassed Penn, 60-20. Hometown hero Brill scored three touchdowns.

The following week, Joe Savoldi's expulsion for violating the school policy against the admission of married students cost the tough Italian-American a sure chance to achieve All-American and Hall of Fame status. Rockne could do little but see him off when it was revealed that Jumping Joe had not only been married, but filed for divorce in a South Bend court. By filing the petition locally, he delivered his own exposé to the door of the *South Bend Tribune.*

Another dull Drake game followed the Penn massacre. Standing at a perfect 7-0 and looking very much like repeat national champions, Notre Dame hoped to see an increase in ticket demand for the remaining games.

Also undefeated at 7-0, Northwestern was expecting a good draw for the Notre Dame match. With the Chicago economy suffering, the president of Northwestern approached Notre Dame with a proposal to move the game from Northwestern's Dyche Stadium to Soldier Field. Extra proceeds from Soldier Field would then be used to benefit the local relief fund for the poor. The expected benefit was $100,000 for charity. Though Notre Dame officials agreed, Big Ten Conference member Northwestern needed conference approval.

Despite good intentions, the venue change was denied by conference representatives in a perplexing, if not strictly anti-Catholic, decision. Thus, instead of playing at Soldier Field, the two teams met in the much smaller forty-eight-thousand-capacity Dyche Stadium with the scalpers instead of homeless families reaping the benefits. While Northwestern fans sat in their high-dollar seats and lamented their team's performance, the press bemoaned the lost opportunity to help the indigent. Rockne's boys outscored the Wildcats, 14-0.

The next weekend, Soldier Field would see another opportunity for a broken attendance record when unbeaten Army faced the Irish on November 29. Though the rainy weather didn't cooperate, the fans still came. Sitting in the foul Chicago chill, a capacity crowd saw both teams operate conservatively from their tight formations with a typical scrimmage down resulting in twenty-two unidentifiable players sloshed together in a murky, mud pie. The power slogging of Marchie Schwartz eventually gave the Irish a 6-0 lead and Carideo tacked on the extra point, but Army responded late with a blocked punt for a touchdown. Luckily for the Irish, Army missed the point-after, and the game ended with a 7-6 Irish victory.

After the usual Irish whistle-stop tour through the Southwest on the way to Los Angeles, a victory over rival USC could complete the perfect season of 1930. The Trojans with eight wins was a pretty decent football team, but on that Saturday afternoon, they were completely outclassed by the visiting Irish in a 27-0 shutout. Rockne's 1930 squad stood alone at the pinnacle of perfection. Four days after the USC game, the team returned to Chicago to a tickertape parade along a route of blue and gold banners. In an outflow of accolade previously reserved for such icons as Lindbergh, seven different media sources named the Fighting Irish as national champions.

As a player and star of the Gipper game, Jack Chevigny had played a key part in college football's greatest moment. In just his second season as a coach, Chev's loyalty and hard work had resulted in his being granted access to the inner circle of football's royal court, embraced by the king, and appointed to supervise the greatest backfield ever assembled. While millions of American lives descended into the dark days of hunger and hopelessness, Jack Chevigny's stock soared in his first season as a college football coach.

But soon he would suffer his own personal Black Tuesday. For Jack, it would be the day that would change forever the course of his life's design.

# CHAPTER NINE

# *The Crash*

Rockne basked in a bright future of coaching school contracts, spokesperson endorsements, and rolling thunder of the nation's best recruits. After the disappointing 1928 season in Jack's final year of eligibility, Notre Dame followed up with national championships in 1929 and 1930. It was the dawn of America's darkest decade, but the future of Notre Dame football had never been brighter.

On Tuesday, March 31, 1931, somewhere in a Kansas field, the spotlight went dark. As he rushed to the origin of a loud noise in a nearby field, thirteen-year-old James Easter Heathman found the body of Knute Rockne and seventy-seven years of personal fame lying about a Kansas airplane crash site. In embracing Rockne seekers for over seven decades, an aging Heathman, a witness to the scene of the crash of Transcontinental and Western Flight 599, willingly relived the memory that would serve as a catalyst for those seeking closure of their own personal Rockne quest. Regularly repeated was his most vivid recollection, that of the smell of "hot oil and gasoline." He wouldn't remember seeing more than a little blood at the site. But for the remainder of his days, he could smell the hot oil and visualize the deep lacerations of the passengers' bodies and the crushed remains of the pilots buried under the plane's main engine. Found lying just left of what remained of the main fuselage was Knute Rockne's body.

> "Of course we didn't know who those people were, not until the next day anyway. But I always remember putting one fella on a stretcher. He had long black rubber bandages around his legs. They were wrapped around his legs but had come unraveled. They were hanging down on the ground so I remember running over and taking the end of the bandage and stuffing it back up his pant leg so the ambulance driver wouldn't step on it and trip. I remember reading that Rockne had phlebitis and he used to wear those kinds of rubber bandages around his legs so I figured that was him. I didn't know it at the time though."

> —*James Easter Heathman to Joe Casey, MD*

After managing his phlebitis and returning to a state of good health early in 1931, Rockne aggressively pursued his interests beyond coaching and working with Studebaker. As documented by his activities outside of football, Rockne's last days were typically energetic.

Just as his understudy Jack Chevigny would one day circulate Hollywood's inner circles, Rockne owned his own backstage pass in Tinseltown. Like Dempsey and Ruth, Rock had taken to working the West Coast circuit in search of greater fame and fortune. Following the back-to-back national championships, Rock was invited by Hollywood to join the stars with a contractual offer from Universal Pictures.

In his last day at the university, Rockne requested a meeting with Notre Dame's poet-president, Father Charles O'Donnell. The purpose of the meeting was to discuss the offer from Universal Pictures. Rockne wanted permission to travel to California in order to help develop a film glorifying both him and Notre Dame football. It was a project that offered Rockne fifty thousand Depression-era dollars.

The master of the Notre Dame shift was acutely aware of the current university president's less than sympathetic view of Notre Dame as a national football factory. A subscriber to the tenets of the Carnegie Report, which condemned the usurpations of amateurism as a cancer in the nation's football factories, Father O'Donnell was on record as to his pro-Carnegian view of the role of big-time college football at Notre Dame.

Coincidentally, or perhaps not, President O'Donnell was out of his office on the day the coach stopped in to traverse the topic of the studio's offer. Indeed, the president's unavailability to comment on the travel request made no difference to the coach. In typical Rockne fashion, the iron was already fired and the trip arranged. As O'Donnell had no knowledge of the request and had made no approval, Rockne left a note for the university president. He would be at the Hotel Biltmore in Los Angeles on Wednesday. Rockne deflected any direct implication that the reason for the trip was his own personal entrepreneurial interest, indicating to O'Donnell that his main reason for pursuing the matter was that his involvement might benefit Notre Dame. Jack's mentor knew that the characterization of the trip as something educational and beneficial to Notre Dame's academic mission would make his absence more palatable to the poet-president. Rockne's misdirection play in the matter illustrated the well-known acumen of the legendary coach when it came to dealing with insurmountable obstacles.

Successfully failing to see President O'Donnell, Rockne left South Bend for Chicago where he later enjoyed dinner. From Chicago, he took a train to Kansas City where he would see his two sons, Knute Jr. and Billy. In a commonly unfortunate circumstance of timing, the popular mass transit vehicle of the day, the train, was running behind schedule. Rockne's boys, returning from Florida to their Pembroke Country Day School, missed the meeting with their father in Kansas City.

At 9:56 a.m. on the last Tuesday of March, Knute sent a telegram from Kansas City to his wife Bonnie in Florida. Minutes later, Rock boarded Transcontinental Western Airlines (TWA) Flight 599. The temperature was 32°. The sky was overcast with slight sleet and snow flurries beginning to fall.

↔

TWA Flight 599 utilized the best of its stable, the Fokker F-10A Super Trimotor, which in this case was tagged with the registration number NC999E. Described by its builders as a stately airship, it was an iconic image of the era of handcrafted motor vehicles and aircraft. Designed to carry twelve passengers in the comfort of a private flying salon, the structural components of the plane were assembled in the Glendale plant of Marshall County, West Virginia.

During the construction process in the foothills of the Appalachians, the huge cantilever wing of the Fokker F-10A was built entirely of wood. Sheets of plywood of graduated thicknesses were glued together, and then wrapped around ribs that were located in the hollow core of the wing. Craftsmen using carpenter's planes sculpted the airfoil angle, so that the wing sloped upward from the center. No apprentice laborer touched the Fokker F-10A; the workman's precision was commonly noted to be consistent within one thirty-second of an inch.

Upon completion of the meticulous construction task, the wings were bolted to the fuselage. Along with the wings were bolted two Pratt and Whitney 450 horsepower Wasp outboard engines, each attached to maple block sections that had been added to the wing. The third motor, a center engine of identical make and power, was located in the nose of the airplane.

Later in production, the fuselage was covered with linen that was stretched and coated with a specially colored dark red paint.

Designer Anthony Fokker commented on his preference for the wooden wing construction, saying that he preferred wood over metal because it was easier for the mechanic to repair. A wooden wing could be repaired more quickly than a metal wing.

With a full load of fuel, the $40,000 Fokker F-10A had a range of 600 miles. Able to carry 10 passengers and 2 crew members, the Fokker F-10A could cruise at 125 mph at 4,000 feet.

Serving the public principally as mail carriers throughout most of the 1920s, the Fokker F-10A was a workhorse of the American aviation industry. After General Motors (GM) acquired 40 percent of Fokker Aircraft Corporation of America, Fokker president Harris Hanshue and chief engineer Anthony Fokker hoped that GM's cash infusion into the company would provide Fokker a more competitive posture in the airline travel industry. Their hopes were partially realized after Fokker stock jumped significantly following General Motors' investment.

On the public relations front, Fokker gained even more ground with Commander Richard Byrd's much publicized use of the Fokker Trimotor in his trek over the North Pole in 1927. Paradoxically, Byrd's unheated *Josephine Ford* was financed by Henry Ford, Fokker's sole competitor for the Trimotor commercial sweepstake. Later, the Fokker image was further enhanced when Byrd went transatlantic in a Fokker named *America*. Adding even more positive press linked to the Fokker name, Amelia Earhart flew her Trimotor, *Friendship,* across the Atlantic, capturing the crown of being the first female to fly across the big pond. In the 1920s, Fokker owned the air over America.

↔

By the scheduled departure time of TWA Flight 599, temperatures along the planned itinerary were dropping. Along the route of Kansas City to Los Angeles via Wichita, Amarillo, Albuquerque, and Winslow, the temperatures ranged from the high of 32° Fahrenheit in Kansas City to a low of 6° Fahrenheit in Dodge City. In an ominous condition, given the disparity of the weather conditions immediately east and west of the destination, the sky was clear and sunny over Dodge City, just 169 miles west of the Wichita destination. The variation of temperatures along the route signaled an approaching strong eastward cold front.

In a post-mortem examination of the weather data, Anthony Fokker, in defense of his plane's design would protest that the Flight 599 should have been canceled. However, pilot Bob Fry, with well over two thousand hours of experience, didn't hesitate in lifting off into the front's heading.

Some accounts state that Fry, known as Joe Pete to his friends, was bullied by Rockne's forceful personality. It was rumored that as Fry recalculated the storm's strength, Rock approached Fry, telling him to get going. Rockne had paid for his ticket and expected to be on his way. Most likely, that account is just another Rockne legend. It was Fry's call whether to take off or delay the flight, and it's difficult to imagine that a Marine sergeant with combat experience could be bullied by anyone, even the great Rockne.

Once airborne from Kansas City, TWA Flight 599 co-pilot Jesse Mathias radioed the Wichita tower at 10:22 a.m. Requesting an updated weather condition, he reported the plane's location as thirty-five nautical miles from Cassoday, Kansas. In responding to the transmission, TWA Wichita station operator, G. A. O'Reilly reported to Mathias that the weather in Wichita remained clear. But for Flight 599, the eastbound onrushing weather front seemed anything but clear.

Following Flight 599's initial transmission to the Wichita tower, Mathias radioed O'Reilly with the news that the crew had decided to turn around and go back to Kansas City. O'Reilly remembered Mathias reporting the weather being too rough to navigate. At that moment, NC999E, call-sign *Fokker Niner-Niner Easy*, had been airborne for one hour and seven minutes.

Although severe thunderstorms weren't active in the flight path, the approaching cold front lowered the cloud ceiling and severely affected visibility. Drizzling rain, sleet, and snow—constant companions of the prairie's low skies—spread throughout the weather front.

The plane was plunging into a soup of foul weather when Mathias's garbled transmission to radio operator O'Reilly indicated that he was too busy to talk. Mathias and pilot Robert Fry were totally engulfed in navigating under the limited visibility conditions of the dropping sky.

If the air mass were a typical approaching Kansas cold front, the clouds would have dropped to within two hundred feet of the ground. Such a low ceiling would have forced Fry to take the Fokker F-10A Super Trimotor down near the prairie's fertile earth. The plane would have been skimming the surface in order to maintain visibility.

According to an eyewitness, mail-pilot Paul Johnson, Fry did take his plane under the cloud cover. Flying for National Air Transport, Johnson reported that he had flown alongside TWA Flight 599 for as long as three minutes before the two planes turned in an effort to find an aperture in the clouds. At one point, he observed the markings of NC999E flying at an altitude of no more than fifty feet.

Noticeably off-course to Wichita, Flight 599 entered the storm. Given the deteriorating weather, Fry's efforts to maintain visibility would have taken precedence over his navigation. A veteran pilot of remarkable skill and proven courage, Fry may have tried to navigate by scud-running.

Scud-running was a common navigational practice of the barnstorming era. With visibility conditions worsening, Fry and Mathias may have dropped their plane to a point below one hundred feet and flipped on their running lights. The rails of the nearby *Atchison, Topeka, and Santa Fe Railway* would have shone like beacons as Fry and Mathias turned their plane into an airborne train.

Air pilots such as Fry and Mathias were keenly aware that railroads served as perfect low-altitude navigational tools. Their gradients are minimized and compatible with any airliner's climbing ability. Both pilots would have known that they weren't flying over the flat Kansas prairie of the postcards. Fry was piloting TWA Flight 599 over the rolling Flint Hills, a geographical band of hills running through the heart of the state northward from Oklahoma. However, if Fry followed the tracks, his Fokker F-10A Super-Trimotor could easily clear the rise of any oncoming hill.

Twenty minutes after notifying Wichita, the Fokker F-10A turned and headed back to Kansas City. Soon after heading back, Fry decided to turn again and fly west in an attempt to make Wichita. The weather was intensifying, and he was caught in the belly of the beast. Turning westward seemed to be the better option. Cruising at a speed near 100 mph, Mathias again contacted radio operator O'Reilly in Wichita to inform him that the storm was increasing in intensity. The time of the radio call was approximately 10:50 a.m.

Knowledgeable of the danger of executing a low-altitude 180° turn toward Wichita, Fry would have pulled back slowly on the Fokker's altitude control. As the plane climbed back into the thick cloud cover, Fry and

Mathias became totally dependent on their instruments that were known to be crude and vulnerable to foul weather temperatures.

↔

The aeronautical engineering community in the 1930s generally held that the Fokker F-10A Super Trimotor had two major drawbacks. One was structural; the other was mechanical. Structurally, the F-10A wing utilized a series of interior glued wooden joints. Glued joints meant that moisture could severely deteriorate the joint's stability. In the case of the Fokker F-10A, as little as a 20 percent moisture saturation of the joint would cause catastrophic failure of the wing.

In 1986, retired TWA mechanic E. C. "Red" Long went public with his recollection of an inspection he had performed on NC999E, Rockne's plane. Long's alleged inspection was just days before the doomed TWA Flight 599 lifted off in Kansas City. Long recalled that the wing panels were loose. He had recommended that the plane be grounded until the wing panels were repaired, a process that would take days. According to Long, the supervisor overruled his decision and cleared NC999E for flight. If the wing panels were as former TWA mechanic Long described, TWA Flight 599 was destined for catastrophic wing failure. Prior to Flight 599's takeoff in Kansas City, moisture might have already undermined the wing's stability and dampened the Fokker's chance for a safe sojourn into the Kansas sky of sleet and snow.

With the wing's stability compromised, flutter—the condition under which a surface vibrates at its resonant frequency—would have snapped the wing from the Fokker. The tendency to experience flutter was a recognized flaw of the wooden Trimotor on which Rockne traveled. Airplane designers and pilots of the era knew that once flutter occurred, the pilot had only seconds to slow the plane before it would begin to tear apart due to the vibration.

In addition to the structural issues, the Fokker F10-A had small design flaws that could have caused big mechanical problems for TWA Flight 599. Both the plane's gyroscope and its newly redesigned ailerons, the hinged parts of the wing that allowed the pilot to turn the plane along its axis, were vulnerable to ice formation. A recent redesign of the plane had repositioned the ailerons along the wing, making them more vulnerable to icy conditions.

While the lack of ice formations and evidence of ice at the crash site indicated that the wings did not suffer a catastrophic failure from the weight of ice, the possibility of a mechanical failure of the device that powered the gyroscope remains an intriguing piece of the puzzle. If bad weather had fouled the gyroscope, the air speed indicator would have likely failed. As Fry pulled back on the control and banked the plane upward for a 180° turn, other instruments critical to the pilot's control of the plane could have failed. Pilot disorientation caused by the failing instruments could have caused Robert Fry and Jesse Mathias to lose control in the leveling of their ascent.

If the gyroscope malfunctioned, TWA Flight 599 would have continued to climb and then turned over in a downward spiral from several thousand feet. As the plane's nose rolled downward, Rockne's aircraft would have accelerated downward out of control with engines screaming.

While he was feeding his cattle on a Kansas ranch near Bazaar, approximately seventy-three miles northeast of Wichita, Robert Blackburn heard a plane revving its engine in the overcast sky. At the same time Blackburn heard the plane, Easter Heathman's teenaged ears perked.

Hearing the revving engine, he thought an impromptu car race was about to occur down the road.

Once the plane entered a steep dive with the three Fokker engines racing, the flutter phenomena would have begun to rip the plane apart. As a flutter countermeasure, Robert Fry would have yanked the throttle back. The engine would have likely backfired as a result of Fry's action.

Prior to the plane falling, an explosion in the sky was heard by some witnesses. Robert Blackburn recalled that it sounded like an engine backfiring.

Most of the witnesses' reports consisted primarily of those sounds heard before the crash, and it was on the basis of these reports that crash inspectors theorized the final moments of TWA Flight 599. Investigators speculated that in the fated plane's final moments, Fry shut down one of the three engines in a last ditch attempt to stop the vibration that was caused by the rapid descent, but Fry's shutdown caused greater vibration, affecting the wing that held the second of the three engines. The crew and passengers were doomed when the excessive vibration of the second engine ripped off the wing and sent the ten-seater commercial airliner cartwheeling to Earth.

This scenario fit the kind of compromised wing structure reported by former TWA mechanic Red Long. If the wing was compromised as Long claimed, the excess vibration would have initiated catastrophic failure of the wing's structure.

No one can be certain of the exact cause of the crash. Only the outcome is clear. An engine revved out of control, and the plane went into a steep dive that tore the wing from the plane. The crew and passengers had just enough time for a private thought.

Easter Heathman arrived at the site of the crash only minutes after its impact with the Kansas earth. Contrary to numerous legends, he repeatedly stated that he didn't see the plane go down.

On the day after an earthquake devastated Managua, Nicaragua, leaving three Americans dead, fifteen thousand homeless, and some two thousand dead or missing, two-inch headlines of the *Chicago Sun* declared, CITY HONORS ROCKNE TONIGHT. A ten-inch by eight-inch telephoto transmitted by International News Photos, Incorporated, anchored the front page. Depicting the graphic destruction of the wreckage, the photo projected an indiscernible image of broken plywood and twisted metal tubing. A narrative on the right hand corner of the paper stated that the train carrying Rockne's body would arrive at the Dearborn Street station at 7:45 p.m.

Strewn about the crash site were bags containing the latest Wilson-Western tennis racquets, golf equipment, and tennis balls. Many of the bodies were entangled in wreckage debris. With the pilots' remains buried under the Fokker's main engine, horses had to pull the engine away, so their bodies could be recovered.

Nine hundred yards away from the wreckage, one of the plane's wings lay. Investigators theorized that it was the wing that had separated from the plane in midair.

Rockne had perished with seven other seemingly nameless, faceless, humans. As with any national tragedy, the people wanted to know more while the news services scrambled for what was known of the personal lives of the legendary coach's fellow passengers and crew. Surely, there had to be more to them than names. There was.

Along with the legendary football coach, onboard NC-5999E were passengers H. J. Christen and John Happer of Chicago; Waldo D. Miller of

Hartford, Connecticut; C. A. Robrecht of Wheeling, West Virginia; and Spencer Goldthwaite of New York.

Other than the information indicating that he was a financially fit designer of department store fixtures, not much is known of H. J. Christen. Supposedly, he was on his way to California to reconcile with his estranged wife. His attorney, Murray Miller, revealed that prior to leaving on his trip, Mr. Christen had withdrawn $58,000 from his bank account. With the recovery of only $400 from Christen's clothing, speculation would swell regarding the thought of a small fortune lying out in a Kansas field waiting to be found. In a later press release, both Miller and Christen's secretary confidently reported that the successful businessman would not have personally carried that much cash. Christen's attorney and secretary were right. Within two weeks of the crash, the money was found in a safe deposit box of a Chicago bank.

When he boarded the ten-passenger plane in Kansas City, passenger John Happer would have squeezed down the cabin's short narrow aisle. Formerly a comptroller for the parent company of Wilson-Western Sporting Goods, Happer had recently worked in Buenos Aires and was familiar with Rockne. The golf and tennis equipment found at the crash site belonged to Happer; he was scheduled to collaborate with Rockne on the West Coast account. As usual, Rock had finagled a way to kill two birds with one stone, fulfilling duties in his role as advisor and spokesperson for Wilson-Western Sporting Goods while formalizing a six-figure offer from Universal Pictures for his collaboration on some football short films.

Rockne's partnership with Wilson resulted in several innovations. Most significant of these developments was the valve implant under the laces. Replacing the outward stem, the valve implant gave the ball a smooth surface. With the valve implant positioned under the ball's laces, the spiral pass was possible. An evolution was sparked in the game of football.

Following the crash, the fortunes of the Happers would experience a spiral of their own, a downward one. With John's death at the cusp of the Great Depression, the professional's wife and six children were left alone without an income. Financially, John Happer's family would never recover.

Due to their marketing strategy being tied so closely to Rockne, Wilson Sporting Goods would also suffer from the crash. With the flamboyant Rockne gone, Wilson turned to Nebraska head football coach Dana X. Bible as its chief consultant. And while Bible's association helped improve the design of Wilson helmets and shoulder pads, the company's football-related fortunes stalled out after Rockne's death. In extracting itself from the wreckage of *Fokker Niner-Niner Easy*, Wilson Sporting Goods would shift its focus from football-related products to developing and marketing products for the game of golf.

A third passenger, Waldo H. Miller, still had sound footing in the perilous financial world of the deepening Great Depression. Entering the workforce with Aetna after his graduation from Wesleyan College in the spring of 1924, the twenty-nine-year-old Aetna supervisor was the only child of itinerant Methodist minister Reverend Edward F. Miller and his wife of 1 Logan Street, Lawrence, Massachusetts. A single young professional scaling the Jazz Age corporate ladder, Waldo lived in a Hartford, Connecticut, apartment with fellow insurance professionals. Recently promoted to a supervisor of sales personnel and field operations, Waldo Miller took the *Twentieth Century Limited* to Chicago, then traveled a later train to Kansas City where he joined Rockne and his fellow passengers and crew. The dapper executive with the receding hairline and stylish, round horn-rimmed eyewear planned to spend two weeks working in Los Angeles. Following the completion of his primary obligations, Miller arranged for a working sightseeing tour of the upper West Coast. TWA Flight 599 was Miller's first plane flight.

Also taking his place in one of the five passenger seats was Charles Robrecht, president of his Wheeling, West Virginia, namesake company, C. A. Robrecht Produce. A widower for several years, Mr. Robrecht controlled a Depression-era estate worth six figures. He had been called to the Texas Panhandle to provide emotional support in a dual circumstance of family need. In Amarillo, he intended to look after the needs of his daughter, Teresa Robrecht who was suffering from a severe illness. At the same time, the produce distributor, father, and grandfather would also comfort another daughter, Mrs. George Hermann, in the circumstances of the death of her daughter, his granddaughter, three-year-old Marguerite Elizabeth Hermann.

Of Rockne's five fellow passengers, the most intriguing personal life was claimed by twenty-five-year-old Spencer Goldthwaite. With his father listed in Albert Marquis's 1916 edition in *Who's Who in New England,* Goldthwaite's family was as influential as anyone could be in turn-of-the-century New England, and after the baby's birth on December 8, 1905, the father named his son in proper New England fashion with the child's first name being that of his mother's family name, Spencer.

An advertising executive on a meteoric rise in the financial world, Spencer's net worth was still untouched by the darkening doom of the Great Depression. A little more than a month after the young professional's death, a probate court would estimate his dollar net worth in the hundreds of thousands. Reports of the crash indicated that the Connecticut native perished on a trip to see his father in Pasadena, California, where Spencer owned a home at 1105 Glen Oaks Boulevard. His will would leave $40,000 to a cousin and $20,000 to a friend in New York. Other significant persons in Spencer's public life shared significant amounts of cash in life insurance policy payouts.

Friends of Spencer were shocked to find that one of those significant persons was a closeted romance interest. Spencer maintained a Manhattan residence only blocks from Times Square and unknown to some of his influential East Coast family and friends, he had been involved with a woman. With his wavy hair and the pedigree of a proper New England family, the Williams College graduate probably could have gained the eye of any young woman. He chose Mary Johnson of Brooklyn.

Following the crash, Miss Johnson would offer proof that Goldthwaite had intended to marry her. In court testimony, she stated that the marriage was called off when doctors found that she had a serious heart condition. The medical recommendation was that she should never marry. Apparently, the heart condition left Mary unfit for later child-bearing.

According to Mary, Spencer Goldthwaite had recently decided to inform his father of his love for Mary and his intention for her to be included in his will. Thus, a few days before his flight, Spencer wrote a letter to his father in Pasadena, stating that if anything should happen to him, Mary Johnson should get one-half of the proceeds of the sale of his house and furniture. The letter was a key piece of evidence in the ruling against Spencer's father in his opposition to Miss Johnson's court petition. Some months after the crash, Miss Johnson's representatives produced a copy of the letter to the court. Two years following Spencer Goldthwaite's death, Los Angeles Probate Court Judge May Lahey ruled in favor of Miss Johnson in January 1933, giving her one-half of financial executive's estate on the basis of Spencer's alleged letter. The judge's curious ruling ensured that, as breadlines snaked through the Big Apple, sickly Mary Johnson of Brooklyn would never know hunger.

Because TWA had discontinued the use of flight attendants in the months prior to March 31, 1931, copilot Jess Mathias was the lone assistant to the pilot and passengers. Mathias, known as "Math" to his friends was a fearless type of flyer who had worked in the Pacific Coast region prior to his service with TWA. As the years passed, much of the controversy over Bob Fry's actions during the last moments would surround Math's last words to the Wichita radio operator. Sadly, Math's personal life and the crash's effect on his family would be relegated to the footnotes of the story.

Like Mathias, pilot Bob Fry was known as an aggressive but competent flyer. Employed with TWA Incorporated since July 1930, the veteran airman was popular with his colleagues. While anecdotal evidence implied most pilots of the era were apprehensive of flying the wooden Fokker F-10A Trimotor design, no such apprehension can be attached to Bob (Joe Pete) Fry. A man who stood with a swaggering aviator's lean, Fry often sported a double-breasted pilot's jacket with the fashionable wide lapels. Wearing his pilot's hat tilted to one side in the manner of the cocksure man of the day, the thirty-two-year-old Fry was a native of Canton, Ohio. A veteran pilot of the Great War, Joe Pete became internationally famous when his plane was forced down over China in 1928. Held captive by the Chinese rebels, Fry was eventually released and declared a national hero.

When she heard of the Fokker's crash over the radio at her home in Milwaukee, Bob's mother, Lena Fry, collapsed. His father, John Fry, rushed home from work.

Wild speculation of the causes of the crash would eventually wind down to a negligible determination that Fry became disoriented and thus put undue stress on the Fokker's design. Even though the wooden winged

Fokker F-10A had gained a reputation as something of an airborne death trap, difficult to maintain, and prone to structural failure, Robert Fry would take the fall for the Fokker's failings.

Like his more affluent passengers, Fry's personal life would take center stage following the crash. As Mary Fry, the pilot's wife of little more than a year, left Los Angeles to claim his body, the national news media found out that the couple acted as foster parents to a nephew, ten-year-old James Adams Jr. With the crash of Flight 599, young Adams had endured a macabre string of circumstances in just a year's time.

Adams's stepfather, Lieutenant Herbert J. Fahy, an endurance flyer, had died in a recent airplane crash. Just seven months later the boy's mother, Claire Fahy, also a pilot, had died from injuries suffered in a December plane crash in Tonopah, Nevada. Now his foster father, Uncle Robert Fry, had perished. In just over twelve months, the boy had lost three parents.

Adams's parents, Herbert and Claire Fahy, were the Gable and Lombard air couple of the barnstorming days. Dining with stars and celebrity makers such as Howard Hughes, the vibrant couple made front page news on a regular basis. Herbert Fahy's 1929 Los Angeles solo endurance flight of thirty-six hours, fifty-six minutes, and thirty-six seconds had secured an international posture for Lockheed, while Claire delighted the avant-garde air chic crowds with monthly air derbies and competitions. Claire often accompanied Herb. And he would follow suit, sometimes trailing Claire in her competitions and acting as her mechanic. As aviators who pushed the mechanical envelope of 1930s air designs, the couple faced death with every working breath.

A pioneering aviatrix, Bob Fry's sister-in-law, Claire Fahy, often faced harsh odds for survival. Proof of the difficulties faced by the early mistresses of the sky could be found in cases such as Marvel Crosson's death in August 1929. The darling of the aviation industry, when others such as Amelia Earhart could only chase her stardom, the flamboyant Crosson was killed during a cross country race from Santa Monica to Cleveland. Amidst a flight of other famous female aviators, Marvel's plane fell mysteriously from the sky. In the same derby in which Crosson's plane entered a fatal tailspin from over one thousand feet, the center section wires of Claire Fahy's plane snapped, forcing her down near Calexico, California. Herb Fahy, the protector and overseer of Claire's competitions, was present to evaluate the plane. When he found that acid had been used to weaken the section wires, Herb advised his wife to drop from the competition. Not coincidentally, during the same competition an act of vandalism also forced down German aviatrix Thea Rasche. She had received anonymous notes prior to the competition warning her to "beware of sabotage." On a single day, three of the top female aviators of the day had fallen victim to a plot to end their lives. No one ever determined the identity of the saboteur.

That same year on May 23, young James came dangerously close to losing both parents when Herb Fahy crashed a fresh-off-the-assembly-line Lockheed Sirius. Coming along for the ride, Claire accompanied Herb to the Durant estate in Roscommon, Michigan. Aviation enthusiast Cliff Durant had agreed to purchase the industry's cutting edge in technology and speed; however, as a condition of the sale, he wanted Fahy to demonstrate that it could take off and land at his private airfield. With Herb at the controls, the couple landed safely, and after a brief visit, they were ready to jump off to Detroit. Upon taxiing down the strip, the Sirius began to lift when a tree stump snagged its landing gear and sent the plane flipping tail over nose. Herb Fahy, the pilot who would go down as the first man to operate a camera in an airplane, never regained consciousness.

While Claire Fahy escaped with only minor scratches, the love of her life, her mentor, protector, and son's stepfather was gone.

Not one to push her luck and cognizant of her role as a mother, Claire scaled back her competitions, but later accepted an invitation to make an appearance to help publicize the December 22, 1930, opening of an air school in the fading boom town of Tonopah, Nevada. Attempting to take off for her return to Los Angeles, her Waco taper wing biplane inexplicably left the runway and gathered sagebrush in its undercarriage. Moments just prior to the biplane's liftoff, Claire Fahy was seen to be struggling with the controls when the biplane suddenly jerked approximately fifty feet into the air. At that point, the plane promptly stalled and fell like a rock. This time, it was Claire's injuries that were serious. In addition to deep lacerations, the renowned aviatrix suffered cervical spinal fractures and severe head trauma.

Lockheed ordered their fastest plane to fly Doctor Stanley Anderson of Los Angeles out to the desert to treat Claire. Upon his arrival in Tonopah, Doctor Anderson treated Claire's head injury and by the middle of the week even offered a cheerful diagnosis. But the famed flyer took an overnight turn for the worse and died on Friday, December 26, 1930.

Claire's sister, Mary Fry, agreed to foster parent young James. Together, Mary and her new husband, TWA pilot Bob Fry, would offer the boy a safe and loving home. Then for the third time, death made other plans for James Adams's upbringing.

←—→

In South Bend, no voices of 1931 were left untouched by the tragedy of *Fokker Niner-Niner Easy*. In fact, the day the coach died ripped the fabric of an entire country.

For the first time in its history, the solid foundation of Notre Dame football cracked. The Fighting Irish wouldn't see another perfect season until 1947, many years after Rockne and Chevigny.

Rockne had been heard more to proclaim the future of sports team travel to be in the air. He said that a good pilot and a good plane made flying as safe as any other method of travel.

On March 31, 1931, the greatest of all football coaches was indeed served by a good pilot. Unfortunately, what most people in America thought to be a very good plane was found to be complex in maintenance upkeep and vulnerable to catastrophic failure. Following the publicity over Rockne's crash, compartmentalized wing structures and wooden planes became as dinosaurs, practically extinct overnight. Fokker's competitor, Ford, moved quickly to abandon its own Trimotor configuration.

Worldwide, both the air-traveling and non-air-traveling public knew of the plane that killed Rockne, and TWA immediately set out to push forth their dream of a single-engine, all-metal, stretched model, passenger plane. With airplane maker Boeing committed to TWA's rival, United Air Lines, TWA mogul Jack Frye contacted Donald Douglas of Douglas Aircraft. Charles Lindbergh was requested to fine-tune the design efforts as the TWA team set out to build the blueprint to the airliner of the future, the DC-2.

The DC-2 would spawn the plane that put the American aviation industry on top of the world—the famous DC-3. When democracy came under attack in 1941, the DC-3 would serve as the workhorse of American aviation history and a principal weapon against Mussolini, Hitler, and Tojo. Thus, it is reasonable to suggest that the crash of NC599E and Rockne's untimely death jumpstarted modern air travel and ultimately led to America's upper hand in troop and material transport during World War II.

Though the role of the crash in the development of the Douglas airliner is a matter of historical record, many details of the personal costs related to Rockne's plane crash were lost to the pages of family Bibles and forgotten cemetery plots.

A large part of Johnny Chevigny died in that field with Rockne. The crash unhinged Jack's life and reshaped his destiny. Nothing would ever be the same. Jack's scrapbook would be filled with condolences sent via Western Union, evidence that the coach's devotee was eternally devastated. Film footage of Rockne's funeral shows a grieving Bonnie Rockne clinging to a young man for support throughout the ceremony and graveside service. News photos of the funeral scenes identify the consoling figure as one of Rockne's sons. In a way, they were right. During Rockne's funeral service, Jack Chevigny never left Bonnie Rockne's side. It was the spring of 1930 again, Jack was sitting at Rock's Mayo Clinic bedside. Number twelve, the surrogate son, was again doing what he did best. This time instead of one for the Gipper, it was one for the Rock.

In that Jack was known for his supreme fortitude and loyalty during his playing days, it is easy to see how the young assistant coach stepped forward at Rockne's funeral. But what was the cost to the one left behind? Did the loss of Chevigny's King Arthur mortally pierce the French knight's armor? If there ever was such documentation, it has been lost to time. Possibly Jack's grief was just too immense to have been recorded. What is clear is that the crash of TWA Flight 599 and the death of Rockne left Jack adrift in the world of coaching. He wasn't ready to sail alone.

After the Bazaar, Kansas, crash, the young James Henry Adams Jr. became something of a media darling. In one photo, photographers posed him full-faced to the camera. Dressed in a pilot's headgear with the goggles pulled over his head, James held in his left hand a large model monoplane.

The child appeared strangely focused and serious. The April 6, 1931, photo was wired nationwide, further personalizing and extending the sadness of those touched by the crash while at the same time offering a sense of dignity and hope for those readers affected by the Rockne tragedy. The American public was assured that this young heart would prevail and continue to dream of flying. If this boy could face that type of loss and still dream, the world, America, and Notre Dame could again dream.

Despite the need for loose ends to be tied and the country's collective need to put a resolute face forward, nothing said could offset the loss of March 31, 1931. The dreams were dead for Jack, the Happers, the Rocknes, the Frys, and Anthony Fokker. For practically everyone touched by the crash.

The encouraging resolution of media-darling James Adams Jr. to be a pilot one day was revisited in a later news article. It was only a blurb regarding his formal custody hearing. The article relates that while the boy once dreamed of being a pilot, he wasn't so sure now.

Jack Chevigny understood completely.

# CHAPTER TEN

# *Shaken by the Thunder*

In South Bend, Western Union's wire service was overrun by condolences from every place imaginable. One telegram arrived from a grade school class in the Texas, another from the King of Norway. Just forty-three years old when his life ended on the Kansas prairie, Rockne was a global luminary.

Along with assistant coach Hunk Anderson and other Notre Dame officials, Jack traveled south to meet Rockne's body.

A candid photo of the group was snapped at the Kansas City station. Waiting at the boarding platform with several Notre Dame concierges to Rockne's remains, the impeccably dressed Jack wore a camelhair overcoat, fedora, and leather gloves. His empty dark eyes stared at the camera. Standing beside Jack and the other important men from South Bend was Hunk Anderson. He appeared worn and haggard, the perpetually lit cigarette dangling from his fingers.

Both Hunk and Jack were still young men. Both faced an unclear future made murky by Rockne's loss.

Adding to the confusion, their immediate careers are collectively put in limbo when neither of Rockne's trusted assistants received a ringing endorsement from their alma mater. The announcement was made that

Notre Dame would have no head football coach in the following season. It was a bewildering move by the administration.

Following Rockne's funeral, Hunk and Jack were knighted with titles remarkable only in their ambiguity. Hunk Anderson and Jack Chevigny would lead the 1931 edition of the Fighting Irish in nebulous dual roles. Ordered to lead the nation's greatest football team collaboratively, Hunk was named the senior coach, while Jack was the junior coach. In a half-baked pronouncement that would go down as one of the most ridiculous and inept administrative decisions in collegiate sports history, Notre Dame President Charles O'Donnell had written a recipe for the destruction of a football dynasty.

From the beginning, neither Anderson nor Chevigny was happy about the arrangement. Compounding the incomprehensible hierarchy, Hunk fell ill soon after President O'Donnell announced the succession. With the senior coach incapacitated, Anderson's opportunity for establishing his leadership role was disrupted. In his absence, the squad's rudder would turn at the order of Jack Chevigny, the twenty-four-year-old novice junior coach. As a result, what little fruits he and Jack could have borne together soured into a distasteful and contentious relationship. For the 1931 Notre Dame football season, the miserable road paved by Rockne's death had just taken a turn for the worse.

Once he returned to campus, Hunk began to reassert his status as the alpha dog. From his own perspective, Jack felt he had performed masterly in Hunk's absence. Simultaneously resenting Hunk's absence and his return, Jack bristled at Hunk's assumed restoration, and the dysfunctional relationship between the two men soon evolved into a coldly silent but disruptive feud. As Rockne's coaching godson, Jack felt that he alone was privy to the intended roadmap of the future

Rockne had passed away, but the legacy of his ambiguous leadership lived on. In an impalpable leadership style similar to that of future president Franklin Delano Roosevelt, Rockne never shared a whole piece of the pie with any one assistant coach. As to their leadership style, both Rockne and FDR were masters of the gray art of ambiguity. Rockne's indefinable management style had established the competitive posturing between Hunk and Jack. In fact, numerous Rockne-ordained successors to the head coaching position at Notre Dame could be found on both coasts.

For Jack, the right of inheritance was personal. Jack lived in the Rockne family inner circle. On many occasions, Jack, the student whom Rockne inspired to drop out of medical studies so that he concentrate on football, the young man to whom Bonnie Rockne clung in the church and graveside photos of Rockne's funeral, would have been told that he was to be the face of the future for Notre Dame football. After all, Jack was a true Notre Dame man, a Notre Dame graduate completing a Letters of Law, while Hunk's legacy as a Notre Dame man was one of a shushed shame.

To establish himself as the greatest lineman Rockne had ever coached, Heartley "Hunk" Anderson would start every game in each of his four years of college eligibility. As a guard on Rockne's first football team in 1918, Hunk provided the interference for the immortal George Gipp, the Calumet, Michigan, hometown buddy of Anderson's. However, in Jack's perception, Anderson was a damaged legacy. Jack knew that during Hunk's senior year at Notre Dame, Anderson was snared in a scandal, an amateurism rule violation.

Though marquee college football players of the era often played professionally during the college season, the rules of amateurism nonetheless forbade such activity. After the Great War in the faltering postwar economy, the frequency of rule violations escalated as star college players found a way to generate income by taking an active part in the promotion of these professional contests while making sizable wagers on the games in which they played. Such was the environment of college football.

During his senior season at Notre Dame, Hunk and two other Notre Dame stars were accused as suiting up for the Green Bay Packers of the American Professional Football Association. But because the accusation occurred after Hunk's final season, no permanent harm was done to his eligibility. The only penalty was that Hunk Anderson, Ojay Larson, and Hec Garvey were barred from further participation in Notre Dame varsity sports. Additionally, the Notre Dame Faculty Board of Control of Athletes withdrew the varsity letters of the three athletes.

The punishment was little more than a slap on the wrist. Each of the three boys would land on their feet in making the Chicago Bears roster the following year: Anderson at guard, Larson at center, and Garvey at end.

For Jack, a man of law, the record of Hunk's rule violation was much more meaningful. While Hunk Anderson was a tenacious player and an on-the-field terror for opponents of the postwar era, to Jack he was best known for leaving the grace of Rockne to strike out on his own at Saint Louis University. Add to the equation, Hunk's black mark for losing his senior letter, Jack felt Anderson to be less of a Notre Dame man than he.

Jack's urbane persona contrasted sharply with the gruff and unkempt line coach. They were as two pieces of separate jigsaw puzzles forced to fit together, though neither the color nor the shape matched. Anderson was best known for his work ethic and no-nonsense approach to the game. Immensely loyal to his superiors, he was considered the ideal assistant coach, a perception later confirmed by the position of trust he earned under pro football's legendary head coach George Halas of the Chicago Bears. As a married man with children, Heartley "Hunk" Anderson was never a man of the society circuit. Hunk Anderson took great pride in being the working man's coach.

Jack was the perennial playboy, the eternal student, lawyer, and son of a physician. When Jack entered a room, conversations would stop and heads would turn. To Hunk, Jack Chevigny was just so much fluff and still had much to learn. Rock was the backfield's orchestra leader. In Hunk's opinion, Jack's role on the 1930 national championship was superficial; Chevigny hadn't earned his stripes the hard way as Hunk had.

Before the 1931 football season would end, the flower of Rockne's contradictable succession and ambiguous management style would bloom in a full and foul odor of dissension between the two men. As senior coach, Hunk Anderson's fate was doomed from the start. No coach—no man— could follow Saint Knute.

Impatient ambition is a classic ailment of many young coaches, and a symptomatic Jack resented Hunk's return in 1929. To Jack, the field had been furrowed for his professional growth and eventual harvest, not Hunk's. Now with Anderson's unexpected return to Notre Dame, the weeds of distrust and professional jealousy would foster a malignancy of ill-feelings toward Anderson. Meanwhile, the media's occasional features describing Hunk as the brain behind the Notre Dame football operation only increased Jack's disdain for Anderson.

Hunk and Jack would remain entangled in the power struggle long after Hunk's spring absence. Thus, the Notre Dame administration could not have established a more dysfunctional work environment if they had planned it. Struggling in the grip of a dark, inexplicably difficult grieving process over the loss of their beloved mentor, these two polar opposites were pitted in a struggle for affirmation. Hunk was close to Rockne, but Jack was a son of Rockne.

For Jack, the instant transformation of his life was almost unbearable. Evidence to this fact is provided by photographs. While photos of Jack typically convey a visible confidence and intensity, photos from the summer and fall of 1931 reveal Jack's discernible sadness and his uncharacteristic look of lost vitality. The Moorhead Coaching School brochure of August 1931 shows an acutely pained and disheveled Jack on the cover, looking more like Johnny after the circus fire than Jack after the 1928 "one for the Gipper" game. Rather than looking like the dashing featured speaker of a large regional coaching school, Jack with his downturned mouth and gray cotton sweat suit, uncharacteristically slouched. It was the only period in his life that Jack was ever photographed without his sharp self-assured persona notably present to the lens.

Despite the tragedy and tension within its football program, Notre Dame—unlike the rest of the country—was weathering the darkening storm of the Great Depression quite well. In 1931, enrollment had reached an all-time high, while the university managed to continue the full spectrum of student services. The football program was expected to continue much as it had under Rockne, except for the compensation offered through off-campus jobs to football players.

Adding to Hunk's troubles, it took less than two months for him to realize that some of the priests felt the time had come to even the score with Rockne's omnipotent ghost. Notre Dame Vice-President Father Michael Mulcaire, the administrator presiding over the athletic director, reinforced the senior coach's anxiety when he commented publically that the days of Rockne's impunity were over. For the smoldering priests who long felt diminished by Rockne's fame and celebrity status, it was their time. While Hunk suggested that he might resign in protest, he complained as to the cuts, tighter policy reins, and the new circumstances under which the football program would operate. Father O'Donnell flatly informed Hunk that he would remain as senior coach and that the matter was closed.

When the back-to-back national champions opened the 1931 season under the split leadership of Anderson and Chevigny, the chemistry that was Notre Dame football was as unbalanced as the unique combination of the dual coaches. Losing most of their stars to graduation didn't help the Irish. Despite the public trepidation as to Anderson's leadership ability, Notre Dame crushed Indiana 25-0 in the season opener at Bloomington. And against Northwestern in the second game, the Irish sloshed across a muddy field to a scoreless tie with the Wildcats. Yet, even though the Irish carried an unblemished record, few of the subway alumni were impressed with what was thought to be substandard Irish performances.

In both the Indiana game and the Northwestern game, Notre Dame's ticket sales were deplorable. The financial despair of the Great Depression combined with a deeper, more personal depression as Irish fans and followers came to the realization that Notre Dame football just wasn't Notre Dame football without Rockne. No Rockne equaled zero ticket sales.

The pessimists had reason to doubt. For the first time since 1903, Notre Dame had failed to defeat the Wildcats, a fact that would forecast dark clouds for the rest of the season. Even from Hunk's perspective, a tie with Northwestern was as good as a loss. Although Hunk and Jack's Irish shellacking of the Drake Bulldogs 63-0 allowed for a peek of sunshine before the storm front, still no fans came. Following the decisive win over Drake, the Irish continued their undefeated season dropping Pitt by a count of 25-12, but a chill crept through Athletic Director Jess Harper's office when he learned that the financial take was just one-third of the gate from the previous year's game with the Panthers.

The wolves were continuing to howl over the tie with Northwestern from two weeks prior when Hunk's methods drew criticism after he was accused of coaching dirty football against Carnegie Tech. Indeed, Hunk may have wanted to exact his proverbial pound of flesh for the blame he suffered in the 1926 ambush. Whatever the reason, Hunk's Irish racked up a large total yardage in penalties in the 19-0 victory over Carnegie Tech. So convincing was the physicality of the Notre Dame victory, football historians would long point to Notre Dame's beating of Carnegie Tech that Saturday on Halloween as the beginning of the Tartans' descent into college football anonymity. Anderson could hardly believe that despite his Irish dismantling the Tartans once and for all, he received not praise, but more criticism.

The following Saturday in a 49-0 win over Penn, the gate receipts dropped even further, totaling approximately one-sixth the draw of the previous season. And against Navy on November 14, the charges of rough play were again publicized throughout the large eastern papers. Anderson's name was becoming daily fodder for the finger-pointers and naysayers.

Ironically, at the time of such discontent over Anderson's leadership, his record as senior coach was a stellar 6-0-1. Yet, it seemed as if Anderson's success was the elephant in the room.

As many supporters were aware, Notre Dame was home to a suitable head coaching candidate whose religion did align with the university's identity. Jack was a devout Roman Catholic. And while Hunk did little more than complain to sources of Jack's inexperience and outright insubordination, the smooth, charismatic Jack Chevigny offered a stark contrast to the abrasive and plain-spoken Anderson.

Throughout the season, authoritative comments hinting of a clash between Anderson and Chevigny continued to be leaked out to the press.

Claiming Jack countermanded his orders during a game, it was a matter of record that Hunk blamed the younger junior coach for undermining his authority with the team. Given the drop in Notre Dame's talent from the 1930 season and the two coaches' feuding, it was amazing that the Irish continued to win.

Carrying an unblemished record through mid-November, the Irish worked to prove that the dynasty remained intact. But by November 21, 1931, the façade finally cracked.

Once-beaten USC, sporting its usual stellar team of the era, came to South Bend for the first time. In paying a debt of long overdue loyalty to Hunk's undefeated squad, Irish fans financed the moment with the new stadium's first sellout crowd. Headlines proclaimed the match was for the national championship. Forgotten in the hype was the fact that both teams had played a remarkably softer-than-usual schedule.

After spotting the Irish a 14-0 lead, the Trojans roared back to capture a 16-14 victory in front of 52,000 plus spectators. For Anderson, the loss wasn't without controversy.

An issue of a questionable coaching strategy on Hunk's part surfaced after the senior coach apologized to the press for sending in the reserves too soon. Once the starters had been removed from the game in the fourth quarter, the eligibility rules of 1931 prevented Notre Dame's starters from reentering the game. When USC regained the momentum against the Irish substitutes, the reserves were unable to stop the Trojan march to a come-from-behind win. For Anderson, the loss and self-admitted coaching error seemed to cement the perception that he was incapable of filling Rockne's shoes or serving as the leader of the nation's premier college football program. What was not publicized was the fact that Anderson subconsciously blamed the USC loss on Jack.

Later, he would blame the failures of the entire season on his junior coach. To Hunk, it was always the fault of the young Chevigny, the one who undermined his direction and field generalship. As the season progressed, their relationship further eroded into a silent stillness. Hunk intimated to friends and press sources that he never wanted Jack as an assistant; Chevigny was forced on him. Hunk stated that because he knew the backfield system quite well himself; he never needed Jack's help. An aged Hunk asserted that athletic director Jess Harper and Father Mulcaire had pressured him to accept Jack in the role of junior coach.

In the final game of the 1931 season against Army, New York Mayor Jimmy Walker, one of Notre Dame's most fanatical supporters, was at his second consecutive Irish football game. Joining him was a capacity New York crowd. The 12-0 loss was a disappointing but somehow expected finish for Hunk's Irish.

Although the Irish finished the season with a respectable 6-2-1 record, most of the Notre Dame supporters had disowned Hunk even before the season had ended. Often vocalized was the opinion that the Irish had seemed to play with little or none of the fighting spirit for which the program was known. Following the two season-ending losses, vocal boosters and critical sportswriters called for Hunk's head.

It wouldn't be that easy. Notre Dame had never been known to bend to outside pressure; in leaving no room for doubt as to Hunk's future, the Notre Dame administration rallied to support its native son. In a short time, the criticism died down as additional Hunk's supporters rallied in his behalf.

Upon the season's conclusion, Anderson used his contacts in the media in an attempt to force Father Mulhaire's hand with regard to releasing Jack. For the voiceless junior coach, the sudden flurry of articles highly sympathetic to Anderson's side of the story provided the personal motivation he needed to resign. Sure in his outlook that Hunk would remain as senior coach and owning the opinion that the administration would grant Hunk more autonomy in 1932, Jack Chevigny decided to leave the one place held dearest to him. The university's blind allegiance to the oafish Anderson had convinced Jack that this Notre Dame wasn't his Notre Dame anymore. Hunk had won the blame game.

Before he had returned to Notre Dame in 1929, Hunk blamed the Jesuit administration for his failure at Saint Louis University. In his inaugural season as the Irish mentor, he had found an easy mark in Jack, the twenty-four-year-old Rockne loyalist. Hunk never admitted that his subversive tongue-in-cheek remarks to the media regarding Chevigny's alleged disloyalty were in themselves disloyal. In an ironic twist, the disloyalty on Hunk's part was a counter-point of the coaches' feuding relationship that few sportswriters brought to light.

Initially, the two men had been appointed co-coaches, but by the Army game, the chain of command had transformed with Jack becoming an unwanted young assistant under Anderson. Notre Dame's aimless decision to split the leadership duties was supremely indecisive. Following the lackluster finish to the Irish season, numerous sportswriters condemned the decision while at the same time expressing some compassion for the administrative confusion. At the time, the university was operating in a state of shock, and the lack of course was understandable.

While Hunk's Notre Dame win-loss record would eventually total a respectable 16-9-2, the numbers were far from Rockne's dominating career percentage. Anderson's righteous embitterment regarding the senior-junior coaching schism of 1931 tainted the next two years of his tenure. In 1933, the bottom fell out of the Anderson regime as the Irish suffered the first losing season in Notre Dame's storied history.

Hunk never had a chance. After two consecutive national titles, Notre Dame football was in the throes of a rebuilding year similar to 1928. Because of the uncertainty of the fiscal outlook in America, every program in the country was suffering from administrative shortfalls in both dollars and vision. Characteristic of most university budget cuts of the time, Hunk's program was drastically slashed. In fact, if TWA Flight 599 had not crashed into a Kansas field in 1931, even the great Rock would have faced some unwelcome and intrusive administrative audits of his operating expenses and expenditures. With Hunk instead of the godlike Rockne at the helm, it became much easier for the good priests of the Congregation of the Holy Cross to rein in the football program.

Thus, in Hunk's evaluation of his situation, history should exonerate him. He faced an uneven playing field and fought unfair administrative policies set against his success. But Hunk didn't leave it at that, either in 1931 or ever. For years, Hunk Anderson continued to harbor resentment toward Jack. In that Hunk Anderson, like Jack Chevigny, wished for nothing more than to remain at Notre Dame for the rest of his days, his own memory of his tenure would be built around a lifelong sardonic assessment of Jack's abilities, one that included inaccuracies and apocryphal anecdotes.

For the rest of his life, Jack would ignore Anderson's deprecating assessments of his job as junior coach. Possibly it was Jack's depth of character that didn't allow him to validate Anderson's whining exculpations. A maturing Jack would eventually accept the way things had worked out under the senior coach's reign. He had wanted the job for himself, but Jack knew that appointing a twenty-four-year-old head coach to fill the chasm of Rockne's death would have taken the courage and vision that only a Father Sorin would have possessed.

Two years before his death, Hunk Anderson reminisced as to the true assessment of Jack Chevigny's forced appointment on Hunk's ability to lead the team. In Hunk's more aged eyes, there were bigger problems at Notre Dame. By 1931, the university's neglect of his needs in recruiting and funding had brought many of their chickens home to roost. Graduation had wiped his roster clean, and he had little chance to appease the spoiled boosters who yearned for the return of Irish supremacy experienced under Rockne. As such, Hunk Anderson came to terms with Jack Chevigny.

After a January visit to the University of Iowa, Jack's name was linked to a position with the Hawkeyes. Anderson's post-season wish was granted when Jack resigned on February 1, 1932. No reason for the resignation appeared in the papers, and President Charles O'Donnell offered no comment.

After a spring of evaluating his options, Jack Chevigny signed a contract on July 8, 1932, to succeed Ernie Nevers as head football coach of the Chicago Cardinals. For Jack Chevigny, attorney at law, an established but struggling National Football League (NFL) franchise would have to do for now. When the time was right, he would return home to Notre Dame.

# CHAPTER ELEVEN

# *Cardinal Blues*

The Chicago Cardinals offered Jack Chevigny his first fulltime legitimate head coaching position; however, in 1932, on football's center stage the NFL wasn't. Though Jack would have been pleased to have garnered the position, he would have confided to his family and friends that he felt he deserved better. Pro football was still in its formative stage. Having experienced a brief period of success during the 1920s, the Cardinals were best known for starting their inaugural season in secondhand faded red jerseys from the University of Chicago. College football was America's game of choice. When contrasted with the top tier of the college game, professional football was a sandlot operation. Jack would have doubted the decision that placed him in the south side of Chicago, coaching second level pros.

Though his career was traveling in a healthy new direction, away from Hunk, Jack remained afflicted with the passion to return to South Bend. Although he told his friends and family he would never lose his desire to be back at Notre Dame coaching Notre Dame men, Jack focused on establishing a quality reputation as a head coach. While waiting for Hunk's inevitable expiration date in South Bend, he would coach the Cardinals.

Chicago provided an open window to the next level in Jack's career and gave him the opportunity to counter Hunk's showering criticism regarding his term as junior coach.

With his character and integrity beset in the press for months, Jack got some satisfaction that Hunk Anderson would now have the chance to show his own ineptitude without anyone to blame. To Jack, the title of junior coach had become a pair of concrete shoes, an affirmation of Hunk's personal disdain for Jack and a daily reminder that he wasn't considered ready or worthy to carry his weight in the Notre Dame tradition. The Cardinal post offered him an opportunity to prove to Notre Dame that they made a terrible mistake by not appointing him Rockne's successor.

After purchasing the team for a little more than $12,000, on July 27, 1929, Doctor Jones was aware of the fact that, for over twenty years, the most notable achievement of the Cardinal franchise was in acting as a thorn in the paw for the Bears.

Doctor Jones, a huge Bears fan and prominent Chicago public healthcare physician under four mayors, was a personal friend of Bears' owner George Halas. One of the founding fathers of the NFL, Halas actually underwrote Jones's purchase of the Cardinals.

Assuredly, Doctor Jones had other friends in the public health field. One of those friends would have been Doctor Julius Chevigny, chief of nearby Hammond, Indiana's Department of Public Health. With his health declining due to congestive heart failure, Jack's number one fan was slowing down. Coaching the Cardinals put Jack in close proximity to his father.

Given the pay for professional coaches during the early days of the NFL and the growing depth of the Depression, Jack planned to practice law during the off-season. The added income notwithstanding, Jack's time spent practicing law would allow him to rub elbows with area power brokers and increase his team's name recognition within the professional circles of the community. As he had learned also from Rockne, it was possible to align the craft of coaching with the realization of financial stability. Chicago offered Jack the ideal environment for expanding his financial portfolio beyond coaching.

Prior to Jack's south side arrival, Hall of Famer Ernie Nevers served as player-coach of the Cardinals. In that dual role of coach and star player, Nevers led the Cardinals to one of the best three-year stints in franchise history, but retirement came unexpectedly for Nevers after a charity game in San Francisco where he was competing on the behalf of the Knights of Columbus. After suffering a serious wrist injury late in the fourth quarter, a worn Ernie Nevers in the locker room after the game announced that he was done. Telling his friends and the press that his resignation was due to the beating he had taken over the years, Ernie decided to return home to the West Coast for good.

Jack's first order of business as head coach was issuing a press release, which stated he would change the Cardinal's offensive style from the Stanford double-wing popularized by Pop Warner to Rockne's Notre Dame shift. Longtime Cardinal fans were thrilled when they heard of the change. Eddie Anderson had used the Notre Dame shift in bringing the Chicago club to within a breath of the championship in 1925.

To enhance his roster with a few familiar Irish names, Jack signed former Notre Dame players Tim Moynihan and Al Culver. Other than instituting a change in the offensive philosophy and signing a couple of Notre Dame graduates, Jack promised the fans that the Cardinals roster would return intact from the previous season.

As the new coach, his first order of business was to attend an NFL rules meeting in Atlantic City, New Jersey. Since he had spent much of his college life in the fast lane, the free-spending bachelor would have looked forward to the quickly arranged trip to the boardwalk.

A 1931 meeting between George Halas and Doctor Jones ended with a legal agreement that the Cardinals would claim the south side of town, while the Bears would remain the team of the north side. In the 1920s and 1930s, Chicago's tough, working class, south side supporters fanatically cheered their team, win or lose. But tough times had arrived for the professional league.

Even though an association of teams first took the field as part of the National Football League in 1923, the NFL was still struggling to maintain solvency a decade later. With the financial malignancy of the Great Depression eroding all levels of disposable income, smaller salaries and shorter rosters highlighted the league's balancing act. Austerity ruled the league as owners agreed that paychecks were to be cut 20 percent.

In their first outing, Coach Jack Chevigny's bright red uniformed Cardinals traveled to Michigan to face the Grand Rapids Maroons in an exhibition game. Accompanying Jack and his thirty professional ball players were team owner Doctor David Jones and trainer George Vichfield. Using the game to evaluate newer players such as Moynihan the Notre Damer, the head coach's close friend and former teammate, Jack saw his Cardinals blank the Grand Rapids group by a count of 13-0. Doctor Jones was impressed with the expert timing of the new offense and Jack's overall generalship.

The following week under the lights, the Cardinals wrapped up their preseason schedule with a 33-0 blanking of the Aurora, Illinois, Yellow Jackets. Describing Moynihan's performance, the *Chicago Press* noted that the tough smart Notre Dame man had lost nothing in his two-year hiatus from competition. After the Aurora contest, Doctor Jones informed the press of his assessment of the Cardinals.

> "They're in excellent shape. I venture to say not half of those men out there smoke cigarettes and practically none drink. Not only that but they conduct themselves in an orderly, dignified manner, reporting on time every morning for practice and get plenty of sleep."

After two preseason victories provided a needed boost of confidence for Jack's Cardinals, the south side gang squared off against the league champion Green Bay Packers in their first league game on Sunday, September 18. It should have been a boisterous debut, but the Cardinals came out flat in the drizzling rain. A paltry three thousand four hundred soaked fans endured the unappealing Chicago weather only to see numerous turnovers quickly dampen their club's chances of upsetting Curly Lambeau's championship squad. Doctor Jones would leave the game disappointed; as most of those in attendance expected, the Packers were dominant from the start.

Possessing interior linemen who outweighed and outplayed the Cardinal front, Green Bay took advantage of the mismatch at the line of scrimmage by blocking two first-quarter punts. Unable to muster much of a run threat, the Cardinals went to the air. As they stood with water puddling in their trouser cuffs, diehard Cardinals rose from their seats as Jack's offense moved down the field with a series of passes. But it was too little and too late; the Cardinals fumbled away their last chance to score.

For the day, the Cardinals attempted fourteen passes, completing six of them for seventy-five yards. Unfortunately for Jack's squad, four of the fourteen passes resulted in interceptions.

Though Jack's ace recruit Tim Moynihan played most of the game at center, it was John "Blood" McNally, an obscure league adventurer known for his tough play and colorful nickname, who shone in the Packers' 15-7 win. The quintessential pre-modern era vagabond, McNally played for five football teams in a sporadic career from 1925 through 1938.

Traveling back to nearby Michigan for the next contest, the Cardinals needed to regroup if they were to prevail against their third non-league opponent, the Battle Creek Maroons. Snapping back to form before a crowd of two thousand spectators, Jack's club demonstrated a new vitality and versatility as three different players scored a touchdown when the offense rolled to 14-1 edge in first downs. With the 19-0 victory, the Cardinals' overall record improved to 3-1.

At this point in the 1932 season, Cardinals owner Doctor David Jones, a man known to love a bargain, stumbled across a Picasso at a rummage sale. In acquiring the rights to a former Oregon freshman phenom, Jones obtained the talent of one of the best black players available, Joe Lillard.

Despite having played only his freshman year at Oregon in 1931, Lillard's well-publicized athletic abilities offered Doctor Jones a substantial payoff for only a minimum investment. Though rumblings from both owners and the white press warned of an oncoming racial storm in pro football, Jones was willing to gamble that the consternation of the white Chicago sports columnists would be offset by Lillard's ability to fill the seats and win games.

The Cardinals were known for passing over proven name stars and signing no-name players from lesser known colleges. Signing Lillard was just an extension of that fiscally frugal policy. However, in that he was unproven star of color and a suspected locker room mustang that did not yield lightly to authority's bit, Joe Lillard was a poster boy for the continued criticism of the Cardinals' front office personnel decisions.

Doctor David Jones countered the disparaging criticisms saying,

"The lowdown is that we are showing up the All-Americans of the big schools, a lot of whom get that way through the efforts of high-powered publicity departments. Look at Lillard, our colored boy. He is one of the best backs in the entire league, yet his entire college experience consists of a freshman year at Oregon. He wanted a job and we gave him one..."

Jack may have appreciated that Doctor Jones thought outside of the traditional white owner's box. After all, Jones had hired a twenty-five-year-old coach with no head coaching experience.

In the NFL of 1932, the signing and utilization of a black player's talent was not without precedent. Unlike major league baseball, pro football had included select African American participation since its inception. Most notable of those early black pioneers was Fritz Pollard. Prior to the Great War, Pollard was an All-American halfback at Brown and the first African American to play in the Rose Bowl. Entering the league in 1919, the Chicago native later became the first African American head coach, directing Jack Chevigny's hometown Hammond Pros in 1921.

By 1931, despite the achievements of Pollard and other black ballplayers, a conspiracy had begun to lurk in the league's closets, a conspiracy to eliminate African American players from the NFL. The country was enduring the deepening global economic depression and with their predominately white fan base suffering from a double-digit unemployment rate, NFL owners foresaw an impending public relations problem. If their teams allowed African Americans to stay in the game and keep their jobs, the league's white attendance would suffer. In the year prior to Franklin Roosevelt's election, the number of NFL teams declined by three in 1931; rosters correspondingly shrunk as well. Many teams were hemorrhaging cash, and financial managers and owners looked to stop the bleeding. To the white NFL owners, it made prudent business sense to phase out all colored players. For several of the more racist owners, the nation's deepening economic downturn justified shuttering the league against African American players.

By reporting late to the team because of a professional baseball commitment, Lillard would have sported a large target on his new Cardinal jersey. As a NFL rookie in 1932, Joe Lillard was exceptional in every way. Several years after starring at quarterback for Mason City (Iowa) High School in the 1920s, he enrolled at the University of Oregon as a four-sport prospective superstar in 1931. Controversy surfaced midway through his sophomore season in Eugene when he was embroiled in a controversy over playing semi-professional baseball under an assumed name. During the week of the USC game, the Pacific Intercollegiate Conference commissioner suspended Joe's eligibility. Declared ineligible on October 16, 1931, Joe decided he would turn professional in baseball, football, and basketball. As much a star on the hardwood and diamond as he was on the gridiron, Joe Lillard was a lightning rod for controversy.

Despite the rumors, Jack may have appreciated the unfairness of Lillard's criticisms. The few sour notes directed at Joe Lillard sounded a harmony similar to the criticisms levied on Jack during his tenure as Notre Dame's junior coach. Nevertheless, Jack had grown tired of taking the field in full gear and practicing with the squad. With a lack of depth in the Cardinal backfield, Coach Chevigny would have gratefully accepted the tardy rookie's signing.

Dubbed *The Midnight Express*, Lillard was a train with its own baggage car. It wasn't long before Jack realized his new running back was no team player. Indeed, when it came to temperament, Joe Lillard was no Fritz Pollard or Joe Louis. If the twenty-seven-year-old Lillard was anything, he was the Muhammad Ali of the pre-modern NFL. Joe Johnny Lillard Jr. didn't buy into the restrained turn-the-other cheek mentality. He was a young black man who strained against the oppressive yoke of racism, and, as would be expected, he was a black athlete who found himself the target of his own white teammates' antipathy.

Attempting to secure his team's unity, Jack's Rockne-styled rhetoric had negligible effect. Lillard's white Cardinal teammates were intent on demonstrating their antagonism toward his skin color.

While, to the African American press corps and community, the responsibility to play humbly and keep his eyes low fell upon Lillard, those bigoted Cardinals who deliberately missed blocks when Joe's number was called took a toll on the temperamental star. Fearful that Joe was carrying the future of the black athlete in professional football on his back, African American sportswriters worried that Lillard's proclivity for petulance would tip the scales of racial injustice.

Al Monroe of the *Chicago Defender* wrote of Lillard,

> "Football players like anyone else, will always be jealous, but a fellow can always clean up such a situation by living, walking, and breathing in a manner that does not bespeak supremacy—a thing Lillard hasn't learned."

Monroe, in his regular editorial *What Say*, continued with his own thoughts on the matter,

> "Truly it would be too bad to see Lillard dropped from football...The Cardinals want him. The coach told me that. But they would much prefer to have him under different circumstances, which is the only way prejudice in his own line-up can be beaten down. Joe and his race are on the spot now. Will he pull both through? What say?"

Imploring Lillard to hang onto "play upon the vanity of the race that outnumbers him 21-1 in every game he plays or suffer the consequences," and hold onto the "lone link in a place we are holding on by a very weak string," Al Monroe knew that Lillard's demise in Chicago would color the league with an even whiter hue of racism.

Against the backdrop of the NFL's finalization of its plan for ultimate racial exclusion, Joe Lillard reported for his first game against the Portsmouth Spartans.

In addition to acknowledging Joe's talent and making him a starter in the backfield, Jack recognized that Lillard was a prodigious drop kicker and punter. With Lillard's leg behind the Cardinals, Portsmouth was unable to capitalize on the field position. Striking first, the Cardinals looked to capitalize on their advantage when Portsmouth's Mule Wilson dropped back to punt from near the Portsmouth goal line. After Wilson's punt was blocked by a mass of Chicago defenders, Tim Moynihan fell on the loose ball for the opening touchdown. On the next play, Joe Lillard kicked the successful point-after.

Later in the second half, the Spartans managed to convert a sputtering drive into a payoff of six points. Dismayed, Jack watched from the sideline as Portsmouth's Glenn Presnell added the important point-after to deadlock the contest at 7-7. At the sound of the final gun, the tie entered the record book. With the stalemate, the Cardinal's league record reflected a winless five-way tie for fourth place.

Attendance records were gloomy all across the league. For the season thus far, less than eight thousand fans had paid to see the Cardinals in action. With the Bears in town for another Chicago-style tango, Doctor Jones's expectations were for a better gate at the next game.

In the manner of Rockne, Jack believed the big game required a tougher practice regimen. Putting this theory into practice in early October as he prepared the Cardinals for their cross-town rivals, the Bears, Jack practiced his team under a Chicago downpour at Mills Stadium on October 4. For the Cardinals, the week resembled an August week of two-a-days. Jack's plan called for three Cardinal running backs carrying the load— Bucky Moore, Walt Holmer, and Tony Holm. The highly-touted Joe Lillard remained in his backup and kick specialist role. Jack felt that Holm, an Alabama sensation who had played briefly for Portsmouth would bring more pro experience to the table.

Sunday, the Cardinals met the Bears in a classic Chicago brawl of south side versus north side. Former Purdue captain and center Ookie Miller served as the fulcrum of a Bear line. Meanwhile for the Cardinal clad lineup, Tim Moynihan made his first start at the center. In stating that neither team enjoyed a size advantage, Chicago sports analysts wrote that the opposing teams each weighed exactly 3,212 pounds. What wasn't recorded was the fact that the Bear backfield was far superior to the Chevigny lineup. For that reason, Jack decided to shake up his roster.

End Chuck Braidwood, having started the season with the Bears, would see more action than usual, while Jap Douds and Elmer Schwartz would be expected to contribute more than their usual minutes.

With the game played on an inundated Wrigley Field, the Bears and Cardinals wrestled to a scoreless tie. For the duration of the game, threatening storm clouds hung over a field of indistinguishable jerseys attached to flailing arms and fists. Dampened on this occasion by the rain and mud, fisticuffs and melees were common in the meetings of these bitter antagonists from the Windy City. Though the mud allowed the Cardinal defense to cage two of Halas's more aggressive Bears, Bronko Nagurski and

Herb Joesting, it was the Cardinals' second consecutive tie of the season. The dual Chicago workhorses of Nagurski and Joesting should have carried the day, but the mud and slop had helped to keep the tandem from executing a consistent drive. And while the Bears' cleats stuck in the Wrigley gumbo, Joe Lillard's agility and open-field running turned the Chicago mud into Kentucky bluegrass. Showcasing his ability to spin away from tacklers, Lillard broke open on several elusive punt returns. To most observers present, Joe was a thoroughbred among the mules and a savior to the Cardinals' cause. When the Cardinals' chance to stay even with the Bears appeared to be lost, Lillard's kicking leg delivered a fifty-yard punt from the back of his end zone.

After several weeks without a victory, the Cardinals planned to board the winning train when the team traveled to Boston for its first meeting with the Braves. On October 16, they would take the field in front of fifteen thousand paying customers, the hometown Braves' largest crowd of the season.

From the opening whistle, Joe Lillard took control of the game as he led the Cardinals on a seventy-yard scoring drive. Later in the game, Chicago added two points. On the first anniversary of the Pacific Intercollegiate Commission's decision to strip him of his college eligibility, Lillard averaged twenty-five yards on punt returns in a game mired by arguments and player flare-ups. Made possible by the Cardinals' 11-4 advantage in first downs, the 19-0 shutout gave Jack confidence that his lackluster offense was turning the corner. Unleashing Joe Lillard had given the Cardinals a new gear offensively. A crowd favorite in Boston, Lillard was nearly untouchable in a broken field of pursuing defenders.

No secret was made as to the gravity of Lillard's every move as the *Defender's* columns continued to express optimism that Lillard's exploits might possibly save the Negro professional football player from the label of *persona non grata* the National Football League was covertly planning to tag on its African American players.

Up next for Joe Lillard and the Cardinals was a trip to Providence, Rhode Island. Having dropped out of the NFL due to the deepening depression, the Providence club remained barely alive as a local professional charter.

A fluke interception of a lateral by Cardinals' left end Milan Creighton (an eventual Cardinals' head coach in 1935) accounted for the game's only touchdown. Joe Lillard's peerless toe nailed the point-after to make the score, 7-0.

Not that the Steam Rollers didn't put up a fight. Providence managed to penetrate the Cardinal twenty yard line an astounding eight times. More astonishing was the fact that the Rollers ran out of steam on each of those eight penetrations. The downside for the Cardinals was that as a non-league game, the win counted for not much more than a shot of confidence.

In the pre-modern NFL, players would often go home from the game hungry. In addition to the low pay, football in the 1930s was a dangerous game played by men who wore little more than a piece of cardboard over the shoulders. Testimony to the dangers of the game came in a *Chicago Tribune* blurb regarding the outcome of a Midwestern semi-pro game. In describing the action, the *Tribune* reported that a hometown player suffered a broken neck playing against another small-time organization, the Coldwater Tigers. Theodore Tremple would no longer dream of the day he would play for the Bears in Chicago's Wrigley Stadium. With a mother and several brothers left at home, he was dead at age twenty-six.

Returning to Chicago, Jack prepared his train-weary squad for another difficult league match, this time against the Brooklyn Dodgers. The

Dodgers carried on their roster a marquee name known since his college days, quarterback Benny Friedman. A crowd favorite, Benny Friedman always brought his A-game to Chicago.

What should have been a routine intersectional meeting turned into a contentious contest when, earlier in the season, Friedman acting as player-coach fired Lou Gordon. Since he had developed into one of the league's best tackles, Gordon landed with Jack's Cardinals. Chicago papers hinted that it would be important for Friedman to keep his head on a swivel if he were to avoid a retaliatory Gordon blindside. One of the other interesting features regarding the game was the match-up between Joe Lillard and Jack Grossman of the Dodgers. With Lillard living up to Doctor Jones's expectations and electrifying the league, the press promoted the clash as a David versus Goliath match between Lillard and Grossman. Grossman, the big name star during his college days at Rutgers and the current league leader in scoring, was Goliath; Lillard, the inexperienced midseason transfer from Oregon, was David. And in a grudge match meeting that had a flavor of familiarity, Cardinal center Tim Moynihan faced former rival Saul Mielziner of Carnegie Tech. Spotting Mielziner forty pounds, Moynihan would have his hands full.

As illustrated by the *Chicago Tribune's* pre-game write-up of the Dodger game, Joe Lillard's talents were characteristically rated with a racial slant.

Noting Lillard's deceptive running style, the *Tribune* stated, "Chicago fans who saw Lillard in action against the Bears on a muddy field haven't any idea of just how fast and tricky he is. At Boston and Providence, he was practically unstoppable...."

In what was described as a tug-of-war between the two squads, the Cardinals and Dodgers battled to a 7-7 tie through three quarters. Aided by a fifteen-yard penalty against the Dodgers for coaching from the sidelines, the Cardinals gained the lead on a fourth quarter drive covering seventy yards. With the final period winding down and Chevigny's Notre Dame shift consistently outflanking the Dodgers, the Cardinals pushed the final tally to 27-7.

The aerial circus master Friedman had failed to make an appearance in the game. Muting Lou Gordon's revenge, Friedman had left for New York prior to the game due to an illness suffered by his father-in-law.

For most of the contest, the highly productive Joe Lillard was left unexpectedly out in the cold, sitting on the sideline for the entire game, except for a brief fraction of the first quarter. With no explanation forthcoming, Cardinal fans wondered about the reason for the star's absence.

It was no secret that the Cardinals' largest home crowd of the year had shown up mainly to see Friedman's passing prowess. Calls flooded the commissioner's office calling for the league to punish Friedman and the Dodgers for his late leave of absence. Doctor Jones filed a formal protest on behalf of the fans, but the protest was denied. Due to the fact that no league rule against such an emergency leave existed, league president Joe Carr ruled that Friedman could not be punished. And in a jab directed at the Cardinals' front office policy of signing nameless players, Carr stated that if anyone in Chicago was disappointed in not seeing an NFL star perform that day, they should blame Doctor Jones.

In acknowledgement of the fans' dissatisfaction with Friedman's nonattendance, Doctor Jones offered a complimentary Packer game ticket to anyone who presented a stub from the Brooklyn game. Going into the rubber match against defending league champion Green Bay, Jack's squad had high expectations. In the first game, the Cardinals had outplayed the

Packers only to lose the game on mental errors. If Jack's squad could hit on all cylinders, they could hand the Green Bay team their first loss of the year.

With no mention of Lillard, the press focused on Jack's commitment to expand and refine his team's passing attack. A Chicago win would be the "shot heard 'round the world," and the Cardinals would move into second place. In Jack's usual manner of preparation for a big game, daily practices went as long as four hours.

In expressing his optimism, Jack remarked, "Given just half the breaks, we should hand the champs their first defeat of the year. We out-gained them from scrimmage in that first meeting and had an advantage in all other departments, except the scoring of points. With our improved passing attack and the speed of Lillard, anything can happen."

Since his high school days, Lillard had been a bit injury prone, but the good dope was that the Midnight Express was healthy and ready to play. During the earlier meeting with the Packers, the Cardinals had moved the ball without Lillard. Certainly, the Red and White would have an even better chance with the "shifty" and "tricky" Lillard in the backfield.

For the Cardinals, the "even better chance" turned sour, when according to the *Chicago Tribune*, "Chicago's Cardinals could not stop Johnny Blood yesterday afternoon at Wrigley field."

A gate of 8,323 spectators, the largest Cardinal crowd of the year, watched the Packers' Johnny "Blood" McNally strike twice with touchdown receptions, while Jack's offense sputtered. The Cardinals' lone touchdown came in the second quarter when Jess Tinsely blocked a Packer punt. Taking the ball on the short hop more in the manner of a St. Louis baseball Cardinal than a Chicago football Cardinal, Tim Moynihan rumbled for Chicago's first score of the day. Trailing just 13-7 in the third quarter, the

Cardinals flubbed their last chance to take the lead with an Irwin Hill fumble and a Green Bay recovery.

Joe Lillard, his name and performance perpetually tagged in white newspapers with the specification of "Negro Joe Lillard," remained hampered by the ankle injury. Still, he excelled at the passing game. Al Monroe of the *Defender* was pleased to report that Lillard led the third quarter drive to near the Packer goal line before the Irwin Hill fumble occurred.

Despite the game remaining close and Jack's Cardinals trailing by only four points, the Cardinals folded their tent after the Packers orchestrated a compelling seventy-five-yard touchdown drive. Again, it was Johnny Blood who administered the *coup de grace*. Catching his third long pass of the afternoon, Blood set up the Packers with a first-and-goal. From that spot, the Pack smashed the ball over the goal line for the win, 19-9.

Their hopes dashed for a final spot near the top rung of the league's ladder, the Cardinals would have to quickly board an eastbound train for a return match with the Brooklyn Dodgers. This time, future NFL Hall of Fame member Benny Friedman would play.

Friedman's Dodgers were eager to break a five-game losing streak. Before a home crowd of seventeen thousand at Ebbets Field, Friedman's play coupled with Jack Grossman's quick kicking to consistently force the Cardinals back near their own goal line. Unable to flip the field position, the Cardinals moved the ball toward midfield, but stalled out each time they approached the fifty yard line. The Brooklyn victory came after a Dodger drive pushed the ball to the Cardinal seven yard line. From there, the multi-talented Friedman split the uprights with his winning dropkick. The Dodgers ended their losing streak with a 3-0 shutout.

←→

That same weekend in an unrelated non-league game, the Sing Sing prisoners football team defeated a Bronx Parkway team consisting of several policemen and local college graduates, 46-0. The news article noted that "for some reason the prison team usually played its best games against teams consisting of law enforcement officers." Inmate Alabama Pitts scored two touchdowns for the prisoners.

During his five-year sentence for a 1929 armed robbery, Edwin Collins "Alabama" Pitts, a tremendous athletic talent, had gained favor with Warden Lewis E. Lawes. Because of his extraordinary abilities in football, baseball, and track, Pitts became a well-known name in New York City, starring on Warden Lawes's rehabilitating sporting teams. Though relishing the status offered him through the great experiment of Warden Lawes and the New York media, Alabama Pitts never accomplished much on the professional baseball diamond or football field. In 1935, Pitts was offered a contract with the Philadelphia Eagles for whom he would play just three games. Though reaching the precipice of a life-changing experience through the opportunity of sport, Alabama Pitts couldn't escape his demons. He would be stabbed to death in a notorious North Carolina roadhouse in 1941 and remain forever a testimonial footnote to the frailty of the redemptive power of sport.

↔

Lacking the services of injured center Frank McNally, tackle Lou Gordon, and fullback Irvin Hill, Jack's Cardinals continued their blitz of the East in search of a victory. The week following the Dodger loss, the team traveled to Staten Island where the New York tour ended badly.

The Cardinals' Walt Holmer, punting in place of Joe Lillard, had an awful day. Holmer's errors provided Stapleton with the edge they needed. Stapleton was a team known for rough play, and the game stopped numerous times because of unruly spectators repeatedly rushing the field. Holmer eventually did complete a late thirty-seven-yard touchdown pass to Chuck Kassell, but for the Cardinals it was too late. Stapleton thrashed the visiting Cards, 21-7. Chicago halfback and triple threat Joe Lillard failed to make an appearance, and with the loss, the Cardinals dropped to 6-4-2 overall.

Upon returning to Chicago, the Cardinals prepared for an 11:00 Thanksgiving Day kickoff against the Bears at Wrigley Field. The Thursday game marked the thirteenth Thanksgiving Day meeting of the two Chicago clubs. Although the Cardinals' hopes for a league championship had vanished, the Bears remained in the hunt for the crown. In order to upset the Bears, Coach Jack Chevigny's team, healthy for the first time in weeks, needed to elevate their offensive production.

In doing his part to provide some spice to the bland production of the Notre Dame shift, Doctor Jones purchased the contracts of two players: fullback Homer Ledbetter from the Providence Spartans and quarterback Barney Finn from the Staten Island Stapleton. Prior to the game, it was announced that Cardinal running back Joe Lillard was not expected to play.

Approximately six thousand five hundred fans made the Cardinal-Bears Thanksgiving clash of 1932 part of their holiday plans. After enjoying their turkey, Bears fans relished Bronco Nagurski's smashing-line plunges. The former Gopher star battered the Cardinals' morale as plays disintegrated into a carnival of fistfights and ejections. Meanwhile, Jack's Cardinals continued to fly on one wing; fumbles, interceptions, and blocked kicks led to three Bear touchdowns. Little could be said of the Cardinals' sad effort. The Bears devoured the miserable Cardinals, 34-0. With Nagurski at full strength, Coach Ralph Jones's T-formation offense was in an elite league.

Carrying a league record of 2-5-2, the Cardinals uninspired return to Wrigley the following week marked the last league game, as well as the final home game. It would be their second game in three days. Planning to boost attendance with the dual celebration of Dollar Day and Ladies Day, Doctor Jones hoped to at least cover his costs. With no time to prepare, the Cardinals ran through light drills on Friday and Saturday.

Against the Braves, the Cardinals' lone spark was a rare sixty-three-yard touchdown pass from Holmer to Martin. Although Jack's squad dominated the first half, they couldn't push the ball over the goal line, and the halftime score stood at 6-0. In the second half, a penalty forced the Cardinals to punt from their end zone. When the punt was subsequently blocked, it ricocheted outside the back line for a safety and two points for the Braves. Holding on to the slim 6-2 lead, the Cardinals kicked off to start the second half. After a sluggish third quarter, Boston's Gipp Battles opened the fourth quarter by running over three Cardinals on his way to the game-winning touchdown. The Cardinals closed their regular season in an 8-6 loss to the newly chartered Boston Braves.

For a game with less than one thousand five hundred paid in attendance for Ladies Day, the only big winner at the gate was the government. A call from the tax man informed the Cardinal front office that they would have to pay a 10 percent tax on over four thousand unpaid spectators. As a result, Doctor Jones could not cover the guarantee to the visiting Boston club.

Traveling to St. Louis for their final outing, the Cardinals closed their season against a non-league opponent, the St. Louis Battery A Gunners. Against the Gunners, Coach Chevigny's red-clad troops jumped off to a quick twelve-point lead after Homer Ledbetter slashed off-tackle. Afterward, the visiting Chicagoans tacked on a third first-half score when the hometown Gunners fumbled in their own end zone. St. Louis eventually responded and the Gunners' Swede Johnson rumbled across the end line, but Chicago prevailed, 20-7.

Three days after the St. Louis game, on December 7, 1932, the *Chicago Defender* reported that Joe Lillard had been suspended from the Cardinal football team. According to the nation's premier African American daily, the suspension was ordered by the Cardinal front office, after Lillard objected to "certain restrictions ordered by the management."

The *Defender* noted that Coach Jack Chevigny had no experience dealing with athletes of color.

> "The suspension of Lillard by the Cardinals is traceable directly to the disfavor he ran into with his coach, Jack Chevigny, former ace at Notre Dame. They don't use Race boys up at Notre Dame, you know, and Chevigny may or may not have been prejudiced against the flashy back. The star is expected to be back in professional football next season."

What Jack felt about Lillard or his skin color isn't documented. Indeed, Jack would have had a problem with Joe Lillard. He was admittedly mercurial. Even in the perception of the *Defender's* staff, Joe's background was spotty, his character in question. Being the consummate team player when he played for Rockne, Jack would have disdained Lillard's individualistic priorities. The two men, just one year apart in chronological age, were decades apart in perspective.

As a player, Jack was known for his physical and mental toughness. During his playing career, sports writers wrote effusively of Jack Chevigny's tenacity and larger-than-life performances. Jack played with concussions and broken bones. He was the ultimate Notre Damer. Contrarily, Joe Lillard's own supporters, including African American star player Ray Kemp, saw Lillard as pouty and angry. On the field, his sulking made him an inviting target of white opponents.

In the *Defender*, it was suggested that Notre Dame's segregationist stance of the 1920s forged a racist value system into Jack Chevigny's structural character, a mores that led him to prejudiced decisions regarding Joe Lillard's role. But the Notre Dame argument ignores the fact that Ray Kemp's playing days were spent as an All-American at Duquesne under another Notre Dame legend, Elmer Layden.

More likely, the rift between Jack Chevigny and Joe Lillard developed because of Lillard's slow recovery from the inopportune ankle injury. It could only be imagined how frustrated Jack felt when his one and only triple threat weapon repeatedly fell victim to what Jack would have perceived as a minor injury. Even though modern sports medicine recognizes an ankle sprain as a serious injury capable of ending a single season, Jack would have had little sympathy for Lillard's slow rehabilitation, especially if the Oregon phenom verbalized his personal grievances or intention to hit the basketball court with Abe Saperstein's Harlem Globetrotters in early December.

The tension line between the coach and player snapped after Lillard missed a Friday night team meeting prior to the Brooklyn Dodgers game on October 30. Because no information of the suspension was put forth in the daily sporting news until after the season, most fans were uninformed of the reason for Lillard's absence.

With only a dozen African American players having participated in the NFL since the league's inception and only two remaining in the league by 1932, Joe Lillard's prospects of remaining with the Cardinals were dim, regardless of his attitude and injury status. Without question, Lillard was a target of his opponents. By November, it was common knowledge that Lillard was a target of his own teammates as well.

The *Defender* publicly warned Joe in an article titled, WATCH YOUR STEP, JOE. With the subheading stating, "Rumors Continue to Fly That Cardinals Are 'Opening Switch' on Lillard," the editorial pointedly rebutted the inaccurate rumors that Joe kept himself sidelined by choice and that the star refused to block for his teammates when he wasn't carrying the ball.

The editor concluded his take on the Lillard rumors.

> "There is such a thing as 'opening the switch,' you know, and when your own team does that you become the target of five and six tacklers on every play. And five or six pro gridders hit you pretty hard, you know."

In 1932, the Cardinals finished a mediocre 7-6-2 overall and a disappointing 2-6-2 in league play. With the writing on the wall, Jack Chevigny cast his coaching hook back into the waters of college football. He quickly got a bite in the form of St. Edward's College in Austin, Texas. His resignation from the Cardinals was effective immediately.

Fifteen days after a new head coach hailing from Joe Lillard's Oregon arrived in Chicago, Doctor Jones welcomed Lillard back with open arms saying, "Joe is a great player and well liked by fans around the circuit. We'd love to have him back under different circumstances than those labored under last season."

The Jones's quote mixed with the *Defender's* "…They don't use Race boys up at Notre Dame, you know… " comment to cement a historical slant that Jack Chevigny wore a black hat in the Lillard affair. Lost in the interpretation of Lillard's separation from the Cardinals was the fact that Jones had supported Chevigny in releasing Lillard after the 1932 season. The "different circumstances" specified by the Cardinals' owner applied uniquely to Joe Lillard and his own behavior. Jones's hiring of Oregon's Paul Schillesler made things easier for the former Oregon freshman to reconcile his return to the Cardinals in 1933.

A symbolic photo was taken in October of 1933. Centered in the lens, Joe Lillard's long-bodied, powerfully athletic torso is frozen in action. Streaking down the sideline on a fifty-three-yard punt return, number nineteen is pursued by Chicago Bear legend Red Grange and another helmet-less Bear. Grange's bareheaded teammate is struggling to gain an angle on Lillard. The aging Galloping Ghost follows just a stride behind the Midnight Express. Lillard's face is relaxed; his stride is long and fluid. Grange and his teammate grimace, their upper bodies tense and bent in a strained effort to match Lillard's speed. As the shutter snaps, the aging Grange realizes the chase is futile.

Joe Lillard scores easily on a run described in the caption as "one of the prettiest ever seen in professional football."

Published exclusively in the *Chicago Defender*, the image of the brash African American star embarrassing Grange, the Babe Ruth of professional football, hinted at pro football's future if the National Football League stayed the course of integration. The photo also served as evidence as to why the NFL would soon take action to align the league with Jim Crow policies.

By 1932, George Preston Marshall had purchased part ownership in the Boston Braves. In 1933, in his first act as primary shareholder, the master showman changed the team's name to the Redskins. Even though the Cardinals' Joe Lillard was a proven draw and a favorite of the Boston fan base, Marshall immediately convened his fellow NFL owners in a star chamber to outline the future of a league without African American players. When the assertive Marshall convinced his fellow owners to go along with his business plan, Joe Lillard, Ray Kemp, and every other African American were voted out of the league. Banned from the game.

Black athletes weren't allowed back on NFL gridirons until after World War II. Even then, the spots were restricted and the league's commitment superficial. George Marshall had a long and powerful reach. Finally in the 1960s, long after his team had changed its name to the Redskins and moved to Washington, Marshall's openly racist stance against signing black players was targeted by President Kennedy and his administration. As the *Chicago Defender* put it, the Redskins were forced to integrate or else.

Time would reveal that the banning of African American athletes from the league in 1933 was a manifestation of the owners' racism, not simply the sound business decision of a few white owners hoping to just make a profit.

The *Defender's* photo of Joe Lillard, the "high-spirited Negro" leaving behind in his tracks Red Grange, the immortal white apotheosis of professional football, served as a window to the future of professional football. In 1933, it was a window that a racist NFL wanted to board shut.

Three decades later, in 1963, Chicago's Red Grange and owner George Marshall were inducted as charter members of the National Football League's Hall of Fame, while Joe Lillard's name would become a footnote to what never was.

Tackled by bigotry, Joe Lillard was stopped far short of the last chalkline. In 1978, the former superstar known as the Midnight Express was found in New York City's Penn Station, unable to speak—the victim of a stroke. Taken to Manhattan's Bellevue Hospital, he died a short time later, forgotten and alone.

For Jack Chevigny in 1933, the train couldn't leave Chicago fast enough. He would take his ball to Texas and build on the experience.

A wise coach once said, "It isn't the success that makes you smarter, it's the failure."

# CHAPTER TWELVE

# *A Box is Shipped to Texas*

In mid-January 1933, St. Edward's president Father Hugh O'Donnell, the brother of Notre Dame's Father Charles O'Donnell, appointed Jack to be head football coach of his parochial Austin satellite school. To the Chevigny doubters in the media and coaching circles, the appointment was something of a surprise.

Stained by the Lillard controversy, Jack's brief head coaching career had accomplished only a single patchy season record with the Cardinals. Even Jack's supporters felt that the "one for the Gipper" legend would have experienced a problem landing a head coaching job worthy of his pedigree. In addition to leading the Cardinals to another futile season, Jack's coaching reputation had been marred by Hunk Anderson's allegations of disloyalty. Now that Jack had landed the St. Edward's position, it was as if the umbrella of Rockne's ghost had shielded the youthful and debonair Notre Dame man from the drizzling criticisms.

In the 1930s, Texas was still considered a nook in a network of college football's back roads. Meanwhile, Austin was considered an idyllic oasis far from the woes of thousands of thirsty, dust-bound farms found across the state. Cold water springs from the Edward's aquifer wafted up to the surface offering a self-renewing stream for Saturday afternoon bathers in an era of breezeways and evening-porch gatherings. Austin was a locale in which people could live and work in relative comfort year round. It was no accident that Austin with its temperate Central Texas climate, pleasing hill country terrain, and refreshing underground springs was selected to be the hub of the state government.

Before the turn of the twentieth century, O'Henry's *City of the Violet Crown* and former home of the Tonkawa Indians had stoked the vision of an ambitious Catholic priest. Father Edward Sorin CSC, the same Father Sorin who founded Notre Dame, decided in 1877 to locate St. Edward's University on a hilltop overlooking the Colorado River and the Austin city limits to the north. From its origin, Austin's only Catholic university maintained close ties with the Holy Cross Congregation's flagship school. In struggling like many universities during the Great Depression, St. Edward's relied heavily on Notre Dame's generosity and support. With Jack traveling south to Austin, Notre Dame had arranged for a favorite son to stimulate the struggling St. Edward's football program's fortunes.

St. Edward's had fielded a football team since its earliest days. Rockne held coaching schools on the St. Edward's campus. A tradition existed there, just not a rich one.

After replacing Michigan native Al Sarafiny on February 1, 1933, Jack reported that he was looking for players who fit the Rockne mold, a mold that Jack had once outlined in 1931 saying,

> "There are four classifications of men who come out for football: the inferiority complex; the know-it-all or superiority

complex; the whiner; and the persevering man. Rock catered to this latter type."

Upon evaluating the talent pool, Jack concluded that the Saints of St. Edward's offered few of the latter type. After Coach Sarafiny left to wear number twenty-four of the Green Bay Packers, several lettermen and squadmen failed to return for the 1933 season. Jack, in his new role as head coach, faced a tough schedule with only twenty-seven players projected to audition for the squad.

As Hunk Anderson had learned in his first year at Notre Dame, America's Great Depression affected all levels of the college sporting community. Across the country, college enrollment declined. Superfluous extracurricular activities suffered from lowered funding and declining spectator interest. Though the economic climate trimmed the squad's size, those players who returned as St. Edward's Saints would be prepared. Spring football with the new coach and his system would whip the boys into shape. Assisted in the spring by John Sherman, formerly a student manager at Notre Dame, Jack was able to install his version of the Notre Dame box formation with an emphasis on the quick flanking backfield shift and its patented perimeter attack. Among the bluebonnets of the Texas spring, Coach Chevigny—with Rockne's ghost as overseer—refined the movements of the famed Notre Dame shift.

During the first year of Jack's tenure as a college football head coach, the NCAA rules committee mandated a major change in the flow of the game action. In wanting to enhance the fluid nature of the game and its popularity, the association enacted numerous football rule changes during the summer of 1933. One rule change in particular, the sideline rule, would drastically change how the game was played.

In what football historians mark as a large leap forward toward the structure and motion of the modern game, the NCAA rules committee changed the rule that required a ball carrier to carry the ball out of bounds in order for the ball to be spotted in the center of the field for the next scrimmage play. Prior to the rule change, when a ball carrier was tackled near the sideline, the official was allowed to place the ball at the exact spot where the ball carrier was tackled, regardless of how near the sideline was in proximity to that spot. Only when the ball carrier went out of bounds would the ball be moved to the center of the field.

"Printing all the news that's fit to print since 1871," the *Austin Statesman* headlined in bold the St. Edward's mentor's take on the new sidelines rule. In the column solicited by the *Austin Statesman*, the lawyer coach explained the rule change in refined legal language, clarifying how it would change the game in the upcoming season.

First, Jack attempted to convey the sentiments of the rules committee chairman Walter Okeson by restating the committee's position that the rule would hasten the pace of the game and improve fan satisfaction. Succinctly closing his highly technical commentary with the prediction that the new rule would allow for a newer, more open style of the game, Jack piqued the reader's enthusiasm for the fall.

He explained that under the new rule, a ball carrier could cut back from the sideline toward the open field without fear of a disadvantageous spot, should he be tackled. Coaching strategies that called for the ball carrier to purposely go out of bounds in order to get the ball spotted near midfield were eliminated. The massive rugby scrums that normally took place close to the sideline would no longer be a part of the game. Following any tackle outside of that ten-yard demarcation, the new rule called for the ball to be repositioned ten yards from the sideline.

Moving the hash toward the field's center increased the scoring potential of the offense, giving the fan more excitement for his dollar. Allowing the ball to be positioned farther away from the sideline for the following scrimmage down opened a gateway to the modern game.

Below Jack's column in the *Statesman* was a small article stating the Texas Longhorns were conducting secret practices at Clark Field in order to prepare for Saturday's home contest at Memorial Stadium against the Texas College of the Mines. At the same time, the St. Edward's Tigers worked hard versus simulations of Baylor University's "strong air game and quick kicks" while sharpening their own offensive scheme.

As reported by the *St. Edward's Echo*, the scribe and voice of the St. Ed's hilltop, Jack's favorite play was a wide lateral from the opposite shift. Diagramming the play for the *Echo*, Jack explained that, after starting in a T-formation, the backfield shifted to the right. This shift aligned the running backs in the traditional Notre Dame box set. Quarterback Bill Cheatham took the snap and executed a half-spin on a fake to the sweeping fullback George Karam. The play called for Karam to dash left. Cheatham would follow Karam and the rest of the backfield in a full student body sweep to the left. Once outside, Karam—whose path was designed to arc slightly deeper than the ball carrier Cheatham—received a pitch from Cheatham and sprinted to the defensive perimeter. With the two backs from the front edge of the box right formation leading the play, the power sweep provided more than adequate interference for the pitchman, Karam. In addition to the two backs leading from the right side of the box, both guards also pulled to the left, providing Karam a total of four blockers.

When the student journalist asked why the play was the coach's preferred choice in a critical situation, the new coach explained that the delayed lateral offered a quick flanking threat to the defense while maximizing the available interference of four blockers pulling in front of the ball carrier. Coach Chevigny remarked, "It is a powerful open field play."

Around the coffeehouses of Austin, Jack's work on the hilltop didn't go unnoticed. After a solid spring of tough drills and team building, summer whisperings of a new attitude and confidence at St. Ed's meandered throughout the smoke-filled board rooms of those Austin oil men and ranch barons who so loved their own Forty Acres, the University of Texas (UT).

St. Ed's wasn't the only team in town looking for a fresh start. Led by their much beloved Orangeblood and seventh-year football head coach, Clyde Littlefield, the University of Texas also strained to see the new horizon.

Littlefield, the first alumnus to become head football coach at Texas, was also the first Longhorn superstar athlete. Earning four letters in each of three sports from 1912-1916, Clyde possessed athletic skills from a future era. In the pre-World War I years, when basketball games were played on a dirt court, Littlefield dominated, averaging nineteen points per game. In those days, such an output was unbelievable. It would surprise no one when Littlefield's scoring average stood as a Longhorn record for the next forty-four years. In track and field, Littlefield's hurdle times ranked with the world's best. As to his skill in football, if a Heisman Trophy had existed in Clyde Littlefield's era, he would have won it.

Named head track coach in 1920 after a stint as a highly successful Texas prep coach, Clyde Littlefield replaced E. J. "Doc" Stewart as head football coach in 1927.

Despite a 24-9-3 record and the fact that Stewart never experienced a losing season, the Ohio native was forced out in an acrimonious atmosphere. Although some rumors of womanizing and female-related indiscretions were whispered about town, the official complaint was that

Stewart, a jack of all trades and owner of many talents, allegedly misappropriated his time.

In 1933, the Texas (UT) athletic dynasty was in the later stage of its formative era. It had begun with Athletic Director Theo Bellmont, a visionary who had come to Texas in 1913 after serving as the YMCA director in Houston. Recruited to the post by millionaire University of Texas graduate Lutcher Stark, Bellmont was a pioneer in strength training and a founding father of modern athletic professional standards. In a time when it was considered unsportsmanlike and sissified to work at gaining an advantage in off-season strength and conditioning, Bellmont held the unconventional attitude that players and coaches alike should abide by a lifestyle of commitment to their skill development, no matter how inconveniently pervasive the training lifestyle.

Supporting Bellmont was the irascibly fervent Stark, a nightmare booster for any coach. In 1910, Lutcher Stark came to Texas, driving a 1908 Hupmobile roadster. In that university regulations forbade students to use cars on campus, Lutcher's family had the rule changed so that he could keep his vehicle. The fact that the pudgy, ostentatious Orange, Texas, native had few friends didn't dissuade him from using his father's millions to ingratiate himself into the Forty Acre's landscape. Like many rich kids, the cloistered Stark didn't have the opportunity to pursue sports in his childhood.

The chance to actively participate in athletics as a football manager infused Stark with an exhilaration unmatched on campus and the Orange millionaire's son often used his own money to arrange first class travel and lodging for the Longhorn teams. Of his many contributions, probably most historically significant was his gift of orange and white blankets to the football team. Emblazoned with the Longhorn logo centered between the words *Texas Longhorns,* this application popularized the heretofore occasional use of Longhorns as the team nickname.

After graduation, Lutcher Stark's weekly trips to Austin helped him maintain a close friendship with Theo Bellmont. The two engaged in regular barbell and weight workouts.

Stark fell in love with strength training after working with Alan Calvert, owner of the Milo Barbell Company. Following his Philadelphia mentor's conditioning regimen, Stark returned to Texas forty pounds lighter and twice as strong. The experience would make Lutcher a zealous believer and practitioner of strength training for the rest of his life.

Unfortunately for Doc Stewart, Stark remained overenthusiastically involved in Longhorn football, as well. Nothing less could be expected of the man who offered 10 percent in matching funds to be added to the coffer of donations acquired to build Memorial Stadium, a site, which, during Texas home games, would become a living monument to those students and staff lost in World War I and all other wars. Lutcher Stark's generosity guaranteed that Texas would join in the celebration of college football by building a stadium worthy of recognition in conversations of the great stadia of antiquity. Its construction was another testament to the 1920s as The Golden Age of Sports. Stark's munificence contributed to the construction of other grand landmarks on the UT campus, as well. And while Stark's one hand gave the gifts of a true Orangeblood, the other hand wielded a hammer that could deliver a malevolent blow to the head of anyone who failed to yield to his point of view.

As Doc Stewart's players gathered in support of their embattled leader, Stark and Bellmont managed to push the Athletic Council to replace the multi-talented coach. In spite of a 24-9-3 record, which included three victories in four outings against D. X. Bible's accomplished Aggies of Texas

A&M, the well-traveled Renaissance man was forced out to El Paso where he coached the Miners for two years. After leaving college football to devote his time to his summer camps near Kerrville, E. J. Stewart was tragically killed in a deer hunting accident.

Camp Stewart, his nationally acclaimed camp for boys established in 1924, continues to exist as a tribute to E. J. Stewart's admirable ability to mesh his entrepreneurial acumen with his sense of service to youth.

After shipping Stewart off to El Paso, the Longhorn administration wasted no time in naming campus legend Clyde Littlefield to the post. Just as he delivered during his days as a UT athlete, Littlefield delivered as a coach on the football field. His inaugural season saw the Longhorns finish second in the SWC with a 6-2-1 record. Then, in his second season, the Horns captured the SWC title with 7-2 record. In his third year Littlefield's good fortunes continued with an 8-1-1 record. After suffering a mediocre 6-4-1 slate in 1931, Littlefield rebounded in 1932, finishing 8-2 and second in the SWC.

Considered a campus mover and shaker, Littlefield evolved the athletic climate at Texas into a contemporary model. From helping to design the basketball uniforms during his days as a player to officially adopting the burnt orange color of the Longhorns during his tenure as football coach, Littlefield was a factor in the genesis of Longhorn athletics. Most famously known for his role as Longhorn head track coach, Littlefield developed the famed *Texas Relays*, a nationally acclaimed meet in which Knute Rockne was a 1929 meet official.

In the spring of 1933, despite having delivered two SWC football titles in five years, Littlefield's struggling offense had led to a state of impatience on the part of the Longhorn faithful. By September, discontent generated by millionaire regent Lutcher Stark rumbled over the Steers' program.

The growing legion of swooning Jack Chevigny followers and the glowing press accounts from the St. Ed's hilltop probably did little to help Littlefield's situation. From the beginning, the local press was smitten with Chevigny.

A.S. 'Hop' Hopkins of the *Austin American* was one of the first to fall under Jack's spell.

> "Chevigny snaps out orders like an army general…There is no doubt Chevigny is a coaching wizard who may some day be back at Notre Dame in a high capacity…Personally, Chevigny is a prince. He has a magnetic personality, which makes friends on all sides. And he is a great leader. His players swear by him. Late in the season a group of powerful Texas supporters were invited out to see a practice at St. Edward's. They left quite impressed with the 28-year old coach."

With his strong personality and reputation as a charismatic speaker, Jack Chevigny was seen as a man of decisive action, a man who wasn't afraid to think outside the box. In accord with the public perception of him as a man of action, the new head coach on the hill didn't hesitate in moving quickly to inspire the hearts and minds of the St. Edward's players. St. Edward's lack of a successful football tradition presented a blank slate for the Rockne blueprint, and Jack retooled St. Edward's from the basement up. Even the vestige of the school's athletic history, the Saints nickname, was reworked. In authentication of St. Edward's long-term objective to forge a winning athletic program, the small Catholic school with its new Chevigny-decreed *Tiger* nickname opened the 1933 season with a train ride north to face a member of the respected Southwest Conference—Baylor.

This was the season that the Baylor Bears were expected to harden into a football team capable of challenging for the SWC title. In a year that presented one of their best opportunities to dominate the likes of conference foes, Texas Christian University, Texas A&M, Texas, and Arkansas, the Waco fans, and sportswriters expected their Baylor Bears to show substantial improvement over their previous season's 3-5-1 record.

Offensively, Baylor used its own patronage to Rockne-ball, and in alignment with the customary strategy of the single platoon era, the Bears started the St. Ed's game with its shock troops, the reserve linemen and backs. Just after the opening kick, the Tigers' Bill Garrett shocked the home crowd with a series of slashing runs that pushed the Baylor Bears backward into the shadow of their own goal posts. Then Jack's boys completed their march to pay dirt when George Karam punched the ball over the white-chalked goal line. Jolted by Karam's score and the Tigers' quick start, the green and gold Baptist shock troopers were replaced by the starters, and Baylor was able to retaliate with its own touchdown just before the end of the half. The game was headed to a halftime deadlock with St. Edward's obtaining a moral victory, but Jack's boys relaxed before time expired. Baylor quickly took advantage of the letdown and struck again for its second score of the first half.

Starting the shock troops at the second half in a repeat of the opening strategy, Baylor Coach Morely Jennings returned to his regulars in the fourth quarter. This time, Coach Jennings's method worked as the much deeper Bears squad wore down the overachieving Tigers and cruised to the 20-6 win.

Every loss was a bitter pill to swallow, but the Baylor game proved to Jack that his St. Ed's men held promise. Karam appeared to be a major talent, and the rest of the boys had played hard. Any coach would have been pleased at the spirit of the fight he saw in Waco. By the final gun of the St. Ed's-Baylor contest, a buzz of admiration for the St. Edward's boys filled the press box. From both on and off the hilltop, fans and writers lavishly praised the former Saints. The word began to circulate that Chevigny was up to his billing as a chip off the old Rockne block. The game's spectators were stunned by the ferocity of St. Ed's defense. The newly-renamed Tigers would be a team to be watched in the Texas Conference standings.

Less than six miles north of the hilltop, Clyde Littlefield's Longhorns played well in their home opener, dispatching the overmatched Miners of Texas College by a score of 22-6; yet, Littlefield's compelling win appeared strangely insignificant when compared to the St. Edward's loss.

All was working according to Jack's plan. By week two of the season, he was coaching the most confident 0-1 team in the nation. Following the Tigers' strong effort at Baylor, Jack and his assistant, former Notre Dame guard Bill Pierce, readied their boys in blue and gold for the most critical game of their season, a night game against favored Simmons University. Slated for a home stand, St. Edward's enjoyed a home field advantage for the October 6 meeting; nevertheless, Jack was the metaphorical long tail cat in a room full of rocking chairs. Following his evaluations of the Baylor game, Coach Chevigny apprehensively shuffled and reshuffled his lineup in preparation for the big game.

At the game, St. Ed's officials reported the largest turnout of fans in several years. Austin area columnists wired praise of Jack across the state, reporting that credit for the crowd should go to the charismatic Chevigny and experience his personal impact upon people.

The "square fighting chin, broad, beaming smile, a pair of light brown eyes that see all, massive shoulders from which hang powerful arms ending in a pair of hands that give you a warm, meaningful handshake…He is all that and more…not to mention, the snappy brand of football…," wrote the *Austin Statesman*.

Using an old Rockne strategy of passing in the face of a superior opponent, Jack's boys struck twice on perfectly executed play-action passes. Simmons earned only one first down in the game, while St. Edward's tallied nine of their own in overwhelming the Cowboys. Dubbed the Four Rockets in homage to the legendary Four Horsemen of Notre Dame, Coach Chevigny's backfield chewed up 242 yards of offense. Equally spectacular was the veteran defense. The St. Ed's defenders, led by Shaw, Guynes, and Al Duderstadt limited the Simmons Cowboys to a scant sixty yards of total offense. For the Tigers, it was a total domination on both sides of the ball. Bill Cheatham's passes combined with the runs of former junior college star Leo "Pope" Dillon to give St. Edward's its first win of the season. The resulting 13-0 shutout of Simmons University stunned the sporting press and positioned the Tigers atop the Texas Conference standings in just the first week of conference play.

In their third outing, the Tigers traveled thirty miles north to meet the Southwestern Pirates of Georgetown, Texas. It was Friday, October 13, but the St. Ed's men had no illusion of superstition as they sought to avenge two recent one-point losses in the series. Garnering a second consecutive shutout, Chevigny and his boys made short work of the former Southwest Conference member Buccaneers, 18-0.

Following the Georgetown win, the Tigers traveled to Brownwood, Texas, where they met the Daniel Baker Hill Billies on October 19. While in Brownwood, Jack and his Tigers surfed a wave of unmatched perfection as St. Edward's five touchdowns overwhelmed the hapless Hill Billies. An intercepted pass, two blocked punts, an off-tackle slant, and a pass provided St. Edward's all the scores they needed as the Tigers pummeled Daniel Baker College.

As the *San Antonio Light* reported,

"St. Edward's University's championship bound football machine had completely outclassed Daniel Baker Thursday night winning 31-0. The Tigers flashed a great exhibition of fancy ball-carrying, fierce blocking, and tackling serving due notice on other Texas conference title contenders…"

To solidify their conference lead the following week, the Tigers needed to pounce on the boys from Austin College with a decisive home win. Pounce they did, scoring three quick touchdowns in the first quarter; as time elapsed in the Friday night game, the St. Ed's men turned out the lights of Austin's House Stadium with a final score of 18-0.

With the Tigers undefeated in conference play, Jack and his assistant Bill Pierce were the toast of Austin. St. Edward's had reeled off four consecutive victories, outscoring its conference opponents, 82-0.

Ted Paulison, an elementary-age student in the St. Edward's prep school at the time, remembered Chevigny's effect on the area's Catholic community.

Paulison recalled, "At the dinner table, my dad used to talk about Jack Chevigny and what he meant to everyone affiliated with St. Edward's. He never missed a game. My dad used to take me to their games. I remember at times just watching Chevigny on the sidelines. He dressed impeccably with a suit and hat. You could tell he was somebody special. My dad just loved him because of what he represented for Catholics."

To the Paulisons, Jack was a hero, a Catholic who was wildly successful and practically worshipped by everyone in the city of Austin. Like other Roman Catholics in the area, the Paulisons acknowledged that the consummate popularity of the brash, young, urban Catholic transplant was no small accomplishment. Depression-era Texas was a time and place of ubiquitous bigotry.

At the same time just across the Colorado River, the Texas Longhorns carried the brand of mediocrity. By midseason, the discontent over the Horns' two wins in five games had become palpable. Disgruntlement and pessimism shrouded Clyde Littlefield's performance. Compounding the dissatisfaction was an anemic Longhorns' offense, which had failed to score in the last three contests versus Nebraska, Oklahoma, and Centenary. Though six games on the 1933 SWC circuit remained, Littlefield was already on the hot seat. The wolves began to howl against the favorite son of the Forty Acres.

Searching for a brighter future, many eyes of Texas turned to the hilltop of St. Edward's. Like Littlefield, Jack Chevigny was a natural heir to a wealth of personal charisma. With his charm, his good looks, and his perceived ability to consistently inspire an average team to a championship level, Jack had displaced the legendary Longhorn as the sports celebrity of Austin.

St. Ed's graduate Ted Paulison remembered seeing Jack Chevigny on the Longhorns' sideline. Jack would hold the down-marker at several of the UT home games. With St. Edward's home games scheduled so not to conflict with Longhorn home games, Jack had the opportunity to make an appearance on the Longhorn sideline. In a tradition that continues in current times, the place to be seen in Austin was on the Longhorn football sideline. Chevigny cynics cited Jack's presence there as a thoughtful marketing strategy, a brazen self-promotion for Littlefield's job. The true motivation remains unknown, but it should be noted that it was a common practice in Texas and other places for local coaches known to the program to assist in such duties as chain crew management and even officiating. As a matter of *quid pro quo*, whenever St. Edward's played a game, it wasn't unusual to see a Longhorn assistant coach on the sideline.

Whether holding the chains or just making an appearance, Jack would have been easily recognizable on the Memorial Stadium sidelines. As a prominent member of the Austin sports community, the neighboring St. Edward's mentor would have explained his presence on the Longhorn sideline as a way to offer moral support for the struggling Horns.

On the hilltop, the outcome of a football season was still to be decided. Even with the Tigers' tightening grasp on the Texas Conference title, Abilene's McMurry College remained a formidable obstacle to the Tigers' sole possession of the crown. Complicating the task, the Tigers would have to make the long trip northwest to play the traditionally troublesome Indians.

Over the last six years, the Indians had lost just once at their home stadium, Donaldson Field. To make matters worse, this tradition combined with early November temperatures, which ushered in another cold dry winter for the windswept West Texas plain. Exposed to strong winds and Abilene temperatures in the thirties, Jack's fair weather Texas hill country boys tackled a strong McMurry club with a decisive home field advantage.

Although most of St. Ed's supporters remained in Austin, the Tigers would not be denied their Chevigny faithful. A leased wire carried the play-by-play report of the game back to the hilltop; a campus public address system broadcast the events of the game to the crowd. It was a subway alumni moment in the Texas hill country. The atmosphere was electric.

The fall of 1933 saw Americans suffering joblessness, homelessness, and hunger in a time of indescribable uncertainty. By the summer, President Franklin D. Roosevelt's first one hundred days had given the country the expected relief, but the programs acted more as a grinding stone of progress than a scythe of salvation.

During the Great Depression, the entertainment dollar was the most valuable dollar spent. Good entertainment allowed people to laugh and cheer—and forget. In November of 1933, few things made people forget their troubles more than a winning football team—Jack Chevigny's football team. While Clyde Littlefield's Longhorns delivered unmet expectations and reminded fans of their despair, Jack's St. Edward's Tigers injected color into the bleak grayness of the hill country's consciousness.

By halftime of the contest in Abilene, those St. Ed's fans who were listening to the game soberly realized that the even an Austin autumn day could turn bitterly cold. St. Edward's Leo "Pope" Dillon gave his teammates the lead early in the third quarter with a nine-yard run. Though Naiser's point-after was blocked, McMurry was flagged for aligning offside. In what turned out to be a bad decision, Coach Chevigny's squad elected to go for two points. On the two-point conversion attempt, Charles "Chili" Stone was stuffed by McMurry's D. H. "Red" Jefferies Jr.

Following an exchange of possession, sophomore quarterback C. L. Harless pierced the St. Ed's secondary with two thirty-yard passes, the first to Amon Harris, the second to Jim McKenzle. With Harless's heroics placing the ball at the Tiger's twenty yard line, the St. Edward's group appeared rattled. Although out of time-outs, Jack sensed his team faltering in their attempt to counter the Indian attack. In an attempt to calm his squad, he decided to take the five-yard penalty for excessive timeouts, but the timeout strategy failed. The Indians continued to slice the St. Ed's defense. After five consecutive plunges through the middle of the line, McMurry's double threat, Harless, ripped through a large hole over St. Edward's right side. Just six plays before the gun sounded, McMurry's Francis Smith kicked the game-winning extra point. Coach R. M. Medley's Indians shocked the Texas Conference, defeating St. Edward's, 7-6.

In what the *San Antonio Express* called the Texas Conference's "most smashing upset," the first-year Texas Conference member McMurry Indians "came from behind in a desperate aerial and ground rally in the fourth quarter to defeat the leading St. Edward's Tigers, 7-6."

Jack's Tigers lost their stranglehold on first place, but still maintained the opportunity to control their own destiny. The Tigers would win the title if they could defeat Howard Payne the following week. McMurry, on the other hand, hoped for a Howard Payne victory or tie with St. Edward's. Either scenario would give McMurry a share of the conference title. And should Chevigny stumble in Brownwood against the Howard Payne Yellow Jackets, Coach Medley's Braves with their win over St. Edward's could claim to be the sole heir to the Texas Conference crown.

The nifty, sure-footed halfback from Notre Dame wouldn't stumble. Neither would his charges.

After traveling the one hundred sixty miles to Brownwood, Texas, a second time that season, the heavily favored St. Ed's squad orchestrated their strategy in workmanlike diligence. Though the game remained scoreless for two quarters and the Yellow Jackets didn't go down easily, Chevigny's *Four Rockets* eventually launched a 7-0 victory. Not much was said of the game other than it was a total team effort. The team train rumbled south with St. Edward's first Texas Conference title in the bag.

Across the Colorado River, the Texas Orangebloods stewed in a pot of disenfranchisement. On November 12, the Longhorns were held scoreless in a three-point loss to the Baylor Bears. Even though Texas fought the good fight against the favored Bears, it was the fourth that the misfiring Horns had been shut out.

By November 1933, Texas sportswriters had begun surreptitiously to position positive remarks regarding Jack Chevigny's leadership alongside negative comments alleging Clyde Littlefield's mismanagement of the Longhorns. The iron was being struck for Littlefield's termination. There would be no sympathy for the fabled Clyde Littlefield. The game was major college football, and it was a dirty business even in those days.

For Jack's Tigers, just two non-conference games remained. The first of those final games was scheduled at home against a talented junior college squad, Schreiner Institute from Kerrville. The second was scheduled in San Antonio against an early season Longhorn opponent, Texas College of the Mines from El Paso. With the conference championship under wraps and the additional motivation of an undefeated season spoiled by McMurry, it would take inspired coaching on the behalf of Chevigny and Pierce if the Tigers were to finish strong,

Few St. Ed's supporters were so football savvy as to appreciate the height of the hurdle that was Schreiner Institute. Coached by former Longhorn star H. C. "Bully" Gilstrap, the Mountaineers played an open style of play similar to St. Edward's. Their attack centered about former Austin High School star, "Pee Wee" Beard. Two other former Austin High Maroon stars, Alvin Eggerling and Moreland Chapman, gave the Mountaineers a sizable advantage over the Tigers on the line of scrimmage.

In addition to posting a laudable lineup, Gilstrap's Mountaineers looked forward to earning the significant prestige of beating the declared Texas Conference champions. Together, the talent and motivation of the Kerrville crew brewed an ale of apprehension for Jack Chevigny and Bill Pierce. On Friday, November 17, 1933, it would all come to a head before an overflow crowd of more than four thousand fans at House Park Field. With limited student tickets available for forty cents, most of the sellout crowd had to purchase the $1 adult ticket.

At 8:00 p.m., the ball was teed up. Within minutes, the Mountaineers' game plan was easily discernible. Showcasing Schreiner fullback Winford Baze, the boys from Kerrville pounded the smaller St. Edward's front. However, Jack's Tigers refused to break. Late in the second quarter with less than a minute to halftime, St. Edward's ignited when Bill Cheatham completed a fifteen-yard pass to Hester Evans. After All-Conference first-teamer Leo Dillon swept the Mountaineers' left flank for thirty yards, St. Edward's owned a new set of downs, first-and-goal at the Schreiner two yard line. Two plays later, Dillon punched the ball over on another end run, this time around the Mountaineers' right side. With Cheatham's point-after kick, the Tigers were able to go to the locker room with a lead, albeit an unimpressive one.

In the second half, the Tigers played ball control, and their threadbare one-touchdown lead held its stitching. When St. Edward's escaped with the 7-0 lead, their record stood at 6-1-1. Their fame already inked in the conference record book, the St. Ed's men, the best eleven ever to grace the hilltop, had only one game remaining between them and Texas Conference immortality.

Depending on the regional preference, the Texas College of the Mines athletic team was also known as Orediggers, Miners, or Muckers. In their home city of El Paso, Muckers was the preferred moniker.

In ore mining, the resulting product of dynamited ore below the surface is called muck. Before the invention of the mucking machine in 1933, the broken bits of product were hand loaded into cars or trucks and transported to the surface where it would be further processed. Miners who loaded and transported the fractured earth, rock, or clay were called muckers. Below the earth's surface, muckers worked at one of the toughest and dirtiest jobs in

America. Only the strongest and most physically fit could call themselves muckers.

Principally a squad of underclassmen, the Texas College of the Mines was led by team captain Lindy Mayhew. An outstanding guard for the Muckers, Mayhew was playing a fourth year in the Orange and White.

Being so far west as to be in a separate time zone from the rest of Texas made recruiting exposure critical for Texas College of the Mines, and San Antonio, known for its fair winter weather and fondness for all types of sporting events from major league spring baseball to horse racing, was the perfect November locale for a neutral site meeting with St. Edward's. Regrettably for Mines coaches Mack Saxon and Harry Phillips, eligibility problems and injuries had emaciated the Orediggers roster. When the train left El Paso on Thursday evening, the *El Paso Herald-Post* reported that the team's Pullman car carried only nineteen players available to face St. Ed's that Saturday afternoon at San Antonio's Eagle Field.

Even though the Muckers weren't in their best shape of the season, the headlines of the *San Antonio Light* encouraged a lively crowd turnout. ST. EDWARD'S MINERS PROMISE CLOSE GAME read the bold print. In something of a footnote, on the same page just below the headlines, was a much smaller article originating in Austin. The smaller article informed readers that the Arkansas Razorbacks had claimed the Southwest Conference; at least they had claimed it on the field. The SWC conference members would meet on December 9 to decide if the ineligible participation of Arkansas tackle Heinie Schleuter should affect the final standings. Headlining the Schleuter article was the announcement, TEXAS BEATEN, LITTLEFIELD SET TO GO.

Sunday's sports pages revealed that the Tiger-Mucker contest was as predicted, a close-to-the-vest punting duel for most of the game. In fact, it was scoreless for three quarters.

The favored St. Ed's squad started slowly. With each team playing for field position and with time winding down, St. Ed's was eventually able to obtain a favorable point from which to launch their Four Rockets. Starting from their own forty-one yard line, St. Ed's Cheatham attempted three straight passes, each falling incomplete. Desperate to get on the board, the Tigers gambled on fourth down. Cheatham scrambled and released the ball late. Although the incomplete pass would have resulted in a turnover on downs to the Miners, Texas College of the Mines was flagged for a personal foul. The fifteen-yard penalty allowed St. Ed's to retain possession with a new set of downs and the ball on the Muckers' thirty-five yard stripe. Bill Cheatham took advantage of St. Ed's good fortune when he smashed across the goal for a touchdown.

With time running out, the Miners attempted one last ditch effort to score, but they could manage only four straight incomplete passes from deep in their own territory. Time expired as St. Edward's beat the Mines and finished its Cinderella season at 7-1-1.

For Jack, the opportunity to try on the glass slipper would soon follow.

# CHAPTER THIRTEEN

# *The Eyes of Texas*

Like the wind scraping away the crayon foliage of a big tooth maple, the Longhorn losses felled the sturdy burnt orange oak, Clyde Littlefield. The 20-6 season-ending loss to the Arkansas Razorbacks dropped the legendary Orangeblood's record to 4-5-2 for the season, his first losing season in seven years. More importantly, it was Texas's first losing season in forty years of football.

As he came to the realization that he had no heart for fending off the attacks led by Texas exe Lutcher Stark, the embattled coach remarked that the football job wasn't worth the price. In leaving his fate to the university leadership, Coach Littlefield emphasized that he would not resign, because he "was no quitter." Qualifying his remarks, the orange-blooded Littlefield admitted that he would welcome being removed from the head football post, so he could concentrate on track.

The man behind making the job too expensive for Littlefield was coach killer, H. J. Lutcher Stark. In displacing Littlefield, Stark allied himself with Hilmar H. Weinert of Seguin, a banker and oilman appointed regent by Governor Miriam "Ma' Ferguson in 1933.

The gruff Texas football letterman Weinert had a reputation for getting what he wanted, when he wanted it. What Weinert wanted was Jack Chevigny at head of the Longhorn herd. It was a wish that meshed with Stark's mission to oust Littlefield and replace him with a *name* coach, one with a registered coaching bloodline. Jack's nationally known football name combined with his Rockne lineage to provide Wienert with the perfect candidate for gaining Stark's support.

As the loose alliance of Stark and Wienert pushed the board toward firing Littlefield, University of Texas President H. Y. "Benny" Benedict took no discernable stance in the matter. The Board of Regents was the sole power behind these types of decisions, and Benedict would not venture in such treacherous political waters unless it concerned the core survival of his university.

Nevertheless, Littlefield wasn't completely stranded. He remained the archetypal Longhorn, and in spite of the recent season, he was a successful football coach with a 44-18-2 career record. One influential Littlefield believer was Texas-exe, Jubal "J. R." Parten.

A model for the sinister J. R. Ewing of the 1980s long-running television series, "Dallas," the real J. R. was remarkably dissimilar to the villain portrayed by Texas-born actor Larry Hagman. Parten attended Texas as a member of the Class of 1917, but he failed to graduate when he answered his country's call and entered the service on August 24, 1917. Although his degree requirements weren't complete, the Madisonville native stayed long enough to complete the summer session and pass the bar exam. Delaying his marriage and his graduation, Parten intended to return to complete his degree after the war.

When Parten returned, he struck it rich in the oil fields of Louisiana and East Texas. Like Stark and Weinert, the oilman was a regular at

University of Texas football games. Colonel Parten was as consumed with the fortunes of Longhorn athletics as he was with the fortunes of his oil exploration ventures. Traveling to see the Longhorns compete in various cities, Parten was more than an avid spectator; he was a recruiter of athletic talent. Each football season, the millionaire oilman would offer detailed scouting reports on northern Louisiana and East Texas high school stars. Not only did Parten locate the talent, he also paid for the talent. In the days before NCAA-sanctioned athletic scholarships, wealthy boosters such as Parten covered the expenses of those athletes who led their teams to victory.

Clyde Littlefield always had high praise for Parten's efforts. Not a man to abandon his friends, Parten stood in Littlefield's corner. Yet, he remained pragmatic; the Littlefield thing wasn't going away. Knowing that the anvil would be struck against Littlefield, Parten decided to hammer a compromise, which met the demands of both Stark and Weinert.

In Parten's plan, Clyde Littlefield's contract would be renewed, even though the coach had stated he had no desire to continue as head football coach. Littlefield would then step down as head football coach but remain as head track coach, the job he most loved. In this manner, the regents and the athletic department would avoid a schism in the university.

Agreeing with the compromise, the board felt it would placate the Littlefield supporters as the university moved forward in constructing a premier football program worthy of more than just regional recognition. In a secret meeting of the university's Athletic Council held on Wednesday, December 5, 1933, Clyde Littlefield was reappointed to another term as head football coach and head track coach. Conjunctive to that reappointment, the coach submitted his resignation along with a prepared statement regarding his decision to surrender his current post as Longhorn head football coach.

With Coach Littlefield's statement held in confidence, former Longhorn head coach, esteemed German professor and Athletic Council chairman, Doctor W. E. Metzenthin released the council's own declaration stating,

> "The Athletic Council by unanimous vote recommended the renewal of the contract of Clyde Littlefield as head coach of football and track for the years 1934-35. Mr. Littlefield appeared before the council and after expressing appreciation, of the action, declared that under the present circumstances he would prefer to be relieved of duties as football coach and be allowed to concentrate on track. After considerable discussion, the council agreed to recommend that a contract on a tenure basis be given Mr. Littlefield to serve as track coach and to perform such other duties as might be assigned by the council. No more formal action regarding the appointment of a head football coach to take Mr. Littlefield's place was taken."

Doctor Metzenthin, in his role as a pseudo-athletic director, (Texas had never filled Bellmont's vacancy after he was reassigned following E. J. Stewart's dismissal in 1927) elaborated that the council had four or five coaches in mind for the position. Action on those names would be delayed until after the national meeting of football coaches to be held in New York during the latter part of December.

Hinting that the fix had been on against Littlefield, the *San Antonio Express* informed its readers that

> "Lutcher Stark of Orange, prominent among alumni and a member of the board of regents revealed that prior to Littlefield's resignation Stark had authorized the sending of telegrams to various prominent football coaches in the country, approaching them as prospects for the job. The final action on the question of retaining Littlefield or obtaining a successor would rest with the regents, the athletic council serving in an advisory capacity."

In railroading Littlefield, Lutcher Stark acquired his third head coach's scalp. In the combined tenure of the three coaches that Stark undermined, the Longhorns had suffered only one losing season, Littlefield's 4-5-2 finish in 1933. Stewart being the second and Littlefield being the latest, the first Stark victim was Berry Whitaker. Outscoring opponents 282-13 in rampaging to a perfect 9-0 slate, Whitaker's 1920 squad is recognized as one of the greatest Longhorn teams ever to wear the burnt orange.

Lukewarm on the idea of Jack's appointment, Lutcher Stark appealed for a nationwide search for the most vibrant and accomplished coach available. At the same time, H. H. Weinert had no intention of deviating from his mission of hiring his daughter's beau and the apple of his wife's eye.

In that Jack was of the Rockne lineage, the Orange, Texas, millionaire was unable to argue that Jack didn't fit his qualifications. Stark was on the Texas sideline in 1913 when Gus Dorias and team captain Knute Rockne helped the Ramblers crush the undefeated Longhorns, 30-7; therefore, Stark recognized the value of a Notre Dame resume.

That game seeded a revelation for Lutcher Stark. For the Longhorns, the road to recognition as a major college football power ran through Notre Dame. And since their first sip from the chalice of Notre Dame's fame, the Longhorns yearned for acknowledgment from the eastern establishment.

Although a rubber match with Notre Dame in 1915 ended in disappointment with a predictable 36-7 Texas loss, a Longhorn visit to Harvard offered another chance at the grail of eastern recognition in 1931. Unfortunately, the two-thousand-mile trip to Harvard yielded only an empty spoon when the Crimson crushed the visiting Texans, 35-7. For the Horns, it was a disappointing loss, which lingered as a stinging rebuke of

Southwest Conference football. The lone highlight of the trip was the $20,000 guarantee.

One year later, St. Edward's Jack Chevigny sat in the wings, hoping to be chosen to round up the Longhorn herd for an eminent fourth run at distinction with another shot at Notre Dame during the fall. But first, Jack had to wrangle the foreman's job.

After the pangs of the Depression prompted UT to freeze Littlefield's salary at $6,000, the Athletic Council dropped the ceiling to $5,000 per year. This anemic salary, even for Dust Bowl times, diminished Lutcher Stark's ability for Texas to find a top applicant and left the university with a limited field of choices. Of that field, Jack was clearly the most qualified and most desirable. Following some bantering among the regents and a second ballot being recorded, Jack was elected to the head football position and awarded a contract worth less than $5,000. The length of the term was a single year.

*January 13, 1934.* It was halftime at the Texas-Baylor basketball game. Jack was standing at center court, his pulse rising with the intensity of the crowd when he was introduced. Chairman of the Board of Regents Beauford Jester walked his new coach out onto the maple floor of Gregory Gymnasium. Only a few fans had left their seats for a concession or smoke break when President Benny Benedict and the Athletic Council Chairman W. E. Metzenthin met Jack near mid-court.

When Jester declared, "...the university had obtained the cream of the crop of coaches available for the place..." four thousand students and fans roared in approval.

Jester pointed to Jack and continued, "We had some mighty fine men proposed. None was too good for our school. But we decided a man we knew already had the stuff. Knute Rockne thought he had great ability, and that is a fine recommendation."

Taking the microphone in center court, Jack offered his thanks to all involved in his appointment and proclaimed that he would do "all in my power to make the flag of the University of Texas fly high among the schools of the nation."

Wired across the country are photos of the dashing bachelor coupled with news articles containing descriptors such as color, verve, *élan*. Though other hyperbolic adjectives are sprinkled liberally throughout the narratives, the question remained as to whether it was Jack's vitality or the paltry remuneration for the head coaching salary that sealed the deal. Despite the incessant crowing of the board as to "the crop of coaches available," no big names had applied for the job. Of the applicants other than Jack, only Lutcher Stark's preference, Northwestern assistant L. B. "Pat" Hanley, had a resume that deserved a second look. Hanley had interviewed first and received a margin of the regents' initial vote of confidence, but the tally was split. Finally, Weinert won over his colleagues on the board.

Though it had been three years since TWA Flight 599 had crashed to the Kansas earth in a twisted mess of metal, wood, and flesh, Rockne's omnipotence continued to boost Jack's status in the coaching world.

Beauford Jester boasted of Jack's close connection to the legendary coach saying, "In my opinion, Chevigny is one of the most promising young football coaches in the United States. Knute Rockne was enthusiastic over Chevigny's capacities and possibilities as a coach and used him as an assistant and also a demonstrator in his coaching schools."

For the St. Ed's boosters, Jack's sudden departure is a bitter tea. It becomes palatable only when Jack's former teammate and hero of the Gipper game, Johnny O'Brien, replaces him on the hilltop. With O'Brien's appointment, eleven more Rockne men are added to the total number of Notre Dame graduates in head coaching positions throughout the country.

In support of the Chevigny selection, the *American-Statesman* indicated that Jester went on to cite what he called a "happy precedent" of the hiring of Billy Disch from St. Edward's in 1911. Reminding the Horn faithful of Disch's outstanding record as a baseball coach at Texas, Jester remarked, "His teams have been dubbed perennial champions, having won championships in 19 of the last 23 years."

The board's final stamp of approval quelled a small storm that had hung over Jack for weeks, a storm generated by his own words. When he was still at St. Edward's, he was asked to provide his opinion on the state of high school football in Texas. Replying that he felt the Texas high school football to be sub-par to high school football in the Midwest, he put a Texas-sized foot in his mouth. Sportswriters such as Bill Van Fleet of the *Galveston Daily News* defended Jack, pointing out the possibility that his evaluation may have been triggered by the fact that few Texas prep players enjoyed the opportunity to further their experience at a prep school or junior college before going on to a four-year institution. Van Fleet suggested this regional disparity is what may have caused Chevigny to misjudge the state of high school football in Texas.

Thanks to writers like Bill Van Fleet and the statewide excitement surrounding Chevigny's appointment as Longhorn head coach, the viral effect of Jack's Texas high school football faux pas was eventually suppressed. Characteristically resilient, Jack had stamped out the fires set by his remarks and moved forward. The milk had been spilled, but it was no time to cry. With his appointment to ride herd on the Longhorns, Jack had triumphed despite the snide remarks of his detractors.

Meanwhile, one of the Four Horseman, Elmer Layden, was signed to replace the displaced Hunk Anderson. With his heart belonging to Our Lady, Jack had pulled out all stops in an attempt to be named Hunk's replacement. He never had a chance.

For the priests of South Bend, the acidity of the senior coach and junior coach disaster had corroded the Chevigny name. Jack would have to settle for Texas. Rebounding from his Notre Dame disappointment, Jack knew that it was monumentally important to infect the rest of the Lone Star State with the same Chevigny fever that had spread throughout Austin after his arrival in town in March 1933.

Jack was an expert card player, and words were Jack's strong suit. When speaking before a crowd, it would be only a few minutes before his hypnotic oratory skills and persona seduced every man and woman in his presence. As expected, after Jack showed his cards in Gregory Gym, the budding student revolution calling for the reinstatement of Clyde Littlefield reconstituted into an emergent Chevigny mania.

If he were to show his wares, Jack needed greater exposure, so in order to get his face in the local papers of the state's farthest reach, the Longhorn coach embarked on a crisscross statewide speaking tour before the various Rotarians and booster clubs. On one circuit, the new coach covered 865 miles in less than a week. After meeting with supporters in the foothills of the western hill country, Jack drove southeast to the Beaumont-Orange-Port-Arthur triangle of ports and petroleum distribution centers. From the Golden Triangle, he then traveled north through the Big Thicket to Lufkin. Ultimately, he returned to Austin by way of Corsicana and the surrounding oil rich upper East Texas landscape. Thanks to Lutcher Stark and J. R. Parten, the Longhorns experienced generous returns from their recruiting investments in the East Texas piney woods and Southeast Texas.

Coach Chevigny had no assistants available to tour with him during the early months of 1934; nevertheless, the delays and slow confirmation process of his new assistants was small potatoes. Jack Chevigny needed no help in selling his program. Always self-reliant to the point of being overconfident, Jack acted on the belief that he was his program's best salesman. In the manner of Rockne, Jack held his recruiting cards close to the chest, maintaining a tight inner circle of coaching confidantes while sharing the spotlight with only a few select individuals who had earned his trust.

Bill Pierce, his line coach at St. Edward's, had agreed to transfer to Texas, but a line snagged in the university's approval process, and Bill signed with Austin College. Tim Moynihan had expressed an interest in the line position, but by the time the board was ready to act, Tim was bound in negotiations with Georgia for the line job in Athens.

Jack needed a Notre Dame man who understood the Irish system of line play. Moynihan, the All-American center at Notre Dame, was an ideal candidate. As Moynihan had filled the dual role of player and coach in Chicago, Jack knew his former college teammate would coach in the same manner he played. Jack didn't give up on Moynihan but eventually snagged a commitment from his old teammate to bypass the Georgia opportunity and come to Austin.

As with the Pierce venture, administrative delays continued to postpone Moynihan's endorsement by the board. Not that Moynihan, the son of a Chicago firehouse captain, would have been much help in recruiting Texas prep stars. Most of what Moynihan knew of Texas he had learned from Tom Mix movies. Although born in Wyoming, Moynihan the Chicagoan would have envisioned Texas as still part of the Wild West, teeming with Indians raiders and Texas Rangers riding white horses.

One of many unique features of Texas is its vastness. By automobile, the Texas landscape covers an area too immense to cover in a single day, or even a week. And because of its size, Texas is home to an exceptionally diverse populous. Though these regional cultures own a range of mores and political priorities, they are seamlessly interwoven with a nationalistic pride that comes from living under the Lone Star flag. Not easily understood by outsiders, the phenomenal sense of identity that comes with being Texan dates back to the days of the Alamo.

Jack could not appreciate that regardless of the depth of his charismatic abilities, no isolated football coach could meet and inspire the entire teenage male populous of such a disseminated and heterogeneous state. Recruiting Texas alone was an impossible dream for Jack. As a French-Canadian Catholic hailing from a prosperous suburb of the nation's second largest city, Jack lacked an understanding and appreciation of the complexities in recruiting the state of Texas. He underestimated the intensity of the nativist Texan consciousness. A product of the Notre Dame system, Jack lacked the instinct and expertise to develop a protocol for competitive college recruiting in such an expansive and diverse environment. Eventually, this amalgam of recruiting ineptitude and cultural oversight would solidify to be an ominous antecedent of the Chevigny legacy at Texas.

By 1934, other Texas universities had begun to embrace a new philosophy in college football recruiting, and whereas Jack's Notre Dame ruled all of Catholic America as well as the densely populated urban and rural areas of the Midwest, Texas had at least five instate peers in the college game. In Houston, Rice was an elite football power. In Dallas, Southern Methodist University had its own aspirations of national recognition and had made progress toward that goal. Located just a few miles away from SMU, Texas Christian University (TCU) monopolized the Fort Worth market, while it extended its reach into West Texas and the Panhandle. Baylor followed up as a source of righteous attraction to Central Texas prep stars and Baptist-affiliated prospects. Adding to the mix, Texas Tech was growing as an influence on prospects who worked their family's farms in the Llano Estacado and western Texas counties. Lastly, rival Texas A&M offered a fine military curriculum and used its Corps of Cadets to appeal to many East Texas boys who wanted a better life through education. With systematic recruiting practices at each of these universities being put in place statewide, it was as if the entire herd planned to drink from what had been an exclusive Longhorn pond. Even as more pickers plucked the prep school peaches the Burnt Orange once harvested by default, Jack failed to hitch his wagon to the emerging trend of a structured recruiting system in college football.

Compounding Jack's problem was another reality. The Board of Regents expected Texas to beat out its rivals in recruiting the gems of the Lone Star prep ranks. As an unmarried Roman Catholic from Indiana, Jack Chevigny faced a tall cultural hurdle as a recruiter of high school talent in the Lone Star state. A proper vetting may have revealed his experience as a recruiter to be insufficient; but neither he nor the Board of Regents appreciated the recruiting intricacies and pitfalls of the progressing college game. Compounding that deficiency was his previously admitted disdain for Texas high school football.

In fact, Jack was inclined to believe most young boys out of high school were interested in helping their family make ends meet, not playing football. He knew no amount of suave recruiting talk could fill the bellies of their hungry brothers and sisters. It would take cold cash to convince the best to drop everything to go kick around a football for four years. From the perspective of Jack Chevigny, the importance of the development and maintenance of a standard Texas recruiting plan was moot. His recruiting success would be found in the pockets and judgment of boosters such as J. R. Parten and Lutcher Stark.

In a 1937 *Saturday Evening Post* story, Lutcher Stark, admitting to funding many of Texas's best athletes including the legendary Clyde Littlefield, said,

> "After the athlete has met the requirements for eligibility, then it makes no difference whether his family is going without an automobile to send him to school or his education is being paid for by his uncle, the fire department, chamber of commerce, or myself. Why not be honest about it and recognize and regulate subsidization?"

Stark considered it ridiculous to expect to stand by idly, while talented students were unable to afford the opportunity to help his alma mater achieve recognition, be it through athletics, science, or the arts.

The lumber and oil tycoon explained, "Some men paint, but I don't. Some men write, but I can't. And I won't have anything to leave behind except the men I rear."

On such a foundation Jack Chevigny's recruiting rested. And after the brief Rockne-like triangular tour of his most fertile recruiting territories, the newest high priest of the Texas football flew to Chicago on the fourth of February to attend the wedding of his sister, Graziella. In sealing the Chevigny name to the Galvin family, Graziella strengthened an already firm Chevigny bond to Notre Dame. His new brother-in-law, Tim, a prominent Notre Dame alumnus, would remain one of Jack's closest friends throughout the remainder of his life.

Soon after the wedding, Jack returned to Austin with his parents in tow. Doctor Chevigny, a fanatical supporter of Jack's career, wanted to experience the excitement of his son's new position. A snow-less Travis

County offered the elder Chevigny's ailing heart a more agreeable February climate.

Upon Jack's return to Austin, the Longhorn staffing needs were met. In the middle of February, Tim Moynihan signed a one-year contract for $3,000. Jack also felt satisfied about the remaining staff members: Mike "Marty' Karow, John Dibrell, Curtis "Shorty" Alderson, and Bill James. Alderson and James would direct the freshmen.

Alderson was a Littlefield holdover as was Bill James. His value would be in helping Jack negotiate the treacherous political waters that ran through the Forty Acres.

Marty Karow's football background as an All-American fullback and team captain at Ohio State would make him another essential cog in the Chevigny machine. Karow's greatest legacy would be leading the Ohio State baseball program to a national championship in 1966.

John Dibrell arrived on the Forty Acres immediately after completing his studies at St. Edward's in June. His affable nature and his playing experience at St. Ed's provided Jack with a trustworthy end coach, one who was already versed in Chevigny's version of the Notre Dame system.

With his parents settled in at a local hotel and his staff in place, Jack left on the lecture circuit. Moynihan was left in Austin to acquaint himself with the team, while Karow, Alderson, and James helped Moynihan negotiate the ropes of assimilation. Upon his return to Austin, the head Longhorn would ready his team for spring practice.

A primary focus of the spring session would be refreshing the stale Longhorn offense, which during Littlefield's last season, accounted for an anemic total of just forty-four points against nine of its top tier opponents. As the end of spring contact drills was slated to coincide with the alumni-centered Round Up weekend, the publicity savvy Jack planned the first

Orange-White intra-squad game as an additional opportunity for the students and Texas exes to enjoy. Burnt Orange electricity sparked throughout the state and the alumni circles. The Chevigny touch was paying dividends.

The offense wouldn't be the only thing Jack would change. Abandoning the traditional all-white Texas helmet, Jack designed an orange panel that would be splashed across the front of the headgear. Unlike his brief stopover at St. Edward's, there would be no drastic changes. As a Notre Dame man, Jack knew better than to tug on the cape of tradition, and he knew better than to alter the burnt orange, which, thanks to Clyde Littlefield, was licensed as *Texas orange*.

In 1934, every new program proclaimed to provide its players, students, and boosters a New Deal, and Jack's installation as head coach gave sportswriters the opportunity to compare the new coach's challenges with those of the new president, Franklin D. Roosevelt. In cards, getting a new deal means a chance to start fresh with a new hand. In that he was a poker player, Jack would have liked the phrase. Borrowing from President Roosevelt's promise of a new beginning, zealous sports editors from across Texas painted the opening of the 1934 season as a bright new orange sunrise for Longhorn football.

Overlooked by the sportswriters was the fact that during its run of forty-two seasons, Longhorn football had experienced only one momentary eclipse of its winning tradition prior to Littlefield's 1933 season, the 4-4 season of 1917. History had become strangely opaque in the face of Jack's refulgent personality and charm. Like a deer in the headlights, the Longhorn masses could no longer see the program's past glories, the championship seasons under Longhorn bosses Allerdice, Whitaker, and Littlefield.

Some Horn fans questioned why Jack was seen as the savior when Longhorn football had experienced only a single losing season in its entire existence. But that statistic was of no matter. Once exposed to Jack's presence and oratory skill, legions of Longhorn faithful fell under his hypnotic spell. Whether in a group of two or a crowd of two thousand, the diminutive Midwesterner was an exhilarating presence. That spring at the Forty Acres, all who came in contact with him were blinded by the new and brilliant orange son of Austin. It was as if no Longhorn football coach had achieved anything before Jack Chevigny arrived.

Amidst a great fanfare on St. Patrick's Day, Jack Chevigny's New Deal opened in Austin with the customary spring drills. Then in a shock to every player and coach present, tragedy interrupted spring's first full contact scrimmage.

Resting that afternoon in his Austin hotel room located just a couple of blocks from Memorial Stadium, Jack's father suffered a heart attack. Sprinting from the practice field, Jack left Moynihan in charge. Transported to the hospital, Doctor Chevigny died later that evening.

With the coaching staff instructed to continue spring drills under the leadership of Tim Moynihan, Jack and his mother accompanied his father's body back to Hammond the following day. After leaving Austin early Sunday, they arrived in Northwest Indiana on Monday afternoon.

Doctor Julius Chevigny's career was one of service to his community. In addition to his military service during the Great War, Julius served for years at the Simplex Plant of American Steel Foundries. His love for high school football was demonstrated through his decade of service as the medical examiner for Catholic Central High athletes. In the latter years of his medical career, Doctor Chevigny had served on the staff of Burns Funeral Home. Because the Burns and Chevigny families were close, Burns

Funeral Home handled the preparation of the body and services. More than 165 automobiles followed the hearse from All Saints Catholic Church to Calvary Cemetery in East Gary.

Not surprisingly, Knute Rockne's widow, Bonnie, attended the graveside service along with her fourteen-year-old daughter, Mary Jean. Just three years hence, Jack had served as Bonnie's main beam of support during Rock's funeral. On this day, she would be there for Jack.

Three days later on Saturday, March 24, 1934, Jack stood before his charges at Memorial Stadium. Inconsolably grieving, he had lost a father for the second time in his life, but his new mission could not stop for the pain.

An April issue of *The Alcade*, the university's alumni publication, described the excitement of Jack Chevigny's New Deal. Describing the first spring intra-squad game set during Round Up festivities, *The Alcade* proclaimed Chevigny's promotion of the 1934 Texas Longhorns to be a grand idea.

As an *Alcade* author explained,

> "Ex-students like football; everybody knows, and lots of people can prove that old grads are very interested in football...This exhibition will not be a mere scrimmage; it's a real game with all the fixin's, including the rah-rah boys and the band. When the whistle blows it's tooth and nail until the gun shoots."

*The Alcade* reminded the alums that with the installation of the Notre Dame shift, they would see an invigorated Longhorn offense—an offense that was substantially less than vigorous in the last year of the Littlefield era.

Fans in attendance that Friday afternoon saw the Longhorn varsity face a Round Up team consisting of a ménage of first-year men, ineligible players, and alums returning for a glimpse of the old gridiron glory. At the Ex-Students Association luncheon Saturday after the game, Jack again showcased his New Deal Longhorns by awarding medals of merit to outstanding varsity Steers. A strong believer in individual recognition as a necessary entree on the menu of teamwork, Jack recognized numerous players for their performances, including the most outstanding player of the Round Up game. Following the hoopla of Round Up and the conclusion of spring training, Jack Chevigny's New Deal looked forward to its premier on the dusty plains of Lubbock in September.

Less exuberant were the exes and writers who had not yet conquered the gloom of Littlefield's disappointing 3-5-2 finish. They attempted to dissuade Chevigny fans from expecting much success for the 1934 season. For these doubters, even the messianic Chevigny faced a tough row to hoe in the white-chalked fields of 1934.

Given the mixed prognostications, Jack's first Longhorn herd was stocked with some quality head. Jack Gray returned at end, while Joe Smartt, Fred Beasley, Clint Small, Charles Coates, and a muster of other lettermen gave the Horns a talented veteran line. Most importantly, three-year letterman Bohn Hilliard would be on the Longhorn train to Lubbock for the season opener against Texas Tech.

All-Southwest Conference in 1932 and 1933, Bohn Hilliard was what Texas high school coaches liked to call a guy from a "whole nother level." Thanks to the generosity of his fellow Orange native and benefactor Lutcher Stark, Hilliard brought his star talent to Austin where it shone on the Longhorn baseball diamond as well as the gridiron. Having already earned a place in the UT record book with his ninety-five-yard punt return against Oklahoma in 1932, Hilliard impacted any game in which he participated. Of Hilliard's considerable talent in carrying the ball, most significant was his ability to change directions in mid-stride. At broken field running, the Orange, Texas, schoolboy legend was said to better than the legendary Red Grange of Illinois.

After the close of spring drills, Jack would have made some attempt at relaxation. He faced the rest of his life without his two most powerful influences and moderators. Escaping the pain of his loss and the pressures of his new job, Jack would obtain some respite by playing the ponies and sitting in on some poker games with his rich and powerful friends. Betting on horse races had been a favorite pastime of his since his days at Notre Dame. As a social butterfly, who casually flittered among the rich and famous, Jack loved everything about life in the fast lane, particularly pari-mutuel gambling. Back in Chicago, the dashing young Cardinal coach had been a regular at prestigious Washington Park.

Evident by the sprinkling of just a few horse tracks throughout the state, gambling on horses had been illegal in Texas for years. Without legalized pari-mutuel gambling, horse racing in Texas was handicapped and unable to gain any legitimate following. With each new legislative session, diehard thoroughbred breeders continued to fight for legalization, so that they could build a firm infrastructure of homegrown stables and racing facilities. Meanwhile, Texas had its share of derby fanatics, and the interest in thoroughbred racing brought with it the perfunctory element of illegal gambling.

In 1933, horse breeders caught a break in the Texas courtroom following the arrest of two gamblers at Arlington Downs. At that time, the economics of horse racing in Texas was reevaluated by the state legislature, and in a boon for race fans and horse breeders throughout Texas, Governor Miriam A. "Ma" Ferguson agreed with the legislature and signed the pari-mutuel bill into law. Elated thoroughbred enthusiasts learned that Fort Worth oilman William Waggoner, owner of Arlington Downs, would be granted the state's first pari-mutuel racetrack. Construction on new parks, including San Antonio's Alamo Downs, followed.

Opening on April 24, 1934, Alamo Downs was the sparkling wine of Texas racetracks. Its grand opening brought numerous Texas luminaries to the derby. Among the guests of honor on opening day were Jack Chevigny and Governor Ma Ferguson. Even if she was married to one of the most powerful men in Texas, it never hurt a fifty-eight-year-old woman to have a handsome twenty-seven-year-old bachelor in her entourage. The liberal Klan-hating Ferguson and Notre Dame graduate had at least two things in common: politics and a fondness for the derby. Though she was the ranking dignitary on the platform, Ferguson didn't pack a celebrity punch any greater than the debonair Longhorn head football coach.

Proof of Jack's celebrity could be found in the starting gate of the first race, a young thoroughbred from Burnet County, Texas, named Jack Chevigny. The coach's namesake belonged to the stable of State Senator Houghton Brownlee, a close friend of the Texas football coach. Brownlee's dream was for the Lone Star state to depose the Bluegrass State from the throne of thoroughbred horse breeding. The Burnet County rancher had spent the better part of a decade pumping cash into building his stables of dreams.

Two brands of millionaires ruled Texas in the days of the Dust Bowl— the old money rancher and the new money oilman. Socially the inner circle's habits were similar, but each held its own coterie as exclusive. Oilmen held new money, which, during the oil exploration boom, usurped the traditional status of the old money ranch families. Still, nothing in Texas held its value as much as a ranching pedigree. The decisive commonality that the two groups shared was their love of horses and gambling—and polo.

As it is today, polo was a sport of prestige during the 1930s. During the Great Depression, polo's popularity even challenged King Football as the sport of interest among the Texas oil and rancher rich. Accordingly, Austin was home to two of the world's best polo players, Cecil Smith and Vernon Cook. Given the popularity of the sport and the economic vitality of its fans, it wasn't uncommon for tens of thousands of dollars to exchange hands after a polo match. Better trained and less temperamental than its oval bound cousin, the polo pony is no less fierce as a competitor. The vivacity of a team of stampeding thoroughbreds, each valued at hundreds of times more than the lifetime earnings of the average worker, made for a sensational and stimulating afternoon.

Jack's celebrity status and personality provided him an open invitation into the clique of polo and thoroughbred enthusiasts, and with invitation into the lifestyle came the temptation to live the lifestyle. For Jack the magnetic playboy, the problems began with his attempt to maintain that status quo on a coach's annual salary, which was roughly equivalent to less than a single week's income of his friends and gambling associates.

On opening day at Alamo Downs, Houghton Brownlee's three-year-old Jack Chevigny surprised most of the fourteen thousand spectators with a solid show for third place. Obligated to pick his namesake to win, Jack's wallet would have been lightened by the order of finish. Nonetheless, among the dignitaries of the dais, the young thoroughbred would have elicited a buzz of comparisons regarding old number twelve's former speed and quickness on the gridiron.

The remainder of Jack's spring was spent officiating high school track meets and working the lecture circuit. After a series of speaking engagements, Jack would have had the opportunity to look back on the changes the last five months brought into his life. He had returned to near the pinnacle of major college football and was set to get his chance finally to prove Hunk and the doubters wrong. In the span of just three years, Rock and his father were gone. Together they had served as the guidance system for his edgy and sometimes volatile personality. Now, he had neither. His Achilles was exposed.

# CHAPTER FOURTEEN

# *One for the Chevigny*

With the hoopla of Round Up and the memories of spring faded, the Longhorns' New Deal looked forward to its September premier in the dusty Texas Panhandle. The Jack Chevigny era would open at Texas Tech on September 6, 1934.

Longhorn football experts warned Texas fans and students not to expect too much of the Rockne prodigy. In continued finger-pointing toward Littlefield and his disappointing 3-5-2 finish, they said that Chevigny would need time to round up a herd that could compete in the Southwest Conference race. Worn from the disappointments of the previous season, a downtrodden and spiritless Memorial Stadium was expected to be without its traditional September cheer.

If he were to restore the Longhorns' field of glory, the silver-tongued orator would need to remove the ankle-twisting nut grass and re-sod the barren spots with players who bought into his philosophy and system of play. Reaping a plentiful harvest of wins would be difficult in the first year. Although Bohn Hilliard was back for another year, the regents and the Burnt Orange mafia were conditioned to believe it would take Jack a full season to cultivate the many unproven sprouts into a winning crop. Should

Jack need to proceed in a reconstruction mode during the first year of his tenure, the board planned to hold Lutcher Stark on a tight leash.

Looking forward to his first season as a Longhorn, Jack took a moment to address the alumni with an open letter.

"From the point of view of sportsmanship and courage I can say that our 1934 edition of the University of Texas football team will be of the representative quality that the TEXAS alumni strive to attain. The team will be inexperienced at the start of the season and will be handicapped by the introduction of the Rockne system— which few men have played—and the obviously difficult schedule.

"The outlook would be most disheartening were it not for the fact that we feel confident the alumni are wholeheartedly cooperating with us and that the possibility of losing will not distract from this loyalty in its greatness.

"That athletics and studies do not mix well, and that athletics are of no particular value to the student body, seems to be the ideal that is found in the minds of many unacquainted with the facts. Having been connected for the past eight years with athletic work, which has brought me into close contact not only with conditions at Texas, but also with those existing at many other large schools in the United States, I am absolutely convinced that anyone holding such an idea is either ignorant of the facts or narrowly prejudiced.

"These critics overlook or ignore one important (and I think the most important) aspect of the whole question. College is not merely a school; it is a life. It is school life, of course, and the major emphasis, I affirm, is as it ought to be, on study, but it is true that football interest is very great during the first quarter of the school year. However, there are ever so many worse things that could happen to a school, and in my opinion would happen, if that healthy outlet for youthful energy and enthusiasm were closed.

"Man is not all mind. He is a creature of flesh and blood. He has a heart, and the heart, too, must be schooled in the curriculum, which life itself supplies in those four years, crowded with wonder, which make up the college career of the student body.

"The spirit that the men exemplify on the field is what we call the TEXAS SPIRIT—a spirit that is most precious, that adds to the sum of life itself and makes us grateful to the state of Texas." —*Coach Jack Chevigny (Daily Texan)*

After readying the fall practice schedules and conducting their final equipment checks for the opening day of drills, the Longhorn coaching staff met on Tuesday, September 3. Also planning for the Longhorn practices in Memorial Stadium were the numerous colonies of bats nesting near the concrete rafters. Jack recalled it was sometimes hard to determine which was more annoying: the ammonia smell from the continuous bat droppings or the driveling guano from the pens of the newspaper men. Like wasps in a cicada swarm, a cloud of press corps members gathered daily about Memorial Stadium in search of quotes and constant updates on the team's outlook during the opening week of a brutal two-a-days.

When questioned in regard to his players' readiness upon their arrival back in Austin, a tongue-in-cheek Jack summed up what the generous team-sponsored training table meant for farm boys in the third year of an epic regional drought, saying, "I expect that many will be ready for a week of free meals."

Prior to the start of fall drills, coaches Moynihan, Karow, James, and Alderson issued gear to sixty-four athletes. In telling several reporters that he expected the Longhorn squad to increase to eighty participants by the time the school term opened, Jack reminded the press that only nineteen Littlefield lettermen had returned for the 1934 slate. Mumbling under his breath to Moynihan, he would have said that he preferred nineteen seniors.

Like his mentor, Knute Rockne, Jack believed sarcasm to be an effective tool for inspiring athletes. It was a common tool for coaches of the era. Few Rockne men matched Jack's skill at imitating the iconic mentor. In deference to his upbringing, Jack occasionally dropped a cynical snippet regarding his team's chances or abilities.

In a phone interview on September 7, 1934, he commented on the team's outlook versus Pete Cawthorn's Texas Tech squad, and the press locusts devoured the bait, by printing his gloomy prognostication, "Only fifteen more days until we take our first spanking."

On Monday, September 10, Jack opened his first fall drill as Longhorn mentor. Twelve days before the season opener at Texas Tech, local scribes recorded their take on the anticipated opening day, while Longhorn squad members attempted to survive the grueling Rockne-style regimen. His big game theories intact from his days at Chicago, Jack instructed the backs in the "art of sidestepping and broken field running," while Moynihan, in the manner of a sadistic trail boss driving the herd, punished the linemen in drills that were designed to get them to charge explosively off the line.

In the opening days of drills, few reporters were shocked to see Jack Gray in the dual role of a player-coach working at end and instructing the younger players as they ran through various ball catching drills. Jack Gray was a natural leader who could play and coach simultaneously.

When he talked to the press following the long opening day's workouts, the Longhorn mentor made clear that he intended to continue and intensify the practice routine right up until the meeting with the Tech Matadors.

By September 21, 1934, the day before the meeting with Tech, Jack felt that his Texas Longhorns still remained rough around the edges, but it was too late for adjustments to be improvised. The hay was in the barn; Jack's squad would arrive in Lubbock by train on Friday.

A new Chevigny tradition caught the Horns' veterans by surprise when the team found themselves confined to the train overnight. Spending the night on a railway siding was part of Jack's team-building platform. Regardless of the level to which the mercury would fall, it would be four years before a Longhorn football player slept in a hotel room on the night before an out-of-town game. Sitting in the idle sleeping cars on the eve before meeting Tech, Jack and his staff prayed their team was ready to face the favored Matadors.

Collier Parris of the *Lubbock Morning Avalanche* told his Panhandle readers that the large delegation of Longhorn supporters waited for at least an hour past the scheduled time to cheer the arrival of Chevigny's Steers. They waited non-customarily alone.

Because of unfinished campus construction projects, the summer vacation at Texas Tech had been extended. Two new large dormitories designed for the growing South Plains institution weren't completed; therefore, lest they find themselves sleeping on campus benches, Tech students were advised to delay their arrival until the first day of October.

Not many people saw the Longhorns step off the train. The prospect of a fifteen-hour trip dulled the Steers' fans interest in following the team to Lubbock. Four hundred tickets were returned from Austin.

After a brief Friday evening workout under floodlights, Jack informed Collier Parris of his squad's chances. "It is a nightmare to me, this game tomorrow night. I'll be glad when it's all over. It will be a rough, hard game, with no mercy asked or given. We know the Tech boys are ready and waiting for us, and they know we're pretty steamed up ourselves. It will be anything but a pink tea affair. It should be a midseason game. It should be a good one as it is, but if it were played later in the year, it would be a whiz sure enough."

*Lubbock Morning Avalanche* readers noted the homecoming of Sweetwater's Ney "Red" Sheridan, quarterback of the Longhorns. Sheridan was a dynamo who had been recruited to Texas. His high school teammate, Sammy Baugh, wanted to go to Texas with him, but Longhorn baseball coach Billy Disch told him he couldn't play both sports, so Baugh signed with TCU. In the Horn backfield alongside Bohn Hilliard was Irwin Gilbreath at right halfback. Backing up Hilliard in Chevigny's famed Notre Dame shift was burner Hugh Wolfe.

Wolfe, a world class speedster, would rarely touch the ball during the 1934 season, serving mainly as a blocker. The scarcity of his playing time and carries in the 1934 season would puzzle the affable Wolfe for the remainder of his long and successful life.

Assessing both teams in the straight-talking parlance of a West Texas sportswriter, *The Avalanche's* Collier Parris compared the two teams:

> "Added up, the dope looks mighty like a tie, with lucky breaks figuring in the scoring, if any. Both teams are strong defensively with Texas having the edge. Tech's offense may click more smoothly, the Matadors being more experienced with the Notre Dame system instituted only this spring by Chevigny at Texas. Neither team has had time to learn all the frills and furbelows that may be worked from the Rockne formation, so it probably will be a game of straight, fundamental football."

For the fans with a yen for wagering, Parris added,

> "There does not seem to be an unusual amount of watering on the game, and what money that does change hands probably will do so on an even exchange. Prevailing odds seem to be 3 to 2 on Texas Tech but few indications of wagering have been noticed."

With a Longhorn fan risking fifteen dollars to win just ten, betting on Texas was a risky proposition for a Depression Era gambler. The lack of significant action on the betting line reflected the Austin-based gamblers' perception that the odds should have been weighted more heavily in Tech's favor. This perception was based on two factors: Tech's home field advantage and Jack's pre-game poor mouthing about his Longhorn's lack of expertise in the complex Notre Dame system.

Regardless of his players' lack of proficiency in the Notre Dame system, Jack decided to pull out all stops for the critical opening game win. In an act that would give birth to his Southwest Conference reputation for gamesmanship and chicanery, Jack orchestrated a personnel sleight-of-hand in deceiving the public address announcer and Texas Tech head coach Pete Cawthorn prior to the kickoff. Initially announcing his shock troops as the starting lineup, Jack hurriedly ran his true starters on the field only seconds prior to the 8:00 kickoff. Though the Horns' deceptive strategy was precisely orchestrated, the Longhorn starters couldn't force a break in the static defense of Tech's own shock troops. Predicted in Jack's deprecating pre-game remarks, the game eroded quickly into a defensive struggle, which seemed to numb the spectators.

The hometown Lubbock newspaper labeled the Matador offense "positively pitiful at times."

It would be the second quarter before the Longhorns' Phil Sanger awakened the slumbering crowd when he blocked a Tech punt at the Matador ten yard line. The ball ricocheted out of bounds at the six yard line. From that point, Horn fullback Buster Jurecka bulled into the end zone to put Texas up, 6-0. When Hugh Wolfe missed the point-after attempt, the score stood until near the end of the third quarter.

Late in the third quarter, another Tech punt pinned the Steers inside their ten yard line. On the next scrimmage down, Hilliard took the center's direct snap and charged straight over the right side. Breaking free and bouncing toward the sideline, Bohn Hilliard went the distance on a ninety-four-yard dash that put the Horns on top, 12-0. Longhorn fans gasped when, after crossing the goal line, Hilliard collapsed.

Hushed Longhorn fans stood on the edge of their seats, straining to catch a glimpse of the stretcher upon which the Texas trainers laid the star halfback. With Hilliard out of the game, the contest returned to a sluggish stalemate until late in the game when Tech pierced the goal line on a late razzle-dazzle counter. On the receiving end of a series of laterals, former Notre Damer Ed McKeever notched the home team's first points of the 1934 season, giving the Marauders their first edge of the contest. For Tech, the former Notre Dame man's heroics came too late in the game. Hilliard's ninety-four-yard gallop had sealed the victory. Jack's Longhorns brought home a tough 12-6 triumph.

Up next for the Longhorns was an opponent that presented Jack with the once-in-a-lifetime opportunity found only in the dreams of those who have been so scorned—a lover's revenge. Texas would travel to South Bend to face the Fighting Irish of Notre Dame. With the *Longhorn Special* rumbling south toward the Forty Acres, even Hilliard's doubtful outlook for the Notre Dame game couldn't discourage Jack's fervor.

In Austin, the Longhorns met an emotionally charged group of students and fans ecstatic over their team's first win. Allotted an extra week to prepare for the Fighting Irish, the Horns could take a moment for a slap on the back and bask in their fans' shining exaltations.

While an open date allowed Chevigny's Longhorns an extra week to sharpen their skills in the box offense, the real benefit was the two-week window available for Hilliard's recuperation. The Horns had little chance to beat Notre Dame if the two-time All-SWC honoree Hilliard remained hobbled. Riding a wild bronco of media adulation, Jack used the time to work the area high schools and wow more small-town Chevigny converts.

Friday night found Jack thirty-two miles southeast of Austin in Lockhart, Texas, where he would help dedicate the new high school football stadium.

During the fall of 1934, federal dollars available through FDR's Keynesian economic policies were being used to inoculate numerous Texas communities against the spreading plague of financial collapse, and future president Texan Lyndon B. Johnson headed many of the Texas initiatives. In conjunction with President Roosevelt's alphabet soup of community assistance policies, groundbreakings on federally-funded football stadiums throughout the state provided jobs and paychecks, and resulted in fresh, sparkling new venues for the Lone Star state's principal religion, high school football. Fortunate school districts such as Cleburne Independent School District received new stadiums courtesy of the federal government.

Just southeast of Austin, Lockhart was one proud locale that opted for fully privatized funding, and on September 28, 1934, hundreds of Lockhart area fans turned out to dedicate their new Lions stadium. The local news reported that while the Lions' contest with the Texas School for the Deaf would be interesting, the events not to be missed were the festivities surrounding the dedication of the new football stadium. New floodlights had been installed along with a newly-leveled playing surface, seeded and manicured even better than the lawn in front of the governor's mansion. Starting at 7:30, activities under the Friday night lights opened with the fireman's band rendition of *Lockhart High Forever*. One-minute speeches by four local sports dignitaries and remarks by Texas head football coach Jack

Chevigny followed. Even more celebrated than the actual game was the fact that midway through the thirty-minute program, the Texas Longhorn band, dressed in full colors, marched to the cheers of the capacity crowd.

Since there would be no Longhorn game the following day, Jack accepted the petition of the Lockhart boosters to officiate the night's contest. In doing so, he was to evaluate closely the skills of Lockhart team co-captain W. H. Moore. Dubbed "Pete" by his classmates, the strapping 195-pound Moore was a track star capable of clocking a fifty-second quarter-mile. The prospective Longhorn was a near clone of Bohn Hilliard.

Failing to disappoint the comparison, Pete Moore delighted the Lockhart rooters late in the third quarter when he broke through the opposing defense for an eighty-five-yard touchdown run. Moore's dash, the final event of the evening's celebration, gave the Lions a 6-0 win over the Silents from the Texas School for the Deaf.

On the drive north to Austin late Friday night, the game's referee would have removed the silver-plated whistle from his neck and reached for his recruiting notebook. Fumbling deep in the glove box for a pencil and pad while holding the wheel with his left hand, he would grasped what he needed with his right hand, then used the dash to support his writing. Living up to his reputation as a hard driver with an affinity for fast cars, the speeding Jack might have flown through the rusting stop sign at the intersection of the Old San Antonio Road, that part of a three-hundred-year-old Spanish artery from the Alamo city to Louisiana. The interior of the dark coupe would have been illuminated only by the blur of oncoming headlights. Paying little attention to the road, he would have been more focused on holding his pen and pad to the light. In that brief moment, the Texas coach who had allegedly once berated the quality of Texas high school football might have hastily scribbled "Moore, Lockhart ace."

Although the Lockhart venture allowed Jack a short vacation from the stress of the upcoming Notre Dame contest, in the short time it took to return to Austin, he would have resumed fretting over the biggest game of his life. This game was bigger than the Gipper game, the game that had made Jack Chevigny a living legend. His thoughts would have turned to a scrimmage scheduled for the following day. Saturday, the Horns would undergo a controlled contest in which his freshman would act as a mock Notre Dame team. On the coaches' office wall, the calendar held a boldly inked star. All of the preceding days had been crossed out with an ✕. Eight days remained until kickoff.

With Moynihan close, Jack rested on one knee at the forty yard line of Memorial Stadium. Twirling his whistle lanyard around his right index finger, the two old Notre Damers contemplated their next move. Saturday's scrimmage was a success. The Horns were in the locker room. It was a spirited, fun scrimmage. Moynihan suggested that in following week, they should push the boys harder. Replying that he would prefer to see that the squad conclude their full-contact rehearsals without injuries, Jack disagreed. Moynihan expressed his concern when the timing of the Notre Dame box offense continued to hiccup. Allaying the old center's worries, Jack pointed out that during the scrimmage, Hilliard and Jack Gray exhibited their usual superb skills.

Jack Gray was a Texas trophy fish. A speedster with feather-soft hands, he offered that elusive big catch capability for the quarterback skilled in the art of passing. Lamentably, the Horns owned no such quarterback. With Texas featuring Bohn Hilliard in an attack built around the shifts and misdirection of the Notre Dame box, Coach Chev fretted as to how he could tap Gray's wealth of talent.

During the era of 1930s college football, a ticket to an intersectional skirmish between two football powers was similar to an invite to the presidential inaugural. With Elmer Layden facing off against Jack Chevigny, the additional bunting of two Rockne disciples on the balustrade heightened the interest of every sports celebrity and journalist from Oakland, California, to Lowell, Massachusetts. Press coverage of the Fighting Irish-Longhorn contest would be coast to coast with live radio feeds through most of the East and Southeast. A whole country of sports fans was aware that on Saturday, October 6, Elmer Layden's untested Irish would tangle with the Longhorns of Jack Chevigny.

It was as if the teams were two trains arriving from opposite sides of the continent. Optimism waved the pennants in Austin, while pessimism stained the bleacher seats in South Bend. New coach Elmer Layden, the fourth horseman of Grantland Rice's biblical metaphor, recently had been appointed to wake up the echoes of Notre Dame football, an appointment complicated by an administrative mandate to upgrade the players' performances in the classroom.

Prior to the Layden era, Notre Dame athletes had to maintain only a passing average, a numerical average of at least 70 percent. With the death of President O'Donnell, new president Father John O'Hara's first decree was to require all athletes to maintain a 77 average in order to retain their eligibility.

O'Hara's second decree addressed transfers. Foreseeing the coming transfer restrictions in college football, Father O'Hara limited the eligibility of Notre Dame students to eight total semesters of play, inclusive of the athlete's time at another institution.

Layden accepted O'Hara's charge with angst and consternation. When he arrived at South Bend to replace Hunk Anderson, Elmer was appalled to see before him a football wasteland. By 1934, Notre Dame wasn't Notre Dame anymore. Rockne's Notre Dame had disappeared, his stadium remaining as a ruin testifying as to the existence of a once powerful civilization. Elmer Layden realized that he faced a total rebuilding program. After his first day of contact practice, the fourth horseman reported that of the over one hundred Fighting Irish varsity squad members, only one knew how to block.

In Texas, following a varsity-freshman scrimmage in which the varsity triumphed 35-0, six thousand students and other fans filled Gregory Gym for a Tuesday evening pep rally. Standing on the stage was Jack and his team. Next to Jack, just inches from the band's tuba player stood Governor-elect James Allred.

Holding the microphone with both hands, Allred led the crowd in a rendition of "The Eyes of Texas" after which he stated, "Following this Saturday's game the song, 'The Eyes of Texas Are Upon You' will be changed to The Eyes of America Are Upon You."

Taking the microphone from Allred, Jack promised the band and those in attendance, some from as far away as Brownsville, that the flag of Texas would fly high with pride in South Bend. The largest pep rally in years closed with the cheers and exhortation, "On to Notre Dame."

Across the Lone Star State the first week of October 1934 brought with it a string of unprecedented intersectional matches. Three Texas teams would travel to Indiana. Railing north alongside the Longhorns was Texas A&M and Rice. The Aggies would be spending most of the week in Indianapolis preparing for Pop Warner's Temple University squad. The Rice Owls would travel to Indiana to meet Purdue.

In a show of regional fraternization, Rice University boosters offered Texas Longhorn fans the opportunity to share a Rice-Texas special to

Chicago. Meanwhile, funds had been raised for the Longhorn band to travel to South Bend with the team.

Completing the next-to-last leg of their journey to South Bend, the Longhorns arrived in downtown Chicago. Like most of his teammates traveling outside of Texas for the first time, end Jack Gray saw his first skyscraper, the Marshall Field and Company Building. Amazed at the sight of the forty-three-story tower framed by four twenty-two-story wings, one of Gray's buddies blurted, "Hey, boys, wonder how many bales of hay you think you could stack in that building?"

Traveling with the Longhorns were some locally known Austin gamblers. No doubt, more than a few cows (one hundred dollar bills in Texas gambler parlance) were wagered on the game. The line as reported in the Port Arthur, Texas, daily had Notre Dame favored by thirty.

Jack, indicating that it would fulfill his greatest hope to hold the Irish to just four or five touchdowns, remarked, "It seems impossible to think we can stop such stars as Melinkovich, Elsiner, Carideo, Vairo, and Bonar."

As kickoff drew near and Jack continued to play down his Longhorns' chances, unknown to practically anyone except the Longhorn team members, the cat was in the bag. The team arrived in Chicago with a mission and a plan. At the center of the plan was a web of deceit.

Not only did October 3, 1934, mark the Longhorns' first visit to the "House That Rockne Built," it was the afternoon of game seven of a classic World Series. The St. Louis Cardinals had fought, sometimes literally, tooth and nail with the Detroit Tigers for six games, and the series was now tied, 3-3. Due to its geographical status as the southernmost major league baseball franchise of the time, St. Louis enjoyed a large following from the nation's dispossessed farmers and southern poor. On their route to the

World Series, brothers Jay Hannah "Dizzy" Dean and Paul Dean combined to earn forty-nine victories from the mound.

Facing the Cardinals at Detroit's Navin Field were Mickey Cochrane's Detroit Tigers, champions of the American League. With over one hundred wins, the underdog Tigers had rocketed to excellence after spending years in the shadows of mediocrity. Together the two major league baseball teams were followed by a heterogeneous mix of fans—Hollywood stars, politicians, Arkies, unemployed machinists, Okies, working men, and old money. All groups and social strata took sides. It would be one of the most diversely attentive World Series in history. Adding to the excitement was the fact that for the first time in history, a suffering patchwork nation could come together in their living rooms to listen to a live radio broadcast of the World Series.

Immediately following the Series finale, the two major radio networks would switch to the Notre Dame-Texas game. In New York City, both WEAF-NBC and WABC-CBS would transmit the Notre Dame game. Across the nation, numerous other local radio stations followed the network feeds, making the game heard nationwide.

A pragmatic Layden admonished the overtly pro-Notre Dame press and the overenthusiastic bookmakers in New York and Chicago. "Everything has to be developed," said Layden. "Sure we are going to lose games this fall, especially through the line, where there are gaping holes to be filled by inexperienced men. Frankly, it takes four games for a coach to get a fine line on his players and we're going to give every one of the three hundred candidates a big chance."

Privately, an affirming Layden knew his team had a more personal motivation than Our Lady, the fans, or the coach could provide. His name was Johnny "Tex" Young.

Layden would have sensed a willingness of the team to win one for Johnny. Unlike the inspiring Gipper legend, the squad's sentiment to "Win One for Johnny" was one of intimate heartfelt reverence. Johnny Young was a lost brother-teammate of every member of the 1934 varsity squad. Layden, the plain speaker, wouldn't attempt to hype the facts of the Johnny Young story in order to win a game. His was a recent and painful loss that would not be exploited in a ballyhoo of halftime exhortations.

Not just some reserve player, John Young was a returning letterman from Anderson's last squad. Proving his ability in spring ball, he was expected to start on opening day against Texas, but the right halfback fell ill shortly after the end of spring practice. During the early days of summer vacation, a staph infection spread from Young's neck, hospitalizing the twenty-two-year-old senior. Treated at St. Joseph's Infirmary in his hometown of Houston, the former St. Thomas prep star passed away in the presence of his parents on July 6. Four months later, Young's death remained a tragedy and a damper to Irish morale.

Layden was not of the mold of Rockne and Chevigny. Providing honest insight to the game and the personnel match-ups, Layden told it like it was. Correct in his unbiased observation that an offensive line often took two weeks to develop into an effective unit, Layden knew that his inexperienced line wouldn't perform decisively for at least three to four weeks. Texas was week one. Mixed with the squad's horrendous hangover from last year's 3-5-1 season, the loss of Johnny Young combined with an inexperienced line to make the Fighting Irish just another average college football team of 1934.

Inside information is critical to setting the odds of any athletic contest. Oddsmakers don't set a line to pick a winner; they set a line to get a split between the number of winners and losers. The oddsmaker hopes to make money on the juice, a set percentage the bookie charges to handle a bet. The oddsmaker's plan is to gain enough inside information to set a line that is equally tempting to both fans on both sides the stadium. What the bookies should have considered in this particular outing was the fact that Jack held a decisive wild card—the Bohn Hilliard trump card.

Being the stone-faced poker player that he was, Jack publicly qualified Hilliard's status as doubtful for the game. Supposedly, the ankle was still bothering him from the Tech game. In reality, Bohn Hilliard was as healthy as he ever had been. Into his second week of rest and recuperation from a slight ankle sprain, Hilliard was at full strength. In fact, Longhorn insiders such as J. R. Parten and Lutcher Stark doubted Hilliard was ever injured at all. They believed the entire Hilliard injury scenario was an elaborate Chevigny ruse, which began with Hilliard falling to the turf after his long touchdown run against Texas Tech. With a healthy Hilliard, Texas was an even bet. Without Hilliard, Texas was a solid three-touchdown underdog. Jack's successful misdirection regarding the health of Hilliard's ankle would have provided his traveling Austin gambling friends with a large edge on the line.

Historically, Jack's Texas critics have censured him for a perceived lack of substance. In their arguments, they often highlight Jack's preference for deceptive strategies, his lack of diligence, and his obstinate arrogance. Chevigny detractors elicit visions of the traveling snake oil salesman riding his wagon into town to shop his illegitimate health care and home goods to the poor and uneducated. But during the 1930s, it was common for coaches to mislead the public as to the health of a team's superstar, as well as numerous other facets of the program's outlook.

On October 3, 1934, the salesman arrived home in South Bend. Prior to entering the house that Rock built, Jack would sell every drop of Burnt

Orange tonic and snake oil he had to the Texas Longhorn football team. What remained to be answered was would they swallow it.

Enhancing the national hysteria of the Notre Dame-Texas gridiron battle, the multitalented entertainer Phil Harris saluted both universities on his "Listen to Harris" program aired nationwide on the NBC affiliates. In addition to his regularly scheduled programming, the popular singer-humorist took time to examine the "social fanfare" of the game, taking a sociological peek behind the curtain at what went on at the two campuses in the week prior to kickoff. A popular baritone who would perform for over four decades, Harris was a star in several genres. His immortality would eventually arrive in the acclaim and adoration he received for his work as the voice of Baloo the Bear in Disney's 1967 hit, "The Jungle Book."

Friday afternoon before the game, Layden's men in blue worked out behind closed gates. Jack had publicly hinted of his plan to use Buster Jurecka in place of Hilliard. In telling the press that he might not utilize Hilliard at his regular backfield position, Jack's intentionally loose lips tightened another spoke in his wheel of deception. With Layden's defensive plan designed to stop Bohn Hilliard, Chevigny's subterfuge regarding the All-American's status must have been unsettling for Layden's coaching staff.

That Friday, the Longhorns held their own pre-game walk-through under wraps at Cartier Field. Jack's heart would have pounded in his chest as his boys went through their final signal checks. He was back at the scene of his past glory, returning to coach where he had always dreamed of being a head coach. Dusk shadowed the Golden Dome as Jack's boys huddled around him, each on a knee awaiting their coach's final preparatory summation. Looking down into their eyes, Jack may have felt uneasy as to how things could get any better.

In only his eighth month on the job, in just his second game as head coach, he stood before his squad on Cartier Field on the eve of what could be the capstone of his entire coaching career—past and future. No one expected him to win, but what if things went as planned and he defeated his alma mater, his personal exemplar of college football? Where would he go from here?

Game day, minutes before kickoff; Jack Gray, Clint Small, and reserve J. Neils Thompson recalled their coach pacing in the locker room; the team mulled around him. It was just before kickoff, and the visitor's locker room appeared to exist in another dimension without sound and motion. Jack Chevigny began to speak.

More than the years that have since passed, it was the emotion of the moment that blurs the memory. No one has ever accurately recalled what Jack Chevigny said. What has been precisely remembered is the power of the moment and the conviction that he communicated to his boys. According to Texas football historian John Maher, Jack Chevigny's words collectively reign as number one on the list of most inspirational speeches given by a Texas coach of any sport.

Some of his players recall Jack bringing forth the memory of his dead mother to inspire the Longhorns. But his mother was alive and reasonably healthy back in Hammond. Other players remember that Jack centering his speech on his father's desperate health, saying that the doctor's only desire before he died was to see his son beat Notre Dame. But his father had passed away in Austin months earlier. Like Rockne's Gipper speech, numerous accounts differed as to the facts of what was said. Like Rockne's Gipper speech, it didn't really matter what was said.

In their account of that day, Jack Gray and the others do agree on one thing. When the Horns leapt to their feet to take the field, not a dry eye was left in the locker room. One misty-eyed player tripped as he pushed through the door.

The players had the right emotion. Jack had the right plan. It was time to let the cat out of the bag. Hilliard would start the game.

As important as Hilliard's true status was the fact that Jack had convinced the team that the coin flip would land in favor of the Horns. In the week before the game, Jack drilled his premonition into the Horns; their break would come on the opening kickoff. Like the pre-game speech, accounts differ widely as to the precise details of Jack's plan, but the outcome remains etched in history.

Center/linebacker Charley Coates would kick off. Notre Dame's game-breakers, George Melinkovich and Fred Carideo, were set deep near the ten yard line. Having coached Melinkovich in 1931, Jack knew of George's potential to quick-six the opening kickoff. Fred, the cousin of Hall-of-Famer Frank Carideo, was a lesser-known standout to Jack. Both Fred Carideo and George Melinkovich had already earned their place in the Notre Dame record book, George with a 92-yard kickoff return in 1931 and Fred with a 72-yard interception return in 1933. Kicking to either might invoke a Faustian toll for Jack's decision.

Longhorn annals record Jack as directing Coates to kick off to one particular Irish deep return man. Whether he targeted Melinkovich or Carideo remains in dispute. Possessing insider knowledge regarding Melinkovich, Coach Chevigny likely would have planned to kick to Melinkovich. Jack may have felt Melinkovich's best days were behind him. Allegedly, Jack told his squad that Melinkovich had issues with securing the ball and was prone to muffing the kickoff. George had missed the 1933 season due to an off-campus accident and had not been expected to return with his old form. Numerous Longhorns remembered Jack predicting that

George Melinkovich would fumble the opening kickoff. Jack told his Horns that if they hustled down on the kick and sold out, they would pull off the play of the game and shatter Notre Dame's confidence.

With the teams lined up for the opening kick, a brisk north wind made the strategy's execution tricky, but Jack remained true to his plan. Coates kicked deep to Melinkovich. Receiving the ball near his five yard line, Melinkovich bobbled the ball as he attempted to break up-field. A host of Longhorns blasted Melinkovich, and the ball squirted loose. As predicted, Jack Gray recovered for the Horns near the fourteen yard line.

In one of the earliest versions of the scripted offensive series used in the modern college game, the Longhorns rushed three times in rapid succession for a first down. Then Bohn Hilliard knifed through the Notre Dame defense for an eight-yard touchdown. After Hilliard split the uprights on the point-after, Texas led, 7-0. According to the Longhorn legend, it happened exactly as Jack had predicted.

In many ways, the game evolved to be similar in style and substance to the Gipper game. Like Army in 1928, Notre Dame flubbed more than one chance to tie or win the game. As it was the opening game of the season in a new system, the Irish could not sync the blocking schemes with the backfield action. Their best chance to tie the game came when the Horns' Buster Baebel, standing on the Texas nine yard line, muffed a catch of a Notre Dame punt. The Irish recovered, and Melinkovich bulled through the Longhorns on a fourth-and-inches run, but Wayne Millner missed the tying point-after. With the clock running down, both Notre Dame and Texas failed to capitalize on other scoring opportunities deep in their opponent's territory. After the game ended in a 7-6 nail-biter, stunned Notre Dame fans milled about the stadium in disbelief.

Jack had disdained his reserves to shoot the works on his core players. As a consequence of the strategy, only fifteen Longhorns contributed to the victory. The most important Longhorn, Bohn Hilliard, carried the ball twenty-five times and played defense the entire game. Across the field on Layden's sideline, it was a different story altogether. In the loss, Layden activated every one of his blue-clad Irish with each player having a role in the game. For this tactic, Layden was heavily criticized.

After his substitution strategy was blamed for the loss, Layden responded, "A coach can only get to know what his players can do by letting them play. Furthermore, I always felt that a coach owes it to his team to let as many people play as possible. Nobody wants to practice all week and then spend the game on the bench."

For once, Jack was speechless. Supposedly, he failed to meet the equally dapper Elmer Layden at midfield to shake his hand. Jack was too stunned.

The fourth horseman walked across the field to find the Gipper legend sitting on his bench with his head in his hands mumbling, "We did it. We did it. We really did it."

Avenged was the rejection Jack had suffered in 1932, and again in 1934. Unable to resist a final jab at the university's choice of Layden, Jack topped the win with a singular sharp comment regarding the game's outcome. "Notre Dame looked pretty terrible, but they ought to have a good ball team before the year is out," Jack remarked to the Austin press.

Attorney Jack Chevigny was masterful in his use of the language. "Notre Dame looked pretty terrible," was a slap directed at the hiring of Elmer Layden, an accomplished gentleman coach with a proven record. The conditional clause, "…but they ought to have a good ball team before the year is out," was meant as a condescending remark.

Jack loved Notre Dame beyond measure. He was a true Notre Damer. Now, the relationship had come full circle. The French knight had pillaged his homeland, his birthplace.

When the team's train arrived back in Austin on the following Tuesday at 7:00 a.m., Governor-elect James Allred and half of the city of Austin was present to meet the team. For Jack, the celebration was over by the time the reserved Pullman rolled to a stop. He had less than four days to prepare his team for Oklahoma.

On Wednesday, Jack put the team through a series of full contact drills designed to sharpen the passing game. The Horns still lacked a quarterback who could get the ball to Gray. It was the week of the state fair game in Dallas. While Oklahoma newspapers announced that Charles "Pretty Boy" Floyd was officially a suspect in the June 17, 1933, machine gun slaying of four Kansas City lawmen, most Texas newspapers focused on the festive opportunity of the state fair.

Dozens of papers advertised a special rate for a roundtrip train ticket to the fair. Longhorn fans from Galveston could purchase a weekend roundtrip coach ticket to Dallas for $5.87. First class tickets went for $11.75.

The fans that made the trip should have brought their umbrellas. A terrific rainstorm flooded the stadium aisles. Drenched in the torrential second-half downpour, the Oklahoma University (OU) Sooners were failing to weather the storm. Swamped by Irvin Gilbreath's two second-quarter touchdowns, a lack of production on the part of the Sooners' stagnant offense opened the floodgates on their porous defense. Accumulating a total of eighteen first downs, Texas tromped Oklahoma before an estimated count of twenty-one thousand wet souls. With the exception of some fists thrown the way of Jack Gray, the Sooners offered little resistance to the Horns' rushing attack.

Everything had gone the Horns' way. Jack started the game with his reserves, but when the game stalled in a scoreless tug-of-war during the second quarter, he inserted his prime lineup. At that point, Gilbreath's heroics thrilled those Orangebloods clustered under the wet newspapers and umbrellas. By the second half, the region of North Texas known as Tornado Alley rumbled as sheets of rain obscured the action on the field. Players of both teams seemed to dissolve into an anonymous mud-caked mob.

In the third quarter, an even more sinister cloud darkened the Horns sideline after Bohn Hilliard left the game with a rib injury. Though Hilliard's injury was judged to be minor, Jack elected to keep him out for the remainder of the game. In addition to handling the place-kicking duty for the Horns, Hilliard was an important part of the revamped Longhorn passing attack, his arm contributing to a pair of Gilbreath's three scores.

The 19-0 shutout provided little joy to the tired Horns. As an ailing Hilliard was helped to his seat, the mood of the team boarding the train to Austin was as dark as the Dallas storm clouds. A more thorough examination of Hilliard revealed the possibility of a torn hip ligament. The team doctor's diagnosis implied Bohn Hilliard would be able to contribute little of his immense talent to the Longhorns' future contests.

Despite the bad news, Jack and the team stood at a perfect 3-0. More than one national poll had the Horns at the precipice of the number one ranking. One more victory and Jack's boys would be standing atop the summit of college football. As Governor-elect Allred anticipated, the eyes of the entire country were upon the Texas Longhorns. Next was a non-conference trial in Austin. The opponent: Centenary of Shreveport, Louisiana.

Founded in 1825 in the village of Jackson, Centenary is the oldest institution of higher learning in Louisiana. Long after the college moved north to Shreveport, independent funding allowed for the establishment of a highly successful football program. Competing with programs such as Arkansas, Southern Methodist, Baylor, Iowa, Texas A&M, and Texas from 1930 to 1933, Centenary's win-loss record was 29-6-6. The Gentlemen of Centenary were anything but gentle. They had not lost a game to a Southwest Conference opponent in three years.

From the week's outset, Bevo sensed bad omens. Hilliard was confirmed as out for the Centenary game. Worse than the news of Hilliard's status, sports columns had already begun to tout the match-up between Rice and Texas. An Associated Press wire reported that the Rice game was a sellout with only a few temporary end zone bleacher seats available. And those seats were expected to sellout by noon the following day, ten days before game day. For the contest that would likely determine the Southwest Conference champion, the Owls' fifteen-thousand-seat stadium would overflow to standing room only. Jack attempted to focus the Horns' energy onto the visiting Gents, telling the press, "I regard Centenary as a very formidable foe, despite the false idea in some quarters that the Gents will be nothing more than a set up. Back in 1932 it will be recalled Centenary surprised Texas with a 12-6 victory. While we will do our utmost to prevent such an occurrence, I realize it will take alert, head-up football to turn the trick."

On the same day that President Roosevelt ordered Secretary of the Interior Harold Ickes and Federal Relief Administrator Harry Hopkins to keep financially strapped school districts in Texas open at the federal government's expense, the city of Austin officially proclaimed October 20, 1934 as *Jack Chevigny Day.*

Hitching his political wagon to Jack's soaring popularity, Mayor Tom Miller, in an open letter inviting nearby communities to the game wrote,

> "The Texas University has won three very important football games this year in the victories over Texas Tech, Notre Dame, and Oklahoma University. This coming Saturday, October 20th, Texas will play Centenary College, and in honor of Jack Chevigny, the successful coach of our University, Austin and the people of Central Texas are setting aside this day as 'Chevigny Day.' As Mayor of the City of Austin, I realize that the Texas victory over Notre Dame has increased the presence of the state of Texas, not only in athletics but has also heightened our standing in every way. I will appreciate greatly your doing everything possible to proclaim 'Chevigny Day' in Austin by urging your people to come to Austin and see the game as appreciation of the team can be best shown by a large attendance…"

Predicted to play a larger role in the offense, Stephenville's Hugh Wolfe practiced in tandem with the hero of the OU game, Irvin Gilbreath of Wellington. It was the best plan Jack could muster as he juggled the lineup in an attempt to replace Hilliard's firepower. After the win at Notre Dame and the short turnaround against Oklahoma, the Longhorns had fallen predictably flat by Thursday's practice. By Friday, October 19, the day before the game, several newspapers across the state were predicting a Centenary upset victory. The good dope was that Texas wasn't in the right frame of mind for the game. Neither were they the same team without Hilliard.

As Longhorn fans continued to look past the Gents to Rice Institute, the undisputed top-ranked team in the nation, according to the prestigious Dickenson system, their lack of regard for Centenary resulted in poor ticket sales for the Longhorns' first home game. Less than ten thousand tickets were pre-sold.

Austin's mild weather provided a gorgeous day for a parade and a football game. Enhancing the pre-game distraction, *Jack Chevigny Day* festivities opened on the morning of the game with the mayor leading a parade of floats, the Longhorn marching band, fraternities, and sororities before Jack and thousands of students and alumni. Standing in review, Jack may have wondered if Centenary had scheduled the morning's activities. The pre-game activities could not have been designed as a better distraction.

Winning the coin toss, Jack Gray elected to receive and the Horns' shock troops took the field. Failing to advance the ball, Texas was forced to punt into the wind. Centenary took over, pushing the ball to the Texas thirty-one yard line behind the running of Buddy Parker. At that point, Jack inserted his regulars who promptly repelled the Gents' advance. Penalties and punts reflected the frustration of both teams with the Longhorns spending the entire second quarter at the brink of disaster as the Gents advanced close to the Texas red zone on several occasions. At halftime, the game was scoreless.

Texas opened the second half with a series of miscues. After a series of punts, the Longhorns lost the ball on a fumble that Centenary returned to the Texas twenty-one yard line. When Jack Gray blocked a Centenary twenty-three-yard field goal attempt, the Gents' wasted their fourth scoring opportunity of the day.

The day's cliffhanger came when Hugh Wolfe appeared to cross the goal line as he juggled the handoff. When the ball squirted loose, players from both teams dove into the end zone in a mad scramble. Peeling the players from the pile, the referee found Hugh Wolfe to be in possession of the ball and awarded Texas the first score of the day.

The game seemed in hand after another empty Centenary possession was followed by a slightly productive Longhorn offensive series. Then calamity lined up to punt for Texas.

Timing his charge, Centenary's Conway Baker pinched through the protection. After the punt careened off his hands, Baker continued up field and scooped the ball from the Memorial Stadium turf. Securing his own blocked punt, Baker sprinted untouched to the Longhorn end zone.

On the point-after attempt, Centenary's kicker suffered the same misfire that Texas had experienced earlier. The point-after failed, and the game remained tied at 6-6.

After Centenary's score, Chevigny's boys felt as if their backs were against the wall. A tie was a Centenary victory; more precisely, a tie was a Longhorn loss. The Horns responded to the Centenary score with a flurry of desperation passes, and with the game drawing to a close, desperation spelled disaster after the Gents' Pug Crowther intercepted a Buster Jurecka pass.

Crowther's interception return brought the ball to Longhorn eighteen yard line with time left for the Gents. Advancing to the Texas seven yard line, Centenary elected to kick a field goal for the win. Despite suffering an earlier blocked field goal and a later blocked extra-point, Buddy Parker pierced the uprights with less than a minute left on the clock. Maintaining its three-year unbeaten streak against Southwest Conference opponents, Centenary defeated Texas, 9-6.

With their glass slippers shattered, the orange-on-orange Horns congratulated the white-jerseyed Gents and shuffled back to their Memorial Stadium locker room. Jack told the team that they had only a few hours to sulk. In Houston, the undefeated Rice Owls awaited.

Other than a loss of their national title hopes, Texas had lost little prestige in the game. Centenary was a known giant killer, a habitual thorn in the paw of the Southwest Conference. On Monday, the press rebooted the hype machine. Boldly printed headlines hailed the upcoming occasion of the meeting between Rice and Texas.

Rice's undefeated season with wins over Loyola, Purdue, SMU, and Creighton had earned the Owls the respect of the Southwest Conference. Tying Senator Huey P. Long's powerful Louisiana State squad solidified their position as a national power.

Remembered as the first super fan of the Louisiana State University (LSU) Tigers, Long was more than a natural showman. Reared in the backward piney woods of Winnfield, Louisiana, he was a self-made man, self-educated. After stumping his way to the governor's mansion with his political promises to represent the poor, Governor Long siphoned the excesses of the offshore oil exploration companies and utility companies, and gave the money back to the people of Louisiana in the form of paved roads, bridges, free textbooks for their children, and a modern state police force. Evolving into a dangerous demagogue, Huey consolidated his power in the manner of a European dictator, turning Louisiana into his own personal banana republic. Every school teacher and state employee were required to sign an oath of allegiance to Long, their loyalty measured in the form a payroll deduction, which funded future Long political campaigns.

Prior to some LSU away-games, Senator Long could be seen leading the Tiger band from the train station to the stadium. Most of the train tickets were purchased by Long and dispensed to the students, so they could cheer on their Tigers. On the sideline at the games, it wasn't uncommon to see him throwing tantrums. More times than not, Senator Long would suggest plays and strategies the coach could not refuse. With first right to the locker room speeches proprietary to Long, it was said that in a battle of speeches, an inebriated Long would have shamed the great Rockne. Huey's best football speeches were said to have been made when he was drunk.

The media followed Long's antics at every LSU game. Disturbed over the upset tie suffered in Houston, the Kingfish had some things to say about the game.

Implying there were some Rice shenanigans in maintaining the condition of the turf at Rice Stadium, the Democratic frontrunner to challenge FDR in 1936 said, "That game should never have been played! If I'd a-been there, it wouldn't a-been, either. Why the grass on that field was three feet high…"

Granted, Jack stubbed his toe against the Gents, but the fervor of the impending contest for the Southwest Conference title eased the pain. Though everyone agreed the upset loss to the Gents cost the Horns a chance to be named national champions, the Southwest Conference title wasn't something mythical; it was concrete and indisputable. Whereas the national title would be awarded through a disputable rating system, the Southwest Conference title would be won on the field. If the Steers were to win at Rice, they would gain the pole position in the race for the Southwest Conference championship.

Wednesday before the match with Texas, barred gates locked out reporters and onlookers as Coach Jimmy Kitts installed four new plays and honed his team's defensive game plan against the expected return of Bohn Hilliard. Kitts remarked that he wished the Horns had beaten Centenary. "I figure the loss to Centenary will make Texas about twice as tough when we play the Longhorns," Kitts quipped.

In Austin, Jack offered no definitive statement as to Hilliard's condition; however, Austin reporters indicated that the Horns' star halfback was seen going through a light workout in track sweats on Tuesday. Avoiding hysterics, Jack chose to calmly counsel his team. The Steers were to forget the Centenary loss, focus on Rice. Wednesday, he put the team through a "lively scrimmage."

In an unusual public statement to the gamblers, Jack set the betting odds at 4-1 in favor of the Owls. Bohn Hilliard had been unable to bounce back from the hip injury; the Longhorns confronted what Jack called the "battle of the century" without their superstar leader. A pile of orange money was dropped after the Centenary upset. In going public with his take on the odds, Jack wanted to make clear the risk that his big money boosters were taking if they chose to root with their wallets.

Thursday, Jack arrived at the Rice Hotel in Houston to speak before a civic organization alongside Rice coach Jimmy Kitts. Tickets were fifty cents, and the event was sold out. Kitts's demeanor differed from that of the stern taskmaster Jack Chevigny. A precise tactician with little empathy for anything less than a player's maximum effort, Jack was cut straight from the cloth of Rockne's knickers. When he sensed a lack of intensity on the practice field, Jack's sharp tongue diced the offending players into small bits of quivering attentiveness. Kitts was known for his good humor, especially on the practice field. At Rice, sportswriters often witnessed an ongoing series of witty exchanges and wisecracks between the players and coaches. Although the coaches exhibited different coaching styles, both coaches enjoyed the total devotion of their players.

By Friday, Rice Institute athletics manager Doctor Gaylord Johnson was taking considerable heat regarding to the stadium's small seating capacity. In response, the Rice administration approved statewide broadcasting of the game. Meanwhile, Johnson sweated the details of attempting to squeeze an overflow of twenty thousand fans into the stadium.

On Saturday, the game-time temperature was a sweltering 90°. Jack's thirty-four Longhorns readied themselves to ground the Owls. After a week of practice during which Tim Moynihan emphasized hard line charges, and Marty Karow emphasized ball security with the running backs, Jack felt the staff had done all it could do.

Newspapers across the state devoted entire columns to the Hilliard effect. It was generally accepted that the Horns had not much of a chance without the senior running back.

At Rice, if not for the oblivion delivered upon the Burnt Orange in a scant fifty seconds, Texas would have again shocked the football world. Along with hundreds of boys who viewed the game from atop the stadium fences, the official gate of seventeen thousand ticket holders saw the Steers alternating field position with the Owls for more than three quarters. Trailing by only one point with five minutes to play, Buster Jurecka dropped back to pass from his own goal line and threw a dart to the open Jimmy Hadlock. His reception put the Horns in scoring position at the Rice eleven yard line. After three line plunges, the Horns faced a fourth-and-two at the three yard line. Jack inserted Hilliard to kick the field goal. Despite kicking from a nasty angle, the All-American lived up to his press clippings and split the uprights.

Throughout the press box, typewriter keys clattered as reporters composed their leads detailing Hilliard's heroics. But just as most writers struck the "d" key for Hilliard's name, Rice erupted.

With two minutes left, Rice controlled the ball at its own twenty-five yard line. Texas owned the lead, 9-7.

Positioned in the Texas four-man box secondary were three sophomores. Having the game of his life at quarterback, the left-handed Bill Wallace dropped back to pass to big Ray Smith, an Owl reserve player who was lumbering down the sideline. Wallace lofted the ball and in his angle to overlap the underneath coverage zone and break up the pass, the Texas safety broke too flat. Seventy-five yards later, Smith planted the ball in the end zone for the score. With less than two minutes to play in the game, Rice led, 13-9. Three plays later, the Owls returned a twenty-eight yard interception to make the final score, 20-9.

Texas had had its chances, but lacking the Hilliard punch, the Horn running game was impotent once the offense moved inside the Owl red zone.

Jack received immediate criticism for his decision to implement the box secondary alignment. He retorted, "It wasn't the scheme; it was the inexperience of our defensive backs that cost us."

On the short train ride back to Austin, Jack paused to reflect. If his team were to regain their confidence, they would need a win. Along with Bohn Hilliard's tendon, the heart of the team had been torn. They would have to fight harder if they were to overcome the loss of his rushing production. The following Saturday, the occasion of the SMU Mustangs' visit to Memorial Stadium, would be the Longhorns' final opportunity to break the Hilliard curse. If they failed, their year would collapse into a miserable repeat of Clyde Littlefield's last season.

Southern Methodist University was known for its aerial circus attack. Knowing SMU's reputation, the miserable memory of the defensive secondary's performance at Rice sent a chill through Longhorn coaching staff.

Several thousand Mustang fans planned to attend the game at Memorial Stadium. In preparation for the big game, a special roundtrip train with a dining car and a separate baggage car was made available for the SMU faithful. Scheduled to leave Dallas at 7:30 a.m., Southern Methodist fans would arrive in time for the game and return at midnight. Tickets for the junket were pricey, $3.50, but SMU enthusiasts, being the wealthiest fans of the SWC, could have afforded an even higher price.

Near the SMU campus, a sad incident affected the revelry of a Dallas Halloween night when Mustang mascot, Peruna, wandered into traffic and was killed. The popular Shetland pony, so small it could fit in the back seat of a cab, escaped its stall after returning with the team from New York on Tuesday. Campus officials suspected that the pony's death was a prank gone wrong.

In Austin on Friday, Bohn Hilliard was seen in full practice gear as if he were planning to play against SMU. Meanwhile, Jack Gray suffered from a seriously bruised leg; he would be out against the Ponies. Speaking to the area papers, Jack Chevigny reported his team ready for the SMU arsenal of trickery, which included the infamous SMU unwinding huddle. On Friday night, thousands of Texas fans participated in a "Faith" pep rally complete with fireworks. Approximately twenty thousand Orangebloods showed their faith in Jack and the Horns by purchasing tickets to the game.

Unlike the Texas fans, most of the press had little faith in the Horns. The snide Notre Dame jabs had already appeared in print. Regarding the priorities of Texans, Associated Press sportswriter Bill Parker, in an unsubtle message to Jack commented, "Texas (fans) had rather win this game than beat Notre Dame twice a year…"

The previous week in New York, SMU had executed its unheralded rushing attack to perfection against Fordham, but against the Horns the plan backfired. The Ponies fumbled on just their third play from scrimmage. Texas recovered. Jimmy Hadlock attempted to cap a thirty-three-yard drive with a one-yard touchdown plunge, but the ball was knocked loose. Luckily, guard Joe Smartt snatched the ball and pushed over the end line for the Texas score. With the successful point-after, the score was Texas 7, Southern Methodist 0.

SMU spent the remainder of the half, attempting to flank the Longhorns' perimeter and stretch the defensive pass coverage zones. The result was an uninspired flailing of bodies near the middle of the field with nothing to show for their efforts. Finally, the Ponies struck pay dirt on a spinner play over right tackle. The point-after tied the game at 7-7.

The Horns didn't want to settle for a tie. From his own fifteen yard line, Hilliard launched a wobbly fifty-five-yard pass to Jimmy Hadlock. Two SMU players went for the interception. Memorial Stadium shook when Hadlock wrestled the ball from them and broke free for the end zone. Unbelievably, just as he was about to break past the last defender to score the winning touchdown, a Mustang punched the ball from Hadlock's grasp. In a stumbling attempt to scoop the ball, Hadlock fell at the SMU twenty yard line. With the Horns awarded the ball for one last play, Hilliard's last gasp pass to Phil Sanger sailed incomplete over the back line. In tying one of the toughest teams in the Southwest Conference, Jack's Steers had regained some of their confidence, but they had wanted more.

Bohn Hilliard's return to the field confirmed everyone's suspicion that his presence was the key element to solving the team's chemistry problem. The following week, a faltering Baylor Bear squad would travel south from Waco to meet the Horns. Though managing only two wins against non-conference opponents, Baylor had lost narrowly to Texas Tech, Arkansas, and Texas A&M. Their largest margin of loss was seven points at Arkansas.

Apprehensive of the strong arm of Baylor's Joe Jack Pearce and in hope of preventing a fatal coverage error like that suffered in the Rice game, Jack drilled his secondary relentlessly against the pass. The Baylor contingent, with their black bear mascot in tow, arrived in Austin on Friday. The inside dope was that Baylor, with its anemic running game, would pull out all stops in an airborne attack on Texas.

*Saturday, November 10, 1934.* Baylor kicked off. Buster Baebel returned the Bears' opening kickoff to the forty-three yard line. After the Texas punt pinned Baylor on their fourteen, the Bears failed to move the ball. Soon after taking possession near midfield, the Horns stampeded the Baylor defense with Bohn Hilliard slashing off right tackle for a thirty-seven-yard gain. After a Hugh Wolfe carry, Bill Pitzer attempted to take the ball over the goal line where he was hit hard by Baylor's Joe Jack Pierce. Pitzer's fumble was recovered by Baylor at the three yard line, ending the Texas drive.

After Baylor punted from their own end zone, Pitzer redeemed himself when he dashed thirty-nine yards for the Horns' first score. Hilliard added the point-after and Texas led, 7-0.

Following the coordinated execution of a series of seven consecutive plays in which Bohn Hilliard played the primary role as a ball carrier, passer, or kicker, the Longhorns increased their lead to 13-0. As the Orangebloods expected, Texas was having its way with the Baylor defense.

In the second quarter, Baylor's Aubrey Springer put the Bears on the board with an eighteen-yard touchdown reception. The extra point was missed.

Jack grimaced when a bone-jarring tackle sent Hilliard limping to the sideline. He sent Jake Verde in to relieve the stunned Hilliard. With Hilliard out, Baylor immediately picked Verde's first pass to regain possession of the ball on the Baylor forty-five yard line. Now enjoying some momentum, Baylor attempted to march the ball downfield, but time ran out on the Baptists' revival. The Longhorns left the field holding a 13-6 cushion.

Opening the second half, it was Hilliard and Baebel working in tandem to bring the ball down to the Bears' twenty-two. After two more Hilliard runs and an attempt by Hugh Wolfe to break the plane of the goal line, Wolfe bounced off left tackle for the touchdown. Texas led, 19-6.

Later in the game, Hubert "Buster" Jurecka sealed the win with a twenty-one-yard burst to pay dirt. In taming the Bears, Jack's Steers had rampaged for more than three hundred yards of offense, most of it accomplished on the ground.

For the Horns, it was a landslide victory credited to Bohn Hilliard's rejuvenating presence on offense and defense. Given Hilliard's performance, few Longhorn fans couldn't help but think of what might have been two weeks earlier at Rice. If Hilliard had been available in the secondary when Rice went deep for the go-ahead score, the Horns would have been standing undefeated atop the conference standings.

Wishes couldn't change history; the Texas Burnt Orange would have to settle for trying to finish strong in the conference race. In Fort Worth, the Horned Frogs from Texas Christian were winning. If a team's performance against a common opponent provided a reliable guess as to the outcome of the competition, the Horn's back would be to the wall against TCU. Earlier that season, the Horned Frogs had destroyed Baylor 34-12.

Contrary to its name, the Texas horned frog is a lizard, not a frog. The odd-looking creature's primary mechanism of defense is its ability to shoot blood from its eyelid into the face of a threat.

Even with Hilliard, the Texas Longhorns faced a bloody battle against the 6-2 Texas Christian squad. Cocked and ready to avenge the blowout loss they had suffered at the hands of TCU during the previous year, the Texas Longhorns looked forward to returning to Fort Worth.

Meanwhile, Texas Christian's fuel for victory was enhanced with its own motivational additive. Texas would serve as the Horned Frogs' homecoming date. If needed, Dutch Meyer's Frogs would spit blood from their own eyelids.

Supported by a Texas-sized offensive line, the largest in the Southwest Conference, sophomore Sammy Baugh led a purple-clad offense that combined a deft passing game with a bruising running game. The high school teammate of Texas's Ney Sheridan was starting in his first year of eligibility and quickly becoming known as a passing phenom.

Printing that the first two periods of the game were "insane football," the *San Antonio Express* reported the game to be "crammed with mad passing, crushing power plays, fatal fumbles, and numerous injuries." Another paper called the game "…a rough and tumble affair throughout. As it ended, a Texas player tried to punch umpire Jack Mahan, but Coach Chevigny pushed him away and shook hands with the official."

It was the Horns, not the blood-spitting Horned Frogs, who drew first blood in the game. Midway through the first quarter, Stephenville's Hugh Wolfe gored TCU with a sixty-four-yard touchdown run. Hilliard's point-after gave the Horns a 7-0 lead.

Baugh responded by zipping passes downfield, bringing the Horned Frogs down to the Texas twenty-seven yard line, and with the game quickly disintegrating into a slugfest, Texas was hit with a personal foul that put the Frogs at the Longhorn fifteen with a fresh series of downs. Just a few plays later in the second quarter, Taldon Manton passed to an open Will Walls for the Frog touchdown, but Manton missed the always critical point-after. Texas held on to a fragile 7-6 lead.

After Irvin Gilbreath returned the Frogs' kickoff to the Texas thirty yard line, Gilbreath attempted to slant outside, but Wilson Grosclose ripped the ball from his grasp, and Taldon Manton recovered for Texas Christian. From there, Sammy Baugh went back to work, hitting Walter Roach in the flat. Snagging the ball with one hand, Roach rambled twenty-nine yards for the TCU score. Taldon Manton again misfired on the point-after, but the Frogs were now on the top side of the board with a 13-7 lead.

The remaining minutes of the second quarter allowed each team to display the best of its offensive arsenal. At halftime, the score remained 13-7 in favor of the Horned Frogs.

Dampening the homecoming crowd's enthusiasm, Texas opened the third quarter with a methodical march seventy-one yards for the tying score. Wolfe's touchdown plunge from the one, and Hilliard's point-after provided Jack with a one-point lead over Leo "Dutch" Meyer and the Frogs. With the game growing more physical with each snap, Tim Moynihan's crew of Coates, Smartt, and Small dissected the Frog defensive line. A Bohn Hilliard touchdown run then insured the Longhorn's advantage. With the missed extra-point, the Longhorns led, 20-7. Throughout the rest of the fourth quarter, Sammy Baugh attempted to piecemeal the Horns' pass defense with his brown leather spirals, but Hilliard's leadership held the young group together. In another thrilling contest, perhaps the best of the SWC season, the Longhorns had scolded their critics and prevailed.

Out of the conference race but in it for pride, a group of highly-motivated Chevigny men headed southward in their Pullman sleeper. On

Monday, their trail boss would map a course to Fayetteville, Arkansas, and a meeting with the Razorbacks.

Pleased with the execution of his offense and defense against TCU, Jack decided to put the boys through two standard workouts only. On Monday, he sped the team through a practice designed to work out the kinks and reinforce the systematic rhythm of the Notre Dame shift. As did most teams of the era, the Horns scheduled their long distance travel on Tuesday. Once in Fayetteville, Jack put the team through just one more workout before standing down in a chalk-and-walk mode for Saturday. Jack's days as a Notre Dame Rambler had taught him long train rides were leg killers.

The Hogs had never defeated Texas in Fayetteville. In fourteen previous meetings since 1894, Arkansas had beaten Texas only once. That win came in a 20-6 victory over Clyde Littlefield's Horns in 1933. As far as the Porker fans were concerned, it was time for breaking free of tradition.

In support of the team, ninety-six Fayetteville businesses agreed to close on game day from 2:00 to 4:00 p.m. Except for drugstores and gas stations, practically every business would be shuttered during the game.

No sooner had Jack and the team arrived at their hotel than they were surrounded by rabid Razorback students calling the hogs.

To anyone but the Razorback fan, the ineffable hog call is an egregious assault on the human ear. A tradition that began in the 1920s, the cheer has an expanding dimension of sound rivaled only by the archangel's trumpet. It is easily the most identifiable and spirited cheer in all of college sports.

Pasted on page four of the *Fayetteville Daily Democrat* was a large photo of Irvin Gilbreath. The photo's title read, ARKANSAS MUST STOP HIM. In the subtitle was the name in bold print, **IRVIN 'DUKE' GILBREATH.**

News of Irvin's three-touchdown performance against Oklahoma had reached Fayetteville.

Despite the backing of the area merchants and the spirit of the *Fayetteville Democrat* sportswriters, only about three thousand five hundred of the expected ten thousand showed up to call the hogs. *The Democrat* expressed its disappointment with the turnout in Saturday's evening edition.

A battered Arkansas squad took the field. Several key players were out for the season.

Taking up where they left off against TCU, the Longhorns put together a long opening drive covering seventy-eight yards. Marked by the dominating offensive line play of Joe Smartt and Jack Collins, the drive highlighted the running ability of Hilliard, Gilbreath, and Pitzer. Closing out the punishing Horn assault, Gilbreath capped the scoring drive with a twenty-three-yard reception of a Bohn Hilliard pass. With Hilliard's point-after, the Horns led 7-0 in the first quarter.

In the second quarter, a Bill Pitzer punt to the thirty-nine yard line couldn't dig the Horns out of the hole, and four plays later, Porker senior Clark Jordan passed to senior Elvin Geiser for a score. Geiser's point-after attempt was wide, but the Razorbacks were on the board.

After an exchange of possessions, the Horn defense was pinned near their end zone where they held the Razorbacks on a goal line stand. Pitzer was again challenged to punt the Horns out of trouble. On this opportunity, Pitzer responded to the challenge and got all of it, blasting the ball out to the Arkansas forty yard line.

Owning the momentum and cheered by the three thousand five hundred Arkansas fanatics roaring "Wooooooooooo, Pig! Sooie!" the Razorbacks charged. Caught flat-footed, the troubled Texas secondary relinquished another quick score when Herman Ray flipped a thirty-two yard scoring toss to Paul Rucker. Senior Ralph LaForge missed the extra point, but the Razorbacks were on top by a score of 12-7 as the halftime gun fired.

In the second half, the Razorbacks charged again when Ralph LaForge burst through the Longhorn middle for a forty-yard gain. Eventually held in check by the Longhorn defense, the Razorbacks chanced a poorly conceived thirty-yard field goal. Slicing off the right and partially blocked, the kick had no chance. Texas gained possession at the twenty.

With the game on the line and the box offense locked down, the Horns called on Jack Gray. Two consecutive passes to Gray put the Hogs on their heels. Then Gray hauled in an eighteen-yard touchdown pass from Buster Jurecka. Hugh Wolfe attempted the extra point, but missed. Texas led, 13-12.

Early in the fourth, Arkansas attempted to answer with a long, forty-seven-yard field goal from an angle, but the low kick barely cleared the line of scrimmage. Then Hilliard took over. Carrying the ball exclusively on a drive, which started from the Horns' thirty-seven, the All-American clinched the game with a thirty-eight-yard touchdown run. Fatigued, the Razorbacks couldn't answer. With the 19-12 final score, the Texas win streak continued at Fayetteville.

Idle the previous week, rival Texas A&M would come to Austin for Thanksgiving, and though the Maroon and White held a 2-6-1 record, Jack knew that the Aggies were no turkeys. More than twenty thousand were expected for Thursday's Thanksgiving Day battle. For the Aggies, it was the most important game of the season, and a Rice loss to TCU had given the Horns new life in the conference race. This game could make or break the season for either club.

Leading up to the event would be the Longhorn frosh taking on the Aggie frosh on Wednesday afternoon. Following the freshman game, the

Aggie Corps of Cadets planned to conduct yell practice at the annual bonfire. Scheduled to leave College Station on Wednesday, the varsity Aggies would spend the night in Taylor, Texas. After eleven days of rest, the Aggies wouldn't need much of a good night's sleep. Lacking only one offensive threat, Bill Couser, the boys from College Station were primed for their final test. Coach Homer Norton declared 1934 to be a year that the visiting team takes home a win. With the win, Norton, in his rookie year at A&M, could salvage a wrecked season.

In Austin, tens of thousands of eyes were on Waco. If a Longhorn win combined with a Rice loss at Baylor, the Longhorns would win the Southwest Conference championship. For Longhorn fans, the one moment of distraction from the Baylor-Rice topic would have been the Aggie Cadet Corps's traditional march from their train to Memorial Stadium. One of the most impressive sights in college football, the Texas A&M Cadet Corps's military procession gave goose bumps to even the most orange-blooded Texas fan.

On game day, Aggie fans held optimism that Texas's slashing run game would be slowed by the twenty-four hours of rain that had soaked Memorial Stadium's playing surface.

In addition to Bohn Hilliard, both Jack Gray and Phil Sanger were slated to play their last collegiate game. Coach Chevigny had commented more than once that both Gray and Sanger were the greatest ends he had coached.

As the Aggies teed it up, a strong north wind skirted through Memorial Stadium. Because of it, neither Jack nor Homer Norton could expect any consistency from their kicking game.

Texas's running game threatened first, pushing the Aggies back to their three yard line, but the Aggies held and took over on downs. Early in the second quarter, Texas A&M attempted to take advantage of the wind at their back by quick-kicking on second down. With the Maroon punter aligned deep in his end zone, the Aggie's punt moved the ball out to the Aggie forty-five yard line. With the Steers' offense moving against a strong wind, Homer Norton's boys loaded up against the run.

Bohn Hilliard crossed the Aggies with a surprise pass to Bill Pitzer, the completion moving the ball inside of the Aggie fourteen yard line. Texas was again in business. From there it was Wolf; then Hilliard; then Wolfe from one foot out. Hilliard missed the try for the extra point, and the Horns led by six.

Late in the fourth quarter, the Texas run attack wore down the Aggie front. A Hilliard pass to Phil Sanger finished the Aggies. Hilliard tacked on the extra point as the Texas lead increased to the final count of 13-0.

It was a sloppy affair. Homer Norton's passing game failed to show up for the game. Overall, it was a disappointing finish to one of the gloomiest years in Aggie football history.

The Memorial Stadium crowd gave Charley Coates and Bohn Hilliard a standing ovation. With tears in their eyes, all of the Longhorn seniors came together as the band played "The Eyes of Texas."

Jack Chevigny had returned respect to the program and brought the Horns to the foot of the Southwest Conference throne. To learn of their final conference standing, the Longhorns had to wait until Saturday and the Rice-Baylor game. Hanging in the balance of that contest was a conference crown for Jack's inaugural squad at Texas.

# CHAPTER FIFTEEN

## *An Assassin's Bullet*

No one expected Baylor to beat Rice, but that didn't mean Baylor couldn't pull off the upset. As the Horns found out against Centenary, upsets are a part of the pageantry of football.

The Bears had endured a less than stellar 3-6 record, but their average margin of defeat against Southwest Conference opponents was just seven points a game. On any given Saturday, the Bears could hang tough with the Owls. With Rice traveling to Waco, anything could happen. Lighting a votive candle that Saturday, Jack prayed it would.

An estimated crowd of eight thousand, almost half of them Rice supporters, turned out for the game. Even with the small crowd, the atmosphere was unexpectedly tense, especially for the Owls' followers. Rice fans sat on the edge of their seats as Baylor held the Owls scoreless for the first period. But after a Bill Wallace touchdown pass put Rice on the board, the Bears met their Old Yeller. Wounded with their confidence shaken, the shaky Baylor squad collapsed. Soon after Wallace's score, the Owls were in flight to a 32-0 rout of the hapless Bears.

↔

Hilliard's third consecutive All-Southwest Conference nomination and eventual selection to play in the East-West All-Star game confirmed what everyone in Texas already knew. Losing Hilliard cost the Longhorns the gold ring.

In spite of Texas failing to win the conference crown, most of the state realized how close the Longhorns had come to a national ranking and having the eyes of a nation thrust upon them. Jack was the toast of the town. His New Deal for Texas football had been delivered.

Given Jack's charisma, the sky would be the limit in recruiting the Class of 1939. If Jack could only refill the coffer with enough supporting talent to assist the returning Hugh Wolfe and Irvin Gilbreath, the Steers would get another opportunity to claim the SWC title.

After the season, Jack's boys returned triumphantly home to parties and parades. Sealy greeted Buster Baebel with newspaper headlines and cheering relatives, while Port Arthur heralded Bohn Hilliard's homecoming as if he were Caesar returning from Munda. Hugh Wolfe would go home to a grand Christmas in Stephenville. He had dreamed of playing for Notre Dame, and he returned home as the star of the Horns' victory over his beloved Irish.

On December 29, 1935, *Salt Lake City Tribune* subscribers read of a football coach receiving an expensive car for winning "six football games." To a lot of the readers who lived with no indoor plumbing, it was puzzling as to how winning a few silly games could result in such an incredible dividend.

The article was in error; Jack had won seven games, not six. And while the car he received was of the Cadillac family, it was only a nephew of the Cadillac, the newly designed 1934 LaSalle.

←→

A companion car of the Cadillac, the LaSalle was scheduled to be discontinued in 1934. Given the declining fortunes of the industry, several other competing brands had already dropped their mid-high companion car lines. At General Motors (GM), the sales of the once popular LaSalle line dropped to a record low.

When the legendary Harley Earl toured Europe to review the latest European auto styles, designer-artist Jules Agramonte, in a last ditch effort to save the LaSalle name, developed a set of drawings and concept models to present to Earl upon his return. Agramonte's artwork was so striking; it inspired Harley Earl's collaboration in bringing Agramonte's design to market.

Ordering a quick briefing, Harley Earl showed General Motors' managers the Agramonte models and made just one statement. "Gentlemen, if you decide to discontinue the LaSalle, this is the car you are not going to build."

Harley Earl's presentation floored the bookkeepers and executives. Speechless, management acquiesced to continuing the line for 1934. With the new LaSalle entering the market, GM enticed an unexplored niche of car buyers to look outside of their normal shopping boundaries. The new LaSalle provided buyers with an exciting opportunity to obtain affordable luxury. Uniquely innovative, the LaSalle's freshly designed body by Fleetwood was streamlined for speed. The low windshield, telescoping biplane bumpers, and art deco portholes combined with other equally aesthetic features. Three stylish unique chevrons on the front of each forward pontoon fender blended into the car's posture to give the car a distinct stance and appearance. The refined narrow grill, low catwalks, and protruding pressed taillights made the 1934 LaSalle look as if it were speeding from a standstill. Adding to the illusion of speed were the long teardrop headlights and the torpedo hood ornament, which were kept from the 1933 model. The two-door LaSalle Series 350 coupe came standard with a leather rumble seat and was powered by the *straight-8* engine built in GM's Cadillac factory. Priced from $1,495 to $1,595, the Series 350 coupe was an instant classic, a car built for Jack Chevigny.

←→

At the annual letterman's banquet, the most eligible bachelor in Texas gladly accepted the keys to his black LaSalle Series 350 hardtop. With the LaSalle's service as the official pace car of the 1934 Indy 500, Jack would have had great appreciation for the Series 350. For an Indiana bachelor, an Indy pace car model was a gift fit for royalty. Given his driving habits, Jack was the quintessential driver for such a car.

←→

In the spring of 1935, the Chevigny name was popularly regarded across the Lone Star state. In the recruiting game, little damage had been done by Jack's initial misreading of the Texas prep environment, but the ante had increased. Jack needed a stellar class if he were to replace players such as Jack Gray, Charley Coates, and Bohn Hilliard. Thin numbers continued to plague the Longhorns; only fifteen lettermen returned from the previous season. For Jack, the dwindling roster made the statewide recruiting game a high stakes table. To win that game, Jack would have to cash in on his name recognition.

Inexplicably, Jack never brought his chips to the window. In his first real recruiting year, instead of building upon the foundation he had established through his success at Texas and St. Edward's, Jack acted as if he were coaching in Indiana instead of Texas. In the second recruiting faux pas of his short tenure in Austin, Jack chose to center his recruiting on Chicago and the Midwest.

College football recruiting had evolved into a turf war by 1934 with the exchange of scholarships for play remaining a product of an underground system; thus, Jack's targeting of the Midwest was strange and questionable as a strategy for future success. While coaches accepted the unwritten rule that a program could covertly and illegally recruit its own state or region, recruiting efforts that crossed state lines, especially regional boundaries, was a violation of the code.

Missouri coach Don Faurot didn't hesitate to slap the first hand that he caught in his Missouri cookie jar when he accused Northwestern, St. Louis, Centenary, and Texas of offering inducements to Missouri prep stars. Don Faurot was as much Missouri as Jack was Notre Dame. Faurot, the rightful father to the triple option series and a future legend of college football, was once heard to say he would rather coach Missouri for nothing than get paid to coach Ohio State. It came as no surprise to his fellow head coaches when Faurot stepped into the street at high noon and drew a bead on his competition's illegal recruiting of Missouri high school football stars.

By avoiding a direct response to Faurot's accusation, Centenary's Buddy Parker and Northwestern's Kenneth "Tug" Wilson's muted response would have forced the controversial remarks to die a death of quiet scorn, but Jack was not cut of Parker or Wilson's cloth. By believing that the finger Missouri pointed at Texas was the ignominious one, Jack took Faurot's comments as a personal attack.

Jack took the offensive against Faurot, "Your statement is absolutely absurd. We do not have a single Missouri athlete either on our varsity or freshman teams. You will have to substantiate your remarks with proof or apologize to the university alumni. Apology must be forthcoming within limited hours."

Not satisfied with knocking Faurot to the ground, Jack kicked sand in the eyes of the entire state of Missouri by reminding Faurot that the last time Texas faced Missouri, the Longhorns under Littlefield destroyed the Tigers, 65-0.

"I can't imagine why anyone would want to subsidize Missouri athletes," Jack added.

Apology offered but point made, Faurot backed down. The *Kansas City Star* didn't. Conducting their own inquiry, the *Star* found hard evidence of least one Kansas City boy receiving a job for attending Texas. Two others were promised financial aid. Ridiculing Jack's admonishment of Faurot, the *Star's* headline story, JOKE ON CHEVIGNY—TEXAS U. FOOTBALL COACH DOESN'T LIKE MISSOURI BOYS, BUT HIS ALUMNI DO, revealed unflattering details of the Longhorn boosters' roles in the enticement of Missouri athletes.

Although the mud ultimately dried and the slinging ceased, it would take months for the Missouri feud to die. With the *Star* catching a Longhorn in the hen house, most of Missouri guffawed at Jack's expense. Even the coach of the Missouri State Penitentiary piled on.

Offering his take on the controversy, Leroy Munyon observed, "I notice that Texas coach says he wouldn't bother to get a Missouri boy. Well, our worst players come from Texas."

The Faurot incident wasn't the only problem Jack created for himself. Earlier in March, during the time in which he should have utilized his veteran Texas staff members to map out his instate recruiting, Jack fixated on restructuring his coaching staff. Texas veterans Bill James and Shorty Alderson were out, but not without a cost.

With every withdrawal from the bank of trust comes a debit from the balance, and the termination of two popular longtime Texas assistants was a questionable withdrawal from Jack's public relations account. Both James and Alderson were institutions of an era, Alderson in particular. They had friends and connections, but Jack neither liked nor appreciated James and Alderson. Riding high from the season's accomplishments, Jack knew he could axe both men without seeing so much as a twitch from the alums. The tired Orangebloods, especially Bill James, had to be purged from his new system.

Bill James was an elder of the Texas *good ole boy* coaching system. Like Shorty Alderson, the longtime coach had friends everywhere: high places, low places, and places other than the Forty Acres.

Against Rice, the game that would ultimately decide the conference championship, Bill James invited three Houston friends to sit on the Longhorn bench with him. All were Rice alumni; one was a former Owl football star.

Coach James's allowance for three Rice products on the Longhorns' bench was unconditionally counter to Jack's "all in" philosophy of the game. To Jack, the other team was the enemy. Should they beat him, they would jeopardize his livelihood. Should they win, all the hours of practice and pain would be lost to nothing gained. His team was his family and the only thing that mattered. The act of Bill James patronizing three Rice Owls during the conference title game was unimaginably traitorous.

When Jack noticed the circumstances during the Rice game, an animated discussion ensued and unfortunately for James's future, he didn't back down. On that Saturday, his ticket was punched for a permanent ride out of Austin. Additionally, Shorty Alderson with his homey bantering and gregarious personality (it was said that if he fell in a lake, he would just talk underwater) would have irritated Jack simply for no reason other than his nature. Jack was cool and reserved regarding his game-day affairs, while Alderson was playful and light-hearted.

While Horn basketball coach Marty Karow was also let go from the varsity staff, Jack offered him the chance to stay as a freshman coach.

Again the question of Jack's respect for football played in the Lone Star State floated about the state. As expected, *The Port Arthur News* obliquely attempted to connect the terminations of James and Alderson to Jack's distaste for the homegrown Texas football produce. In the end, Jack's firing James and Alderson sold some newspapers but not much more.

As expected, Lutcher Stark weighed in. To him, the firings were not of anyone's concern other than Jack's. Stark said that James and Alderson had been given their opportunity to coexist with the new head coach; it was time to leave gracefully. Stark added that he never felt Karow was anything but a basketball coach anyway. With his remarks, Stark quelled some of the anti-Chevigny backlash, but his support for Jack wasn't unconditional. Stark qualified his support saying that, should Jack stumble, the board of regents would take similarly quick action on the head coaching position. Stark and others hinted that in the final analysis, Jack's axe-wielding was just a simple withdrawal on the bank of goodwill, one that could be easily overshadowed by a good season.

Demoted to the freshman staff, Marty Karow would now serve in the role of assistant to his former player, Jack Gray. Both Jack Gray and Buster Baebel returned to the Forty Acres as coaches. Bohn Hilliard, only three years younger than Jack, was expected to coach the varsity running backs, but Bohn decided to try professional football.

The shakeup was to be expected. His emotional outlook firmed by his experience under Hunk Anderson, Jack Chevigny was known to be temperamental and inflexible. A genius at the X's and O's, Jack felt that few contemporaries had more answers than he. Hunk's belittling left a chip on Jack's shoulder, making him hesitant to seek counsel in his coaching peers and subordinates. Jack felt more comfortable around his former players, the young men who were family. The one job counselor from whom Jack would have accepted advice was Rockne, and he wasn't around.

The only Rockne presence in Texas was a small village in Bastrop, County. Following the crash, some of the children of that community decided that the townsfolk should honor the football coach by taking his name. Initially, the vote was split evenly between Joyce Kilmer and Knute Rockne. The boys voted for Rockne; the girls voted for Kilmer. The following day little Edith Goertz changed her vote from the poet to the coach. Today, a bronze bust of the Notre Dame legend is found in the only town in America bearing his name—Rockne, Texas.

With his misguided recruiting philosophy and the firings of Littlefield's remnant coaches, Jack played into the stereotype that he was an outsider who didn't respect the Texas high school coaching culture. Carrying the gasoline to help fuel the wildfire were his Southwest Conference rivals. By April 1935, his old quote about the Texas high school players not being on par with players from the Midwest had resurfaced. Although not yet personally aware or concerned as to the damage he was self-inflicting, Jack should have realized that his negligence in winning over the Texas high school coaches had already dug a deep recruiting hole from which he would not climb out.

Compounding Jack's recruiting problem, the Southwest Conference was expected to demonstrate solid improvement from Houston to Fayetteville. Though the Depression seemed to bleed the Longhorns of talent, the other Southwest Conference teams grew stronger. Sammy Baugh returned for TCU, and Bobby Wilson rejoined SMU. In addition, numerous other stars from Rice, Arkansas, and Texas A&M were scheduled to return to the field. Conversely, Jack's recruiting of the Chicago area had yielded little more than Nick Frankovic.

Nick would challenge for a line spot along with his fellow sophomores, Robert Keeling of Dallas, Tarleton "Tiny" Jones of Vernon, and Hagan McMahon of Tyler. But his success was atypical of Jack's Midwestern recruits.

By the summer, the help that Jack needed to win in 1935 had failed to arrive. Then an unexpected blow hit Jack's midsection when Hugh Wolfe, scheduled to undergo eye surgery, elected to sit out the 1935 season. His loss would cripple the Longhorns. The numbers were low and the talent level lower. Even Jack's famed number twelve jersey had to be reissued to an untested track man, Jud Atchison. Sportswriters ranked the 1935 sophomore class one of the weakest in history. Longhorn baseball coach Billy Disch, whose word carried more weight in Austin than Moses's tablet, forecast a terrible dust storm for the Longhorn football landscape.

Uncle Billy remarked, "Jack had the biggest bunch of misfits for a freshman eleven last fall that I ever saw. Besides that, he lost a lot of men to graduation and because of scholastic reasons. It will be a hard fight for him."

In the phraseology of football coaches, *horse* is a popular metaphor for "talented player." In just his second year at Texas, Jack had run out of horses.

Regardless of the bleak outlook, autumn would still arrive and the season would have to be played. Prospects may have been slim, but Jack assured the fans that his boys could win some games and keep things close in others. Team captain Joe Smartt from Austin was expected to provide leadership in the line. Senior Moreland Chapman, also from Austin, and senior Woodrow Weir of Georgetown added two letters to the ranks. Breckenridge letterman Harold Griffin would attempt to fill the shoes of All-SWC center Charles Coates, while tackle Clint Small of Amarillo anchored the inexperienced line. Another prospect expected to challenge for a line spot was Bill Hughes from Van Alstyne, Texas. Harris Van Zandt from Fort Worth and Jack Collins of Denton would replace Jack Gray and Phil Sanger. Charles Johnston of Kerrville and Ney "Red" Sheridan of Sweetwater would compete for the quarterback spot, while senior Jimmy Hadlock of Marshall and senior Buster Jurecka of Robstown hoped to act as catalysts for the Horn rushing attack. Bill Pitzer, also from Breckenridge, would bring his booming leg back for another season of punting. Most notably, junior Irvin "Duke" Gilbreath of Wellington returned at end.

Of the eighteen to twenty prospects who could contribute to the 1935 varsity effort, only one player hailed from Jack's ground zero of recruiting. In the close knit world of Texas high school football coaches, the disparity between Jack's investment and return became fodder for numerous jokes made at his expense.

Not only had Hugh Wolfe's unintended sabbatical crippled the Horns' chances of winning, the Longhorn football schedule included four top-ten teams. In 1935, Jack's misfit Longhorns would stand toe to toe with LSU, Rice, SMU, and TCU.

Being an avid horseman, Jack probably realized this was no season to bet the orange ponies. Yet, betting was one thing from which Jack could not abstain. Though deficient in the game of high school recruiting, Jack continued to drive in the fast lane of the Austin high life. His friends and peers remained the oilmen and ranchers with money to burn. While his poker-playing friends and pony-playing peers remained insulated to the woes of the Depression, Jack's government subsidized salary sat at $5,000 a year.

Jack's financial compensation for his June 4 appointment as Longhorn athletic director had offered little to boost that figure. To support his lifestyle, Jack was forced to practice law on the side. It was said that on some occasions, Jack would fail to show for practice, leaving the leadership of the team to line coach Tim Moynihan.

Like his mentor Rockne, Jack spent an inordinate amount of time off campus. Although, the purpose of Rockne's travel was to accumulate more wealth, while Jack's travels centered on supporting his goal to make Texas a national program. Jack ignored his floundering numbers and team's personnel issues and scheduled an intersectional game versus powerful Minnesota. During a week on the Minnesota campus, Jack negotiated a deal that would bring Texas to the Twin Cities in December 1936.

When an emergency appendectomy sidelined Jack just before the start of the 1935 spring practice, some persons expected him to discontinue his newly-established tradition of the orange-white game. The spring game continued in spite of his surgery.

A reputed "clean liver, who neither smoked nor drank to excess," Jack was a young man in excellent health. While Jack loved his scotch whiskey and an evening smoke, he kept his days healthy with exercise and a good diet at the training table of Ma Griffith, the dorm mother he had hired for the benefit of providing the boys a maternal presence at their new athletic residence.

Regardless of what his detractors may have said about him, Jack was no muscle-headed football coach. Conversely, he was a cerebral football generalissimo always thinking of a new strategy, a new innovation, or a new con, as his detractors liked to say.

By the second game of 1935, he would need all the cons he could manage. After an opening victimization of Texas A&I, the Horns traveled to Baton Rouge to tangle with Louisiana State University.

In the previous week, the Longhorns had had fun plastering Bud McCallum's Texas A&I squad, 38-6.

There was to be no fun in Baton Rouge. There, a grieving crowd at Tiger Stadium mourned the loss of their patriarch, Senator Huey P. Long.

◄—►

Once photographed outside Capitol Hill in his silk pajamas, the Kingfish with his motto "Every Man a King" was expected to launch a serious challenge to Roosevelt for the 1936 Democratic Party nomination. Worshipful Louisiana voters believed Huey P. Long single-handedly brought the citizens of their impoverished state out of the dark ages and into the twentieth century. Senator Long was to pull America from the stagnant well that was Roosevelt's New Deal.

On September 8, 1935, the vibrantly exuberant Huey Long, the visionary who had captured the nation's attention with his Share Our Wealth program, was shot by a Baton Rouge doctor in the Louisiana State Capitol building he had built to watch guard over his Louisiana Renaissance. Despite the rush of doctors sent from Oschner's in New Orleans, United States Senator Huey Long died on September 10, 1935.

The greatest benefactor of LSU football who ever lived was gone. So attached to Long was the LSU football team, for decades it was taught in schools that as Huey P. Long lay dying in Our Lady of the Lake Hospital, his last words were "What will my boys at LSU do without me?"

Huey built the Depression era football power that was LSU. Like Texas's Governor Allred, Huey Long understood the value of a championship football team representing the state's premier public university. Over 225,000 mourners viewed the senator's body lying in state. On September 12, 1935, the Kingfish was laid to rest on the capitol grounds.

←→

Whether Huey P. Long's popular socialistic Share Our Wealth program would have usurped the faltering New Deal in 1936 remains an ongoing historical debate. What was not a matter of debate was the gravity of Long's assassination on a talented and determined group of Louisiana State Tigers; it and its conjunctive distractions darkened the Tigers chances of beating another solid edition of Rice Institute football. The Tigers' chances of victory were compounded that night, as the defending Southwest Conference champions' roster included most of their starters from 1934. With the odds stacked against the Tigers that Saturday, the visitors from Houston escaped Tiger Stadium with a 10-7 victory.

One week later, LSU hosted the Longhorns. And with the post-assassination game behind them, the renewed Tigers of the lighted Baton Rouge lair sought restoration from loss suffered at the hands of the Rice Owls—and Doctor Carl Weiss. Sharpening their claws, the Bayou Bengals looked forward to devouring the visiting Steers.

Regardless of the Tigers' motivation to rebound after the Rice game, not everyone in Baton Rouge expected the Longhorns to herd meekly to the slaughterhouse.

One paper reported, "Chevigny had assembled one of the country's classiest squads…He is aiming at a national championship and Rose Bowl bid in 1936 and is doing what he can to chalk up an impressive record."

Apparently, few Pelican State sportswriters had done their homework on the Horns. For that matter, neither did the bookies. The Tigers enjoyed only an eight-point spread over the visiting Horns. Some dailies across the country even picked the game as an upset special.

Whatever the odds, the LSU coaching staff wasn't overlooking the Horns. Their scouts reported that Jack would utilize a new form of the spinner against the Tigers. While sweating through two days of full-contact drills, Bernie Moore's boys practiced deciphering the Texas double spinner formation. Practicing his squad hard at stopping the circus-style series, Moore knew that Chevigny's version of the Rockne system would exhibit a shower of laterals and delayed passes.

Most effective of the Chevigny-Rockne spinner series was the double spinner play. In the double spinner, two backs aligned side by side reach to catch the ball after it is passed backward from the center. One of the backs catches the ball, but both backs spin counter to the line of scrimmage. Bursting apart, the first back continues in an overemphasized crouch, faking that he has the ball. By imitating the action of the first back, the ball carrier keeps the ball deceptively hidden on his hip as he spins through a hole created in the offensive line. Simultaneously meshing in the blink of an eye, the spinning backs disrupt the defensive reads and create confusion. It was an ideal coordinated series to use against a superior opponent.

Because of speedy sophomores John Morrow, Jay Arnold, Judson Atchison, and Morris Sands, the spinner action meshed in a blink. In the prior season, those four Longhorns had made their mark as the backfield quartet of the Longhorn frosh team. This season, they were ranked as third, fourth, fifth, and sixth on the preseason depth chart. Because of the depth chart listings, sportswriters suspected that the announcement of the four as starters was just another one of Jack's infamous schemes to psyche out the competition. But Jack insisted they were the one of the fastest backfields he had seen coaching.

In a proclamation of faith, Jack commented on the expectant roles of Morrow, Arnold, Atchison, and Sands:

> "I will not hesitate to send Morrow, Sands, Arnold, and Atchison, as a unit, into the LSU game, as I feel that extraordinary speed will help Texas to win. I am inclined somewhat to the belief that sophomores are not so inexperienced as most coaches would have them. LSU's great center, Stewart, is a case in point. He played as a sophomore, did he not? And he acquitted himself pretty well, didn't he? I see no reason why I should not use my fast backfield against the Tigers, even if three of the four men are sophomores."

How could a backfield of inexperienced no name sophomores be expected to tangle with the LSU Tigers? They couldn't.

The quote was indeed another one of Jack's translucent diversionary tactics. Obsessed with teasing the media and his opponents, he promoted misleading pre-game information to the scouts, media, and bookmakers on a weekly basis.

Tuesday, October 2, 1935, was travel day. As the Horns packed onto their express train, Jack hopped into his LaSalle to attend "Football Day" with the Seguin Rotary Club. Moynihan was left to coordinate the team's preparation for the trip to Baton Rouge. After he downed his usual morning cup at the restaurant owned by the father of a young Cater Joseph, Jack left a dime, ruffled the youth's hair, and hurried outside. He was late for an appointment. Pointing the chrome torpedo hood ornament to the southeast, Jack popped the clutch and floored the accelerator. As he leaned back into the plush LaSalle bench seat and used the same straight arm technique he once used against Navy, his right hand would have gripped the wheel near the 1:00 position. His left elbow would have rested on the sill of the open driver's window. Reaching the outer limits of Austin, Jack's lead foot and the Cadillac *straight-8* would have pushed the LaSalle coupe to 85 mph or more.

When Jack arrived on time, clean and debonair for the lovely ladies of Seguin, he took his seat with Mr. and Mrs. H. H. Weinert. Coach E. L. Carter stood to introduce the 1935 Matadors of Seguin High.

The entertainment for the high school season kickoff luncheon was courtesy of the high school orchestra. Behind the lectern, the headliner of the program, Longhorn head football coach Jack Chevigny began his delivery of a poignant affirmation of the sport he coached. Outlining what that sport should mean to the town of Seguin, Jack called the speech, "Football and Playing the Game."

Prior to his time on the dais, Jack remarked to Weinert that in preparation for the Tigers' traditional night game environment, he had practiced the team under the lights. The night practices would prepare the Longhorns for the shadows of the artificial light on Saturday night, Jack told the regent. What the Horns couldn't practice was the oppressive humidity of a Baton Rouge evening.

After returning to Austin later that afternoon, Jack, his super sophomores, and the rest of the unbeaten Horns, boarded the train to Baton Rouge.

Once the Longhorns stood taut with LSU on the lush Bermuda grass of Tiger Stadium, the super sophomores with whom the media were so infatuated would be nowhere in sight. Jack opened the game with his hardened veterans. Ducking under a snarling LSU defense, Jimmy Hadlock thumped the Tigers' noses with a fifty-five-yard run. Reliable Bill Pitzer smashed over from the five, and the Horns led 6-0 early in the first quarter.

After the Bengal Tigers roared back with a long drive, which moved the ball to the Longhorns one yard line, halfback Bill Crass, an LSU Tiger captured in tiny Electra, Texas, rammed the ball over to tie the score, 6-6. For the remainder of the half, the game stood at a stalemate.

In the second half, LSU probed the inexperienced Texas team between the tackles. Behind the plunging dives of halfback Bill Crass and junior halfback J. T. "Rock" Reed, LSU marched downfield in total control of the line of scrimmage. But when the Tigers advanced to the Horn's ten yard line, Jack's boys stiffened and turned away the Tiger threat.

Then purple lightning struck. A Texas punt traveled deep to the Tiger forty-eight where LSU's Reed scooped the rolling ball. LSU's J. T. Reed's electrifying punt return was good for six points and the first Tiger lead of the evening.

By this time, Jack's boys were as battered as General Hood's Texans staggering down from the Devil's Den of Gettysburg. Roaring forward, the boys in purple and gold pinned the Horns against the Texas goal line for a third time.

After securing a third-goal-line stand and taking over on downs, Texas launched an air assault from their end zone. Refusing to surrender without a fight, Buster Jurecka dropped back to test the Tiger secondary with a thirty-four-yard pass to Bill Pitzer.

Tiger Stadium roared as LSU's Gaynell "Gus" Tinsley pressured Jurecka. Because of Tinsley's pass rush, Jurecka's pass wobbled downfield where it was picked off by Jesse Fatheree, another LSU senior who would go on to earn conference honors.

With the final gun fired afterward, Fatheree's interception return for a touchdown mercifully ended the Battle of the Baton Rouge Alamo. The Horns had spent the entire second half defending their last ten yards against an onslaught of a superior force. Boarding the *Longhorn Special* on the bottom side of the 18-6 loss, the pain of their black eyes and bruises was dulled by the knowledge that they had met a team that possessed more talent but not more heart.

It was a classic game of the era. The Texas boys had fought hard against the eventual Southeastern Conference Champions, and although denied by an assassin's bullet the future benefits of Huey Long's patriarchy, LSU set in motion a glorious run. From the 1935 Texas game to the start of the 1938 season, LSU would go 27-4-2 with three Sugar Bowl appearances. Huey would have been pleased.

His Austin-bound train skirted the gator-infested swamp of the Atchafalaya Basin, while Jack ruminated. Thanks to his boys' showing against the Tigers, he knew that if the cards fell right, his boys had a chance against anybody on their schedule. Even the LSU fans acknowledged that the toughness and competitive spirit of the Horns made the game closer than it should have been. Going into the Oklahoma game, Jack felt good about his squad.

Though the celebratory preparations for the 1936 Centennial edition of the Texas State Fair in Dallas had shifted into high gear, Oklahoma brought a perfect record to State Fair Stadium in Dallas. Under new coach Lawrence "Biff" Jones, Oklahoma had undergone more than just a few cosmetic changes since the previous season. Not only did the Sooners own a new water wagon with pneumatic tires, Captain Jones of Army fame brought to Oklahoma a modern system of play with liberal substitutions, laterals, and a playbook replete with misdirection plays. Once holding less value than an acre of dead cornstalks, tickets in Norman were now something to be bartered. Adding to the excitement in the Sooner state was the fact that it would be the first time in years that Oklahoma took the field favored over the Burnt Orange. Over forty-five thousand fans were expected to attend the big game.

After a late evening session of signal drills, which coordinated the offensive aspects of the game plan, the *Longhorn Special* left Austin early Friday morning.

In Dallas, Texas surprised the Sooners, 12-7. After the game, Sunday's press lauded Jack's coaching.

The Associated Press lead read, "Skilled backs using all the running and passing tricks that Jack Chevigny brought down from Notre Dame delivered Texas over Oklahoma."

When he released his entire stable of ten running backs into the fray, Jack pushed the super sophomores into action and enabled heretofore unknown Morris Sands to step into the limelight. Whether he knew it or not, it was a big political victory for Jack.

Prior to the OU game, the orange-clad boosters cared less about the strength of the Longhorn schedule and more about the weaknesses of the Longhorn team and its coach. Rumors surfaced as to Jack's apparent change in intensity. Winning the crucial Red River battle as a decisive underdog wheeled the merry-go-round press back to Jack's side for another week.

Centenary, with its Southwest Conference streak intact, returned to Austin on the following Saturday. For the admittedly weaker 1935 version of the Horns, the Gents presented the same obstacles as the year before. Centenary was a tough group with experience.

While Rice and SMU settled who was number one in the Southwest Conference as well as the country, Texas battled the underrated Gents. It was a close game, but Gilbreath continued to struggle with ball security. His first quarter fumble opened the door for the Gents, and Centenary had no problem capitalizing on the error in quickly taking the lead, 7-0. But just as

Buddy Parker's boys appeared ready to break the game open, the Longhorns came back to life. The Steers hit pay dirt when Jud Atchison lofted a pass to reserve Johnny Morrow in the corner of the end zone. Clint Small's kick tied the score at 7-7.

Though erratic, the Texas box showed flashes of the dominant running game exhibited by the Horns during the previous season. The game was similar to a tug-of-war. The Longhorn offense appeared to push harder than the Gents' offense, but the rematch would come down to the closing minutes.

As he did in the Oklahoma game with Morris Sands, Jack called upon an unknown Longhorn to seal the victory. With the Memorial Stadium clock hand sweeping to zero, the Horns highlighted Jay Arnold's punishing line smashes at the center of the Gents' defense. On ten consecutive carries, Arnold rushed the ball, his final carry moving the ball within the Centenary one yard line where Bill Pitzer's last second leap over the white jerseys clinched the win, 19-13. Arnold's legendary last drive heroics would forever entertain the ghosts of Memorial Stadium as one of the greatest single performances of Longhorn lore. The Longhorns had exacted their proverbial pound of flesh from the Gents.

Following Jay Arnold's punishing debut, newspapers from across the state centered their sports sections around a photo of the bullnecked Longhorn junior. Arnold was a huge back for the era. In Chevigny pounds, Arnold's weight was 205 pound, but Arnold's press day photo showed a young man at least thirty pounds heavier.

Jack had an eye for talent. After graduating from Texas, Arnold would go on to play seven seasons in the NFL.

After the Centenary game, Morris Sands fell ill. Having found his niche in the Longhorn rushing attack, he would remain hospitalized for a bronchial condition, while his teammates played the Rice Owls without him. With Buster Jurecka and Irvin Gilbreath returning full speed to the lineup, Jack hoped to lean on his veterans. New running plays and special pass plays that had been held in reserve would be released on the Owls' return to Memorial Stadium.

Jack had done it at Notre Dame. He had done it in Dallas against the Sooners. Now, everyone in Austin waited to see what kind of Jack-magic would be used on Rice.

Orangebloods were disappointed in the show when the only Longhorn magic of the game exhibited was the lost ball trick. For the third consecutive game, the Horns coughed up the ball on its opening possession. Converting two of the fumbles for touchdowns, the Rice Owls gained the early momentum.

Still, Rice wasn't finished with just the two opening scores. With time remaining in the first period, the Owls intercepted a panicky Longhorn pass. From that turnover, Rice scored a third time in the first quarter. Falling behind 22-0 in the first quarter, the Longhorns junked their running attack, but could not make up the ground. Though the stadium was electrified by four touchdowns being scored in the fourth period, fans wearing the burnt orange and white went home disappointed by the 28-19 final. The game was never close to ending in a Longhorn victory; the divide between Rice and Texas football had widened.

For the Texas students and exes, the ease of the Rice victory revealed an ugly truth. SMU and Rice had forced the eyes of the nation upon the Southwest Conference, not Texas. Now that the conference Texas had built was being hailed in the East and Midwest as the greatest of all, the Longhorns were a second tier football program.

The Mustangs owned the nation's number-one ranking and six consecutive wins, and they were expected to stampede the Horns in front of their homecoming crowd in Dallas. Debating the validity of SMU's ranking and their six-game run, supportive Orangebloods encouraged the Horns by making note of the Ponies' soft non-conference schedule. Working through the weakest non-conference schedule of the SWC prior to meeting Texas, the Mustangs had defeated such weaklings as North Texas, Austin College, Tulsa, Washington of St. Louis, and Hardin-Simmons.

In Dallas, Jack opened with a strategy to frustrate SMU with a multiple passing attack designed to exploit the underneath zones, but the plan faltered when the Texas receivers continually failed to gain any significant yardage after the catch. Both teams employed spread formations utilizing the passing game; yet, it was the Mustangs who had their way with the Longhorns.

Southern Methodist proved they were no pretenders to the national crown by opening with a dominating first half performance behind the running of 148-pound All-American Bobby Wilson. Leading 14-0 at half, the SMU reserves cruised through the second half and handed Jack the first shutout loss of his Longhorn coaching tenure. Securing a 20-0 win over the Horns, the Mustangs set their sights on the long-awaited trip to Los Angeles and a date with the University of California (UCLA).

On the following Saturday, Texas encountered another motivated team possessing six consecutive wins—Baylor. A much improved team from 1934, the Bears' one loss came against Sammy Baugh and TCU. After being dissected by the SMU buzz saw, the Horns would make another tough road trip, this time only a short distance north to Waco. Even though the green and gold Bears owned a stellar 6-1 record, the media held little esteem for the Bears. The dope was that Jack had only two chances to capture a conference victory; one of them was against Baylor.

Back in Austin, an embarrassing silence blanketed the week's preparations. Rather than sparking on Jack's genius, forums were limited to discussing the Bears' chances of complicating the SWC race with a win over the hapless Horns. It was wasted speculations. Saturday, in a sharp rejoinder to the doubters, the young Steers surprised the SWC with an easy 25-6 win at Baylor. Jimmy Hadlock, Ney Sheridan, Jay Arnold, and Jack Collins rose to the occasion in the game. It was a stunning outcome, one for which their coach received some unfamiliar high praise in the local papers.

Waco was an uplifting vacation from the tough losses, albeit a short vacation. The Baylor game proved that as long as the deck wasn't stacked, Jack's boys could play a mean game of football.

In the following week, TCU would be dealing the cards. And the Frogs held the ace of aces, Sammy Baugh. In the process of leading the Frogs to eight consecutive victories, Baugh completed 45 of 81 passes and scored 11 touchdowns. Behind a veteran offensive line built around All-American center Darrell Lester, Baugh shredded the Frogs' competitors.

Outlining the week's preparation, the normally tongue-in-cheek Jack took a dark tone. Jack reflected on his team's chance of winning, "All I can hope is that we keep the score down."

His forlorn elucidation indicated the depth of the malaise that shrouded the Texas Longhorn football program. On Saturday in Austin, Sammy Baugh and TCU would deepen the Steers' pool of misery when the Horned Frogs recorded a quartet of touchdowns for an easy 28-0 win. For the Frogs, it was their fifth shutout win.

Though reeling, the Horns could still finish with a winning record. Jack had to make his team regain only enough confidence to win out against a two-game lineup, which included a mediocre Arkansas team and a cellar-dwelling Texas A&M squad. Having the advantage of facing the Hogs in Austin, the Horns would need only to break the Kyle Field jinx in College Station.

As the Aggies enjoyed the advantage of an open week to prep for the Longhorns, Arkansas packed its 3-5 record and boarded the next train south to Memorial Stadium. Throughout the week of practice, Jack instructed his staff to emphasize perfecting the Horns' blocking technique. He further stressed that the staff refine the erratic passing attack led by converted halfback Buster Jurecka. Seeing little improvement and less enthusiasm during the week's preparation, Jack publicly expressed dissatisfaction with the attitude of his regular starting lineup. Informing the press that he intended to allow several untested squadmen a chance to play on Saturday was Jack's way of challenging his veterans.

Back in action for the first time in weeks, Jimmy Hadlock responded to Jack's challenge. Returning a punt deep into Arkansas territory early in the first quarter, Hadlock set up a Morris Sands' touchdown, and the Horns were up 6-0. But Arkansas executed a fake punt and the point-after to take the lead, 7-6. With the minutes ticking away in the second half, Jack's boys threatened to respond, but time ran out on the Horns with the ball at the Razorback's five yard line. With the half ended, Arkansas took a one-point lead into the visitor's locker room.

Opening the second half, the Hogs took command of the game with two third-quarter touchdowns. Although Jack's Notre Dame shift rambled for 23 first downs and 279 yards, costly turnovers continued to sabotage the Longhorn offense. Burnt Orange ticket holders watched in disbelief as Arkansas exploited the Longhorn mistakes with a timely passing attack. Ultimately, a desperation scoring attempt from deep in Longhorn territory allowed the Hogs to tack on a fourth-quarter touchdown. For the Steers, it was an emotionally devastating defeat.

With the 28-13 loss, the Texas Longhorns now had to return from Kyle Field with a win or face the shame of a losing season. Jack Chevigny was a besieged football coach. He needed to regroup his staggering Longhorns if they were going to beat the equally inept but feisty A&M squad.

Prior to the 1935 season, the Texas A&M Aggies had fired their coach, Matty Bell. With Bell now the head football coach of the nation's number one ranked SMU Mustangs, the Aggies ventured closer to the dissolution of their football program. Winless in the Southwest Conference, the 1935 Aggies had seen victory only twice. Each win was against sublevel competition.

Most Orangebloods felt the Longhorns' greatest obstacle to defeating the Aggies would be the Kyle Field jinx. The Horns had won at Kyle Field only once since 1915.

On Thanksgiving Day at Kyle Field, the spiritual heart of Aggieland, two besieged coaches met at midfield before the game. After the opening kickoff, Buster Jurecka put the Horns up with a thirty-eight-yard run in the first quarter. Strengthened by the cheers of the Corps, the Aggies countered the Longhorn march when sophomore Jimmy Shockey and the Aggies went to the air. Although the Maroon and White threatened to score just before the first half ended, the Longhorns held.

As they left the field for halftime, the Longhorns appeared joyless, visibly void of any initiative and drive. Walking from the Texas sideline, they appeared dull and listless. Fans noticed the Orange and White moving slowly and quietly to the locker room. Meanwhile, the Aggies roared off the field in anticipation of what could be accomplished in the second half.

In the third quarter, the Aggies predictably added two more touchdowns against Jack's lifeless herd. Kyle Field, one of college football's premier venues, erupted as the clock wound down on the Aggies' 20-6 rout. The win signified the beginning of an incredible turnabout for the downtrodden Aggie program.

Headlines recounting the Thanksgiving Day match pronounced the Longhorn Band as something of which the Texas exes could be proud; not so much their football team. During the 1935 conference race, the Aggies and the Longhorns achieved only one conference victory each, but with the Aggie frosh blanking the baby Horns earlier that week, Texas A&M fans had faith in the future. In Austin, the Orangebloods weren't so pleasantly expectant.

For the first time in SWC history, the Texas Longhorns owned the conference cellar. In just one season, Jack's Texas temple had collapsed into rubble. If the football god were a merciful god, Jack Chevigny's stay at Texas would have ended the day after his loss to the Aggies.

A merciful god, he isn't. As sudden as an assassin's bullet would come Jack's betrayal at the Forty Acres.

# CHAPTER SIXTEEN

# *At the Alamo*

Following the Longhorns' surrender at Kyle Field, Texas sports journalists assailed the man said to be responsible for the disintegration of the Texas football program. Uncle Billy Disch's foreboding assessment of the 1935 Longhorn varsity had been conveniently forgotten. Critics from Pampa to Port Arthur called for Jack's immediate dismissal. The sudden fall of the Horns was inexcusable.

Standing in the way of Jack's dismissal were H. H. Weinert, J. R. Parten, and the last year of a contract extension. Though the student body howled for Jack's resignation, the regents took no action and hoped that the howls would subside into muffled gnarls.

Amidst the castigation, Jack took some time to retrain his muscles and football instincts. Joining him at Southwestern's campus in Georgetown for a charity football game was Tim Moynihan. Although it was to be a smalltime affair, some big names were in attendance. Texas Governor James Allred kicked off to start the first half, while Austin Mayor Tom Miller agreed to put every ounce of his 265 pounds into the second half's opening kick. Adding to the fun, Marty Karow and a supporting cast of former Longhorns such as Buster Baebel, Jack Gray, Charley Coates, Ox Higgins, and Joe Smartt agreed to join Jack and Moynihan in the game against Southwestern's varsity. Most of the proceeds would go to the Will Rogers Memorial Fund.

Along with celebrity pilot Wiley Post, the nation's best known personality, had perished in an August 15 plane crash in Alaska. So popular was the Oklahoma native Rogers, his funeral was recorded to have seen the largest turnout of mourners since the services for Abraham Lincoln. In that Knute Rockne and Will Rogers were acquainted, Jack would have felt especially close to the humorist. Like most of America, he wanted to do something to honor Rogers's memory.

Eighteen days after the Will Rogers Memorial Fund charity game, Jack looked forward to returning to the comfort of his hometown friends. Loading his LaSalle for the trip to Hammond, he felt invigorated by the gridiron romp with Moynihan and the boys.

Riding shotgun was Longhorn Bill Forney. His home in Valparaiso, Indiana, was near Hammond, and Jack was glad to have the company of one of his players on the drive home.

The New Year opened with Jack staying at his mother's home on Hammond's Wildwood Road. He had left his trials back in Austin and planned to relax and enjoy the company of his brother-in-law Tim Galvin and his old Hammond High classmate and best friend Ed Burns.

Not only had 1935 been a disappointing year for Jack Chevigny the coach, it was a tough year for Jack Chevigny, the thoroughbred. After appearing at Rockaway with Seabiscuit and the best of the circuit, Jack Chevigny was caught in a blood-doping investigation in Nevada. After his trainer was found guilty of injecting the thoroughbred with a performance-enhancing drug, the young horse's reputation was smeared. Jack Chevigny soon disappeared from the circuit's top cards.

While Jack was back in Hammond, rumors emanated from Austin that the board of regents had sent an emissary to the American Football Coaches Convention. The emissary's mission—surreptitiously contact former Texas A&M and current Nebraska coach D. X. Bible and frame the foundation for a deal to be struck, a deal, which would bring Bible to Austin for the 1936 season. Even though Weinert's influence and the remaining year of Jack's contract continued to restrain the board, conjecture remained that Jack may not finish out the final year. In the case of Chevigny abandoning ship, Lutcher Stark and others wanted the program to have a lifeboat in D. X. Bible.

Known to be a tough sell, Bible turned away the Texas overture. His one concession to the Texas overture was that he may reconsider the offer after the close of the 1936 season.

Whether Jack ever learned of the board's covert mission is unknown. H. H. Weinert would have waged a bloody war on anyone who attempted to break Jack's contract, so it is unlikely that anyone other than a handful of closeted insiders knew of the plot to hire Bible in January of 1936. Had Jack learned of Bible's recruitment, it would have been wise for him to leave Texas. He still had the Rockne and Notre Dame credentials, and in the long term, the split decision of his Texas tenure would not have negatively affected his resume. Indeed, Stark may have intentionally leaked information regarding the Bible contact in order to provoke the reactive Chevigny. Nonetheless, if Jack did know of the plot, he characteristically didn't bite the bait. Although only twenty-nine, Jack was a coach with a worn pea in his whistle, far too insightful and strong-willed to be subversively cajoled into a knee-jerk reaction. The Bible rumors quickly dissipated.

Though the Bible chapter closed without incident, January 1936 would ring in more than a new year. Just prior to New Year's Eve, the University of Texas elected to non-renew Tim Moynihan's coaching contract. Even before Jack returned from Indiana, Tim had packed up his family and left for Chicago. *The Daily Texan*, by now a vehement anti-Chevigny campus news source, scooped the mainstream papers with the story on January 3, 1936. Subsequent scuttlebutt rumoring that Moynihan committed illegal recruiting practices and other malfeasance surfaced, but no reason of any substance was ever formally announced. Some media sources hinted that Jack had made Tim a scapegoat for the Horns' poor performance and left town so that his hands appeared clean in the matter. Whatever the truth, with the longtime bond of the Chevigny-Moynihan coaching duo shattered, the turbulence of Moynihan's abrupt dismissal would continue to rock the boat for months.

President Benedict's action in the Moynihan matter assuredly was just another prong of the Lutcher Stark assault designed to provoke Jack's resignation. Three years of personal rumors and innuendo had undermined Jack's prestige with the administration. By Jack's third spring training, President Benedict had developed a strong personal and professional dislike for Jack. Typical of most school administrators, Benedict had never offered more than protoplasmic support, a backing continually reshaped by the ebb and flow of Jack's popular appeal. With Jack's popularity at an unprecedented low after the 1935 season, Benedict's door opened wide to those who would shoot arrows Jack's way.

Meanwhile, Jack's very real gambling problem undermined his enthusiasts' efforts at keeping the Chevigny ship afloat. His gambling had become a dead Texas albatross hanging about his neck.

In his love of the playboy lifestyle, Jack circulated Austin with oil men and ranchers who played with wheelbarrows of large denominations. Considering Jack's net worth, he was of the nature of a gambler who plays with the mortgage and the baby's milk money. Thus, while cavorting in a social circle that was out of his league financially, the Longhorn head football coach ceaselessly built gambling debts he could not cover. Jack needed the inflated pockets of his closest friends to keep him afloat.

Whether he turned to H. H. Weinert for help in the matter of his gambling debts is unknown. With Weinert being almost a surrogate father, Jack may have been embarrassed to call on him. Weinert may have been sternly averse to his mentee's gambling. What is known is that Jack asked Weinert's fellow regent, oilman J. R. Parten, for a large sum of money on at least two occasions.

Three years of collaborating with Jack Chevigny in the recruiting game cultivated a close friendship between one of Texas' richest oilmen and the young celebrity coach. Parten acted as the sympathetic rich uncle, the associate upon which Jack could rely to bail him out of jail without condemnation. Periodically throughout Jack's tenure at Texas, J. R. Parten's deep pockets enabled Jack's gambling habit. A personal loan of thousands of dollars was of little significance to Parten. Besides, he liked Jack a great deal and was known to be quick to Jack's defense.

In the Texas oilman's culture, gambling was seen as a right of passage and a means to express your manhood. It was a privilege of the successful. Self-made men such as Parten were less condemning of a young man dropping a few dollars at the track or around the poker table. In fact, Parten had made his millions gambling. He had won betting on what lay beneath the dirt clods of worn-out cotton fields and piney wood thickets. Given Parten's wealth, the few thousands that he used to bail Jack out of an occasional jam was no more significant than paying one of Jack's many parking tickets. And while it is certain that Parten remained covertly silent as to his periodic cash bailouts of Jack's gambling debts, Austin in 1936 was a very small town.

Austin may have remained relatively quaint in 1936, but the state of Texas was at the doorway of a population boom. The summer celebration for the state's centennial anniversary had been in the planning for approximately three years. Texas helium floated the celebratory balloons over the state fairgrounds, while the state positioned itself to become the free world's largest source of oil and gas.

At about the same time Texans enjoyed a grand festival in Dallas, much of the world assembled in Berlin for the opening curtain of another festival, one designed to promote racial superiority and the perfection of a nationalistic order of hate. In the state fair's "Hall of Negro Life," visitors celebrated the contributions of black Texans to the Lone Star State, while in Nazi Germany, Jesse Owens strode onto a swastika-draped center stage of Aryan supremacy. In Berlin, Ohio State's Buckeye Bullet stained Adolph Hitler's showcase of the new Germany and its self-perceived Aryan athletic prowess, his four gold medals grossly undermining Hitler's pageant of racial elitism. For both the colored athletes of America and the U. S. State Department, Jesse Owens's superior performance was a prewar political coup over the Aryan propaganda of the Nazi regime. Even a prejudiced white America exalted Owens for his role in refuting the ideology of the *master race* and embarrassing Adolph Hitler.

In addition to Owens, another non-Aryan, Japanese Imperial Army officer Takeichi Nishi arrived in Berlin with a quest. Nishi hoped to earn his second gold medal in the equestrian show jumping event. Though expected to manage easily a repeat of his 1932 victory, Japan's Takeichi Nishi would cause no similar Jesse Owens embarrassment of *Der Fuhrer*. The good soldier Nishi would finish twentieth, ending any hope for another medal finish.

Given the games were during the negotiations for the signing of the Anti-Comitern Pact, the anti-communist mutual defense treaty between Germany and Japan, some historians theorized that Nishi's sub-par finish was intentional. Because racism was the linchpin of the Nazi ideology, a second gold medal by the non-Aryan Nishi could have jeopardized the agreement between Germany and Japan. Nishi may have been ordered to accumulate his twenty faults. It's also been theorized that Baron Nishi, being an Army officer of noble heritage, may have conceived the idea that throwing the competition would best serve his emperor. As an adherent to the Bushido Code, Nishi would have willingly abdicated his desire for personal glory in deference to the good of his emperor and country. The truth is unclear, but many historians believe that Nishi took one of the most transparent dives in the history of sport.

↔

In Texas, far from the political intrigue and implications of the Berlin Olympics, Governor James Allred enjoyed the glorious centennial fair in Dallas. When the $25 million Texas State Fair opened on June 6, 1936, it marked a new day for the entire state. Texans saw in the distance a glimmer of sunshine.

In the Longhorn locker room, the glimmer was dying. Summer offered little respite, as weekly columns across the state postulated of the September hurricane predicted to strike Jack Chevigny's house. Jack had been under attack since the final week of the frustrating 4-6 finish of 1935, and only a small minority of Horn fans doubted a similarly disastrous outcome of the upcoming season.

Harshest of those critics relentless in their pursuit of Chevigny's termination was chief editor of the *Daily Texan*, Fred Shaffner. A student manager under Clyde Littlefield, Shaffner attacked the embattled coach with every printing. Most venomous of Shaffner's minions was Joe B. Frantz, a milk-sopping transfer student from Weatherford College in his first year at Texas.

Frantz was the first to tag Jack with the oft-repeated obloquy, "snake oil salesman." Strangely, Frantz, the venerated historian of later years, never reconsidered the validity of a non-athletic journalism student's four-month assessment of one of the best known football strategists and motivators of that era of college football.

Shaffner's *Daily Texan* may have led the campus termite swarm, but it wasn't the only destructive force eating away at Jack's base of support. Even though the new 1936 Hereford version of Bevo would have made for some fine barbeque, the mainstream media decided to turn up the heat on Jack instead. Stoking the fire under Jack's pant seat, the *San Antonio Light*, formerly one of Coach Jack Chevigny's strongest advocates, printed the details of a covert interview in July with "one of Jack's tried and trusted players." The player confessed that the entire squad knew that Jack's time was up after the next season. According to the unnamed Longhorn, Lutcher Stark had approached several of his teammates during the off-season and had personally guaranteed that Chevigny would be fired within the year.

Positive press regarding Jack Chevigny was a premium in the summer of 1936. Several Longhorns grumbled to reporters that Jack spent too much time at his law practice. As if to support the stories of Jack abandoning his Longhorn coaching duties for the occasional court appearance, statewide papers informed their readers that Longhorn head football coach Jack Chevigny recently had argued a legal case before the state's railroad commission. In no silent hint of Chevigny's uncertain future as Longhorn head football coach, the article stated that Jack's law degree was his "ace in the hole."

Even Jack's gambling, never a closeted facet of his bachelor lifestyle, found mention in the area rags. In August, Jack won $1.50 in a match against a local golf hustler. The win made the sports pages.

No matter how insignificant or trivial, every blemish found its way into the newspapers. Earlier that spring, page four of the *San Antonio Express* mentioned that Jack had been ordered to appear in court over a parking ticket.

Thanks to the subversive Lutcher Stark and the attack dog tactics of Fred Shaffner, Jack was a lame duck coach before blowing the first whistle of preseason drills.

On September 10, 1936, the first practice whistle welcomed a meager thirty-eight Longhorns. Half of them were sophomores, recruited by Chevigny after the successful 1934 season. Just eight seniors returned for the fall. Together, the coach and squad faced insurmountable obstacles. An unpopular coach emasculated daily by the school newspaper and mainstream press corps, working with a newly configured coaching staff, leading an inexperienced and sparsely talented squad, and facing the toughest schedule in college football, Jack was standing alone at his Thermopylae.

Like the 1935 edition, Jack's 1936 Longhorns would tackle four teams predicted to finish in the elite top-twenty national ranking. By season's end, Southwest Conference foes Arkansas and TCU would finish eighteenth and sixteenth respectively, while the late Senator Huey Long's LSU Tigers would continue its dominance of the Southeastern Conference and finish second in the nation. Ironically, Jack had added another tough outing to the schedule. The Horns' final opponent of the 1936 season would be Minnesota led by the sober Bernie Bierman. Savoring a twenty-four-game win streak, the Golden Gophers would go on to cement their dynasty with a third consecutive national championship in 1936.

With the honeymoon forgotten and the marriage crumbling, Jack braced himself for a tumultuous twelve-week season. Fortifying himself with a bunker mentality, Jack cut off the media by ordering sequestered practices for the first time that anyone on the Forty Acres could remember. Limited to knowing not much more than the Horns' practice attire for the day, the press was provided minimal information as to the details of each practice. It was a defensive policy that increased the alienation of the sports reporters. Nevertheless, the policy was a typical Jack Chevigny response. Jack was a peach to those who liked him, a bitter fruit to those who didn't.

Now that the inexorable Moynihan no longer was serving as the tenacious point man of the coaching staff, Jack expanded his own role as the trail boss. Players soon found that Moynihan's absence served only to sharpen Jack's naturally sarcastic coaching persona. In the previous two years, the players had grown accustomed to Jack's coaching style, a style fostered by the prodigiously acerbic Rockne, but now the verbal jabs no longer came across as lighthearted and playful. Several linemen expressed their indignation to the press over what they felt were disparaging remarks directed at the team. Jack was no longer the buoyant and brazen Notre Dame legend with the golden oratory. A once cajoling Jack Chevigny had devolved into a weary and circumspect Jack Chevigny carping his players into submission.

By early September, proof of Jack's darkening mentality could be found in his press offerings. Allowing media access to the Horns' practice for the first time, Jack's infectious optimism had run empty even before the first game. His hollow promises were now just nonexistent.

Degenerating from his pledge to hoist the Texas flag high over the nation, a battered Jack Chevigny in the fall of 1936 could muster no more than, "It's not so far up from the bottom of the ladder."

Pressed for a prediction of the conference outlook, Jack demurred in giving the nod to TCU, "I rate them, Texas Christian, Texas Aggies, Arkansas, Baylor, Rice, and SMU. I don't know where my Longhorns will finish."

A sense of doom clouded the Horns' preseason as preparations for LSU continued. Visiting Austin for the first time in twenty-six years, the Bayou Bengals would arrive on October 3. The 1935 edition of the Tigers had finished 9-2 with a close loss to TCU in the Sugar Bowl. LSU was again ranked among the nation's premier programs.

After scouting the Tigers' 20-7 win over Rice, Jack realized that the Steers' defense would need to be reinforced if it were to hold up against the arsenal of LSU's weaponry. Most of the week's practice efforts were directed toward the installation of multiple defensive fronts that would be used to confuse LSU's linemen. Offensively, the chips would be placed on the affable and talented Hugh Wolfe. Once Wolfe returned to action after sitting out the 1935 season, his speed was a solitary beacon in the dim prospect of Jack's third season as the Longhorn's head football coach.

When the locusts come, they eat everything that's green; so goes a West Texas proverb of woe. For Jack and his 1936 Longhorns, it was an aphorism that rang loud and true.

With opening day of the Steers' season approaching, a flu bug hit the athletic dorm, striking down five varsity players. Two of the five influenza victims were linemen. A swarm of football locusts had come to Austin and eaten everything green.

Exacerbating Chevigny's concerns, a preseason malaise had made its way into the Longhorn practices. Jack scolded the team, saying the players were not giving enough effort and failing to mentally focus in practicing their special team duties. Frustrated, Jack halfheartedly offered a steak dinner to anyone who would "show any speed" during one of the team's punt coverage drills. Jack yelled to the boys that if the Longhorns were expecting sympathy from the nationally ranked Tigers, they would be disappointed.

In Jack's eyes, on October 3, twenty-two men with no excuses would meet on a football field in Austin, Texas. This fact was the essence of the game of college football and the reason for its allure to thousands of Americans who lived week to week on a loaf of bread and hope.

Few in the media shared Jack's succinctly pure analysis. Just two days prior to the game, an Associated Press release throughout the state outlined three reasons the Longhorns would suffer a disastrous rout at the hands of the Tigers: Jack Chevigny failed to schedule an opening game with a weaker opponent; Jack Chevigny disenfranchised his home fan base by conducting practices behind locked gates; and LSU is "an eleven-cylinder juggernaut...headed for a national championship..."

Standing on the sideline versus LSU, the snake oil salesman, who neglected his coaching duties, saw the game start just as he would have scripted it. It was a defensive struggle.

The strength of the Longhorn team, its backfield led by Hugh Wolfe, consistently rattled the Tigers' cage as Jack's defensive plan stuffed the LSU running game. It wasn't long before Wolfe broke the game open with a spectacular thirty-seven yard run that gave the Longhorns the lead midway in the second quarter. It addition to Wolfe's dazzling performance, hard-tackling Longhorns punished the Bayou Bengals, forcing numerous LSU turnovers, two of them coming as the Tigers pushed within the shadow of Memorial Stadium's goal posts.

Only a Jay Arnold fumble at the Longhorn thirty-six yard line saved the Tigers from dropping a goose egg on the scoreboard. Following Arnold's miscue, LSU, behind the slashing runs of Pat Coffee, was finally able to move the ball downfield. Once inside the ten yard line, Art Morton burst off-tackle for the tying score. The scoring ended there.

In a shockingly unexpected upset tie, tenacious Texas claimed a 6-6 deadlock with a powerful LSU squad that was destined to finish the 1936 season at 9-1-1. Yet, absent from the post-game hurrahs were the glowing press accounts regarding Jack's defensive genius in holding the Tigers to just six points.

It would be the only time that season that LSU would not score at least two touchdowns in a game. (Later that year, LSU would score 93 points against Southwestern Louisiana.) Another remarkable statistic was Stephenville native Hugh Wolfe's lone touchdown run, one of only five touchdowns scored against LSU that season.

The Horns' effort may have shocked the nation and the *Daily Texan's* Joe Franck, but Jack and his boys would have no time to revel. A trip to Dallas highlighted the Longhorn travel itinerary for October 10.

In the previous two meetings, Oklahoma had failed to find the key to unlocking Chevigny's defensive scheme, and for the third consecutive season, the Sooner offense struggled to move the ball against Jack's Longhorns. At the final gun of the twenty-first meeting between the Red

River rivals, the Burnt Orange Texas fans of the bicentennial state fair celebrated a 6-0 win. In a bit of coaching genius, Chevigny's late third-quarter decision to remove the backfield shock troopers and reinsert his starters prompted Bill Pitzer's fourth-quarter fifty-five-yard pass to Homer Tippen. For the third year in a row, Texas knocked off Oklahoma. The Sooners fell to 1-2, while Jack's surprising Longhorns evened their slate at 1-1.

As it turned out, the Longhorn win accomplished little more than a yawn from the Chevigny detractors. One day following the shutout win, the *San Antonio Light* questioned whether Chevigny could survive the season; the following Saturday's game against Baylor would offer no redemption for Jack's coaching. An expected win over the visiting Baylor Bears standing at 1-2 would hardly change anyone's mind.

In an acknowledgment to the existence of regional prejudice, the pens of Texas sportswriters were as poisonous as diamondbacks, while Jack's native Midwestern press wrote that the Longhorns' last two outings were evidence of an impending Texas run for the Southwest Conference championship. Indiana and Illinois newspapers reported that in a reversal of the misfortunate 1935 season, Jack had again hailed the Texas flag high over college football.

Unfortunately the members of Jack's varsity leadership council didn't get the *Chicago Tribune*; they were more influenced by the pundits who wore the ten gallon hats. As preparation for Baylor's visit continued, the upperclassmen showed only a modicum of enthusiasm for their opening conference clash.

It was only the third game of the season, but the yearlong anti-Chevigny diatribes and rumor mill had soured the Longhorn's watering hole. In practice, most of the upperclassmen showed contempt for Jack's leadership and coaching. Simulating Baylor's plays against the varsity defense, the Longhorn frosh breezed through the Steer's front.

Tuesday's sports headlines informed the public that rather than focusing on the Baylor Bears with their lone win against Hardin-Simmons, the Texas head football coach's attention was on the surprising 1-1 Longhorns.

In Jack's assessment, the Longhorn varsity was overconfident. They failed to appreciate the intensity it would take to defeat any Southwest Conference opponent, including a conference stepchild like Baylor. Well aware that a Baylor loss was something the alumni wouldn't stomach, Jack set about tearing into his squad's apathetic mindset, further distancing himself from the hearts of those boys whose egos were cut by his sharp-tongued criticisms. Blasting the Horns' effort in the Monday newspapers, Jack was unsympathetic to their lack of emotion and intensity.

The headlines read, CHEVIGNY DISPLEASED WITH SHOW OF VANITY. War had been declared on the Forty Acres.

As a motivational ploy, Jack's public reprimand of the varsity for Monday's apathetic scrimmage against the Longhorn freshmen backfired. Instead of accepting the challenge of their head coach, the Horns chose to sulk and grumble. At kickoff, a determined Baylor Bear squad coming off a successful 8-3 season in 1935 aligned across from a fractured and disassociated Longhorn club.

Amazingly, given the week's rocky practices, the Horns found themselves leading 18-0 in the fourth quarter. Steer fans were pleased to see that their superior Longhorns seemed to have the game under control. Writing their Sunday leads, press box columnists acceded the fact that Jack's whip-snapping practices and public reprimands appeared to have awakened the Longhorns from their slumbering mindset.

By the start of the final quarter, the Memorial Stadium crowd was as quiet as a catacomb, lulled to sleep by fans' early departures and conversations of the upcoming November election. Roosevelt's power base had eroded due to the stagnating results of the New Deal measures; the buzz about the nation was whether his race for a second term would end in success.

A favorite adage of Texans is "If you don't like the weather in Texas, all you have to do is stay in one place long enough and it will change." Though the Bears hadn't shown up for most of the game, the weather in Memorial Stadium was about to change.

At the start of the final quarter and trailing by three touchdowns, Baylor faced a fourth and goal situation. There was no alternative for the Baptists but to roll the dice. Sweeping around the right side, Lloyd Russell, the singing back from Waco, put the Bears on the scoreboard. Though still down by two touchdowns, Baylor owned the momentum.

Minutes later, Russell struck again. This time it was on defense. Intercepting a Longhorn pass at his own twenty-five yard line, Russell weaved his way downfield to the Texas thirty-four where he was finally brought down by several Longhorns. With a fifteen-yard penalty for unnecessary roughness tacked onto Russell's return, the Bears were in business inside the Texas twenty yard line. A quick twelve-yard pass completion brought Baylor just yards from pay dirt, but the Bears' running game continued to struggle. Finally, Baylor's Carl Brazell punched the ball over for Baylor's second score. With the point-after good, Baylor now trailed the Horns by just four points.

At this point, the various interpretations of Jack's coaching decisions that afternoon become muddled. Having struck the Horns with two quick scores, Baylor was on fire. In fact, the Bears owned most of the second half, pushing the Longhorns around during most of the third period before piercing the end zone early in the fourth. Jack felt his front line was spent and possibly shell shocked by the Russell interception. In response, Jack decided to insert some fresh men, substitutes, into the game.

Mindful of the lethargic practice week shown by his regulars, his confidence was shaken by Baylor's fourth-quarter charge. In that state of mind, Jack decided he to take out the starters of the game and go with some of the lesser, yet hungrier players. Only the outcome of the game would decide whether Jack's substitution strategy was brilliantly bold or rabidly reckless.

Relentless, Baylor regained possession of the ball inside Texas territory. In just a few plays, Lloyd Russell struck again on a short pass from Hillsboro's Billy Patterson. Successful on each of their three point-after opportunities, Baylor claimed the 21-18 conference win in Austin. Syndicated sportswriter Paul Michelson proclaimed the Bears' victory as the greatest comeback of the October 17 football weekend.

Baylor's Billy Patterson was especially gratified by the upset win. Since high school, Patterson held a grudge against Texas coach Jack Chevigny. Seven decades later, the sting of Jack's perceived slight to Patterson remained fresh in the Hillsboro native's memory. Jack recruited Patterson in 1934, arranging to meet the schoolboy at Andrews Café in Hillsboro. Coach Jack Chevigny never showed up. Receiving no follow-up phone call, Billy was stood up by the Longhorn coach. When Patterson and his teammates upset Texas by scoring those twenty-one points in the fourth quarter, he experienced great pleasure in taking part in the action. For the next seventy years, beating Jack Chevigny remained one of Billy Patterson's greatest memories as a Baylor Bear.

Despite gaining Patterson's revenge, a single conference loss to the Bears caused only minor damage to the Longhorns' SWC title hopes. Still, Jack awoke Sunday to find a fog of despair lingering over Memorial Stadium. No Texas coach who lost to Baylor had returned the following season. Though the Horns had tied a nationally ranked LSU squad, beat Oklahoma, and suffered just one conference loss, Bob Ingram of the *El Paso Herald-Post* subtitled his October 20 column with the words, "Chevigny's Job Shaky."

Writing of the Longhorns, Ingram called Texas the most uninspired eleven in college football history.

> "If the Texas alumni are yelling for Chevigny's scalp after such a disgraceful finish on the part of the Steers, it will be no surprise. That game may cost Chevigny his job."

In Kerrville, where the second-generation German Americans brewed their own beer and loved a good chorus, no one was adding an impromptu "C for Chevigny" line to Jimmie Rodgers's "Blue Yodel #1 – T for Texas." Like the bluegrass yodeling superstar with the house on the hilltop, Chevigny worshipers were now dead and gone.

Days before the Rice game, *Kerrville Times* sports columnist Neville Johnston chimed,

> "…He must either produce this year or be fired. Possibly critics of the Notre Dame style of football are right. Maybe it isn't the right system after all. Those who teach it say they must have good material. Chevigny has plenty of good material to work with. If he couldn't whip Baylor - he is sure to have plenty of trouble with the rest of the conference teams."

As the hairless D. X. Bible continuing his winning ways at Nebraska, the sands of the Texas hourglass drained for the hirsute Jack Chevigny.

Though the Longhorns had suffered just a single loss, newspapers across the state spurred the cantering anti-Chevignyism. The Texas love affair with Jack was now an ongoing ugly divorce proceeding.

Other than providing an occasional snippet of information to the press, the twenty-eight-year-old head coach remained steadfastly defiant to the negativity. Jack knew that hope was to be found in Houston where a faltering Rice program awaited the Steers. With a win, Texas could even its conference record and rejoin the title race.

Having endured a recent decline in talent, the Owls would wave no white flag over the corner of University and Main Street. Rice had five games under its belt, while the Horns had faced just three opponents. Although Jack never lost to rival Oklahoma, he had never beaten Rice.

With two games experience as an advantage, Rice enjoyed an even greater advantage in the category of personnel injuries. Texas quarterback Bill Pitzer, hero of the OU game, would not suit up for Rice. Mauled by a group of Baylor Bear tacklers, Pitzer injured his shoulder. With Pitzer reported out for the next several weeks, Jud Atchison stepped in the starting slot in an attempt to infuse the anemic Horn offense with some scoring potential.

Against Rice, a modestly talented Atchison would be out of his element. Atchison and Hugh Wolfe did manage to cut through the Owls' line for an occasional gain, but even Dr. DeBakey couldn't have saved the Longhorn offense. The Texas offensive punch died another death on the chalklined operating table.

Kerrville's Neville Johnston was right. Unable to beat Baylor, Texas would have even more trouble with the rest of the conference.

It was another close game. In Houston, the relentless Owls shredded the Longhorns' line for most of the game. Nevertheless, the Horns' tough linemen turned away two scoring threats and seemed destined to pull out the draw. Fading in the fourth quarter, a desperate Rice made its final march deep into Longhorn territory. The subsequent precision execution of a fake forty-eight-yard field goal attempt brought the Owls to the Longhorn eleven yard line. Just seconds from the final gun, future Rice baseball captain Tom Vickers smashed over from the winning score from one-yard out.

A Fort Worth native and star shortstop, Vickers was best known for his fighting temperament on the football field. After graduating from Rice in 1939, Vickers served his country in World War II when he flew missions over the Mediterranean as a B-26 Marauder pilot. Major Vickers earned a Distinguished Flying Cross and Air Medal with seven oak leaf clusters. Surviving aerial combat, the man who beat the Longhorns and sealed Jack Chevigny's fate at Texas would perish in a 1944 domestic crash of an observation plane.

Standing at 0-2 in conference play, the Horns were out of the SWC race. Upon arrival in Austin, Jack was greeted with jeers and chants of "We Want Littlefield."

With Clyde Littlefield's success as the Steers' freshman coach, the *Daily Texan* called for the legendary Longhorn to be reinstated to the position of head football coach. The Baby Bulls' win over the Slimes (an analogy of Rice Institute's freshman being akin to the primordial ooze of life's evolution) had generated dope around town that the beloved Littlefield would return to his old position as trail boss and drive the main herd against SMU on the following Saturday.

The fact that Jack ignored the clamor for his immediate resignation spoke volumes in articulating his tenacity as an athlete and man. With a splintered coaching staff, a fractured team, and a campus undivided in its contempt, Jack Chevigny turned his battered ship into the wind to face Southern Methodist on Halloween.

"Not so fast," wrote the *Houston Post's* Lloyd Gregory.

First, there was some salt to be rubbed in Jack's wound. By midweek, Jack was under attack on multiple fronts. The *Daily Texan* and local print media hadn't quite measured their pound of flesh for Jack's blackout prior to the LSU game. More of Jack's hide needed to be cut and weighed as redress. Out of Houston came charges that Jack had exhorted his Longhorns to do whatever it took to beat the Owls. Gregory, a 1922 graduate and former Longhorn tennis player, accused Jack of encouraging the Horns to engage in dirty football.

Perhaps Gregory felt the discussion would tip the scales in favor of Jack's abrupt dismissal. Possibly, the nationally recognized journalist was simply exposing what he felt was a perceptibly nasty aspect of his alma mater's style of play. Gregory was no Chevigny fan, and his attitude toward the Indiana native was not without accoutrements of the standard regional prejudices of the era.

Though he sparked the fire, the esteemed Gregory couldn't anticipate the back draft of his accusation. Surprisingly, several Texas sports columnists defended Jack against the "dirty football" charge. Other wire stories from Associated Press and United Press also defended Jack. News articles quoted players who not only denied the charges, but also stated that their coach had reminded them to "by all means, keep it clean."

The rebound effect of the dirty football accusation distracted the circling buzzards and allowed Jack to circle the wagons. By the end of the week, even his harshest critics became leery of making further assaults. Throughout the turmoil, Jack remained silent on the charges, choosing instead to focus on grounding the aerial circus of Southern Methodist

University. Coming within seven points of winning the Rose Bowl and an undisputed national championship, the Ponies returned a squad strong enough to ride to another national title.

In the pre-game conferences, Mustang coach Matty Bell attempted to downplay the disparity between the two squads, saying he just wanted to escape Austin with a one-point win.

Meanwhile, Jack took the opportunity to backhand the critics who alleged that he had inspired his team to play "rough" in Houston, saying, "I can only hope the boys play as hard and clean a game as they did against Rice last week."

Though October 31 was the scheduled kickoff for SMU, the better news was the continuing duel between the scribes of the *Houston Post* and Jack's scattered defenders. One remarkable Chevigny defense was a tongue-in-cheek chronicle penned by Abilene's colorful sportswriter, H. L. "Prexy" Anderson. Responding to the ongoing tilling of the Rice controversy, Anderson recounted Jack's personal rebuttal in an Austin newspaper and included a testimonial from an official of the Rice game. In the editorial, the Longhorn coach quoted "umpire Higgins of SMU."

Higgins, who spent the entire Rice game stationed just behind the defensive line, stated, "It certainly was not a dirty game in any sense of the word, but a good tough football game. It was a great game with both teams ready for battle. It was one of the cleanest games I have ever officiated."

The fact that Jimmy Higgins was the brother of famed Longhorn Ox Higgins, a man who happened to be one of Jack's most loyal friends, allegedly had nothing to do with his perception as a Southwest Conference official. But clearly, Jack had pulled nothing in his counterpunch to Lloyd Gregory's scathing pen.

In his defense of Jack, Prexy Anderson showed that he had a bone to pick with the *Houston Post* and one writer in particular named Bruce Layer. A pioneer in electronic media throughout the Houston market, Layer got his start with the *Post*.

In reporting on the October game, Layer finagled a private viewing of the Rice-Texas game film. The filming of games as an instructional tool was a technological leap forward for college football, and Layer understood its value as an interpretive aide to reporting on the game.

Following his film session, Layer wrote,

> "After watching the pictures, we suggest changing the Texas University from Longhorns to Cowboys, for the Texas tacklers turned in a fine bulldogging performance. There are those who contend the Texas team was mistreated by officials. Let them take a glance at the pictures. Let them see Clint Small, the Texas captain try to twist Buck Friedman's head from his shoulders. Let them watch Mittermayer smash ball carriers under the chin instead of tackling. Let them look at a few of the Texas boys pile on after a play is over."

Countering with a narrative aimed at Layer's comments, Prexy Anderson's sarcastic saber wit sliced at the *Post's* literary brigade. "It all seems to boil down to the question of whether the officials or the motion picture camera had a better view of the game."

For Anderson and most other sports fans in 1936, the human eye was far more trustworthy than the moving pictures. In this film, it was Jack Chevigny who was being framed.

While the debate continued right up to the SMU kickoff, one news article commented that the Texas gate would be unexpectedly larger because of the hundreds who would attend the game just to see if the Longhorns did indeed play dirty football. By game time at Memorial Stadium, Texas's dirty football was the talk of the campus, town, state, and nation.

"Many will go the game with field glasses to get a close-up view of every play, particularly any that may involve a penalty. Likewise, sidelines photographers will probably spend as much time attempting to catch action pictures which show 'dirty' work at the same crossroads, as they will snapping shots of brilliant play....When the opening whistle shrills...all of the 'down with Chevigny' shouters will be present, looking for additional reasons for their shouting to further convince themselves that they are justified. Since the Rice game, this group had been particularly adept at picking Chevigny's record to pieces."

*—Austin American Statesman*

Against the SMU Mustangs, the Longhorn players exhibited none of the enthusiasm present the week before in Houston. It was if they had been spanked on the hand for their aggressive play at Rice. Jack could only stand by as his Longhorns genteelly waltzed about the grass-covered dance floor of Memorial Stadium. The Horns brought another loss home to Ma Griffith's boarding house.

Although the 14-7 score was much closer than the Chevigny-haters wanted, the advantage in Mustang first downs marked the growing despair in the Longhorns' offensive production. The Notre Dame box, crunched and battered by three consecutive losses, was barely recognizable as a descendent of the shifting and spinning Rockne mechanism of tornadic destruction.

It wasn't that the Longhorns didn't have their chances against the Ponies. For the third time in three weeks, the game was decided in the closing moments. Looking down from the rafters of self-righteous judgment, the boo birds were doubtlessly disappointed to see Jack's Longhorns take an early lead and hold on until the middle of the third quarter. After the Mustangs took the lead, a last-ditch drive carried Jack's Steers deep in SMU territory where it appeared that the Burnt Orange would tie the game, but the heavily favored Mustangs nabbed an interception, turning back the Horns and securing the win.

Jack's post-game statement was positive, if not tinged with a lingering bitterness toward the *Houston Post* articles of the previous week.

> "Matty's team has potentialities equal to the Rose Bowl team of last year but it doesn't have the polish yet. I'm proud of my Longhorns for their clean, hard fight. It's no disgrace to get licked by Bell's team."

Four days later, the Rice accusations resurfaced in print. This time it was Bill Van Fleet of the *Galveston Daily News* who exhumed the dirty play accusations. Van Fleet had attended the Texas pep rally in which the students mocked Lloyd Gregory and the *Houston Post*. Particularly distasteful was a satirical song directed at Gregory and the Chevigny-haters at the Post. The Galveston sportswriter remarked that the song was "funny enough if you forget that it is doing injustice to a guy who had the nerve to write what he saw."

> A gridiron's just for tea and toast
> Take it from the Houston Post.
> If a man would run and twist
> Only slap him on the wrist.
> Tomorrow, we play S.M.U.
> With pretty colors, red and blue.
> Tickle, tackle all you please
>
> Do not slap or pinch of squeeze.
>
> (Chorus)
>
> Tackle, tickle take a chance
> Get your fans and do a dance
> Tickle, tackle, and be sweet
> But don't knock 'em off their feet.
> Romp and play with S.M.U.
> Tickle, tackle, let' em through

Then they'll think we're oh, so nice.
And let us win the same as Rice.

(Chorus)

Listen, you rough college boys,
Don't use slang or make loud noise
If you do, you wait and see
You'll hear from Lloyd Gregory.
When he was in the Varsity,
A football man of note was he,
He did his playing in the band
Went off tackle, flute in hand.

(Chorus)

Upset that the song chided fellow UT alum Gregory, Bill Van Fleet, a free press zealot and Clyde Littlefield man from his days as the first publicist for the Texas Longhorns, penned a rasping rebuttal.

Writing that a perplexed Orangeblood heard that Texas captain Clint Small was booed at Rice, Van Fleet remarked, "They did, brother. And while you may sometimes convince this corner that a couple of newspapermen may be wrong, you never can make us believe that four officials and eighteen thousand fans all were wrong."

Granted, Bill Van Fleet had not been privy to umpire Jimmy Higgins's observations. No matter, the rough play vampire would continue to rise again and again throughout the remainder of the season.

With the SMU loss, Jack felt as if his own coffin was being nailed shut. The Horns had lost three conference games and were in sole possession of the cellar. Each of those losses had swung on a fourth-quarter pendulum; their outcomes could have gone either way. Now, it would be Jack who would surely feel the swinging of the blade.

In Fort Worth, wrangling most of the Southwest Conference as a hardened rancher would a yearling; Slingin' Sammy Baugh of TCU waited for his turn at some Bevo barbeque. Whether it be roping mavericks or throwing pigskins, the slender Baugh needed little practice. Nursing a badly sprained ankle, he wouldn't get much. Nevertheless, the TCU ace was a ballplayer with the heart of a West Texas rancher. Raised in an environment in which a farm boy rose before 5:00 a.m. and trekked outside into a blistering arctic wind to feed the livestock before he had so much as a biscuit in his own belly, Sammy Baugh was unaffected by bruises and sprains. Sick days weren't part of his vocabulary.

As Baugh rested on the Frog practice field sideline, the Hatfield-McCoy feud between Jack and the press reloaded for another skirmish. This time it was Jack who fired the first shot.

When Jack was asked about how anyone could beat Sammy Baugh and Texas Christian, his admonishment was curt, "That's easy, you've got to outscore them."

A day later, the Longhorns traveled to an unknown location near Fort Worth to practice. Snubbing his nose at the press's ardent barking at his heels, Jack returned to the public relations stance he had assumed before the season opener against LSU.

By denying the press access to the Longhorns' workouts, Jack fended off attacks regarding his coaching and the low productivity of the hop-scotching Notre Dame box offense.

On November 8, 1936, newspapers across Texas peppered headlines across the state announcing that Jack Chevigny would not be the Longhorn head football coach in 1937. Discussions had already emerged as to whether Texas should make the leap forward to raise its head coaching salary to the level needed for snagging a man who could lead the Horns from the abyss. In most cases, the author of such articles pointed out that given his paltry $5,000 salary, Jack was the best for which the Longhorn backers could hope. Once associated with flying the flag of Texas high over the college football world, the name of Jack Chevigny had become synonymous with a commitment to mediocrity.

Information gleaned from a leak inside the Texas attorney general's office revealed that pending his release from Texas, Jack would be hired as an attorney for the state. Three days before the TCU kickoff, Jack issued a press release denying the rumor.

Four games remained, including a tussle with the top team in the nation, Minnesota.

Given his 4-2-1 record and custody of the nation's most prolific passer, TCU's Dutch Meyer had none of Jack's problems. Neither would Baugh have any problems with the Longhorn secondary, firing four touchdown passes while leading Texas Christian to a 27-6 win.

Again the dirty play accusations stole the headlines as P. D. Eldred's Associated Press wire took note of the dirty play of Clint Small. The Longhorn team captain was caught repeatedly kneeing downed Horned Frog ball carriers after the whistle. Two flags against Small led to the fourth and final score for the Horned Frogs.

Jack's Longhorns had finally folded their tents. No Texas Longhorn football team had ever lost four consecutive SWC games.

Strengthening the call for Texas to enter the sphere of big time college football, the *San Antonio Light* announced the 1937 football schedule just days before the Horns left for Minnesota. Not only would the regents need to flex the salary level, they also would have to stand behind a tougher football schedule.

As athletic director, Jack had pushed for this move when he composed the 1936 schedule, a schedule that the Associated Press ranked fourth in the nation in difficulty. As a battered coach, Jack now reaped the bitter harvest of such a schedule. One day after practicing for the Gophers, Jack turned his sleek LaSalle coupe southeast toward Houston.

Almost halfway between Austin and Houston is a sleepy little town known for its quality milk cows and high grade feed grass, the combination of which made for the highest quality ice cream in Texas, if not the country. Texas powerbroker J. R. Parten was waiting at Brenham's Crocket Hotel, most likely having a piece of pie and a dab of Blue Bell ice cream.

Jack decided he had had enough and was notifying his principal backer Parten of the decision. What Jack wanted in return for his resignation was the word of the regents that President Benedict would refrain from any public criticism of Jack and desist from initiating administrative proceedings aimed at terminating his employment. Parten attempted to sell Jack on fighting on through the season and tabling the issue until the end of the season, but after some discussion, Parten relinquished to Jack's wish and guaranteed that his two conditions would be met. Warning Jack that he was opening a door through which he could not return, Texas's most influential oilman shook Jack's hand and headed home to Madisonville.

An arctic cold front had pushed into Texas; the Panhandle was already frozen solid. As the Canadian blast pushed southeast, a crisp November chill crept downward into the heart of Texas. The LaSalle headed west, skimming along the southern edge of the front. On the drive back to Austin, illumination from the car's teardrop headlights pierced the blackness as Jack's mood swirled in an antilogy of exhilaration and deep sadness. For the first time in his life, Jack Chevigny had admitted failure. He pressed the accelerator to the floor and rolled down his window. He always felt better when he drove fast. Cold air whistling past his window would have brought his thoughts back to Hammond and South Bend. Snow. Family. Friends. The Cadillac-built *straight-8* purred as the narrow right lane blurred into racing partitions of concrete. Jack's body was speeding back to Austin, but his heart was traveling in a new direction.

AUSTIN, Nov. 11 (AP) –Head Coach Jack Chevigny of the University of Texas' downtrodden football team today had assured the "wolves" they "could not sit back and relax—I will not be an applicant for reappointment."

Target of alumni and newspaper fire during the current losing streak of his Longhorns, Chevigny announced on the eve of today's departure for Minneapolis, where the Steers clash with Minnesota Saturday, that he would not seek reappointment.

Chevigny, whose third season contract expires February 1, finished a brief speech before a banquet throng of Longhorn well wishers with his startling statement.

Chevigny's announcement surprised many of his listeners although he had been under fire because of his team's poor record. Starting auspiciously by holding Louisiana State to a tie and then defeating the University of Oklahoma, the Longhorns slumped to the Southwest conference cellar with consecutive defeats by Baylor, Rice, Southern Methodist and Texas Christian.

"As to my future," Chevigny said, "I feel that other business opportunities will possibly overshadow my desire to be with the University."

The coach, who has a law degree, indicated he was considering taking up the practice of law. His statement lent credence to recent rumors generally denied, that he was to become an assistant to Attorney General McCraw.

In answer to public accusations that his team had played rough football, Chevigny said: "To a few whose prejudiced views were presented in print I hope that by our efforts to play the game as it is to be played, we will convince them to join us in the sportsmanship that this team has displayed at all times."

Chevigny's announcement was expected to precipitate a flood of applications for his position. Clyde Littlefield, coach of freshman football and track who preceded Chevigny as head mentor, was reported favored by a number of "old guards." The athletic council had taken no public cognizance of recent "howling of the wolves."

Prior to the coach's talk, which was made at a dinner honoring the Longhorns, Captain Clint Small of the team praised Chevigny highly and pledged the squad's co-operation for the remainder of the season. After the Minnesota game, the team faces Texas A. and M. College and Arkansas.

"I sincerely believe the team has played as great a brand of football every Saturday this season as could be seen anywhere in the nation," Chevigny said.

"I would like especially to commend the boys of the squad whose spirit has never faltered and who have given their best always, often under trying circumstances."

Chevigny came to the State University from St. Edward's University of Austin. —*Austin Statesman*

Facing a Minnesota juggernaut, the Horns played as well as could be expected. Though Jack inspired his team with a police escort through Chicago's Loop district to Soldier Field where they were put through the paces in their dress orange and white, the Golden Gophers represented another level of competition, a level, which super booster Lutcher Stark and the football frenzied press hounds of Texas wanted to attain. Arriving in Minneapolis to meet their opponent, Jack Gray and Hugh Wolfe, no tiny man, saw the 1936 Gophers as though they were the descendants of Paul Bunyan. One Texas lineman was heard to say that the Minnesota front line looked like no trees from Texas he had ever seen. The game was over before it had begun; Bernie Bierman's Minnesota Gophers expectedly crushed the Longhorns.

Colorful game accounts described the game with phrases like "brute force, bowled over, battered, hammered, bruised," and "ripped the Texas line to shreds." Of the forty-four thousand fans in attendance, most would have agreed with the adjectives. Minnesota hammered the Longhorns, racking up 547 yards of total offense.

Only Hugh Wolfe measured up to the Nordic supermen. He returned a kickoff for ninety-seven yards and a touchdown late in the third period. But the future plant nursery magnate's kickoff return offered no fertile ground for a Longhorn comeback. For Bierman's Golden Gophers, Wolfe's spectacular run was little more than a bump in the road as they cut ruts in the undersized and overwhelmed visitors, 47-19.

With two games left, the lame duck coach, saddled with a guaranteed losing season and a legacy of a sub-500 career winning percentage, was expected to stand to the task of upholding a Texas tradition. The Longhorns had lost at home to the Texas A&M Aggies just once in forty-three years.

Carrying a 6-2-1 record into Austin would mean that the Aggies held their best hand ever for trumping the forty-three-year series jinx. Only a year earlier, the possibility of dropping the sputtering Aggie football program volleyed about College Station. Sparked by their 20-6 thrashing of the Horns the previous Thanksgiving, the Aggies resurrection had sparked a new resolve amongst the corps and their fans. Last year's dominance over an apathetic Longhorn squad still remained a fresh memory for every Aggie.

Almost as prevalent as the anti-war columns debating the political winds blowing across Europe and Asia were the continued anti-Chevigny articles. Stanley Gunn of the *San Antonio Light* reported that the Longhorns' lawyer-coach intimated in his best legal language that Jack had not resigned at the Texas football banquet; he had merely stated he would not seek reappointment to the post of head football coach. Jack's backpedal sent every newspaper in Texas scrambling for a quote regarding this apparent change of direction. Whether the sleight of hand originated with Jack or whether it was just another anti-Chevigny plant to reignite the flames of controversy during the dull twelve-day stretch before the A&M game, selling papers was indeed the business of a Depression-era newspaper.

In Austin, the November 26 sunrise finally arrived, bringing with it the hated Aggies. For the moment, Jack Chevigny was no longer in the spotlight. Courtesy of Lutcher Stark's generosity, the forty-four-piece Orange High School Bengal Guards entertained an anxious home crowd on Thanksgiving Day in Austin. At center stage along with one of the Golden Triangle's most revered bands were Clint Small, Hugh Wolfe, Red Sheridan, and Jud Atchison. Could they hold the line and maintain the winning home tradition against the favored Ags?

Despite the high quality sounds of Stark's alma mater drum and bugle corps, a substantially greater entertainment value was provided by Sweetwater native Ney Sheridan when he provided the scoring punch in a tight defensive game.

Surprisingly, with the 7-0 victory, a swell of support for Jack Chevigny's return as head coach gained an inexplicable momentum and threatened the established structures in place for Jack's dismissal. Talk bandied about town; Jack's coaching may have been unjustly criticized. The Indiana showman's team had put together a strong showing against several quality teams. Texas A&M had been poised to secure the conference championship with an upcoming showdown with SMU, but the Horns trampled their aspiration.

While Chevigny critics pointed to the erratic week-to-week play of the Horns as more evidence that Jack should be dismissed, supporters counted that Jack had the Midas touch, able to turn chicken excrement into a palatable chicken salad. Only Jack could have beaten Texas A&M when it counted. Indeed, across the Forty Acres, the general consensus was that the Aggie game was the only one which counted.

Riding high after the players put together a late-November petition for Jack to withdraw the statement that he would, in Calvin Coolidge fashion, "not choose to run" for the appointment as head football coach, Jack now had something of a different take on his future at Texas.

No one can be sure of Jack's motivation for riding the seesaw of public opinion toward his reappointment. His motivation may have been related to a common strategy used by a coach under siege; solidify the scattered base of support by offering a resignation.

Regardless of his personal objectives or exit strategy, Jack played the reappointment controversy like a Stradivarius. And with the Texas A&M win steeling his resolve, he now appeared publicly willing to ride out the storm and let his influential backers such as H. H. Weinert and J. C. Dolley speak on his behalf. In the meantime, Jack also had managed to recondition his image on campus. By the week of preparation for Arkansas, many students were heard to be in support of Jack.

In a trend that disturbed President Benedict and the other policy-makers, the quantity of those students vocal against Jack's return was dwindling. A road win over a 6-3 Arkansas squad would reinforce Jack's recovery and possibly offer him a real chance to compete for his reappointment in January. In that campus controversy is the bane of every college president, the emerging controversy over Jack's future as head coach threatened Benedict's hope for a dispassionate and bucolic transition for the Longhorn football program.

Likewise holding a special interest in the Arkansas-Texas contest was Nebraska coach, D. X. Bible. The *Houston Post* had prematurely named Bible as Jack's successor. As Jack would have hoped, the announcement formed only another wave of pro-Chevigny sentiment.

In Little Rock on December 3, 1936, both coaches needed a win. Being a gambling man, Jack knew the stakes. His Longhorns typically achieved when expected to fail, and failed when expected to achieve. Against Arkansas, Jack would have to push his remaining chips to the center of the table. A win against the conference leader would make Jack the pot leader in the high stakes game that was his coaching future. A loss would mean he was finally tapped out.

When a muddy field slowed an already stagnant Longhorn offense, Jack went bust in Arkansas, 6-0. That Saturday, Arkansas squeaked by the Horns when a third-quarter pass gave the Hogs all the leverage they would need to secure the win and the 1936 Southwest Conference title.

It was the Longhorns' fourth conference loss by a touchdown or less. Not only did the six-point Razorback victory guarantee a vacant seat at the head of the table at Ma Griffith's boarding house, it also secured Jack's place as the only coach in Longhorn history to finish his career with a losing record.

Upon seeing the Arkansas score, D. X. Bible told his wife Rowena to gather some boxes and pack the delicates. They would be moving to Austin soon.

# CHAPTER SEVENTEEN

# *One Big Inch and Ten Yards to Go*

The weeks following Pearl Harbor saw America's military infrastructure grind its gears as the nation attempted to abruptly shift its war materials production from a blunt deterrent of war to a sleek spearhead of destruction. Integral to this structural shift was the supply and delivery of domestic oil. As the first Japanese bomb dropped on Hawaii, 60 percent of the world's oil supply was being pumped from United States soil, principally Texas and Oklahoma.

Approximately 95 percent of the Texas oil supply was shipped to the Northeast via tankers traveling from the Gulf of Mexico north along the Atlantic coast, a route infested with German U-boats. Less than three months after America's entry into the war, these U-boats were feasting on the northbound oil tankers. President Roosevelt's advisors recognized that without the uninterrupted flow of both crude oil and refined oil from Texas and Oklahoma, America would be unable to wage war effectively. For those individuals assigned to oversee the transportation of oil from the Gulf of

Mexico ports to New Jersey and New York, it was a time of tireless days and sleepless nights.

Government officials felt that a pipeline connecting Texas to Philadelphia would be the most effective countermeasure to the threat of German attacks on the oil resources flowing eastward from Texas and Oklahoma. Two parallel pipelines along this route would change the rules of the game. Dubbed the Big Inch and Little Inch pipeline projects, the Big Inch line would deliver 250,000 barrels of crude oil a day, while the Little Inch delivered another 200,000 barrels of refined oil products such as fuel for automobiles and planes.

Though a state of war called for unilateral cooperation between the various energy-delivery occupations, political jockeying delayed the laying of the pipe as junior U. S. Senator Claude Peppers of Florida used his growing clout to lobby for the continued construction of the Intracoastal Waterway. Fearful that a quarter of a million gallons piped directly to the Northeast would cost them their niche in the economics of the oil delivery system, Texas oil refinery barons also objected to construction the Big Inch and Little Inch pipelines, while additional opposition came from the railroad men who saw pipelines as a death knell to their way of life. Also bowing their collective necks against any mention of pipeline construction were the West Virginia coal miners whose livelihood depended on the railroads. They were steadfastly against any intersectional oil pipeline and the apparent government trend toward a de-emphasis of coal fuel.

In spite of the well-organized anti-pipeline lobby, the federal government moved forward with its plan to utilize some facet of a trans-regional oil pipeline. To further its progress, FDR appointed Jack's ally and benefactor from his days with the Longhorns, Texas oilman J. R. Parten, to the lengthy title of transportation director for the Office of Petroleum

Coordinator for National Defense. Parten possessed the skill set to navigate the pipeline plan successfully through the rough waters of opposition generated by the Texas refining industry, Claude Peppers, the railroads, and the coal miners. Six years removed from the petty politics of the University of Texas Athletic Department, Parten's job would be to move the nation's oil from Texas to the shipping ports of New York and beyond. By overseeing the transport of oil energy from Texas to the East Coast, Parten had graduated from negotiating on behalf of the Longhorns' football coach to arbitrating on behalf of the free world's energy supply. Placating the discontented factions with concessions, the Texas oilman quickly secured the funds for constructing the Big Inch to its eastern terminus at Norris City, Illinois.

Just forty-three miles west of Norris City was oilman Jack Chevigny's residence in Mount Vernon, a boarding house at 121 North 12th Street. Former Longhorn Hugh Wolfe, on a trip to New York, once detoured through southern Illinois to visit his old football coach. Driving to where he was told that he could find his former mentor, Wolfe was greeted by an unexpected spectacle. Wolfe recognized Jack out in a field nearby a well site. He and his oil workers were engaged in a full-contact scrimmage, Jack in his suit pants, white shirt, tie, and suspenders, coordinating the action as oil-soaked roughnecks and tool pushers in greasy overalls shifted in the backfield with perfect Rockne cadence. Stepping out of the car, Wolfe was immediately recognized by his former coach and asked to join in the game. Though the Stephenville speedster declined the offer, he would never forget the gleam in Jack's eyes when a ball carrier, weaving and lateraling his way amongst the oil-covered coveralls and steel-toed boots, scored the last touchdown in near darkness. It would be the last time Wolfe would see Jack Chevigny.

On February 13, 1943, the first shipment of Texas crude arrived in Norris City, Illinois, via the Big Inch pipeline. The eastern terminus had been reached.

Visiting his official residence of 10 Vine Street, the home of his sister Graziella Galvin, Jack would have taken little note of Parten's accomplishment. As a result of the threat of war in Europe and the Pacific, the first peacetime draft in American history was instituted in 1940. The Burke-Wadsworth Act, approved by a single vote in the House, cleared the Senate easily and was signed by President Roosevelt. All men ages twenty-one through thirty-five were to register for the draft. If selected in the lottery, the length of service for each man would be twelve months.

Thanks to the Burke-Wadsworth Act and a lottery pick, Jack's number had come up. Ordered to report to Indiana's Fort Benjamin Harrison for induction and processing, the thirty-six-year-old oilman and former football coach was drafted into the United States Army.

The Indianapolis military installation of Fort Benjamin Harrison had conducted its first training exercise in June of 1906, two months prior to Jack's birth. At the time of Jack's wartime induction into the Army in March 10, 1943, Fort Benjamin Harrison was the nation's largest facility for induction and reception of military draftees during the war.

In his attempt to join the service during the early months of the war, Jack was rejected due to an old knee injury suffered at Notre Dame. However, with the war escalating in two theatres, the conditions for a draftee's fitness became less stringent. Once denied the opportunity to serve, patriotic individuals with borderline physical disqualifications were now deemed acceptable.

Though Jack would have welcomed his draft notice and eagerly answered his country's call, his letters home from Fort Benjamin made it clear that the thirty-something bachelor wasn't a good fit for the Army. Always impeccably dressed as a civilian, Jack despised Army life and the baggy, hewn uniform of the enlisted man. Indeed, his attitude didn't help his predicament. Inducted as a buck private, Jack's days in basic training were highlighted by punishment drills and extra duty assignments. Exhibiting no desire to tap into the celebrity status and leadership skills of Private John Edward Chevigny, the Army quickly demonstrated that it hadn't much use for an aging prima donna Notre Dame football legend. Peeling potatoes and saluting second lieutenants were persistent reminders to Jack that he held no distinction in a mass of indifference. Jack struggled through his first three months of enlistment and eventually graduated the rigors of intake and basic training at Fort Benjamin Harrison, but his next assignment at Fort Lawton in Seattle failed to improve his lot as a member of the United States Army.

Located just above Puget Sound, Fort Lawton served as a training base and transition hub for troops bound for the South Pacific. Later in the war, the Seattle military base would experience its own day of infamy when several hundred black soldiers attacked a handful of Italian prisoners of war. The Fort Lawton riot ended in the lynching of one Italian soldier and the court-martial of forty-three Americans. Twenty-eight of the black soldiers were convicted and sentenced to terms ranging from six months to twenty-five years.

Since his first day on the Fort Benjamin Harrison grounds, Jack had worked his political connections, so that he might get out of the Army. But it wasn't a desire to leave the service that prompted his machinations; rather, it was his drive to better serve his country. Jack wanted to be a Marine. Not unlike thousands of American boys, the Gipper legend saw the United States Marine Corps as the nation's elite branch of service. To Jack, the Corps was the Notre Dame of America's fighting forces. Within a month of arriving in Seattle, Jack's political connections and savvy paid off when U. S. Army Private Chevigny was appointed a first lieutenant in the Marine Corps Reserve.

In a letter to Maurice D. O'Hern, Hammond native Howard J. Gescheidler recalled seeing his friend Jack at Fort Lawton. Gescheidler wrote,

> "...I was the Personnel Sergeant Major at the Seattle Port of Embarkation...Fort Lawton was a Staging Area and we had four or five thousand troops who were returning or leaving for overseas. I will never forget one morning the name Jack Chevigny crossed my desk and I saw he was in the Staging Area at Fort Lawton. I immediately went out to see him. He was dressed in poorly fitted army fatigues. As a matter of fact, he looked rather bad, and I said, 'Jack, what in the world are you doing out here?' Jack replied, 'I'm waiting for a commission in the Marine Corps and as soon as I get notice, I'll be out of here.' Jack was a well known personality. He said he had been on KP duty which started at 4 o'clock in the morning, ever since he had arrived at the Staging Area...I told Jack that the orders for him to be discharged from the Army to join the Marines would come over my desk and as soon as they were received from Washington, I would let him know. It wasn't but a few days later that we did receive the orders. I immediately went out to Fort Lawton and advised him that the orders would be good that day and he would be released to the Marine Corps the following day."

Gescheidler noted that in anticipation of being transferred, Jack had gone to Seattle's Bon Marché department store, a store once owned by the family of Nordy Hoffman, the starting right guard on the 1931 Fighting Irish—the team over which Hunk and Jack split the head coaching title and authority.

The next time H. J. Gescheidler saw Jack, the newly commissioned first lieutenant was dressed in a tailor-fitted Marine officer's summer uniform. The uniform would have set him back $65.00. Individually, the officer's cap cost $12.95, and the Jarman cordovans with lace would have put an $8.95 hole in his wallet.

That same day, the Marine Corps capitalized on the celebrity status of their newest officer by shooting a promotional photo of a dashing First Lieutenant Chevigny escorting an attractive female Marine reservist down a dusty Seattle street. Gescheidler remembered that he last saw Jack at the Fort Lawton staging area finding great satisfaction in receiving the continuous salutes of the Army second lieutenants who days earlier had outranked him.

The Associated Press wire photo of Jack with Marine Corps Woman's Reservist Agnes Plesh at his right elbow was a public relations coup for the Marine Corps. The physically fit, dark-haired first lieutenant with a cinematic profile, strolling along in conversation with the captivating former model made morning papers across the nation. As Agnes beamed over Jack's right shoulder, the camera lens seemed to catch a glint of light in his eyes. Illuminated in the moment, the faded "One for the Gipper" star had returned to center stage of America's consciousness.

The transition from Army sad sack to Marine Corps poster boy wasn't the only transformation in Jack's life. While in Washington, he met Eugenia Purdy, a slender, five-foot two-inch, doe-eyed bank employee. Always having an eye for the ladies, Jack had noticed the smallish but athletically built Seattle native while making a downtown bank transaction in his private's uniform.

The college-educated granddaughter of a pioneering Northwest Territory timber-cutting family, Eugenia's friends called her Gege, the nickname being pronounced with the soft "G" and long "E" sounds. The avid Mount Rainier skier, tennis player, and award-winning equestrian was over a decade younger and much more reserved than the worldly thirty-five-year-old private. Called to provide a fourth for a Bridge game at the home of John and Mary English, Jack the expert Bridge player, fell hard for Gege's wit and quick laughter. After he witnessed her card-playing ability, the ladies' man known to stop every female's heart in the room fell for the girl.

The atypical Jack Chevigny female acquaintance, Gege was a straight-laced Catholic girl, fiercely independent, and private. For Jack, Gege was something special. Her forceful personality and intelligence gave her the ability to match the dynamic Marine officer at every step. Embarking on the typical wartime romance, Jack and Gege were the perfect couple.

It was Gege who had accompanied him on the proudest day of his life, the day he picked up his tailored uniform from the Bon Marché store. Dressed in his Army private's uniform, Jack asked her to come along for a drive. When they arrived downtown, Jack asked her to wait in the car. After some time, Gege wondered what could be taking him so long. Beginning to believe she may be stranded, she looked up from her window and saw Jack exiting the front door of the Bon Marché. Sporting the summer dress uniform of a Marine first lieutenant, Jack slid in behind the wheel.

For the rest of her life, Gege remembered the look of pride in Jack's reflection of the side view mirror. From that day, Jack's life changed. He was a Marine officer, and he had found his soul mate. And from that moment, Gege would practically have to pry Jack from her side just to get a breath of fresh air.

For the rest of the month, their relationship sped forward in the typical wartime manner. After graduation from officer's indoctrination school, Jack participated in physical training school at Camp Pendleton. Chaperoned by her cousin, Gege trekked the Pacific Coast highway to San Diego to visit Jack that August. Riding in her cousin's red convertible, the coastal drive from her driveway on Federal Drive to Camp Pendleton had a storybook feel, the ocean's crisp breeze lifting her hair as the powerful coupe tooled down the Pacific Coast Highway, inarguably the most picturesque highway in America. Awaiting her and her cousin, Buzz Berg, were the most crowded one hundred twenty-five thousand acres on Earth.

Upon their arrival in the Camp Pendleton area, neither she nor Buzz could find any lodging, but the resourceful Jack arranged for her to stay with a woman named Angel. Spending her nights with Jack in Los Angeles at the Ambassador Hotel's Cocoanut Grove, Gege and her star-struck Marine would sip King's Ransom Scotch Whiskey and dance on the smoke-clouded floor filled with servicemen and celebrities. For the couple who now seemed to be developing a more serious intention, time sped; the days evaporating into minutes. In the blink of an eye, Gege was on a train back to Washington.

Enjoying the weekly letters arriving from Seattle, Jack attempted to refocus on his duty assignment, learning to become a better Marine officer. At the same time, across the Forty-Eight in North Carolina, the Marine Corps was assembling a football program.

The wartime Corps' new athletic mission statement was to upgrade the Camp Lejeune football team to the standard of a championship caliber intercollegiate program. The Corps' brass hoped that the policy shift toward upgrading the Lejeune football program would enhance camp morale not only at New River but across the country. Locally, the Lejeune command felt that providing the diversion of a high quality football team that could compete against major universities and naval bases would provide an exciting collegiate atmosphere for the thousands of Marines who had nowhere to go for the weekend. Taking command of the base in June 1943, Brigadier General Henry L. Larson issued a directive aimed at the establishment of a program on par with the college football powers of the Southeast.

Commenting for the *New River Pioneer*, Larsen stated "his wish was the Marines might use this undertaking as a way to make Camp Lejeune famous throughout sports circles in the same manner as the famous Quantico teams of the 'twenties'."

Marquette football and basketball letterman, First Lieutenant Marvin Bell was assigned the task of organizing the team. The *New River Pioneer* reported that on Monday, August 2, 1943, an orientation was to be held at 2030 in Area 4 Gym. An open invitation for all men who wished to tryout resulted in 140 candidates.

In alignment with the goal of the Lejeune recreation office to provide more weekend entertainment and enhance base morale through the experience of a collegiate home game atmosphere, Bell, whose coaching resume included five years of service at Marquette, indicated that he hoped to schedule nine home games against quality competition.

In 1943, "quality competition" meant any university that possessed a V-12 program, a military program that trained college men to become officers in order to supplement the pool of wartime naval officers. It was a win-win proposition for the Navy and the participating colleges. Because of the war, America's colleges and universities had experienced a drop in enrollment. The economic effect on some of these institutions was disastrous, and several colleges faced closure. The Navy's V-12 program compensated for the inability of the United States Naval Academy to supply an adequate number of officers needed for the war while subsidizing the anemic enrollment numbers in many universities nationwide.

Consequent to the V-12 program was the clandestine shuffling of some of the nation's better football players to select V-12 colleges. Often, V-12 colleges possessed the services of college stars who had transferred to avoid an immediate deployment as an enlisted man. In the V-12 program, these football stars could train to become an officer while continuing to play football. Thus, the federally funded V-12 program became a conduit through which star athletes could be enticed to a university where they would receive a uniform and $50 a month until graduation. Following graduation and upon conclusion of their ability to pass muster in boot camp, the men received commissions as Navy ensigns or second lieutenants in the Marine Corps.

Despite the ease of obtaining star athletes for certain bases and programs, the Navy and Marine Corps ironically took little consideration of the student's value to his football team once the cadet completed the V-12 regimen. Invariably, if the coursework ended and the V-12 requirement was met, the athlete would be shipped off to basic training. One such noteworthy case was Notre Dame's Angelo Bertelli. Enrolled in the V-12 program so that he could continue to play ball at Notre Dame, Angelo Bertelli participated in just six of ten games of the 1943 season before being ordered to report to duty immediately. However, all was not lost for Notre Dame when Bertelli in his Marine uniform accepted the 1943 Heisman Trophy.

←→

At the organizational meeting of Camp Lejeune's football all-stars, 1st Lt. Bell greeted 121 prospects. Nineteen names on the signup sheet had experienced cold feet. From this July assembly of rough talent, Bell was ordered to build a team expected to be capable of challenging the South's established programs; Georgia, University of North Carolina, Villanova, Wake Forest, and Temple. Regardless of the individual talent on the Lejeune roster, it was an ostentatious short-term goal for a startup football team,

Announcing that he would stress the "team and performance angle," Bell told the mixed group of officers and enlisted men that "more than a good college or pro record would be necessary for any performer to win his position here."

If prior to the orientation, the brass's intent was to field a team that would challenge the powers of the South wasn't made clear to Bell, it became blatantly apparent the night of orientation when he saw before him some of the nation's best football players. Attending the meeting were more than a dozen men who had exhibited stellar abilities in the NFL and college ranks. Lt. George Speth and Charles Behan of the Detroit Lions were in attendance along with Lt. Chuck Dralis of the Chicago Bears; Jim Cotton of the Philadelphia Eagles; Lt. Larry Sullivan of Notre Dame; Lt. John Baklarz from Arizona State; Lt. Joe Sebasteanski of Fordham; and Lt. Bob Fitch, an All-American from Minnesota. Highlighting the backfield roster would be Ray Terrell, a speedster running back from Mississippi. A judo instructor at Camp Lejeune, Terrell had played the previous season for the Jacksonville, Florida, Naval Air Station.

With the Lejeune roster flush with former pro and college stars, the local media tagged the team with the nickname, All Stars. But even stars need the proper equipment. The kickoff against the Duke Blue Devils was less than a month away, and the delivery of the team's equipment had not yet arrived. Coach Bell and his All Stars worked "with one eye on the ball and one eye on the calendar."

Seeking its fourteenth consecutive winning season, Duke was a solid favorite to win its conference. In their opening game, the newly constituted Lejeune All Stars would challenge a deep Blue Devil team rife with numerous returning lettermen supported by their own V-12 players. Sixteen days before kickoff, First Lieutenant Bell cut the roster to forty-four Marines. Meanwhile, a few more experienced players matriculated into the program, including Lieutenant John Greer of Colgate and Corporal Wally Feter of Ohio State. Daily workouts continued behind the Protestant chapel. Meanwhile, the recreation department encouraged other Marines to organize a band and cheerleading squad.

The *New River Times* reported that

> "A college-like atmosphere will prevail at the games, with cheerleaders, a band, organized cheering, and all the other stuff makes rah-rah football—especially in the South, the spectacle that it is."

By September 9, some but not all of the tackling dummies and other equipment had arrived. For Marvin Bell, the gear's arrival offered only a slight relief from the growing pressure of putting together a competitive team from an aggregate of teenaged high school heroes, major college stars, and crusty professionals. Drills continued with an emphasis on tackling and hitting, while the staff attempted to stabilize the depth chart, a task made difficult by the stronger efforts of the underling Marines with semipro and high school experience.

Through each day of work, Bell noted that these projected "lesser" players outperformed the more experienced professionals and former college stars. Some of the more talented Marines were developing an attitude problem. They weren't hungry; they weren't motivated.

Indeed, if the Marine Corps wanted rah-rah football at Camp Lejeune, they had picked the wrong man to lead the cheers. Marvin Bell wasn't much for grandiose praise, memorable speeches, or inspirational quotes.

Regarding the status of the team just nine days prior to the All-Stars first game, Bell reported to the New River Pioneer, "The future isn't too dark."

*Friday, September 10, 1943.* Thirty enlisted men and eighteen officers boarded the bus to Durham. Game time was set at 1530 hours, Saturday. This was no intramural outing. The forty-eight men on that bus represented not just Camp Lejeune; they represented the entire Marine Corps. No other Marine base had assembled such an all-star squad; Camp Lejeune's team was the Marine Corps' team.

For Bell, the blistering heat of the North Carolina afternoon hadn't evaporated the problems of the previous weeks. Even up to game time, the veteran players continued to show little enthusiasm and accomplishment. Lacking confidence in several of his former professionals, Bell would have nervously picked at his depth chart in hope of finding the right chemistry.

The afternoon's result was predictable. Duke, led by its veteran roster and two V-12 players, former Wake Forest standouts Johnny Perry and Pat Preston, systematically dismantled Bell's newly mixed amalgamation of fresh high school graduates and grizzled former NFL stars. Though Bell's Marines battled the Blue Devils for a quarter, Duke rolled to a 19-0 halftime lead over the disjointed and uninspired All Stars. Lieutenant Walt Bergman's thirty-nine-yard broken-field run was the lone highlight for Camp Lejeune as the Lejeune Marines fell to Duke by a margin of 40-0.

Although the All Stars had been pegged as underdogs, no one expected them to be routed. The Lejeune roster was stocked with the best football players the Marine Corps could muster.

On this trip, more than the bus engine had backfired. The plan to inspire morale across the nation's Marine bases had exploded in the face of Brigadier General Larsen. Telegraph wires hummed with the news of Camp Lejeune's rout. Marine bases across the nation learned of the loss.

Embarrassing a Marine general who carried Navy Crosses and two Silver Stars on his chest wasn't something that went unnoticed in the Marine Corps. Even before the billowing dust settled on the road leading back to Camp Lejeune, plans were in motion. Like the worn brakes of their rickety green bus, Lieutenant Marvin Bell's Marine coaching career was screeching to a halt. As Bell prepared for the All Stars' next game, a contest against the region's powerhouse military base football squad from Bainbridge, Maryland, Naval Air Station, orders originating from New River passed from one desk to another until they reached California.

In just a few hours, the burly Larsen and his Old Breed connections acquired the answer to his gridiron problem. A direct descendant to football's greatest dynasty was an over-age first lieutenant in San Diego, California. Larsen arranged for his transfer. By September 11, 1943, First Lieutenant Jack Chevigny was en route to Camp Lejeune, North Carolina.

Jack's family was relieved. It appeared that Jack's wartime duty would be to simply fulfill the Marine Corps' mission of establishing a championship caliber football program.

Bainbridge Naval Training Station opened a seven-week home stand for Lejeune's All Stars. The military football power of the East Coast, Bainbridge set the standard for base football teams across the country. Coached by Ensign Joe Maniaci, formerly of the Chicago Bears, Bainbridge arrived at Camp Lejeune as heavy favorites. Ten thousand available seats were added, rows of bleachers overlooking the freshly manicured field. With a full complement of male and female cheerleaders and a rousing spectacle of hundreds of the Marine Women's Reserve in attendance, Lieutenant Bell's All Stars hoped to provide a spirited defense of the base's honor.

Assisted by a new first lieutenant, fresh in from Camp Pendleton, the Marines exhibited a revamped offense and a rejuvenated lineup, but they could do little against the tough Maniaci-coached defense. Still, the All Stars put on a good show for the estimated crowd of ten thousand fans who, as a Marine public relations measure to unify the locals and base personnel, were allowed free admission.

Holding Bainbridge scoreless in the first half, the Marines employed a tough leatherneck defense against the fast sailor halfbacks; Bainbridge's running attack was stuffed by the quick line slants employed by Bell's defense. Forgoing the ground attack against the entrenched Marines, Bainbridge eventually found success through the air when Bill DeCorrevant of Northwestern completed four consecutive passes. When DeCorrevant fired his fifth completion, it was a nineteen-yard touchdown to Howard "Red" Hickey. Harvey Johnson's sixteen-yard field goal provided the cushion needed to secure the nine-point win for the Navy. It was a tough loss for First Lieutenant Bell and his boys, but they had shown great improvement from the Duke disaster two weeks earlier.

For Red Hickey of Bainbridge, the game would be a forgotten footnote. After the war, the former Arkansas Razorback would return to the NFL where, as head coach of the San Francisco 49ers, he would revolutionize the passing game by developing the modern shotgun offense. For General Larsen, the Bainbridge loss tossed a back-breaking straw onto the camel's back. In the *New River Times*, alongside a column on the Bainbridge loss was an article titled, LT. JACK CHEVIGNY NAMED HEAD COACH HERE.

Marvin Bell was ordered to concentrate on the intramural sports program at Camp Lejeune. The following Monday, First Lieutenant John E. Chevigny assumed full command of the All Stars.

Handed a 0-2 squad of celebrated individuals, Jack would have to succeed where a pattern of failure had already been established. Still the expert card player, his ace in the hole would be the Notre Dame box. Although the popularity of the Notre Dame box offense had declined in recent years, the scheme remained an effective offensive stratagem. More importantly, practically every player on the squad had played in some form of the box offense. Charged with instilling virility into the impotent Marine offense, Jack coordinated changes in personnel and blocking assignments as the All Stars prepared to entertain the University of North Carolina.

First Lieutenant Chevigny's first action was to bench Mississippi speedster Ray Terrell along with four other starters. Jack proved that he would emphasize hustle and spirit; Terrell's benching made a sharp impression on the younger players.

Before Jack's arrival on base, Corporal Al "Junie" Kleinhenz, a high school star from his days at Louisville, was an unappreciated practice dummy. Meeting the new coach's expectations, Junie's stock shot suddenly upward.

Remembering his coach as being tough and a no-nonsense type of guy, the Louisville native remarked,

> "He was very sharp, an expert at blocking schemes and defense. And he didn't put up with any funny business from anyone. He had a reputation of being a great pre-game and halftime motivator. I remember one game we were losing at halftime. We weren't playing well; we were sloppy. We were expecting him to give us a Rockne speech. Tell us something to fire us up. He was known for that kind of thing. But he told us to stay in the locker room and just sit there without

saying a word. He left the locker room and closed the door. We waited and we waited. We could hear the noise from outside that signaled the beginning of the second half but Coach Chevigny kept the door closed. After several minutes, the door creaked open and he stuck his head in. He said, 'Well, if you boys are ready, the men out here are ready to see you play some football.' We roared onto the field without warming up and came from behind to tie the game. Thanks to him, we almost pulled off the win. I played ball for several years and I never had a coach like Chevigny. He was tough and demanded nothing short of your best effort at all times, but you loved him. He took an interest in each man on the team. He was a winner."

Standing on the field during the pre-game of his first game as Camp Lejeune's head coach, Jack may have allowed his thoughts to drift back to 1936. He may have imagined flashes of orange and white on the field, ghostly apparitions of almost a decade ago. Possibly he was focused on the task at hand. After all, he was a Marine officer. Trivial thoughts found no asylum in the mind of a Marine officer.

In what would have been a ruinous life-altering failure to the average man, Jack had been run out of Texas's Forty Acres and branded a loser. Although he had come out on top with a more prosperous career venture in the booming exploration industry, the Longhorn experience had indelibly soured his taste for the game. Rather than allow his coaching to be scrutinized again by the know-nothing types of Joe B. Franck, Lloyd Gregory, and H. Lutcher Stark, Jack had vanished from the game. Now, as an officer in the Marine Corps called to coach, he stood on the Lejeune sideline. Was Jack seeing the ghosts of Jack Gray, Bohn Hilliard, or Hugh Wolfe? In the light of seven years of reflection, even Jack may have admitted that he had fumbled the ball at Texas. Now, he had the chance to regain possession of his legacy. Looking out over the freshly chalked white lines of

Lejeune's Camp Field, Jack would have realized that this time, it was more than a game.

No longer the boy wonder of college football, Jack exuded confidence in the manner of a mature Marine officer. His week of hardnosed practices and sweeping personnel changes gave the All Stars the look of a team of Marines rather than an assortment of individual luminaries. In addition to shelving Ray Terrell, Jack had benched former All-American Bob Fitch and the pro out of Detroit, Charley Behan. Gone was the nickname, All Stars; Jack ordered the team to be referred to as the Leathernecks. Under Jack's leadership, the team would have no stars.

The October 7, 1943, *New River Times* reported, "All this week the Leathernecks have been taking verbal lashings and working hard as a victory over North Carolina could very well act as a springboard towards a still successful season."

It was of no matter that North Carolina sent their "B" team to meet the Leathernecks. For Camp Lejeune, this was a big game. Jack reached deep into his bag of psychological tricks and moved Bob Fitch back to the starting lineup along with John Bochynski and "Bus" Bergman. Against an outmanned North Carolina sub-varsity team, Jack substituted freely in the 26-0 win. Thirty-seven Marines saw action. One of the benefits of the substitutions was the opportunity for Ray Terrell's redemption. In breaking out of Jack's doghouse, the Ole Miss star notched a rushing touchdown and an interception return for a touchdown.

First Lieutenant Chevigny's strategy against North Carolina kept his team healthy for the following week's opponent, the soldiers from Fort Monroe. Against the junior Tarheels, Lejeune's newly diversified offense provided more excitement and a greater punch. They would need it against the Fort Monroe Gunners. Earlier that season, the Gunners had defeated the Norfolk Marines, 18-0. Though the Gunners also lost two other contests, they were expected to be much bigger and stronger than North Carolina's sub-varsity.

Jack was shocked when the outcome was an unexpected lopsided win. Camp Lejeune trounced the soldiers from Fort Monroe, 51-0. Seven Marines scored, while Fort Monroe netted minus-nine yards on the ground. Meanwhile, the Marines assaulted the visitors with 465 yards of total offense, 399 of them earned on the ground.

Jacksonville Naval Air Station (NAS) was next up for the Leathernecks. With the game dedicated to Camp Lejeune's Naval Construction Battalion (Seabees), the base increased the Camp Field capacity to fifteen thousand, adding five thousand free seats to the public. For the tribute game to the Seabees, First Lieutenant Jack Chevigny announced that his captains would be Jack Fitch of the Coast Guard and Jim Meek.

The Air Raiders of Jacksonville NAS arrived in camp with a 2-2 record, but one of those wins came over a tough Fort Benning club. After dropping an egg against the North Carolina Tarheel varsity, the Air Raiders were expected to be out for blood. Like many naval air station teams across the country, Jacksonville's roster was loaded with former college stars and professionals. In many ways, Jacksonville NAS was the model of military base football, the model Camp Lejeune hoped to emulate.

For Jack, the Jacksonville game would be another weekend's redemption. Statistically the contest would end almost even, but on the scoreboard Camp Lejeune claimed its third consecutive win, 20-7. It was the first significant action for Junie Kleinhenz, while veterans Paul Dubenetzky, Charley Behan, George Murphy, Bob Fitch, and Chuck Drulis delivered their best performances of the season. Kleinhenz's receiving and rushing led to two of the Leatherneck scores.

The following week, a 14-0 shutout win over Camp Davis, earned the Lejeune Marines respect throughout the military football world. Camp Davis, with its record of four wins in five games, entered the contest as a favorite to beat the Leathernecks. Ed Sexton and George Speth each scored as Jack's boys downed the acclaimed Blue Brigade before a standing-room crowd of soldiers, sailors, and Marines. It was a hard fought victory with Corporal Alex "Junie" Kleinhenz Jr. emerging as the leader in the Camp Lejeune backfield. In addition to nabbing a drive-killing interception, Junie rushed twenty-one times for seventy-seven yards. The six interceptions snagged from the Blue Brigade airways sparked the shocking upset.

In fear of damaging base morale with a broadcast of a Leatherneck defeat, WHTT radio had refused to broadcast the Leathernecks' game. Hinting the station should dine on crow Saturday after the game, the *New River Times* chided the short-sided decision.

Playing to sellout crowds, Camp Lejeune was on a four-game winning streak. Brigadier General Larsen had put the right Marine in charge.

A 55-6 rout of the Norfolk Fleet Marines put Jack and his Leathernecks in a position to capture the mythical North Carolina's Service Team Championship. To claim the title, the Leathernecks would have to defeat Chapel Hill Naval Preflight.

Like Jacksonville NAS, the Cloudbusters of Chapel Hill favored the air attack over the ground game. Standing at 1-4, Preflight's latest loss had come at the hands of Wake Forest, a meaningless loss in the bragging rights of the various East Coast military bases. Not so meaningless would be a loss to Camp Lejeune.

In order to beat Chapel Hill, Jack's forces needed to control the clock and put up an impenetrable air defense. Controlling the clock would be a matter of Camp Lejeune continuing to exert its muscle in the running game. For the season thus far, the Leathernecks had rushed for 1335 yards in five games, while the defense had allowed a meager total of 87 rushing yards. To beat the Cloudbusters, the Leathernecks would need to continue their pick-pocketing ways that had accounted for ten interceptions over the last two games.

The last road trip for Camp Lejeune was the Duke disaster over two months ago. Now, Jack's Leathernecks traveled to Chapel Hill. It would be the first time in seven years that a Jack Chevigny-coached team had played on the road.

PreFlight jumped out to a surprising 14-0 lead. Showing little emotion, it appeared as if Jack's Leathernecks had left their pride back at Camp Lejeune. Furious, Jack sent them in the locker room and locked the door. This was the game that Junie Kleinhenz remembered.

Jack's full halftime of silence spoke the greatest halftime speech Kleinhenz had ever heard. As a result, the Marines roared back in the second half to tie the Cloudbusters. And as the Leathernecks pushed toward the decisive score, time ran out.

Because Wake Forest canceled at the last moment, the disappointing 14-14 tie would remain a bitter taste in Jack's mouth for two long weeks. The Leathernecks would have practice through another open date before their rematch with Jacksonville NAS.

Two weeks of practice paid off when, in another second half turnabout, Jack's Marines came from behind to claim a 13-6 win. For Camp Lejeune, it was a sterling finish to its first competitive season. Earning six wins and a tie, Jack Chevigny had turned a winless team into a winner. In his first season back on the sideline, the old Notre Damer had not lost a game. Jack Chevigny the Marine officer, had redeemed the legacy of Jack Chevigny the coach.

←→

Supplemented by the rarely connected transcontinental phone call fraught with screeching static and dropped lines, Jack and Gege had kept up their letter writing. In less than six months, more than twenty-five letters, many adorned with Jack's elaborate sketches relevant to nature's exhibitions of grace and beauty, arrived in Seattle. The topics of discussion ranged from Jack's disgust of the coaching effort he found on his arrival at Camp Lejeune to his aching pleas begging Gege to pack her bags and move out to North Carolina for good.

In writing of his anxieties and personal yearnings, he told Gege that he had grown tired of training men to fight while staying safe in North Carolina. He had grown tired of life as a single man. In begging Gege to come out East, his letters expressed a longing for her permanence. At the same time, he doubted that her happiness would find fruit with a wartime Marine officer. He knew the pitfalls of planning a wartime marriage. He had heard the horror stories.

Often, groups of enlisted Marines gained permission for their wedding, only to have a carload of brides-to-be stepping off at the New Roads depot to learn that their Marines had been shipped out to the Pacific. Jack knew that it was a sad fact that most of those vows delayed would never be rescheduled. Some of the expectant brides would go on to find other grooms, while some girls would wait for Marines who never came home. Being acutely aware of the mental trauma suffered by the young Marines and their sweethearts, Jack wanted no part of that experience for his "dearest Gege."

During his time as the base recreation officer and coach, Jack saw thousands of boys come through Camp Lejeune. He knew that a lot of them wouldn't be coming home. Jack realized that if he were the leader he was perceived as being, he couldn't sit out the war as Camp Lejeune's football coach.

Just after Christmas of 1943, Jack sat on the front steps of his mother's home in Hammond. With a cigarette in hand, Jack informed his brother Jule and his brother-in-law Tim that he had asked for a transfer to combat duty. After seeing all the boys back at Camp Lejeune go off to war, Jack could no longer stomach being left behind. The thirty-seven-year-old Marine first lieutenant stated that he would go overseas in combat to "be with the boys." He told Jule that he had heard all the dope regarding a big push that would soon be made against Japan. A new Marine division, the 5th Division, was being structured to support this venture.

After nearly a month's leave granted to him in thanks for the job he did at Camp Lejeune, First Lieutenant John Edward Chevigny was detached to Headquarters Company, Headquarters Battalion, 5th Marine Division, Fleet Marine Force. The date was February 24, 1944.

# CHAPTER EIGHTEEN

# *The Eve of Dawn*

Iwo Jima, a pork-chop-shaped island in the Pacific Ocean, location 24.3 degrees north, 141.5 degrees east, is a submarine caldera with a history of non-explosive eruptions. Oriented north-northeast to south-southwest, its subdued elevation made the island a perfect locale for wartime Japanese airfields. After carrier attacks, bombardment, and photo recon missions against the Japanese-held Sulfur Island during the summer of 1944, the Joint War Plans Committee in Washington proposed the capture of Iwo for use as an island carrier, which could service Army Air Corps operations.

On October 7, 1944, Admiral Nimitz, Commander in Chief of the Pacific Fleet and Pacific Ocean Areas (CINCPAC), issued orders to Marine General Holland Smith. He was to seize Iwo Jima. At age sixty-two, it would be General Smith's last undertaking as a Marine Corps commander. His assignment, Operation Detachment, encompassed several dimensions and four basic objectives.

Washington's plan for the capture of Iwo Jima would provide: an operational base from which American forces could attack the Japanese home islands; the ability to protect American forces in the Marianas; the ability to conduct search operations of the approaches to the Japanese home islands; an airbase to provide fighter escort for long-range operations against the Japanese home islands. Written in characteristic military speak, Admiral Nimitz's manifesto to Smith was a dry preamble to one of the greatest human dramas in the annals of military history. After Nimitz's directive to stage Operation Detachment, a date was planned for the largest military operation ever attempted by the United States Marine Corps.

Upon seeing photoreconnaissance obtained during late October 1944, General Smith voiced his concern as to the cost effectiveness of an Iwo invasion. To Smith, the validity of the operation suffered from fractured reasoning. The photo evidence had convinced him that thousands of lives would be lost taking an island that had little strategic value. After a tepid Smith expressed his qualm that the cost in American blood would outweigh the benefits of the island's capture, Admiral Raymond Spruance, the senior admiral who had first suggested the invasion to Nimitz, uncharacteristically reevaluated his supportive position on the operation. Spruance couldn't deny Smith's evidence; the island had been heavily fortified since his conception of the invasion. Taking the island now would cost thousands of lives. Like Smith, Spruance was gnawed by an angst that the invasion wouldn't be worth the lives lost; however, by December 1944, it was too late. Operation Detachment was a behemoth in motion. It couldn't be stopped.

Aware of the apprehension voiced by Smith and Spruance, General Hap Arnold of the Army Air Corps continued to assert his position that Iwo's use as an airbase for the P-51 Mustang would validate the expense of its capture. Arnold was desperate to legitimize the B-29's deployment against Japan. The B-29 program had been disappointing, almost an embarrassment, to Arnold. He was desperate to find a way to improve the productivity of the long-range bomber. Arguing for the invasion of Iwo

Jima, Arnold assuaged the Joint War Plans Committee concerns regarding Iwo's usefulness as a fighter base. In doing everything he could to support the strategic bombing program of his 20th Air Force, Arnold insisted that Iwo Jima would provide the long-range P-51D fighter the ability to escort B-29 bombing raids and attack enemy positions located six hundred seventy miles away in Japan. Insisting that the taking of Iwo would take no more than five days, General Arnold formed the vertex of a misguided triangular collaboration of the Navy, Marine Corps, and Army Air Corps regarding the efficacy of Operation Detachment.

During the early stage of Operation Detachment's preparation, optimistic planners initially set the date for the invasion as November 18, 1944. But as the planned D-Day neared, the needed naval forces for the invasion remained entangled in the Philippines. And after the invasion was postponed to February 3, 1945, the massive operation was soon victimized by a second delay. Finally, after some logistical adjustments, the invasion was set for February 19, 1945. Leading the assault would be the 4th and 5th Marine Divisions.

To the Japanese defenders, the five-hundred-fifty-foot volcanic mountain at the island's southern tip was *Suribachi Yama*. To the Marines, the inactive volcano straddling the island's narrow southern shoulders was Mount Suribachi. To guarantee the invasion's success, the 28th Regiment of the 5th Marine Division would receive specialized training for its task of cutting the island in half and capturing Suribachi. Because Suribachi was the ultimate high ground of the island, Operation Detachment planners felt that capturing its heights quickly was the key to taking the island.

The Fifth Amphibious Corps' plan was straightforward. Operation Detachment called for a beach landing and a turn along the island's vertical axis to capture Iwo's airfields and command centers. As the western side of the island was subject to continuous swells, Iwo's eastern beaches were chosen as most suitable for the landing of the Marine divisions. Divided into seven landing zones, the eastern beach stretched from just below the face of Suribachi in the south to a plateau overlooking the northern edge of the beach. From Suribachi north to East Boat Basin, the total length of the seven zones measured three thousand five hundred yards. Each landing zone was color coded and numbered.

Green Beach was designated as the landing zone on the extreme left directly under Suribachi. Led by Colonel Harry B. Liversedge, the Marine's Marine, the 28th Marines would land at Green Beach. The no-nonsense Liversedge was known for his earthy management style and good judgment. Physically imposing, Liversedge in his youth was an outstanding athlete. A bronze medal in the shotput during the 1920 Olympics combined with his reputation as a former football player and boxer to enhance his image to the youthful Marines he commanded.

Liversedge's objective was to cut off the head of the snake by moving across the base of Suribachi to Iwo's west coast. Once the mountain was cut off, the 28th Regiment would wheel left to ascend the high ground. This critical action would secure the beach flanks and the eventual rear of the rest of the operation, while the other regiments secured the beach and pushed west to north in order to take the airfields and capture the rest of the island.

Because the northernmost area Blue Beach 2 was not a suitable landing zone, Blue Beach 1 would be the invasion area on the far right of the main invasion force. Assaulting Blue Beach 1 would be the 25th Marines of the Fourth Division led by Colonel John R. Lanigan. His 25th Regiment would advance under heavy fire to secure Airfield Number One and neutralize the enfilade fire of the northern Japanese positions overlooking the beach landing zones. Later in the battle, with all of the original battalion commanders killed or wounded, Lanigan would personally push his individual companies forward in an effort to get them to advance under fire. For his effort, Lanigan would receive a citation and the satisfaction that his action allowed hundreds of Marines to return home alive.

Just to the left of Lanigan would be the 23rd Marines of the 4th Division commanded by Colonel Walter Wensinger. An Ohio native with a law degree from Michigan, Colonel Wensinger was a career Marine. Notable in his personnel file was a special letter of commendation for his service as brigade adjutant in Nicaragua during the aftermath of an earthquake, which killed over two thousand people in Managua on March 31, 1931. However, because of a plane crash in Kansas, few people back home in the States made note of the disaster or Wensinger's work in the devastated city. Like the thousands of quake victims, Wensinger's accomplishment in Managua would be buried in anonymity under the bold headlines noting Rockne's death.

His acts of heroism ignored in 1931, Wensinger would make headlines after his 23rd Marines stormed onto Iwo Jima's beaches. Landing at Yellow 1 and Yellow 2 beaches, the 23rd Marines' primary objective was to seize the two airfields in the center of the island. It would be in this area that United States Marine Corps Reserve Sergeant Darren Cole's individual assault on five different enemy pillboxes would make him the first of twenty-seven Medal of Honor recipients on Iwo Jima.

Sandwiched between Liversedge's 28th Marines on Green Beach and Wensinger's 23rd Marines on Yellow 1 would be Colonel Thomas A. Wornham and his 27th Marine Regiment of the 5th Division. Wornham would command all the Marines landing in the adjacent zones known as Red Beach 1 and Red Beach 2.

Prior to the landing, a letter from a Marine reserve lieutenant assigned to Wornham's 27th Marine Regiment headquarters staff glowed in its description of Wornham's compassion for his men and his awareness of their value not just as a tool of war, but as men with families and sweethearts back home. In the words of Jack Chevigny, the man who walked with Rockne, the greatest of all motivators, Wornham was a leader who commanded more than boys and men in a time of war; he commanded respect.

Supporting the landing and waiting in reserve would be the 3rd Marine Division. Just a month prior to the Iwo landing, they had completed a protracted and bloody campaign to secure Guam's Japanese stragglers. Even though the island was officially declared secure on August 10, 1944, their work on Guam continued into December 1944. Bloodied from their part in the liberation of Guam and its native Chamorro people, the 3rd Marine Division were to remain in reserve on board ship until D-Day plus-3, the fourth day of the battle. Intent on keeping the 3rd Marine Division as a reinforcing element of the invasion, Operation Detachment planners didn't foresee that the Japanese Army's strategy of delaying the Marine advance through a battle of attrition would force the 3rd Marine Division to help spearhead the deadliest attack in Marine Corps history.

Besides the 3rd Marine Division, also in support of the 4th and 5th Marine Divisions were the underwater demolition teams and the thousands of adjunct personnel. Sailors, army servicemen, pilots, medical personnel, construction workers, all races and creeds would support the initial landing force with their blood. Many who were not frontline Marines would lose their lives and futures in the effort to take Iwo Jima.

Months prior to the landing, in San Diego, Jack and his fellow Marines had no knowledge of Operation Detachment. However, for over a year, talk had been made of something big, talk that had been confirmed with a presidential viewing of a mock invasion of the Southern California coast.

Not that Roosevelt's visit was that extraordinary for Pendleton. The San Diego base was the hub of Marine publicity. In his letters, Jack observed that Hollywood stars were constant visitors to the base. In a photo taken after the parade review of the 27th Regiment, Jack stands next to Bing Crosby, Phil Silvers, and Judy Garland. In the spirit of reciprocity to the Marines at Pendleton, Hollywood stars often served at the behest of the brass.

Mindful of the complementary relationship between Hollywood and the Marines, Jack's commander, Colonel Thomas Wornham, once enlisted Jack's own star power in preparations for the regimental parade. Following an order issued personally by Wornham, Jack scoured the studios for a suitable female star (preferably single) to stand in review as guest of honor for the occasion. Batting about several studios along with his roommate and fellow lieutenant, Robert Daily, Jack eventually pulled into the Metro-Goldwyn-Mayer lot and snagged what would soon be the hottest young name in Hollywood, Ann Blyth.

In less than twelve months, Blyth would be out on loan to Warner Brothers where she would captivate audiences and earn an Oscar nomination as Veda Pierce, the petulant daughter of Joan Crawford's portrayal of an indulgent mother in *Mildred Pierce*. First Lieutenant Daily was speechless as he and Jack returned to base with the raven-haired starlet and her MGM entourage in tow. With Wornham's confidence in Jack confirmed, the Notre Dame legend's own star power grew within the 27th Marines, Headquarters Battalion.

Dallying with a Hollywood starlet was nothing new to Jack. During his playing days, numerous perfumed envelopes originating from a bungalow just blocks east of Hollywood had found their way to Jack's address. When in Chicago, Crosby and Hope played golf with Jack. At places like the Cocoanut Grove, the company of celebrities was a constant offering for the Gipper legend of Notre Dame.

However, after his time at Fort Lawton, the company of Hollywood stars no longer engrossed the junior Marine officer. During these days, Ann Blyth was just an assignment. These days, Jack preferred the light of a Seattle moon over the Hollywood stars. In spite of the wartime travel difficulties, Gege managed another trip down the coast, but, like other wartime couples, the two had little time for courtship.

A serious relationship in the final years of World War II meant either an expedited calendar or an extended hold of long-term plans. Most romantic relationships were sped forward on a clock unfamiliar to civilian life. In the span of wartime courtship, weeks replaced months, days replaced weeks. In her keepsake box, Gege kept a clipping that announced the wedding of another West Coast beauty, Lena Riggi, to one of Jack's regimental sergeants, Medal of Honor recipient John Basilone.

For now, she and Jack would wait. For now, the Marine and his reserved, self-supporting, hopeful postwar bride would continue writing, wiring, and calling.

During the war years, securing a domestic long distance landline connection was often next to impossible. Jack knew that once his division reached Hawaii he would have no chance to hear Gege's voice before he returned. Always the can-do guy, Jack was determined to find a way to maintain voice contact. Just before leaving the states, he succeeded.

Obtaining a wireless radio capable of overseas communication, Jack mailed a receiver to Gege with an accompanying time-zone table for her to use in order to synchronize their time on air. Communication was possible at only certain times, Jack advised her in his letters. Plus, he may not be able to hear her when she can hear him. She was to listen for him at certain intervals of the day. If the distance between them or the weather disrupted the shortwave channel, they would obviate the interference by arranging a secret meeting time under Jack's moon, promising to look up at the night sky at exactly the same moment for a shared cigarette, some words of encouragement, and a moonlight prayer from Jack sealed with a kiss.

Although Jack had decided he would attempt to quit smoking, Jack and Gege would keep their date for each of the nights prior to his landing on Iwo Jima.

Following two months in the Hawaiian Islands undergoing intensive training for an amphibious attack upon an unnamed island beach overlooked by a steep incline, Jack and his fellow Marines embarked for Saipan. From Saipan, the fleet would sail to Iwo Jima.

As a liaison officer during the landing at Iwo, Jack was to maintain communication between the landing beach elements and the headquarters battalion. The forwarding of his information would be critical in coordinating supply delivery and maintaining the integrity of the offensive once the regiments hit the beach. Because his 5th Division was the greenest of the three divisions, Jack's apprehension for his own performance grew exponentially each day.

In the months prior to D-Day, he obsessed about the amount of Marine blood spilled wastefully in the Pacific War. Telling Gege that if it weren't for the skilled leadership of the Marine officers, many more would have died at Saipan; he wondered aloud if President Roosevelt had any empathy for the families of the boys. To Jack, it was clear that the United States had only to starve Japan into submission to close out the war. In his opinion, the careless disregard for individual life and politics were leading the president to call for the indiscriminate waste of young Marines. Months prior to disembarking the mainland for Hawaii, Jack had already calculated the cost of an imminent invasion of the Japanese homeland and wondered in his letters if President Roosevelt cared about anything other than winning a fourth term.

In just twelve months, Jack had gone from being a gung-ho Marine wanting to be there with his boys in combat to one plotting an escape to Canada with Gege. He had grown tired of the "They Were Expendable" attitude of the gray-haired politicians. The young Marines who were being shipped off to unknown pegs of land in the middle of the world's largest ocean were sons, brothers, and friends. He wondered for what valid reason were so many to die when the enemy would have no choice but to surrender or starve to death. But like the boys, Jack had little choice in the end game. He could do nothing but maintain his fighting edge as part of a flotilla of Marines and sailors on their way to an ambiguous destiny.

In this floating steel continent of warriors, Jack befriended a young Marine captain, as unsure and as undesirable of being there as Jack was. George "Sonny" Franck had been an All-American halfback at Minnesota in 1940. An Iowa native, Franck was an athletic prodigy born of German stock. Always confident in his abilities, his talents were noticed by the legendary Bernie Bierman at Minnesota, the same Bernie Bierman who administered the 47-19 thumping to Jack's Longhorns as the Gophers marched to their third consecutive national championship. Sonny Franck was a key element in Bierman's fourth title in 1940. In fact, Franck, as well as his fans, believed that it was he who should have been awarded the Heisman that season, not Tom Harmon of Michigan. Sonny maintained that he was the better player, but Bierman undercut his glory. The authoritarian Bierman thought of Sonny as cocky, so in order to bring

Franck down to earth, Bierman downplayed his role during the 1940 season. As evidence to his allegation, Franck offered the facts of the 1940 showdown between Michigan and Minnesota, a legendary game declared as the "Battle of the Giants." In that match-up of Big Ten powers, Franck and future Minnesota Heisman Trophy winner Bruce Smith beat Harmon's Wolverines 7-6 for the Big Ten title. A 9.6 sprinter in the 100-yard dash, Franck was an excellent kicker who would be named the Most Valuable Player of the College All-Star game during the prewar summer.

That fall of 1941, Franck signed with the New York Giants. After Pearl Harbor, he, along with Giant teammate Jack Lummus, volunteered for the Marine Corps. Now, he found himself heading toward Japanese soil, sailing on the same ship as his boyhood idol, Jack Chevigny of Notre Dame.

Prior to shipping out with Jack on the USS Rutland, Sonny had been a Marine pilot. He never really enjoyed flying; he had an orientation problem—possibly due to an inner ear infection during his youth. But Sonny heard that because of the lengthy training program, a Navy pilot had a good chance to survive the war.

Although the Iowa native did undergo a long two years of training, Franck did eventually see combat action. Shot down in a dogfight over the Wotje Atoll in the Marshall Islands, Sonny lay in a life raft for over two-and-a-half hours, a floating target in enemy waters. After hours of uncertainty, a sea-rescue plane attempted to rescue him but crashed. Ironically, it was when a second sea plane successfully landed nearby and floundered in the heavy seas that Captain Franck's spirit lifted. He knew that a passing destroyer would consider stopping if three pilots were in need of a rescue instead of just one. After some time passed, he and his unsuccessful rescuers were indeed picked up by a passing destroyer.

Swallowing sea water and inhaling the smoke used to mark his position, Sonny would never forget the foul smell of the burning chemicals.

After three crashes and suffering a serious leg injury, his wings were clipped. A reassigned Franck was now onboard a crowded Haskell Class transport loaded with Marine riflemen. The blithe bachelor known for his love of heaping bowls of ice cream, gorgeous blonde singers, and New York City starlets was facing the next thirty-six days participating as a ground-spotter in the bloodiest battle in United States Marine Corps' history.

To pass the time onboard, Sonny spent a lot of time with Jack. The former Rockne football star would gather a small crowd as he walked his superior officer, Franck, through the coaching points for a trapping guard. Twenty years later as Rock Island (Illinois) head football coach, George Franck would use those same coaching points in teaching his schoolboys how to execute the fullback trap.

In getting to know First Lieutenant Chevigny, Captain Franck learned that it was not football but bridge that was Jack's true calling. Jack was the best bridge player Sonny had ever seen. Those Seattle summer nights with Gege as a fourth back in 1943 had kept Jack's game fit for the long slow cruise with a bunch of hot, bored Marines. Along with bridge, Jack enjoyed an almost daily game of touch football on deck.

As expected with Marines, the touch football games quickly morphed into a semblance of a full-scale contact scrimmage on a steel playing field. The thirty-eight-year-old with a bum knee had scant business roughhousing with boys and men in their early twenties, but such was Jack's way. After only a few days at sea, Jack leapt for a pass he should have let go. Pain searing through his left arm, he had to be helped from the deck.

With his hyper-extended elbow immobilized in a plaster cast, Jack was ordered to assume briefly new duties aboard ship. In a letter to Gege, he bemoaned his rusted football reflexes, maintaining that a younger Jack would have deftly avoided the Marine who splattered him as he stretched to receive the pass.

For the remainder of the cruise, Jack would remain a one-arm man flailing about his duty in great pain. The calendar offered no time for a complete recovery; the final days of preparation had arrived. When the tip of Mount Suribachi crested the horizon, Jack's cast was removed.

On February 17, 1945—two days prior to D-Day—APA 196 (the USS Logan) lay offshore of the enemy-held island of Iwo Jima. The underwater demolition teams (the forerunner of the Navy Seals) were mapping the beaches and defusing any hazards to the landing force. Approximately eighty-two thousand United States service personnel had joined together for the assault of the seven invasion lanes on the island's eastern beach.

Jack penned the last of his sixty-eight letters home. It was addressed to Gege's brother, George Purdy, a Catholic priest.

# CHAPTER NINETEEN

# *The Red Zone*

Detached from an infantry battalion since January 15, 1944, Jack had long since gained a seat at the right hand of Colonel Wornham. Though he suffered oscillating emotions over the frustrations of military life and a spiderlike fear of his finality creeping into his daily thoughts, Jack's courage was steeled through continuous training and his adherence to the Marine Corps values of honor, courage, and commitment. In the month preceding Iwo's D-Day, he reminded himself that he had asked to be there with the boys; he had asked for the privilege of being a part of the best fighting organization in the world. A sharp epiphany that he would soon be leading men into a life or death battle forged his sword of determination and courage. Unlike his letters of the fall, Jack's later letters spoke not of doubt or a yearning to abscond with his sweetheart to Canada, but of honor, courage, and commitment to the boys and men with whom he now faced the possibility of spending eternity.

At sea, forty-eight hours prior to H-Hour, Jack wrote to a friend in North Dakota,

> "You will have read about the 5th Division at the time of this reading because right now we're checking over our final signals. I've wanted to be here because I've felt that to have the

information correct you had to get in the position of the 1ˢᵗ team quarter back. Col. Wornham our CO is a regular guy and a naval academy graduate – he has given me the opportunity of being on his first team, so that I could appreciate this condition and now I'm hoping I can perform to his expectations. We will just about know what Tokyo Rose has left when this mission is complete and then the long run out here will be a short way home. My regards to our mutual friends in North Platte, whose hospitality I shall always remember. Appreciate your prayers for the men here who are so close to meeting their Creator. Kindest personal regards to your wife – family and yourself. Jack."

*February 19, 1945.* After the traditional D-Day steak and egg breakfast served at 3:00 a.m., Jack and seventy-four men of his headquarters company readied their gear and climbed down the rope lattice to board the specified landing craft mechanized boat (LCM2). As if the day was planning a celebration of the dawn, the sky was a pristinely serene crystal blue, the sea calm.

Circling according to plan and awaiting the signal to attack was an armada of seventy-five-man LCM crafts and thirty-six-man landing craft personnel vehicles (LCVP). Some crafts carried engineers; others carried combat teams and medical personnel. A few of the crafts carried tanks, many of which would be lost to the combined conditions of the soft terrain and accurate artillery fire raining down from Suribachi, from the heights behind the terraces, and from the high ground of the northern cliffs. At the planned time of 9:00, Jack and his fellow Marines of the Fifth Amphibious Corps' first wave consisting of nearly fourteen thousand Marines would step American boots on the Japanese homeland for the first time of the war.

Jack landed at Red Beach 3, technically not a specified landing zone; rather, it was only a sliver of beach located at the northern edge of the 27ᵗʰ Marines second landing zone, Red Beach 2. Once he found cover, he could liaise with the 4$^{th}$ Division's regiments landing on Yellow Beach 1 and Yellow Beach 2. As Jack moved inland and sought shelter with several of his men, other liaison officers were attempting to do the same thing southward along the beach toward Suribachi. Once in place, these officers would notify the command that enemy fire was light, but forward movement was difficult due to the terrain. On the beach, the coarse ash made for a soft, porous surface. Communications reported that the soft ash was difficult to negotiate with heavy packs.

Digging a safe foxhole was impossible. As soon as a Marine scooped out a sizeable hole, the ash filled the hole. Former farm boy Marines compared it to digging a foxhole in a silo of grain.

The terraces were worse. Less than fifty yards from the water's edge, the first terrace was a wall of loose volcanic ash standing at least fifteen feet high. Advancing over the first terrace, Marines found themselves sinking past their ankles. Complicating the Marines' dilemma, the beaches were filling to capacity with personnel and equipment, while the intensity of the indirect fire of mortars and artillery firing down on them from three sides increased.

Landing in a later wave, Private First Class (PFC) Paul Merriman of Pittsburgh, Pennsylvania, was no farm boy, but he knew enough about farming to know that his landing with the Pioneers had positioned him in no serene field of corn. In the middle of the Pacific on an island of which he had never heard, Paul Merriman was just seventeen years of age. He had joined the Marine Corps on his birthday ten months earlier. Assigned to rescue his fallen Marines, both dead and alive, what PFC Merriman would remember most about his landing on Red Beach 2 was the intimate closeness, the arm-length proximity of nearly every Marine on the beach. Seventy years after his day on the red-stained black ash, PFC Merriman could still recall being able to reach out in any direction and touch a different Marine, each man and boy hunkered down in search of cover where there was none.

Since May of 1944, the Imperial Japanese Army had adopted a more conservative strategy of defending against the U. S. amphibious assaults on their island strongholds. A strong defense of the beachhead was no longer the order of the day. The Japanese strategists decided that inland fortifications and tunnels offered a better chance for victory against an amphibious island assault. Holding back the large portion of his indirect artillery and mortar fire until the beaches were full, General Kuribayashi's plan for Iwo Jima would perfect that strategy.

On Iwo, one of PFC Merriman's first realizations was that the action didn't much resemble the inspirational movies and the newsreels back at home. By thirty minutes past 10:00, rolling barrages of artillery and mortar fire marched north and south along the beach. The beaches were now crowded, and the supporting naval guns had gone silent. With the broken waves of Marines staggering forward in erratic progress, those sailors manning the Navy's big guns couldn't risk their shells landing close to the beach.

Unopposed by any naval gunfire, the Japanese blanketed the beach with artillery and mortar fire. After the battle, U. S. forces would find on cave walls evidence of written coordinates that indicated the Japanese had pre-targeted the spots where they expected Marines to gather.

Along the beach, twisted pieces of equipment blended with mangled body parts. Some Marines saw their buddies disappear in a mist of blood and tissue, nothing left of them but a smoking depression of red-tinged sand and flesh. Scampering corpsmen came across Marines riddled with smoking holes in their bodies. The hot shrapnel would set the Marine's clothing afire at the point of entry.

Dropping out of high school to fight, Paul Merriman wanted to be a radioman in the Navy, but when he got to the post office to join up, the line was long and moving slowly. As the line inched forward, Merriman noticed a Marine in his dress blues standing in a nearby doorway. The Marine told him he didn't need to stand in such a long line; the Marines had radiomen, the man in blue informed him.

"Come on in," the Marine recruiter told Paul.

He reported to Parris Island on June 23, 1944. As a rifleman on Iwo Jima, PFC Merriman's job was to carry litters with wounded Marines back to the medical staging area. When he wasn't carrying live Marines, he was to recover bodies and torn limbs, or anything recognizable as part of a Marine buddy's remains. Merriman found dead Marines with missing arms and legs, but he didn't recover any missing limbs. On Iwo, when an arm or leg was blown off a person with the greatest possible violence, little was left of the limb. In recovering the dead and wounded, PFC Merriman came across numerous broken Marines yelling for help. The dead and wounded of the first wave, "the assault guys" he called them, were everywhere—in front and in back of him. He wondered how anyone could survive the apocalyptic scene.

With most of the attack force stalled before the first of two terraces, the upward slope of the terrain combined with the height of the two terraces to prevent the Marines from seeing the enemy directly in front of them. By 11:00, the first terrace was cluttered with Marines worming their bodies into the black ashen terrace in an attempt to take cover from a rain of flying metal. Still, the levee didn't protect them from the enfilade fire coming from Suribachi and the cliffs above the East Boat Basin. As bulldozers attempted to move forward to slice a path through the terraces, veterans encouraged the green troops to move forward. They would do nothing but die if they stayed on the beach.

One of the assault veterans, Guadalcanal Medal of Honor recipient John Basilone led an early breakthrough toward the 27th Marine's primary objective. After having eliminated a bunker that was firing on the 4th Marines, Basilone and his fellow Marines became pinned down by enemy mortar fire. Taking cover at the edge of the airfield, Sergeant Basilone suffered a grievous abdominal wound. Unable to move, the Marine hero survived just another half hour. PFC Merriman, working that area of the landing, would wonder if he had carried the body of the famous Marine from the frontline.

After more Marines followed Basilone and the advance of fellow machine gunner Chuck Tatum through the bulldozer's cut in the first terrace, the assault teams carved a path westward across the base of Suribachi to the opposite beach. Like French doors hinged on their respective beaches, the two regiments were to swing north and south. Slashing across the island, the 28th Marine Regiment was to pivot southward climb the volcano and cut off the island's head, while the 27th Marine Regiment whipped northward to capture Montoyama Number One Airfield and establish an east-west battle line along the plateau. Despite the horrendous fire emanating from three directions, the Fifth Amphibious Corps' master plan was working.

Still, there were concerns. Large elements of the 27th Marines remained pinned down in several pockets on Red Beach 2. Near the first terrace in one of those northern pockets, groups of the 27th Regiment remained static, held in check by enemy artillery and mortar fire. "The worst ever seen" one lieutenant reported back to the command post.

Near Yellow Beach 1 under a thunderstorm of flying metal, Jack and five of his boys took refuge from the elements.

Like many men of the newly formed 5th Marine Division, Captain George "Sonny" Franck was untested in ground combat. For three years, he had served the Marines as a fighter pilot, not a combat infantryman. Breathing in the hot air thick with shrapnel, he was unnerved by the constant explosions. In an attempt to find some assurance of safety, Captain Franck darted like a rabbit along the beach, carrying as many beer bottles as his pack could hold. Before the landing, Sonny had obscured his captain's insignia and made plans to latch onto the first battle-hardened corporal who loved beer as much as he did. Sonny would trade the beer for the veteran's help in staying alive.

It was now around thirty minutes before noon. Still in search of that special corporal, Sonny continued to dash from spot to spot, leaping over the lacerated torsos and mutilated remains of young boys. As Sonny darted north between the water's edge and the first terrace, his boots splashed through granular pools of a black reddish soup, blood mixed in with the black volcanic ash.

In just over an hour, Iwo's eastern beach had become a grotesque strip of hellish sights. Death came so violently, it was said that even the most hardboiled Marine veteran of the Pacific was sickened by the carnage. One Marine described leaping over what he thought was a large snake. The snake was a Marine's intestine.

Near Yellow Beach 1, Franck spotted a large shell hole and dove blindly into the crater. After approximately one hour on the beach, Captain George "Sonny" Franck had found safety in a large shell hole, a six-foot-wide crater, which had been created by U. S. naval gunfire. About four feet deep, the hole also provided shelter for several other Marines. Like Franck, they were taking cover from enemy fire coming from three directions. Over the din of the screaming mortars and deafening artillery fire, Sonny heard a voice tell him to hold his position if he wanted to live. It was Jack. Along with five other Marines, he had taken cover in that same deep depression of volcanic ash. Though he too had no combat experience, Jack appeared to Sonny as strangely calm and in control. In the midst of the terror about them, Jack assured Sonny that he was in a safe place.

It was because of Jack's confident demeanor that Sonny listened. But within seconds of Jack's assertion, for no specific reason, just as suddenly as Sonny had dove into the shell hole to take shelter with Jack and the other Marines, the twenty-six-year-old Marine pilot bolted over the crater's edge and ran south toward Suribachi. Frantic to find cover, the former Big Ten sprinter and football All-American wasn't sure where on that murderous black beach he could find safety, but something in that crater just didn't feel right.

# CHAPTER TWENTY

# *For the Boys*

With no explanation offered for his sudden evacuation, Sonny Franck had scrambled from the crater filled with his fellow Marines. In his senior years, he would say he thought he may have said something to Jack. Maybe he voiced concern over the crater's safety; maybe he didn't. His only vivid memory was that a tsunami of apprehension overcame him. Something inside his mind told the fastest man in professional football to get out of that hole and run. So he ran.

Somewhere near Red Beach 1 near the second terrace of volcanic ash, Captain Franck found that beer-drinking corporal he had hoped to find. In the din of explosions and flying shrapnel, the corporal pointed out a narrow, waist deep shell hole. Captain Franck later told the *Washington Post* that he curled his body into that foxhole and took refuge until sometime around D+3. But before that day arrived, he would wonder about Jack.

It was the afternoon of D+1 when Sonny recognized a noncommissioned officer who knew Jack. Inquiring of Jack's whereabouts, Captain Franck asked the noncom, "Have you heard anything of Chevigny?"

Appearing to look right through him, the noncom officer replied, "Chevigny and some other guys got hit in a shell hole. He's gone. They're all gone."

The wire from the War Department wouldn't arrive for weeks. Back in the States, Jack's sister Marie waited impatiently for news of Jack. She was beside herself. She knew that if Jack were well, she would have received a letter from him. Fretful wires crisscrossed the country from Marie's Washington, DC, apartment, to Hilda Weinert's home in Seguin, to brother Jule in Hammond, and to Gege in Seattle. No one had heard a word of Jack.

When he returned from Yalta on February 21, 1945, President Roosevelt was informed of the casualties on Iwo. Though he had presided over more than three years of a worldwide conflict that had resulted in millions of lives lost, the nation's longest-sitting president would be noticeably moved by Iwo Jima's casualty numbers. It was said to be the only time during the war that President Roosevelt visibly reacted to a combat casualty report.

The notification arrived at Marie Gaffney's Washington, DC, residence at 4000 Beecher Street, Apartment 301 on March 24, 1945. Thirty-three days earlier, Jack had been killed in action. It read:

"DEEPLY REGRET TO INFORM YOU THAT YOUR BROTHER FIRST LIEUTENANT JOHN E. CHEVIGNY USMCR WAS KILLED IN ACTION 19 FEBRUARY 1945 AT IWO JIMA VOLCANO ISLANDS IN THE PERFORMANCE OF HIS DUTY AND SERVICE OF HIS COUNTRY. WHEN INFORMATION IS RECEIVED REGARDING BURIAL YOU WILL BE NOTIFIED. TO PREVENT POSSIBLE AID TO OUR ENEMIES DO NOT DIVULGE THE NAME OF HIS SHIP OR STATION. PLEASE ACCEPT MY

HEARTFELT SYMPATHY. LETTER FOLLOWS" — A VANDEGRIFT LIEUT GENERAL USMC COMMANDANT OF THE MARINE CORPS

What letter that may have followed from the commandant has been lost. Possibly, Vandegrift remembered Jack's visit to Washington early in 1944 and later wrote a more personal condolence to Marie. Jack wrote Gege that he had visited the general in the hospital after Vandegrift had suffered an injury playing handball. The commandant of the Marines would have remembered the first lieutenant celebrity of the Corps.

By the time of the telegram, most of the family expected to hear the worst but still held hope for the better. When the worst did arrive, Marie called Jule and Gege.

Home in Seattle, Gege felt an empty feeling in her stomach when the call from Marie came. A cousin remembered her response to the news. She ran to her room, crying, and shut the door. No one remembers how long she was there.

Iwo Jima would be declared secure on March 16, but fighting and dying would continue for weeks as Marines and support personnel swept the island clean of stragglers. PFC Merriman left the island on March 10 with a grenade fragment in his lower back. Charging an enemy position with thirty other Marines, he remembers the Japanese rising up from a ridge with a fortified enemy position that was supported by a Nambu machine gun. Realizing that the Japanese were about to mow down what remained of his company, he dove behind a boulder for cover. As his buddies retreated, he was left stranded in the field of fire where he crouched behind the large rock. Beside him was Marine Alfred Ciccocelli. Caught in the crossfire, neither he nor Ciccocelli could move. In describing the action, Merriman remembers that as he and Ciccocelli continued to take withering rifle and machine gunfire upon their position, Ciccocelli decided it would be better to abandon the rock. Rising to sprint back to the friendly lines, Alfred was shot dead, a bullet to the head. With Ciccocelli's body draped over him, PFC Merriman lay square in the middle of a grenade-tossing contest between the enemy and fellow Marines.

Alfred's body shielded Merriman from the Japanese grenades, but his fellow Marines carried the more potent pineapple variety. Like the Americans who would toss back Japanese grenades, the Japanese soldiers would snatch the American grenades thrown in their direction and toss them back toward the Marines. The errant grenades returned from both lines were landing practically in Merriman's lap. After several minutes of grenade volleys, a friendly grenade landed within inches of Merriman. With Ciccocelli's body on top of him, Merriman could do nothing but turn away from the blast. Struck by one of the forty fragments shot forth in the explosion, he felt little pain. Realizing he had been hit, he reached for the wounded area of his back and felt the warmth of the blood flowing from the wound. Remembering his training, he disarmed his weapon and stripped down. He then said a prayer, and like Ciccocelli before him, he rose up to run back to the friendly line.

Merriman got only four to five feet before falling. A corpsman rushed into the line of fire to bandage him, give him a shot of morphine, and move him back behind the line.

After being evacuated and spending three months in recovery, PFC Merriman wanted to find that corpsman and thank him, but he never got the chance. Merriman never learned the corpsman's identity for certain, but he believes it was John Bradley, one of the six renowned flag raisers of the February 23, 1945, Pulitzer Prize-winning photo. Two days after Bradley removed Merriman from the frontline, Bradley was also wounded and evacuated.

By late March, news of Jack's death had been printed nationwide. It was a sad but inspirational story, one of many from a generation of the greatest Americans to have ever lived. Jack's decision to leave the safety of a post on the home front in order to be with his boys overseas elevated him to a wartime icon of service and self-sacrifice. In the closing months of the war, his story was printed in the papers and spoken on the radio almost weekly. Of the many accounts of the men and women who died without a prestigious medal, the account of Jack's last full measure was possibly the most exalted. Even after the war ended, Jack's story remained an inspirational apologue, something of which the federal government took note.

The Treasury Salute Series episode, *First Lieutenant John Edward Chevigny*, aired on August 20, 1945, six days after the surrender of Japan (VJ Day). The treasury department's public relations people correctly guessed that Jack's story would help raise money to pay for the war debt. Written in collaboration with Jack's cousin, Hector Chevigny, the fourteen-minute radio drama detailed the facts of Jack's past sports glory and current military service. His time at Notre Dame, Chicago, and St. Edward's was mentioned. Strangely omitted from the script was an account of his three years at the University of Texas.

Possibly, the omission was just a biographical oversight. Maybe, the omission held meaning.

Hector Chevigny had been in touch with Jack in the years since Jack's time on the Forty Acres; he may have suspected that the nature of Jack's departure from Texas remained a sore point for Jack. Although Jack continued to maintain an intensely loyal bond with several Texas exes such as Jack Gray, Ox Higgins, Hugh Wolfe, and Hilmar H. Weinert, perhaps Hector felt that some of the malcontent and declamatory Orangebloods such as Joe B. Frantz were not worthy of the association with Jack's endowment of courage.

Indeed, who among the living was worthy of any of the lives lost during what was then called "The War?" Thousands of uniquely brave Americans were lost in the war. No one could redeem those whose futures were lost.

Though the Treasury Salute radio show trumpeted Jack's willingness to die for freedom and his countrymen, it was only partially correct. Jack Chevigny wanted to be where he thought he should be, but he also wanted to come home. He wanted all the boys to come home. Jack wanted to survive the war and return to Seattle for Gege. Jack wanted to play bridge, sing around the piano, smoke an evening cigarette out on the front porch, sip his amber King's Ransom Scotch, and look up at the stars that reminded him of the time he spent in Hawaii, talking out loud to the sky while hoping Gege was doing the same. He wanted to spend time with his brothers Henry and Jule, his sisters Graziella and Marie, and his nephews and nieces—especially his nephew, Jack Chevigny. In his heart, Jack was no hero who was willing to die for freedom and his countrymen. In his heart, he wanted to return home alive and in one piece, just like every other Marine who landed on that black sandy hell of a beach on February 19, 1945.

Not unlike other Marines in the last month of their preparations for combat, Jack feared that he would never come home. That uncertainty of survival is why he gave his dress blues to Bob Daily before they shipped out to Hawaii. That fear is why he had once written to Gege that he felt like fleeing to Canada with her to make a new life. Unlike the teenage warrior fresh out of high school, Jack knew what life offered. By age thirty-eight, he had lived a full life, a life full enough to know that he wanted more. He wanted to marry the woman of his dreams, enjoy the fruits of a prestigious career practicing law, have children, and hold Notre Dame season tickets. Jack's courage took all of that from him.

Courage isn't the absence of fear; it is the antithesis of fear. Courage allows humans to make the judgment that something else is more important than the safety offered by their fear. For Jack, the "something else" was the boys. They were his team.

Ask a combat veteran to define the word hero, and that veteran will take you to a national cemetery. Ask a person who knew Jack Chevigny to define the word hero, and that person will tell you about Jack. In a time and place fading from our consciousness into the pages of history books, Jack Chevigny crossed that final line that separates the greatest of us from the least of us, the line that only the courageous may cross.

# Epilogue

By November 1945, Marie still had heard no definitive statement regarding the details of Jack's final moments. She needed to know. Letters had arrived from many sources, some from Marines who were on Iwo, but each account of Jack's death held details that contradicted the other. The *Washington Post* printed Sonny Franck's account of diving into the shell hole with Jack on D-Day, but the facts of the story were entirely different from those in a letter that Sonny sent to Jule Chevigny in July. Wanting the truth, Marie purchased a ticket to the NFL Eastern Division Championship. The game was at Washington's Griffith Stadium. On December 9, she would find a way to speak with Sonny Franck, who, despite suffering a serious wartime leg injury, was now back with the Giants as a punter and halfback.

Exiting the locker room after the game, Sonny recognized something in the face of the ebony-haired woman who was waiting for him outside the locker room. He paused as she approached and introduced herself to the former Marine captain. Marie inquired about the inconsistencies of the accounts of Jack's death; she wanted to know if there was anything more to the story that he could add. As best he could, Sonny narrated the details as he remembered them. After he told Marie more of his last few days with Jack, she left with tears streaming down her cheeks. Sonny never saw Marie again.

Jack's roommate at Pendleton kept Jack's dress blues in his closet for more than ten years. One day he sold the suit in a garage sale for practically nothing. Bob Daily couldn't bear to look at them another day. After selling the uniform, he wished he had kept it. He would live out the rest of his life convinced that Jack's death had saved his life. Upon hearing of Jack's loss, Colonel Wornham ordered Bob Daily to replace Jack as a headquarters and supply officer. Prior to Wornham's directive, Daily was to lead a platoon of riflemen into battle.

Equestrian Takeichi Nishi didn't return from Iwo Jima. It isn't known when the Olympic gold medalist perished, but speculative historians set his death as occurring on March 22, 1945. Subjected to an aggressive propaganda campaign asking for his surrender, Nishi remained with his men. He died for his emperor.

After PFC Paul Merriman's wound healed, he was reassigned to police the citizens of postwar Japan. Returning to Pittsburgh, he moved rapidly up the ladder at General Electric (GE) and married Patricia in 1951. In 1970, Paul Merriman paid $1.00 for Houston Industrial Supply Company (HISCO). When he retired, his Employee Stock Ownership Plan surrendered total control of the $100 million company to his three hundred employees.

Resolutely staid, Gege traveled to attend Jack's memorial service in Gary, Indiana. She brought with her a trunk of Jack's personal effects to give to the family. When Margaret Chevigny, Jule's wife, passed away five months after Jack's death, Gege and Jule grew close. On August 15, 1946, Gege became the mother to Margaret's five children. After adding three children more to the family, Gege and Jule Chevigny remained in Indiana until his death in 1962.

Legends surrounding Jack's death proliferated in the media for seven decades. Most significant of these stories was the gold pen story in which a naval officer obtains Jack's gold pen that he had received at Texas.

According to the account, a naval officer is on the USS Missouri during the signing of the Japanese surrender terms when he notices a Japanese officer using a gold pen with words in English inscribed down the barrel. The officer seizes the pen from the Japanese and examines the inscription. It reads "To an old Notre Damer who Beat Notre Dame." The naval officer recognizes this pen as the one awarded to Jack by the University of Texas. Taking the pen, the officer forwards it to Marie, providing a bit of closure to her inconsolable loss.

Broadcast nationwide by famed radio personality Bill Stern and reprinted year after year, the pen story remains a cornerstone of Jack Chevigny's biography. While not a single line of the fable is true, it continues to capture the imagination of listeners in that it offers value and redemption in the face of a tragic loss. Bill Stern was not only a Radio Hall of Fame sports announcer, but also an entertainer who was a big fan of Jack's. He saw no reason not to create the story. The legend, still taken as truth, is continually reprinted by legitimate publications and continues to herald Jack's message of courage and sacrifice. Given the result, Stern can be exonerated for his lie.

Sometime after January 4, 1949, Jack's body was permanently laid to rest in Hawaii. In Section C, Site 508, just to the left of Mall Drive South in the National Cemetery of the Pacific, the remains of John Edward Chevigny rest with honor. His family decided he would have wanted his body to remain with the boys.

Marie died in 1975, forever heartbroken over Jack's death. She kept his scrapbook for years, and then passed it on to Jack's namesake nephew. The one thing she couldn't give up was the cameo pin Jack gave her.

# End Notes

## Prologue

Information regarding Operation Detachment's planning is from George Garand and Truman Strobridge's *Western Pacific Operations History of U. S. Marine Corps in World War II* Volume 4. Quantico, VA: Historical Division of U.S. Marine Corps, 1971.

## Chapter One: The Last Circus

The information for Chapter One is from Stewart H. Holdbrook's *The Story of American Railroads*. New York: Crown Publishers, 1947.

Various newspapers from the Calumet area and the Midwest covered the train wreck.

Articles dating from June 18, 1918 to November 29, 1918 provided detailed information as to the cause of the accident and the aftermath. These newspapers were located through the online newspaper archive, www.newspaperarchive.com/.

The military record of Julius Chevigny was provided by the military records on file with the Indiana Commission on Public Records.

## Chapter Two: Rally Sons of Notre Dame

The unpublished writings of Maurice (pronounced Morris) D. O'Hern were provided by his daughter, Maureen O'Hern. Francis Meyer's letter to Maurice D. O'Hern was part of O'Hern's personal file.

In 2009, David Kornaus, a Hammond native and Chevigny historian, provided the information from the *Hammond Dunes* edition of 1924.

The Rip Van Winkle prophecy was provided in 2009 by Kornaus, as well.

The information regarding the Quantico affair and Notre Dame's resistance to the Ku Klux Klan was found in Murray Sperber's *Shake Down the Thunder*. Bloomington, IN: Indiana University Press, 1993. Sperber was the first historian to document the Klan's activities with regard to Notre Dame.

Notre Dame graduate Todd Tucker offered a detailed account of the history of the KKK in Indiana and its political conflicts with Notre Dame University. In his *Notre Dame vs. the Klan, How the Fighting Irish Defeated the Ku Klux Klan.* Chicago: Loyola Press, 2004, he offers a precise account of the riot between the Klan and the Notre Dame men and outlined the Klan's plan to challenge Notre Dame with its purchase of Valparaiso—in addition to relating the strife between the Klan and Notre Dame's mission.

Ray Robinson's *Rockne of Notre Dame, The Making of a Football Legend.* New York: Oxford University Press, 1999, provides facts regarding the Klan's activities in Indiana and antipathy toward the Catholic parochial school system.

Details of the Four Horsemen game and Grantland Rice's legendary article were found in Sperber's *Shake Down the Thunder.* Strickler's photo-op is described by Sperber.

## Chapter Three: The Odds Be Great

Jack Chevigny's academic transcript was obtained courtesy of Notre Dame University.

The locker stuffing incident was from an undated Francis Meyer letter written to Maurice D. O'Hern.

## Chapter Four: Loyal to Notre Dame

Facts of the Columbia affair were obtained from Murray Sperber's *Shake Down the Thunder.*

The information on Percy Haughton's death and its effect on Columbia football were found in the *New York Times* archives and from the online newspaper archive, www.newspaperarchive.com/.

Rockne's conversion to Catholicism is mentioned in Sperber's *Shake Down the Thunder* and Ray Robinson's *Rockne of Notre Dame, The Making of a Football Legend.*

## Chapter Five: Carnegie's Echo

The source of Jack Chevigny's nickname was Francis Wallace's *Knute Rockne*, Doubleday, 1960.

In a newsreel recreating a halftime locker room speech, Rockne staged a typical halftime exhortation that captured his speaking style and ability to motivate. The newsreel was not a replication of a particular halftime but was indicative of a typical Rockne pep talk. In the speech, Rockne uses the name "Chev" to refer to Jack Chevigny. The date of the newsreel is likely 1927 or 1928. Available online at

http://archives.nd.edu/research/texts/rocknespeech2.htm.

In *Shake Down the Thunder*, Murray Sperber first exposed the Carnegie Tech affair and Rockne's deception as to the reason he did not attend the Carnegie Tech game of 1926.

Hunk Anderson's perspective of the game was provided by Emil Klosinski in *Notre Dame, Chicago Bears and Hunk*. Ovideo, FL: Florida Sun-Gator Publishing Company, 1976.

Scrapiron Young's account of the Carnegie Tech affair was described in Eugene J. Young's *With Rockne at Notre Dame*. New York: Van Rees Press, 1951.

Gee-whiz journalism is discussed in William A. Harper's *How You Played the Game: The Life of Grantland Rice*. Columbia, MO: University of Missouri Press, 1999.

Other details of the games were found from articles available online through www.newspaperarchive.com/. Financial figures of Notre Dame football were found in Sperber's *Shake Down the Thunder*.

## Chapter Six: Flanagan's Fighting Irish

Murray Sperber's *Shake Down the Thunder* is the main source for information regarding the Carnegie Foundation and the contrasting movement of college football toward larger stadiums, Francis Wallace's counterattack against Carnegie reforms, and Rockne's stealthy response to outside scrutiny of his recruiting practices.

The information regarding Frank Leahy's opinion on Rockne's talent stockpiling and the background on Paul Danculovic was first related by Sperber in *Shake Down the Thunder*.

Hunk Anderson's return to Notre Dame to serve with Rockne is described by Sperber in *Shake Down the Thunder* and Klosinski in *Notre Dame, Chicago Bears, and Hunk*. The Missouri Valley Conference invitation is discussed in Sperber's *Shake Down the Thunder* and Ray Robinson's *Rockne of Notre Dame, The Making of a Football Legend*.

Bronco Nagurski's quote regarding his caused fumble and recovery is from Jim Dent's *Monster of the Midway*. New York: St. Martin's Press, 2003.

Details of the games of 1926 were found in Sperber's *Shake Down the Thunder* and available online in articles at www.newspaperarchive.com/.

Financial figures in this chapter and others regarding Notre Dame football are from Sperber's *Shake Down the Thunder*.

Rockne's resignation is from Sperber's *Shake Down the Thunder*.

Information regarding the Notre Dame nicknames and the relationship of Albert Erskine, as well as numerous details regarding the 1927 season's games, is found in Murray Sperber's *Shake Down the Thunder* and Ray Robinson's Rockne of Notre Dame, *The Making of a Football Legend*.

### Chapter Seven: One for the Gipper

Jack Chevigny's scrapbook was provided by Jack and Babs Chevigny; it held letters and telegrams regarding his performance. The Rube Wagner quote is from an unknown newspaper source found in Jack Chevigny's scrapbook. On many of the old papers found in his scrapbook, the banners were torn or missing.

An analysis of the Notre Dame shift and the Georgia Tech offense was available from footage of the 1928 Georgia Tech game, compliments of Notre Dame Archives. The description of Georgia Tech's fans' taunts is from Sperber's *Shake Down the Thunder* and Robinson's *Rockne of Notre Dame, The Making of a Football Legend*.

Financial figures are from Murray Sperber's *Shake Down the Thunder* and Ray Robinson's *Rockne of Notre Dame, The Making of a Football Legend*. West Point's unique eligibility practice was first discussed in Sperber's *Shake Down the Thunder*.

The facts and controversial remembrances of the apocryphal One for the Gipper are discussed at length by Murray Sperber in *Shake Down the Thunder* and Ray Robinson in *Rockne of Notre Dame, The Making of a Football Legend*.

Francis Wallace's *Knute Rockne* provides the traditionalist's viewpoint of the legend. Murray Sperber's research indicates the Jack Chevigny exclamation never occurred; a screenwriter first used the phrase in a scene from the 1940 movie "Knute Rockne, All American."

Details of other games of 1928, including Mills's quote, were found in Sperber's *Shake Down the Thunder*, Robinson's *Rockne of Notre Dame, The Making of a Football Legend* and in newspaper articles available through www.newspaperarchive.com.

### Chapter Eight: Just Before the Crash

Referenced Rockne historians are Murray Sperber and Ray Robinson.

Details of the financial benefits of Rockne's coaching schools are found in Murray Sperber's *Shake Down the Thunder* and Ray Robinson's *Rockne of Notre Dame, The Making of a Football Legend*.

The Texas College affair is from Sperber's *Shake Down the Thunder*. Stewart Tolnay and E. M. Beck, *Reasons for Southern lynchings* are from *A Festival of Violence, An Analysis of Southern Lynchings 1882-1930*. Champaign, IL: Board of Trustees of the University of Illinois, 1995.

Rockne's injury is discussed in Ray Robinson's *Rockne of Notre Dame, The Making of a Football Legend* and Murray Sperber's *Shake Down the Thunder*.

Information regarding the early history of the treatment of phlebitis is from the numerous works by Alton Ochsner, MD, and Michael DeBakey, MD, found at DeBakey Library and Museum at Baylor School of Medicine in Houston, Texas, and a conversation with orthopedic surgeon, Mark Adickes, MD.

Rockne's time at the Mayo Clinic is described by Sperber in *Shake Down the Thunder*, Robinson in *Rockne of Notre Dame, The Making of a Football Legend*, and in the letters and telegrams from Jack Chevigny's scrapbook provided by Jack and Babs Chevigny.

The growing cynicism of the press toward Rockne is discussed in Sperber's *Shake Down the Thunder* and Robinson's *Rockne of Notre Dame, The Making of a Football Legend*.

The effects of the Great Depression on the attendance figures of college football are detailed in Sperber's *Shake Down the Thunder* and Robinson's *Rockne of Notre Dame, The Making of a Football Legend*. The pre-game scalping of Notre Dame-Army tickets is detailed in Sperber's *Shakedown the Thunder* and Robinson's *Rockne of Notre Dame, The Making of a Football Legend*.

Rockne's ambiguity in recognizing a clear successor is outlined in Sperber's *Shake Down the Thunder* and Robinson's *Rockne of Notre Dame, The Making of a Football Legend*.

Details of the 1929 games were found in Sperber's *Shake Down the Thunder*, Robinson's *Rockne of Notre Dame, The Making of a Football Legend*, and in newspaper articles available online at www.newspaperarchive.com.

That Rockne's travels strained his relations with Notre Dame's administration is documented by Sperber in *Shake Down the Thunder*.

The details of the Northwestern Charity Game, the season-ending win over USC, and the Chicago tickertape parade are from Sperber's *Shake Down the Thunder* and Robinson's *Rockne of Notre Dame* and Robinson's *Rockne of Notre Dame, The Making of a Football Legend*.

Rockne's quote regarding Schwartz is from various sources including Jack Cavanaugh, *The Gipper*. New York: Skyhorse Publishing, 2010.

The facts of the Joe Savoldi divorce and subsequent separation from Notre Dame are first discussed by Murray Sperber in *Shake Down the Thunder*.

### Chapter Nine: The Crash

The days and events preceding Rockne's trip and the reason for the trip are discussed in Sperber's *Shake Down the* Thunder and Robinson's *Rockne of Notre Dame, The Making of a Football Legend*.

Much of the information regarding the Rockne crash is from William Least Heat-Moon's *PrairyErth: (a deep map)*. New York: Houghton-Mifflin Harcourt, 1999. Heat-Moon was the first to document the facts of the principals involved and accurately discuss the factors leading to the plane crash. Heat-Moon was the first to document witnesses' accounts of the crash and crash site.

Technical information regarding the Fokker F-10A was found in Heat-Moon's *PrairyErth: (a deep map)*. *Fokker Niner-Niner Easy*—the call sign for Rockne's plane—is first used in Heat-Moon's *PrairyErth: (a deep map)*.

Additional information regarding the flutter phenomenon is from documents obtained from Rice University's Fondren Library Woodson Research Center.

The background of the Flight 599's passengers was obtained from newspaper articles at www.newspaperarchive.com/.

Doctor Joe Casey's article in *Notre Dame Magazine* provided insight to the sound, sight, and smells experienced by James Easter Heathman on the day of the crash.

Sperber's *Shake Down the Thunder* and Robinson's *Rockne of Notre Dame, The Making of a Football Legend* provided details of the crash.

Additional accounts of Claire and Herb Fahy are from newspaper articles online at www.newspaperarchive.com/.

### Chapter Ten: Shaken By the Thunder

The account of Hunk playing professional ball is from Murray Sperber's *Shake Down the Thunder* and Ray Robinson's *Rockne of Notre Dame, The Making of a Football Legend*.

Information regarding the junior-senior coach arrangement and the resentment of Notre Dame's academic elitists with regard to the football program is from Murray Sperber's *Shake Down the Thunder*, Ray Robinson's *Rockne of Notre Dame, The Making of a Football Legend*, and Emil Klosinski's *Notre Dame, Chicago Bears, and Hunk.*

Hunk's spring absence is discussed in Sperber's *Shake Down the Thunder* and Robinson's *Rockne of Notre Dame, The Making of a Football Legend.*

Additional details of the arrangement are from newspaper articles available at www.newspaperarchive.com/.

The feuding relationship between Jack Chevigny and Hunk Anderson is detailed in newspaper articles available at www.newspaperarchive.com/and in Murray Sperber's *Shake Down the Thunder*, Ray Robinson's *Rockne of Notre Dame, The Making of a Football Legend*, and Emil Klosinski's *Notre Dame, Chicago Bears, and Hunk*. Klosinski's *Notre Dame, Chicago Bears, and Hunk* documents Anderson's perception that Chevigny undermined Anderson. Klosinski records Hunk's demand that Chevigny be released in 1932.

## Chapter Eleven: Cardinal Blues

Information regarding the history of the Chicago Cardinals was obtained from Joe Ziemba, *When Football Was Football: The Chicago Cardinals and the Birth of the NFL*. Chicago: Triumph Books, 1999.

Doctor Jones's quote is from the *Chicago Tribune* archives and Doctor Jones's quote is also found in Joe Ziemba's *When Football Was Football: The Chicago Cardinals and the Birth of the NFL.*

Information regarding the season and games of the 1932 Chicago Cardinals is from the *Chicago Tribune* and the *Chicago Defender* archives as well as newspaper articles available online at www.newspaperarchive.com.

Chuck Braidwood later served his countrymen in World War II. He died in the Pacific of natural causes as a field manager for the Red Cross. Anecdotal sources indicate his death as coincidental to a Japanese air raid on his base camp.

Also, Lillard's high school background and details from his Oregon tenure were found in newspaper articles available online at www.newspaperarchive.com/.

The facts of Lillard's death are found in the *New York Times* archives and various newspaper articles found online at www.newspaperarchive.com.

The quote at the end of Chapter Eleven was made in 1983 by John Carroll (Johnny) Buck.

## Chapter Twelve: A Box is Shipped to Texas

The account of Lutcher Stark's arrival on the University of Texas campus is found in Don E. Carleton's *A Breed So Rare: The Life of J. R. Parten, Liberal Texas Oil Man, 1896-1992*. Austin: Texas State Historical Association, 1998.

The relationship between Theo Bellmont and Lutcher Stark is described in Carleton's *A Breed So Rare: The Life of J. R. Parten, Liberal Texas Oil Man, 1896-1992*.

The information regarding the 1933 change of rules is from the *St. Edward's Echo*, the campus newspaper of St. Edward's University.

Richard Pennington's *For Texas, I Will: The History of Memorial Stadium*. Austin: Richard Pennington, 1992, provides historical perspective regarding the Texas football program.

John Maher and Kirk Bohls's *Long Live the Longhorns: 100 Years of Texas Football*. New York: St. Martin's Press, 1993, provides extensive detail of the history of Longhorn football and the Chevigny era.

A. S. Hopkins's quote is also found in Maher and Bohls's *Long Live the Longhorns: 100 Years of Texas Football*.

A phone interview with Ted Paulison provided information regarding his personal recollection of Jack Chevigny's impact on the Catholic community of Austin and the state of Texas.

Facts regarding the 1933 championship season of the St. Edward's Tigers were found through newspaper articles available online at www.newspaperarchive.com/.

Newspaper clippings from Jack Chevigny's scrapbook, courtesy of Jack and Babs Chevigny, offered details on the 1933 season.

## Chapter Thirteen: The Eyes of Texas

Clyde Littlefield's "no quitter" remark was found through a *San Antonio Light* article at www.newspaperarchive.com/.

Don E. Carleton's *A Breed So Rare: The Life of J. R. Parten, Liberal Texas Oil Man, 1896-1992* provides insight to the life of J. R. Parten and his relationship with Texas football.

Figures relating to Jack Chevigny's salary were obtained from newspaper articles at www.newspaperarchive.com/.

Information about the transition of the head football coaching position at Texas in 1934 is found in the online data base www.newspaperarchive.com.

The account of Dr. Julius Chevigny's death was found online at www.newspaperarchive.com/and through archival documents from the Jack Chevigny file at the University of Texas, Dolph Briscoe Center for American History in Austin, Texas.

The Gregory Gym scene is from the *Daily Texan* copy from Jack Chevigny's scrapbook and various other sources including Maher and Bohls's *Long Live the Longhorns: 100 Years of Texas Football.*

Lutcher Stark's position on recruiting athletes to Texas and offering scholarships is discussed in Carleton's *A Breed So Rare: The Life of J. R. Parten, Liberal.*

Details of the 1934 season were found in archival documents in the Jack Chevigny file at the University of Texas, Dolph Briscoe Center for American History in Austin, Texas, and online at www.newspaperarchive.com.

Newspaper clippings and full copies of the *Daily Texan*, the UT campus newspaper, from Jack Chevigny's scrapbook, courtesy of Jack and Babs Chevigny, offered details on the 1934 season.

Jack Chevigny's love for thoroughbred horseracing is detailed in letters found in his scrapbook, courtesy of Jack and Babs Chevigny.

The account of Jack Chevigny's attendance at Alamo Downs was found in newspapers at www.newspaperarchive.com/.

King Football is from the title of Michael Orland's *King Football: Sport and Spectacle in the Golden Age of Radio and Newsreels, Movies and Magazines, the Weekly and Daily Press.* Chapel Hill, NC: University of North Carolina Press, 2001.

Information as to polo's popularity in the 1930s Texas and Austin is provided by Vernon Cook's grandson, Marshall Law.

## Chapter Fourteen: One for the Chevigny

A daily accounting of the 1934 season and the facts of the recruitment of Pete Moore is found in statewide newspapers available online at www.newspaperarchive.com/.

Jack Chevigny's driving habits are known thanks to court records published in Hammond, Indiana, and Chicago, Illinois, records found in newspapers at www.newspaperarchive.com/.

Details of Elmer Layden's tenure are from Elmer Layden with Ed Snyder's *It was a Different Game: The Elmer Layden Story.* Englewood Cliffs, NJ: Prentice-Hall Incorporated, 1969.

The account of the Notre Dame trip and game is from a Jack Gray, Jr. interview and Hugh Wolfe interview, as well as from John Maher and Kirk Bohls's *Long Live the Longhorns*, *The Alcade*, Elmer Layden and Ed Snyder's *It Was a Different Game,* and newspapers available at www.newspaperarchive.com.

### Chapter Fifteen: An Assassin's Bullet

The background and features of the 1934 LaSalle given to Jack Chevigny at the letterman's banquet are found in Ron VanGelderen and Matt Larson's *LaSalle: Cadillac's Companion Car.* Paducah, KY: Turner Publishing Company, 2000.

The Harley Earl quote is found in VanGelderen and Matt Larson's *LaSalle: Cadillac's Companion Car.*

Details of the Faurot-Chevigny feud were documented nationwide in newspapers available www.newspaperarchive.com/.

The account of Bill James at the Rice game is found in statewide newspapers available at www.newspaperarchive.com/.

Billy Disch's comments regarding the 1935 team are from the archives of the *Daily Texan* and the *Austin Statesman* newspapers.

The "clean liver, who neither smoked nor drank to excess" reference is from Doctor Jones in the *Chicago Tribune* and in Joe Ziemba's *When Football Was Football: The Chicago Cardinals and the Birth of the NFL.*

Cater Joseph's boyhood memory of Jack Chevigny was obtained through a 2004 phone interview.

Jack Chevigny's taste for Scotch whiskey and his smoking habit are mentioned in his personal letters.

Details of Huey P. Long's funeral are found in online newspapers at www.newspaperarchive.com/.

Jack's comment on the expectant roles of Morrow, Arnold, Atchison, and Sands is found in the *Austin Statesman* newspaper, available online at www.newspaperarchive.com/.

Game action and editorials of the 1935 Texas football season were found online at www.newspaperarchive.com/.

### Chapter Sixteen: At the Alamo

The details of the Will Rogers Memorial Fund charity game, Tim Moynihan's termination, and Jack Chevigny's holiday trip to Hammond are found at www.newspaperarchive.com/.

The doping scandal of Jack Chevigny (the thoroughbred) is found in newspapers online at www.newspaperarchive.com/.

Details of Jack Chevigny's gambling and Parten's loans are documented in Don E. Carleton's *A Breed So Rare: The Life of J. R. Parten, Liberal Texas Oil Man, 1896-1992* and in newspapers available online at www.newspaperarchive.com.

Baron Nishi's fall at the 1936 Olympics is a controversy discussed at http://e-edition.metro.co.uk/2011/09/22/70.html.

Joe B. Frantz's relationship with Jack Chevigny and his criticisms are documented in David G. McComb's *Travels with Joe 1917-1993: The Life Story of a Historian from Texas*. Austin: Texas State Historical Association, 2001.

Jack Chevigny's legal argument before the State Railroad Commission was recorded in statewide newspapers available at www.newspaperarchive.com.

Billy Patterson's resentment of Chevigny is recorded on page 227 of the Baylor 2004 Football Media Guide.

Daily accounts of the 1936 season are from statewide newspapers found online at www.newspaperarchive.com/.

The Parten meeting in Brenham's is from Carleton's *A Breed So Rare: The Life of J. R. Parten, Liberal Texas Oil Man, 1986-1992*.

D. X. Bible's enticement to the position of Texas head football coach is recorded in Don E. Carleton's *A Breed So Rare: The Life of J. R. Parten, Liberal Texas Oil Man, 1896-1992*.

## Chapter Seventeen: One Big Inch and Ten Yards to Go

Information regarding the Big Inch and Little Inch pipeline and America's oil delivery system to Europe was found in Don E. Carleton's *A Breed So Rare: The Life of J. R. Parten, Liberal Texas Oil Man, 1896-1992*.

An account of Jack Chevigny's draft notice and the location of his training was found in the *Lake County* (Hammond, Indiana) *Times* available online at www.newspaperarchive.com/.

Stephen Bower's *A History of Fort Benjamin Harrison, 1903-1982*. Ann Arbor, MI: Command History Office, U.S. Army Soldier Support Center, 1984, provided the information regarding Fort Benjamin Harrison.

Private Chevigny's experiences were recorded in an undated letter from Army sergeant major and Hammond native Howard J. Gescheidler to

Maurice D. O'Hern. The letter was found in Jack Chevigny's scrapbook, courtesy of Jack and Babs Chevigny.

An account of the Fort Lawton riot is from Dominic W. Moreo's *Riot at Fort Lawton, 1944*. Lincoln, NE: IUniverse Incorporated, 2004.

Details of the trip to the Seattle department store to buy the Marine officer uniform were told by Gege Chevigny Brennan to Gege Chevigny Beck.

Wilbur B. Jones Jr.'s *Football! Navy! War! How Military "Lend-Lease Players Saved the College Game and Helped Win World War II*. Jefferson, NC: McFarland Publishing, 2009, offers the best historical background on the V-12 program and college football of the wartime era.

Information about the 1943 football season at Camp Lejeune is best examined through archival documents provided by the John A. Lejeune Education Center Research Library, Camp Lejeune, North Carolina, and John Gunn's *(Quite) A Few Good Men*. Costa Mesa, CA: J&J Publishing, 1992.

The Al "Junie" Kleinhenz quote is from a 2008 telephone interview.

First Lieutenant John Edward Chevigny assignment was documented in his Marine Corps service record.

## Chapter Eighteen: The Eve of Dawn

Information regarding Operation Detachment's planning is from George Garand and Truman Strobridge's *Western Pacific Operations History of U.S. Marine Corps in World War II*, Volume 4.

An account of the Hollywood stars' visits to Camp Pendleton and Jack's role in securing Ann Blyth for the regimental parade is from letters to the author from Bob Daily.

Insight to the personal relationship and wartime communication between Gege Purdy and Jack Chevigny was provided by letters given to Gege Chevigny Beck from Gege Chevigny Brennan (nee Purdy).

Details of Sonny Franck's life and wartime service were obtained through numerous interviews with Sonny Franck.

The account of Jack dislocating his elbow was from a letter from First Lieutenant Jack Chevigny to Gege Purdy, courtesy of Gege Chevigny Brennan and Gege Chevigny Beck.

## Chapter Nineteen: The Red Zone

Facts regarding the invasion of Iwo Jima are from George Garand and Truman Strobridge's *Western Pacific Operations History of U.S. Marine Corps in World War II,* Volume 4, and Richard Wheeler, *Iwo.* Annapolis, MD: Naval Institute Press, 1994.

Paul Merriman related facts of his wartime experiences and his combat experience on Iwo Jima in numerous interviews and correspondence.

The account of "Marines with smoking holes in their bodies" is from Richard E. Overton's *God Isn't Here.* Clearfield, UT: American Legacy Historical Press, 2008.

John Basilone's and Chuck Tatum's advance is discussed in several accounts, most notably by Chuck Tatum in *Red Blood, Black Sand.* Stockton, CA: Charles W. Tatum Publishing, 1995.

The description of the "snake" was from Richard E. Overton's *God Isn't Here.*

In an interview with the author, Sonny Franck provided the details of his actions on the beach at Iwo Jima.


## Chapter Twenty: For the Boys

The account of Roosevelt's reaction to the casualty count at Iwo Jima is from Robert S. Burrell, *The Ghosts of Iwo Jima.* College Station, TX: Texas A&M University Press, 2006.

The account of Jack's death was from an interview with Sonny Franck and supporting correspondence sent to Jule Chevigny from other Marines purported to have knowledge of the incident. Correspondence was provided courtesy of Jack and Babs Chevigny.

A narrative describing the supposed location of Jack Chevigny's shell hole is found in John C. Shively's *The Last Lieutenant.* New York: Penguin Group, 2006.

Information regarding the family's receipt of the condolence telegram was provided by Gege Chevigny Brennan to Gege Chevigny Beck. The telegram was found in Jack Chevigny's scrapbook, courtesy of Jack and Babs Chevigny.

The account of Vandegrift's injury and Jack's hospital visit in Washington, DC, was from a letter to Gege Purdy from Jack Chevigny.

The facts of PFC Merriman being pinned down with Marine Alfred Ciccocelli were related in an interview with Paul Merriman.

The Treasury Salute Series episode, *First Lieutenant John Edward Chevigny*, was located in the National Archives Treasury Department audio files in Annapolis, Maryland.

Jack's conflict over serving in a combat zone was the subject of many of his letters to Gege Purdy. The letters were provided by Gege Chevigny Beck.

The "courage is not the absence of fear" paraphrase is based on the Ambrose Redmoon quote and a Mark Twain quote.

## Epilogue

The account of Marie meeting Sonny Franck at the football game was related by Sonny Franck in an interview with the author. Franck told the same story to the *Washington Post* in 1945. Ironically, in a July 1945 letter, Sonny Franck had related a completely different timeline regarding Jack Chevigny's death. He said the letter was probably a fictional account that Bernie Bierman encouraged him to write.

Bob Daily, in a letter to the author, described the garage sale of the dress blues and insisted that Jack Chevigny's death had saved his life.

Equestrian Takeichi Nishi's death was most accurately detailed in Shively's *The Last Lieutenant*.

The HISCO company history was provided by Paul Merriman.

The account of Gege Purdy hauling the trunk from Seattle to Hammond was told to Gege Chevigny Beck.

The legend of the gold pen story was first debunked by the *Houston Post*.

The gold pen account is not supported by Chevigny family records. Marie Chevigny Gaffney's son, Joe Gaffney, stated in an interview that he had neither seen nor heard of a gold pen; he states that it would have been memento treasured by his mother.

Ox Higgins was the lone Chevigny associate at Texas who stated the pen actually existed.

The one treasure that Marie Gaffney did possess was the cameo pin. According to Joe Gaffney, she didn't want anyone in the family to touch it, because Jack had given it to her.

CPSIA information can be obtained
at www.ICGtesting.com
Printed in the USA
LVOW11s1427060618
579809LV00001B/38/P